17

Michael R.
Dept. of Sociology
Hamilton Hall
Univ. of North Carolina
Chapel Hill, N. C. 27514

Psychological Foundations of Attitudes

SOCIAL PSYCHOLOGY

A series of monographs, treatises, and texts

EDITORS

LEON FESTINGER AND STANLEY SCHACHTER

PSYCHOLOGICAL FOUNDATIONS OF ATTITUDES

Edited by

Anthony G. Greenwald   Timothy C. Brock

Thomas M. Ostrom

DEPARTMENT OF PSYCHOLOGY, OHIO STATE UNIVERSITY, COLUMBUS, OHIO

1968

ACADEMIC PRESS   New York and London

ACADEMIC PRESS, INC.
111 Fifth Avenue, New York, New York 10003

United Kingdom Edition published by
ACADEMIC PRESS, INC. (LONDON) LTD.
Berkeley Square House, London W1X6BA

LIBRARY OF CONGRESS CATALOG CARD NUMBER: 68-26639

Third Printing, 1972

PRINTED IN THE UNITED STATES OF AMERICA

List of Contributors

Numbers in parentheses indicate the pages on which the authors' contributions begin.

REUBEN M. BARON (297), *Department of Psychology, Wayne State University, Detroit, Michigan*

DARYL J. BEM (197), *Department of Psychology, Carnegie-Mellon University, Pittsburgh, Pennsylvania*

JACK W. BREHM (277), *Department of Psychology, Duke University, Durham, North Carolina*

TIMOTHY C. BROCK (243), *Department of Psychology, Ohio State University, Columbus, Ohio*

ANTHONY G. GREENWALD (147, 365), *Department of Psychology, Ohio State University, Columbus, Ohio*

IRVING L. JANIS (329), *Department of Psychology, Yale University, New Haven, Connecticut*

ALBERT J. LOTT (67), *Department of Psychology, University of Kentucky, Lexington, Kentucky*

BERNICE E. LOTT (67), *Department of Psychology, University of Kentucky, Lexington, Kentucky*

WILLIAM J. MC GUIRE (171), *Department of Psychology, University of California, San Diego, La Jolla, California*

LEON MANN (329), *Department of Social Relations, Harvard University, Cambridge, Massachusetts*

THOMAS M. OSTROM (1, 217), *Department of Psychology, Ohio State University, Columbus, Ohio*

RALPH L. ROSNOW (89), *Department of Psychology, Temple University, Philadelphia, Pennsylvania*

ARTHUR W. STAATS (33), *Department of Psychology, University of Hawaii, Honolulu, Hawaii*

HARRY S. UPSHAW (217), *Department of Psychology, University of Illinois, Chicago, Illinois*

ROBERT FRANK WEISS* (109), *Department of Psychology, Queens College of the City of New York, Queens, New York*

*Present address: Department of Psychology, University of Oklahoma, Norman, Oklahoma.

Foreword

This work is frankly and explicitly an attempt to present theories about attitudes that are different from theories centering about the concepts of dissonance or balance. Having spent a fair portion of my professional life working on problems of cognitive dissonance, my personal reaction to the book may be of some interest to the reader.

I found the contributions to be mature, stimulating, and provocative. Although each chapter presents a different theory, and different approach, a different emphasis, one does not get the impression of contradiction or controversy. Rather, one gets the healthy impression that all of it is almost within one's grasp for integrating.

The approaches and the theories in the various chapters are not vague verbalisms. They are specific; they are linked to data and they are linked to other areas of psychology. If one remembers what was known about attitudes and attitude change thirty years ago, these chapters indicate great progress and promise for more progress to come.

But what about the integration that seems almost within one's grasp, but not quite there? And what about the relation of these approaches to theories concerning dissonance and dissonance reduction? My guess is that all of these approaches have validity. The processes of attitude formation, maintenance, and change are not simple. Dissonance plays an important role; so do learning and imitation and conflict and reactance. The question of integrating the various approaches is the question of specifying the conditions under which different dynamics come into play.

To achieve this integration will take ideas and much more research. After reading this book I am convinced that the goal is attainable.

New York, New York   LEON FESTINGER
August, 1968

vii

Preface

In the organization and editing of this volume, we have been guided by two conceptions of the current status of the psychology of attitudes. First, we feel strongly that it is meaningful to use the term "attitude theory" to describe an interrelated set of diverse theoretical ideas concerned with "attitude processes." (The terms just used in quotes can understandably be regarded by the reader as vague at this point; it is not until the concluding chapter that we are very specific about what is meant by these terms.) The conception of an integrated body of attitude theory may be contrasted with (a) treatments that separate out "attitude change" as a special theoretical area of interest[1] or (b) treatments that formulate the study of attitudes in terms of the competition among theoretical formulations.[2] The approach of focusing on attitude change can be justified in that attitude change research provides information about many other aspects of attitudes (such as attitude formation and attitude structure), while the analysis of the relative merits of competing theories has the value of being a fairly direct approach to theoretical refinement. In this volume, these values have been incorporated in the form of extensive attention to attitude change research and acknowledgments of conflicting interpretations of data when appropriate. However, we have

[1]E.g., Insko, C. A. *Theories of attitude change.* New York: Appleton-Century-Crofts, 1967; Cohen, A. R., *Attitude change and social influence.* New York: Basic Books, 1963.

[2]E.g., Insko, *op. cit.*; McGuire, W. J., Attitudes and attitude change. In G. Lindzey & E. Aronson (Eds.) *Handbook of social psychology.* (2nd ed.) Reading, Mass.: Addison-Wesley, 1968, in press.

given decidedly reduced attention to questions such as: "Under what conditions will formulations A and B generate conflicting predictions?" and have focused more on the question: "Assuming that there is at least some truth in both formulations A and B, how do they fit together in the larger body of attitude theory?" The former question starts from an assumption that formulations A and B are intended (by their authors) to apply to the same facts; in pursuing the conclusions from this sometimes erroneous assumption, much conceptual and empirical effort may be wasted. The latter question starts from an opposite initial assumption: since different theoretical formulations are typically derived from different observations, it should not be assumed that they are intended to apply to the same data. This typically raises questions such as: "Under what conditions does A apply more than B, and vice versa?" Although this last question is much easier to ask than to answer, the effort spent answering it is quite unlikely to be wasted.

Our second guiding conception was a reaction to particular contemporary developments in attitude theory. It must be obvious to any student of attitude processes that theoretical analyses based on a cognitive consistency principle have dominated research and interpretation of attitude processes for approximately the past decade. While the cognitive consistency principle has done the valuable service of attracting much attention to the psychological study of attitudes, at the same time this attention has tended to obscure a number of important attitude-theoretical developments that do not make reference to the consistency principle. Our view is that cognitive consistency theory is one *part* of attitude theory, a part that is best viewed in the perspective of a variety of alternative (not necessarily competing) theoretical approaches to attitude processes. In reaction, then, to the strong focus of much of the contemporary literature on cognitive consistency theory,[3] this volume has focused specifically on a number of attitude-theoretical formulations that are not based on a consistency principle. Consistency theory is nonetheless given frequent reference in that several of the present authors devote some space to comparison of their own formulations with consistency formulations, and the introductory and concluding chapters, dealing

---

[3]E.g., Feldman, S. (Ed.), *Cognitive consistency*. New York: Academic Press, 1966; Abelson, R. P., *et al.* (Eds.), *Theories of cognitive consistency: A sourcebook*. New York: Rand McNally, 1968, in press; also examine the titles of articles in social psychology journals for the last several years.

with the field of attitude theory in general, treat consistency theory in the context of other attitude-theoretical formulations.

It obviously would have been possible to invite contributions from a few consistency-theory researchers in the interest of being more fully representative of currently active theoretical approaches. However, it would have been impossible to do justice to consistency theory in only a few chapters, and, since consistency theory has been the topic of two recent volumes, our decision was not to include any chapters describing consistency-theory research. For additional coverage of consistency theory, the reader is encouraged to consult those volumes cited in footnote 3.

Chapters 2 through 13 were specially prepared for this volume by researchers actively and programmatically pursuing a variety of theoretical interpretations of attitude processes. Each author was given the task of describing his theoretical formulation and discussing research relevant to it, giving strong emphasis to his own research efforts. In the interests of keeping presentations compact, authors were explicitly asked not to be exhaustive in reviewing literature pertinent to their area.

Our organization of these contributions into major sections on learning-behavior theory and cognitive integration theory represents what seems to us the most comfortable system for designating the major categories of attitude-theoretical formulations. The basis for this category system is developed further in the concluding chapter.

The original impetus for this volume came from a symposium, "Alternatives to consistency theory in the study of attitude change," presented at the September, 1967, American Psychological Association meetings in Washington, D.C. The editors are indebted to APA, and particularly to David O. Sears, who at the time was program chairman for Division 8 (Personality and Social Psychology), for their cooperation in organizing the symposium. Among the contributors to this volume, Baron, Bem, Greenwald, and Weiss presented papers at the symposium, while Staats was a discussant and McGuire was chairman. Barry E. Collins, although not a contributor to this volume, was a stimulating discussant at the symposium.

John D. Edwards, Jeffrey H. Goldstein, and Lorne K. Rosenblood, participants in a seminar on attitude theory at Ohio State University during the winter quarter, 1968, made useful editorial contributions, for which the editors are grateful. We are additionally indebted to the many students and colleagues who, by virtue of their participation in the research programs reported in this volume and their informal comments on manuscripts, have added much of substance to this volume. Finally, we wish to acknowledge with gratitude the assistance of the Academic Press staff, who have expedited the production of this volume at several stages of its preparation during the past year.

A. G. Greenwald
T. C. Brock
T. M. Ostrom

Columbus, Ohio
July, 1968

Contents

xiii

PART III: COGNITIVE INTEGRATION THEORY CONTRIBUTIONS TO ATTITUDE THEORY

9. Psychological Perspective and Attitude Change   217

Thomas M. Ostrom and Harry S. Upshaw

10. Implications of Commodity Theory for Value Change   243

Timothy C. Brock

11. Attitude Change from Threat to Attitudinal Freedom   277

Jack W. Brehm

12. Attitude Change through Discrepant Action: A Functional Analysis   297

Reuben M. Baron

PART I: INTRODUCTION

1

The Emergence of Attitude Theory: 1930–1950

THOMAS M. OSTROM
DEPARTMENT OF PSYCHOLOGY
OHIO STATE UNIVERSITY
COLUMBUS, OHIO

Within a decade of the establishment of social psychology as a separate discipline within psychology, the concept of attitude was thoroughly established as one of its prime substantive areas (Thomas & Znaniecki, 1918). Throughout the first third of this century, however, the study of attitudes was pursued in many disparate fields with little communication or agreement regarding its properties and boundaries. Workers in the fields of experimental psychology, psychoanalysis, and sociology, for example, had investigated such expressions of attitude as set, prejudice, and suggestion. A major integrative influence was provided by Allport in 1935 in his classic Murchison *Handbook* chapter which brought together the divergent prior usages of attitude, distinguished it from other psychological concepts, and unquestionably established its study as a specialty of social psychology.

The two decades between 1930 and 1950 were marked by extensive empirical and theoretical study of attitude formation and change. Despite the countervailing influences of a depression and a world war, a number of influences combined to rapidly advance the understanding of attitudinal processes during that 20-year period: the establishment of social psychology laboratories in the United States, the ascendance of interested scholars who were trained in both fundamental psychological theory and empirical techniques, the integrative influence of Allport's 1935 chapter, the solution of measurement problems by Thurstone and others, and the ubiquitous application of attitudes in explaining important social phenomena. The antecedents of nearly all modern psychological interpretations of attitudes, such as those presented in this volume, can be traced to that 1930—1950 period. The objective of this chapter is to examine the attitude-theoretical advances made during those two decades and to trace the contribution of these conceptual insights to subsequently developed theories of attitude formation and change.

The development of attitude theory has been a major occupation of social psychologists since 1950. At least thirty-four discrete contributions to this development have been formulated in recent years; a listing of these is provided in Table 1. In the preparation of Table 1 an attempt was made to give each contribution a label descriptive of the theoretical innovation which distinguished it from the others. The reader will note that the contributions overlap in varying degrees. Some differ only on minor points, while others are widely divergent in the theoretical constructs offered to account for attitudinal phenomena. Each formulation, however, represents a systematic attempt either to isolate a subset of attitudinal processes (e.g., Festinger, 1957; Rosenberg, 1956), or to provide a broad-based conceptualization within which all determinants and consequences of attitude can be related (e.g., Campbell, 1963; Katz, 1960).

The task of theory classification involves a search for facets of similarity and distinction which capture the fundamental features of the theoretical domain. The organization of theories in Table 1, although the product of such a search, is not regarded as wholly satisfactory. In the final chapter of this volume, Greenwald describes the rationale which lay behind its structure and provides a more extensive definition of each category. The two major categories are learning-behavior theory and cognitive integration theory. The former draws upon principles resulting from the study of human and animal learning, while the latter is based on analyses of the individual's phenomenal representation of his world. The two subcategories under the learning-behavior theory heading are S-R theories and eclectic theories which correspond, respectively, to applications of the mediating processes borrowed from specific learning-behavior theories and to theories which borrow empirical principles and apply them analogically to attitudinal responses. The subclasses of consistency, motivational, and nonmotivational separate cognitive integration theories into those which assume operation of a consistency principle, those which adopt motivationally dynamic assumptions, and those which do not incorporate motivational constructs. Consistency theories are placed

TABLE 1

ATTITUDE-THEORETICAL FORMULATIONS DEVELOPED SINCE 1950

Classification	Psychological process	Contributors
Learning-behavior theory		
S-R	Mediated generalization	Lott (1955), Lott & Lott (this volume), Osgood et al. (1957)
	Concept formation	Fishbein (1967b), Rhine (1958)
	Conditioning	Weiss (1962; this volume)
	Effectance motivation	Byrne & Clore (1967), Golightly & Byrne (1964)
	Stimulus generalization	Rosnow (this volume)
	Reinforcement	Staats (1967; this volume)
	Arousal value	Feldman (1966, 1968)
Eclectic	Symbolic mediation	Hovland et al. (1953), Janis & Gilmore (1965)
	Inoculation	McGuire (1964)
	Behavioral disposition	Campbell (1963)
	Self perception	Bem (1965, 1967; this volume)
	Sequential mediators	McGuire (1968; this volume)
	Cognitive response	Greenwald (this volume)
Cognitive integration theory		
Consistency	Interpersonal orientation	Newcomb (1953, 1961)
	Congruity	Osgood & Tannenbaum (1955)
	Di-graph balance	Cartwright & Harary (1956)
	Dissonance	Brehm & Cohen (1962), Festinger (1957)
	Psycho-logic	Abelson & Rosenberg (1958)
	Logical-affective consistency	McGuire (1960)
	Tricomponent consistency	Fishbein (1967c), Insko & Schopler (1967), Rosenberg & Hovland (1960)

TABLE 1 (*Continued*)

ATTITUDE-THEORETICAL FORMULATIONS DEVELOPED SINCE 1950

Classification	Psychological process	Contributors
Cognitive integration theory (*cont.*)	Belief congruence	Rokeach (1960, Rokeach & Rothman (1965)
Motivational	Self-evaluation	Festinger (1954), Latané (1966)
	Value-instrumentality	Peak (1955), Rosenberg (1956, 1960)
	Functional	Baron (this volume), Katz (1960), Katz & Stotland (1959), Kelman (1958), M. Smith *et al.* (1956)
	Psychoanalytic	Sarnoff (1960)
	Attitudinal involvement	Ostrom & Brock (1968), M. Sherif & Hovland (1961)
	Decisional conflict	Janis (1959), Janis & Mann (this volume)
	Reactance	Brehm (1966; this volume)
Nonmotivational	Belief dilemma resolution	Abelson (1959)
	Cognitive complexity	Brock (1962), Crockett (1965), Harvey (1967), Kerlinger (1967), Schroeder *et al.*, (1967), Scott (1963), Zajonc (1960)
	Assimilation-contrast	C. W. Sherif *et al.* (1965), M. Sherif & Hovland (1961)
	Perspective	Upshaw (1962, 1968), Ostrom & Upshaw (this volume)
	Adaptation level	Helson (1964)
	Commodity	Brock (this volume)

into a separate class due to their large number, the special emphasis currently given them within social psychology, and the lack of agreement among consistency theorists regarding the necessity of assuming that consistency is a psychological need or motive.

No doubt readers will feel that some contributions have been inappropriately identified, either in the labeling phrase adopted or in the other contributions with which it was grouped. Of course, it was inevitable that the author's selection of labels would reflect his own interpretations. Given such a diverse abundance of theoretical viewpoints (and the number is increasing each year) it is clear that further efforts must be expended toward the development of a cogent meta-theory which will permit the integration and differentiation of these individual contributions.

One striking fact stands out when one leafs back through the history of attitude theory. With rare exception, usage of the phrase *attitude theory* was literally nonexistent even through the publication of the 1954 *Handbook of Social Psychology* (Lindzey, 1954); this was so despite the contemporary plenitude of theory. The theories section of that handbook included reinforcement, cognitive, psychoanalytic, field, and role theories, but it did not include a specific chapter on theory of attitude. Even the attitude-relevant *Handbook* chapters on prejudice and on mass communications focused on empirical findings to the near exclusion of theoretical analysis. Likewise, a recent text entitled *Theories of Social Psychology* (Deutsch & Krauss, 1965) and two otherwise comprehensive literature reviews (McGuire, 1966; Moscovici, 1963) did not provide a separate discussion of attitude theories. It was not until 1967 that this developing body of theory was professionally acknowledged through publication of books which use the term *attitude theory* in the title (Fishbein, 1967a; Insko, 1967). Past reluctance to apply the label of theory to attitudes can be attributed in part to a desire to reserve that term for the more traditional areas of perception, learning, cognition, and motivation. Attitudes, however, possess the basic characteristics required of a theoretical construct, that of having multiple antecedents and of affecting multiple responses.

The emphasis in this chapter will be on theoretical treatments of the processes underlying attitude change, since attitude theorists have typically formulated their conceptions of attitude with reference to the change process. Problems of definition and measurement are discussed only when required for understanding the determinants of attitude change as identified in any particular theoretical position reviewed.

The decision to focus on the processes of change had the effect of excluding from present consideration much of the early work in attitudes. Most of the research covered in Allport's chapter (1935), in Murphy, Murphy, and Newcomb's attitude chapter (1937), and in M. Sherif and Cantril's reviews (1945, 1946, 1947) was solely concerned with descriptive analyses, the influence of gross environmental variables, and individual differences. Much of the value of this early empirical work lay in demonstrating the applicability of attitudes to a broad array of psychological problems, in establishing the boundaries of attitude as a psychological construct, and in proving that an attitude was a situationally modifiable characteristic of the individual. The definitional problem has been examined by Fleming (1967) in a historical survey of the conceptual properties of attitude, emphasizing the evolution of the affective, cognitive, and conative components from Darwin and Sherrington to the present. A second consequence of the present focus was to exclude discussion of attitude-relevant research and theory from the fields of sociology, consumer behavior, public opinion, propaganda, and mass communication. An introduction to early work in several of these areas can be found in B. L. Smith, Lasswell, and Casey (1946) and in Schramm (1949).

The next section is organized around specific theorists and their individual contributions to the understanding of attitude change. For some, their original concerns were directly with the theoretical bases of attitude; for others, the theoretical implications had to be extracted from papers written with other objectives in mind. To convey the historical sense of this 20-year period, a chronological order of presentation is maintained.

CONTRIBUTORS TO ATTITUDE THEORY DEVELOPMENT

THURSTONE

Thurstone's most often acknowledged contribution to the study of attitudes was his solution to the problem of attitude measurement. Issuing the imperative that *attitudes can be measured* (Thurstone, 1928), he put an end to much of the unproductive debate of that period regarding the accessibility of attitudes to observation. His methodological innovations gave impetus and direction to research in attitude change for the ensuing decade. Thurstone, however, also made a conceptual contribution which had not been widely recognized or acknowledged either by the researchers who immediately followed his pioneering work, or by contemporary attitude theorists.

Thurstone has been credited only with the inelegant expression that attitude is the amount of affect for or against the attitude object (e.g., Edwards, 1957). His theoretical thinking, however, was far more subtle than this, and contained a view of the attitude change process which has been implicitly accepted by most later theorists.

The concept of attitude denoted, for Thurstone, a very complex and multidimensional psychological construct (1928, 1931). He likened its complexity to such multidimensional objects found in the physical world as a table or a fruit stand. The problem of measurement of such a complex object, especially when the definitional controversy had not yet been resolved, could only become manageable by assessing the object one dimension at a time. Even disregarding the problem of defining a fruit stand, the task of studying differences between fruit stands and the changes in a fruit stand as a function of environmental conditions requires an analytic view of the object.

The most rudimentary system for mapping objects into a number system is the nominal scale. Prior to Thurstone, this was the level of measurement predominantly employed; that is, researchers isolated such nominal classes as personal, natural, and cultural attitudes (cf. Allport, 1935, pp. 835–836). In this way, all the complex differences between one attitude and another could roughly be preserved. The study of ordinal and magnitude relationships, however, required a higher level of measurement.

Even though the attributes of attitude were still being debated, Thurstone noted that all theorists and researchers agreed that attitudes possessed an affective quality which included the properties of directionality (positive and negative) and extremity. Having thus isolated one attitudinal dimension, he set about constructing procedures for measuring individual differences on that hypothesized single-dimensional continuum. The outcome of his efforts is, of course, well-known and well-accepted. Attitude measurement theorists who followed Thurstone (e.g., Guttman, 1944; Likert, 1932) accepted this dimensional analysis of attitudes and the prepotence of the evaluative characteristic.

In the process of establishing measurement procedures, Thurstone made several assumptions regarding the relation between verbal opinion statements and the underlying evaluative disposition regarding an object. These assumptions were never fully articulated at any one place in his writings, but are clearly conveyed in the logic upon which his procedures are founded.

Individuals possess a wide variety of beliefs pertinent to any particular attitude object. These beliefs may be logically incompatible with one another; they may be distortions of reality; they may even be affectively incompatible with one another. Thurstone defined attitudinal affect as being equal to the average evaluative scale value of all belief statements the individual believed applied to the attitude object. The scale value for a belief statement was determined by group consensus rather than on an individual basis (Fishbein, 1967b).

Attitude, then, is a compound in which the elements are beliefs and the affective value of the compound is equal to the average affective value of the elements contained within the compound. This conclusion is based on Thurstone's view that attitudinal affect is most fully described by a distribution of affective values of attitude-relevant beliefs. A frequency distribution can be constructed by taking all relevant belief statements to which an individual ascribes and plotting the number of beliefs the individual possesses for each level of affective value. The average of this distribution measures the level of affect attached to the attitude object. Thurstone predicted that other parameters of the distribution, such as variance, might prove valuable in the study of attitudinal affect. The current work of Sherif on the latitudes of acceptance and rejection (C. W. Sherif, Sherif, & Nebergall, 1965; M. Sherif & Hovland, 1961) has been concerned with a form of this variance parameter. The frequency distribution need not have any explicit shape, as was assumed by early critics of Thurstone (e.g., a normal distribution was imposed by Merton, 1940), but rather can be of any irregular, multimodal form. Regardless of the form, however, Thurstone postulated that the best estimate of the individual's attitudinal affect is the average of the affective distribution of his personal beliefs. A similar averaging view of compound stimulus evaluation is offered in a more quantitative form in the works of Anderson (1965, 1968).

Since, for Thurstone, affect toward an object could be derived from a frequency distribution of the affective value of the beliefs or cognitions one holds about the object, any alteration of that frequency distribution could produce attitude change. Attitude change could thus come about through adopting new beliefs and/or through rejecting previously held cognitions about the object. An attitude could become more pro, for example, by acquiring more favorable beliefs, by rejecting previously held unfavorable beliefs, or both.

There are conditions, according to Thurstone's formulation, under which belief change will have no influence on attitude. This would occur when the acquired (or rejected) beliefs were symmetrically balanced on either side of the mean affective value of the distribution. A second case would be when a rejected prior belief was replaced by a new belief or equivalent affective value. It should be noted, however, that to the extent these belief changes affect other parameters of the distribution, such as homogeneity, other characteristics of the attitude (e.g., confidence and resistance to persuasion) may be affected.

It was this atomistic view of the attitude change process that lay behind most of the early experimental and survey research on attitudes (Murphy *et al.*, 1937). Research on the effects of movies, classroom lecture, regional origins, and socioeconomic status on attitude were inspired by the notion that the information one encounters and accepts is the primary determinant of attitude. Further, it is the evaluative loading of that information, rather than its cognitive content, which influences the individual's attitudinal affect. This fundamental assumption, although ill-acknowledged, has underlain every attitude change formulation which has been developed subsequent to Thurstone's contribution. Its importance is especially evident in the analyses of cognitive integration by Heider (1958), Newcomb (1953, 1961), Osgood and Tannenbaum (1955), Rosenberg (1956), Festinger (1957), Abelson and Rosenberg (1958), Anderson (1968), Rokeach and Rothman (1965), Fishbein (1967b), and Feldman (1966). First, these analyses concern themselves with conditions under which information is accepted or rejected and, second, with the effects of such weighting factors as saliency, polarity, importance, and compatibility, with underlying personality dynamics, on the contribution of each cognition to the resultant attitude. None, however, contest the central role played by the evaluative loading (direction and magnitude) of the relevant cognitions in determining the location of an individual's attitude on the affective continuum.

ALLPORT

In his landmark survey and analysis of attitudes, Allport (1935) devoted only a brief section to the determinants of attitude change. The bulk of his chapter dealt with the history of attitude, various definitions of attitude, the distinction of attitude from other concepts such as needs and habits, and the nominal classification of attitudes. This treatment reflected the major concerns of the preceding two decades; being more involved with the delineation of the domain rather than with the determinants of attitude formation and change.

Allport identified four "conditions for the formation of attitudes" (1935, pp. 810–814), but none were developed in any great detail. Individual experiences with the attitude object combine through *integration* in forming a unified attitude. This was akin to Thurstone's view that information combined to produce the final attitude, but was meant by Allport to include other characteristics in addition to affect. An attitude which is initially gross and diffuse will become more *differentiated* with experience. Having a negative reaction toward being in the dark as a child becomes more and more contingent on other factors, such as who you are with and whether or not you are in familiar surroundings. Permanent attitudes can be formed rapidly and forcefully as the result of a single *traumatic* experience, a third mode of acquisition. Finally, *imitation* of attitudes expressed by friends, parents, or admired others can be a source of ready-made attitudes for the individual.

Although these four classes shared an emphasis on the effects of experience as a determinant of attitude, they did not illuminate the influences of such intervening processes as learning, perception, and motivation on attitude change. They represented, rather, descriptive classes of environmental variables. Indeed, the closest Allport came to examining the psychological processes by which attitudes are formed and changed was in his review of Lippmann's theory (1922) of public opinion. Lippmann, according to Allport, emphasized one function attitudes play in the day-to-day life of the individual. Since it is impossible for the individual to acquire and hold in mind complete knowledge of his world when making his everyday decisions, he must find a way to summarize and classify this information. Attitudes, because of their stereotype quality, permit the person to hold beliefs about and respond to classes of objects rather than having to respond differentially to each individual object in his environment. Allport concludes that it is because attitudes serve this function of cognitive economy that they frequently will be resistant to influence based on direct experience with the attitude object.

LEWIN

Arriving in the United States during the period when some were defining social psychology exclusively as a study of attitudes, Lewin's theoretical orientation (1935, 1951) remained peculiarly aloof from this attitudinal preoccupation. His theoretical concerns were more broadly defined; he attempted to integrate all the determinants of behavior under one dynamic, cognitive system. The most basic proposition of Lewin's system was symbolically expressed by the equation: $B = f(P,E)$. Behavior (B) is a joint function (f) of the person (P) and his environment (E). By this expression Lewin meant to convey more than simply the elementary notion that behavior has two classes of determinants, those unique to the individual and those contributed by the environment. He meant, rather, that behavior was determined by the simultaneous operation of momentary conditions of the individual in combination and interaction with the structure of his environment. Determinants contributed from these two sources were potent only if they were represented in the individual's life space, or his psychological view of the relevant characteristics and forces operating in the present situation. Because of this orientation, attitudes were viewed by Lewin primarily as behavioral determinants rather than as dependent variables in their own right. For most purposes he accepted attitudes as a given rather than examining the determinants of their formation and change as a separate problem area.

The one concept in Lewin's theoretical analysis of life space which comes closest to present-day conceptions of attitude was his construct of valence. A positive valence characterizes a region or object in the life space toward which the individual is attracted (or toward which all "forces" are directed); a negative valence characterizes an object or region which repels the individual ("forces" point away from the region). Such movement toward or away from an attitude object is the resultant of driving and restraining forces operating in the life space.

Lewin used the concept of valence in two distinct ways. One was similar to the dimension of affect identified by Thurstone in that it referred to the individual's feelings toward the attitude object or goal region. The second usage, which was more often invoked in his analyses, viewed valence as a transient state being determined jointly by the individual's present environment, his personal preferences, and his immediate needs rather than as an enduring disposition of the individual. Attitudes, therefore, served as one of several forces operating to determine valence in this second usage. The second meaning was, of course, in greater congruence with his overall view of behavior as a joint function of the person and the environment. However, the first, more restricted usage appeared at least once (Lewin, 1935) in an analysis of the determinants of valence change.

Valence change takes place, Lewin asserted, when the attitude object or goal region becomes imbedded in a new context and thus changes its location in the individual's life space (Lewin, 1935, pp. 167–170). Placing an object of previous negative valence into an integrated relationship with objects or activities of positive valence will cause that negatively valued object to be reassessed in the light of this new context. The negatively valued act of eating asparagus might, for a child, become a positive act when placed into the context of playing a game in which he pretends the spoon is a steam shovel and his eating the asparagus is an excavation project. A second major class of determinants for valence change was reinforcement. Lewin acknowledged that direct or anticipated experience with punishments and rewards would affect the value placed on the activity or object on which the reinforcements were contingent. He felt that the influence of rewards and punishments had the greatest effect on young children who had rather weak functional boundaries in their life space or cognitive structure. For rewards and punishments to be effective in a developed life space, the individual must see their contingencies as being justified; that is, the reward contingencies must be seen in a broader, more integrated context before they will be effective.

One additional determinant of valence change identified by Lewin is satiation resulting from repeated experience of the goal region or attitude object. Satiation operates at the cognitive level in that the second experience with an object will not be identical to the first encounter because the individual has in his past history the previous experience. This logic can be extended to the comparison between experiencing the object a third time compared to the second, and so on. Satiation affects the valence of the goal region relative to the valence of alternative goal regions. In an absolute sense it is unclear whether satiation causes a lowering in valence of the focal region, a positive change in the alternative regions, or both.

Lewin's contribution to the development of theory in the area of attitude change is due less to his analysis of valence change and the influence of valence on subsequent behavior than to his more general view of man as a cognitive organism reacting in integrated fashion to the influences impinging on him. Attitude is not an automatic reflex or immutable disposition, but rather it exists in a personal and situational context. Attitudes, for Lewin, were represented in the individual's life space and imbedded in a cognitive context, with affective and cognitive structures operating in an interdependent fashion to determine subsequent behavior. It was this field-theoretic orientation of Lewin's that set the stage for the subsequent development of the cognitive balance interpretations of attitude change. Modern analyses of cognitive integration (e.g., Abelson, Aronson, McGuire, Newcomb, Rosenberg, & Tannenbaum, 1968; Feldman, 1966; Osgood, 1960; Rokeach & Rothman, 1965) have built upon Lewin's conception of life space as a dynamic system of regions and forces. It is clear that his insightful analysis of behavioral conflicts (approach-approach, approach-avoidance, avoidance-avoidance) has a direct analog in contemporary theories of affective and belief consistency (Abelson & Rosenberg, 1958; Heider, 1958) and their relation to behavior (Insko & Schopler, 1967; Rosenberg & Hovland, 1960). Finally, the study of cognitive complexity draws many of its theoretical concepts from Lewin's structural analysis of life space (Brock, 1962; Crockett, 1965; Harvey, 1967; Kerlinger, 1967; Schroder, Driver, & Streufert, 1967; Scott, 1963; Zajonc, 1960).

individual's policy orientation are two important dimensions of this component.

This differentiated description of attitudes marked an important break with the attitude measurement tradition initiated by Thurstone in 1928. Although Thurstone acknowledged that attitude was a multi-faceted concept and cautioned researchers that his technique measured only one of its dimensions, the only dimension that received substantial empirical attention was the one for which Thurstone provided a rational measure. Smith offered a cogent and meaningfully integrated array of attitudinal facets, each of which was capable of empirical investigation. This represented a stern challenge to theory development in that a comprehensive formulation should be able to account for responses within each of these facets, rather than just affective responses alone. Unfortunately, despite his having emphasized the importance of measurement in the analysis of attitudinal components, Smith provided no clearly specified procedures for their quantitative assessment in his published work.

Smith represented a break with a second tradition initiated by Thurstone by reappraising the role of new information on attitude change. While Thurstone assumed that the acceptance of new information by the respondent led directly and immediately to attitude change, Smith believed that information per se was not a determinant of attitude change. Attitude change could only be accomplished to the extent that the new information was relevant to one of the functions served by the attitude within the personality structure of the individual. Smith suggested that there were five primary personality functions mediated by attitudes.

In serving a *value function*, attitudes represent an expression of the individual's basic personal and social values, a function similar to Sherif and Cantril's concept of an ego involved attitude. Although values can affect several of the characteristics of attitude, Smith explicitly postulated that the intensity of an attitude was a function of first, the degree to which the value is engaged by the attitude, and second, the importance or centrality of all values so engaged. This particular hypothesis was subject to more extensive analysis by Smith (1949) as well as later workers (Peak, 1955; Rosenberg, 1956). The *consistency function* of an attitude reflects the extent to which the attitude is consistent with the individual's characteristic modes of reaction. So, for example, individuals who are extrapunitive (blaming others) in their reactions to a frustrating situation are more likely to develop attitudes of blaming other countries, persons, racial, or religious groups for personal or national difficulties. The *gratification function* expresses the fact that attitudes can serve indirectly to gratify the individual's basic needs. For example, a person's positive attitude toward his employer aids his advancement in the organization. Attitudes can serve a *meaning function* in that they operate to make the individual's world predictable and orderly; they serve to make his knowledge and his experiences more stable and integrated. In performing this function, attitudes may simplify the objective world through wishful thinking. This occurs, however, only to the extent that cognitive distortions do not impair the individual's ability to operate effectively in the environment. Lippmann's theory of public opinion (1922) was based upon this function and the "wishful thinking" postulate reappears in McGuire's research on logical-affective consistency (1960). The *conformity function* of an attitude serves to facilitate the individual's identification with friends or prestigeful persons and, second, to promote their acceptance of him. A basic need for acceptance and approval was postulated as the motivational source underlying this function.

In accordance with each of these functions, attitude change can be obtained by either modifying the individual's value structure, altering his basic personality disposition, introducing disruptive information and experiences, or changing the attitudes demanded for respect and acceptance by valued individuals in his social environment. Themes developed in this early functional analysis were elaborated in the subsequent theoretical treatments by Adorno, Frenkel-Brunswick, Levinson, and Sanford (1950), Smith *et al.* (1956), Katz and Stotland (1959), Kelman (1958), Sarnoff (1960), and Katz (1960).

DOOB

Early S-R interpretations of attitude, offered by Thorndike (1935) and Lorge (1936), were based on the associationistic principles of repetition and reward. Each attitude was an overt affective response which became associated with its own specific stimulus conditions. This view, lacking the conceptual flexibility provided by the later-developed conception of implicit mediating response, failed to engender a following due to its inability to account parsimoniously for the diverse phenomena of attitude (cf., Asch, 1948).

An analysis of the "behavior of attitudes" was offered by Doob (1947) based on the reinforcement orientation of Hull (1943) and Miller and Dollard (1941). Doob viewed attitude as an anticipatory or antedating implicit response which mediates the individual's overt responses. The implicit response mediates by producing stimuli to which overt responses, including linguistic responses, stereotypes, and other cognitions, are conditioned. The attitude is also drive-producing in that its activation creates tension within the individual which can only be reduced by subsequent reward-producing behavior.

This conceptualization led Doob to propose in summary form three classes of variables which would be effective in inducing and modifying attitudes. The influence of *reinforcement* is determined by the frequency with which the attitude has mediated the receipt of a reward, by the immediacy of the reward, and by the amount of the reward. Also, both the distinctiveness of the arousing stimulus pattern and the frequency with which it has aroused the attitude influence the effectiveness of reinforcements in determining attitudes. The tendency toward overt expression of attitudes in a given situation may be altered by changes in the *drive strength of competing attitudes* aroused by the same situation. The final set of factors affecting attitude change are those processes which lead to *forgetting* such as extinction through nonreinforcement.

Doob's contribution stemmed entirely from his theoretical analysis, for he offered no original empirical support in favor of his position. His comprehensive statement, however, gave guidance to subsequent researchers and provided an explicit foundation which others could either build upon or use as a reference point to initiate their own theoretical excursions (e.g., Fishbein, 1967b; Hovland, Janis, & Kelly, 1953; Lott & Lott, this volume; Osgood, Suci, & Tannenbaum, 1957; Rhine, 1958; Rosnow, this volume; Staats, this volume; Weiss, this volume).

ASCH

Representing the Gestalt tradition, Asch and his colleagues (Asch, 1940, 1948; Lewis, 1941) challenged the early learning interpretations of attitude change. The influence of communicator credibility or prestige on the acceptance of a communication was interpreted by Thorndike (1935) and Lorge (1936) as being due to the affective response to the communicator becoming associated with the content of the communication. Asch observed that these early theories treated the objects of judgment, the attitude object as well as the arguments in a communication, as being fixed entities regardless of the source to which the communication is ascribed. These learning theorists appeared to assign little relevance to either the meaning of the specific arguments involved or their personal importance in determining attitude change.

Asch believed that this gave an incomplete picture of the attitude change process, for not only do individuals differ in their perception of an object, but also the meaning of the object can be changed through informational communications. In addition, ascription of high versus low prestige sources to a communication will have a significant influence on the cognitive interpretation it receives. Asch (1948) demonstrated, for example, that the quote, "those who hold and those who are without property have ever formed two distinct classes" has an entirely different meaning when ascribed to Karl Marx than when attributed to John Adams. Thus, the extent to which the person feels positively toward a communication (and, consequently, the degree to which he agrees with it) is largely determined by the meaning which the recipient attaches to that communication. More generally, any background or contextual factors which influence the meaning of a communication, such as its source, will influence the individual's acceptance of its arguments.

The meaning of a message, although not formally delineated by Asch, referred to the type of other beliefs and values which were seen as related to and supportive of the attitude object. The cognitive implications of meaning were treated more explicitly by Heider who is discussed below. One important contribution of Asch's work was to obligate subsequent learning formulations to account for the acquisition and change of meaning (Fishbein, 1967b; Osgood, et al., 1957).

Asch did not compare, either in his 1948 paper or subsequent text book (1952), his cognitive interpretation with the learning formulation presented by Doob (1947). By employing the construct of an implicit response, Doob's formulation was better able to meet Asch's objections than was the formulation of Lorge and Thorndike. Doob explicitly stated in his paper that not only can attitudes be formed through reinforcement, but also that the implicit response can serve as a stimulus for such things as thoughts, beliefs, and other cognitive responses to the stimulus input. It is likely, however, from Asch's cognitive orientation that he would not find this more advanced reinforcement interpretation completely satisfactory.

HEIDER

Although he addressed himself primarily to the study and analysis of interpersonal relations, Heider (1946, 1958) had an important directive influence on the development of attitude theory. Like Lewin's, his analysis was based on the assumption that one must understand the individual's cognitive representation of the environment, his life space, in order to understand the operation of attitudes and their impact on behavior. People, objects, and events are related to one another within a dynamic cognitive system. Having primary significance in the life space are the attribution of causality, the existence of sentiments, the degree of belongingness characterizing pairs of elements, and the extent to which a person ought to or ought not to engage in a particular activity. Of these several basic concepts it was Heider's analysis of sentiments and belongingness which had the greatest influence on subsequent attitude research and theorizing. Assumptions analogous to his principle of cognitive balance have been adopted as the central postulate in the theories of Newcomb (1953, 1961), Osgood and Tannenbaum (1955), Festinger (1957), Abelson and Rosenberg (1958), Rosenberg and Hovland (1960), and Insko and Schopler (1967).

Sentiment is the positive or negative evaluation the perceiving person makes of some object represented in his life space; in addition, one cognitive element may be perceived as possessing positive or negative sentiment toward another element. Unit formation exists between the cognitive representation of two objects when they are seen as "belonging" together in the Gestalt sense of belongingness or unity. Heider borrowed the principles of proximity, equality, and context directly from Gestalt psychology's study of perceptual phenomena and applied them to social perception and cognitive organization. Two cognitive elements will be bound together as a unit if they are seen as different aspects of the same person (proximity), they possess similar attributes (equality), or they interact with one another (figure and ground). A person is likely to see himself in a unit formation with another person or object under conditions of frequent interaction, high degree of familiarity, ownership, similarity of beliefs and goals, and when he is personally instrumental in causing a good outcome for the other. All sentiment and unit relations fall into two classes: either positive or negative. Positive sentiment relations are illustrated by liking and approval, and negative relations by rejection and condemnation; a positive unit denotes the presence of a cognitive unit between two entities, whereas a negative unit indicates segregation of the two entities.

The dynamic element of Heider's formulation is the motive or need to maintain balanced and harmonious relations between cognitive elements. Heider asserted his principle of balance on the basis of a "naive psychology" analysis of such phrases as, "Joe avoids his best friend, Bill." This particular illustration and many like it represent, for the typical "naive" individual, an uncomfortable and somehow contradictory description of Joe's behavior. Two cognitive entities are balanced if both the relations (sentiment and unit) are positive or if they are both negative. Thus, Joe should either begin seeking out Bill or begin disliking him if balance is to be obtained. Attitude (sentiment) change is produced by the occurrence of unit relations which are opposite in sign to the existing attitude.

A second definition of balance is offered for the case in which three cognitive elements (a triad) are involved. The third element can be a third person, or it can be an object, act, or event. Balance is obtained when the relations within pairs of the three cognitive entities are either all positive, or two are negative and one is positive. As applied to analyzing Joe's attitude toward Bill, if Joe believes that he and Bill share common sentiments or unit relations to a third element, he would develop a positive sentiment and unit relation toward Bill to establish balance among these cognitions. Thus, under the principle of triadic balance, attitude change is accomplished through altering the degree to which the individual and the attitude object either share common relations or possess opposite signed relations toward third elements.

Heider's balance principle suggests a variety of specific ways attitude change can be produced, even under the two restricted cases of two and three elements. The variety was greatly expanded by later workers who, for example, examined balance restoring mechanisms not involving relation modification (Abelson, 1959) and who extended balance principles to multiple element systems (Abelson & Rosenberg, 1958; Cartwright & Harary, 1956; Phillips, 1967).

In addition to predicting changes in sentiment, which corresponds roughly to Thurstone's dimension of affect, Heider's principle of balance provided a basis upon which predictions could be made of the association among cognitive elements and their relationship to the attitude object, i.e., the attitude's cognitive composition.

HOVLAND

Carl Hovland entered the arena of attitude theory by way of his World War II research activities with the U.S. War Department's Information and Education Division in the general field of mass communications (Hovland, 1948a, 1948b; Hovland et al., 1949). In his two 1948 papers he divided the communication process into three broad components: stimulus or cue properties, responses of the individual, and the psychological processes which mediate between stimuli and responses. He believed that, while the other social sciences were valuable in delineating important classes of stimuli and responses in the study of mass communications, psychology was uniquely qualified for conducting research and constructing theories regarding the intervening processes.

While harboring an interest in attitudinal responses during this period, Hovland did not adopt them as his primary research interest until after completing the 1949 book (with Lumsdaine and Sheffield) on mass communications. It was then that he instigated the renowned Yale Communications Research Program, funded by the Rockefeller Foundation. The focus and goals of this group, as well as a summary of its early research activities, was given by Hovland in his presidential address to the Eastern Psychological Association in 1951 (Hovland, 1951).

Hovland did not make an effort in this early work to present a systematic theoretical statement; rather, he offered illustrative analyses and applications of psychological principles to communication and attitude change phenomena. Although these may have only been considered illustrative by Hovland at that time, they contained theoretical concepts which were to become central in the later attitude research of the Yale group (e.g., Hovland et al., 1953).

Hovland's contributions to understanding the processes involved in attitude change fall into two categories: his analysis of the sequential steps involved in attitude change and his application of behavior theory principles to complex attitudinal problems. Consistent with his focus on mass communications, Hovland restricted his theoretical discussions to situations in which only one-way, verbal communications were employed.

In analyzing the components of the persuasion situation, Hovland argued that one cannot conceive of attitude change as a single response but rather a resultant of separate subresponses. In his analysis of the effects of intelligence on attitude change (Hovland et al., 1949), he identified four facets of attitudinal responses. The first was simple learning ability, which influences attitude change through the amount of information the individual understands and retains from a communication and thus affects the information on which the final attitude is based. His second facet was acceptance of the material communicated. Intelligence influenced acceptance through both motivational factors and rational analyses of the validity of the arguments communicated. Motivational factors included emotional biases, authoritarian orientations, and personal involvements, whereas rational analyses included an assessment of the comprehensiveness and reliability of the information contained in the communication. The third factor was the individual's interpretation of the arguments presented in the communication. Although interpretations and conclusions may have been drawn in the communication, the recipient will make his own inferences and generalizations on the basis of the material presented. So, such individual difference factors as intelligence will affect the validity of the interpretations made and consequently the extent to which the communication will be accepted. The last facet of attitudinal responses Hovland considered was the prior information or factual basis the respondent possessed at the time of receiving the communication. Individuals who have higher intelligence may be expected to have already collected facts, to have better retained previously acquired facts, and to have spent more time evolving a better integrated and factually based position on the attitude issue.

Although Hovland's analysis was explicitly restricted to the variable of intelligence, it was clear that this analysis could be applied to any other source of individual differences. A second extrapolation could be made in analyzing the effect of environmental manipulations on attitudinal responses. For example, in studying the influence of distraction or stress on the effectiveness of persuasion, the theorist should be able to separately predict its influence on each of the facets of response. Hovland, Lumsdaine, and Sheffield's analysis of the stages involved in attitude change was a forerunner of that presented in Hovland et al. (1953), as well as that offered by McGuire (1968; this volume).

Hovland identified two general classes of processes which mediated between stimuli and responses; one was biological-physiological in nature and the other was due to learning processes. In presenting this dichotomy, he appeared to be using the expression learning to include all psychological processes which are affected by experience. While this presumably included theory drawn from all areas of psychology, he specifically cited five principles drawn only from learning-behavior theory; they were extinction, generalization, discrimination, temporal gradient of reward, and reinforcement. It was his assertion that these principles, derived from the study of organisms behaving in simple, uncomplicated environments, could be satisfactorily applied to attitudinal responses. Hovland et al. (1949), drawing upon such learning-behavior theory principles, proposed a variety of processes to explain the sleeper effect and the relative effectiveness of one- and two-sided messages.

Several alternative hypotheses were tendered in accounting for the sleeper effect. One explanation which later received experimental support (Hovland et al., 1953) distinguished between forgetting of a message's source and forgetting of its specific arguments. On this basis it was possible to predict that a negative source would produce more attitude change after a period of delay than upon immediate assessment. A second explanation suggested was that the information learned from a communication may take on new meaning due to subsequent experiences. The new meaning then makes the arguments more acceptable than they had been previously. This hypothesis, bearing a similarity to Asch's "change of meaning" interpretation of communicator prestige effects (1948), did not directly incorporate principles of behavior theory. A third explanation of the sleeper effect, like the first, employed the assumption of differential rates of forgetting. It suggested that subjects would forget at a comparatively rapid rate the specific arguments incorporated into the communication, but they would retain for a much longer period the general idea or sentiments expressed by the communication. Arguments which are applicable only to one member of a class may later be generalized to all members of that class; the generalization will be produced by rapid forgetting of the specific qualifying clauses which accompanied the original information.

A second phenomenon investigated by Hovland *et al.* (1949) was the effectiveness of one- versus two-sided arguments in producing attitude change. In analyzing the psychological consequences of this communication characteristic, they argued that the respondent makes implicit verbal responses which include both rehearsal of prior beliefs and evaluation of the bias of the communicator. Here, then, was emphasized the individual's cognitive response to a communication, a concept which reappears not only in Hovland's later work (Hovland *et al.*, 1953), but also in Janis's incentive theory (Janis & Gilmore, 1965), and in the work of A. Greenwald (this volume).

Hovland's major contributions lay in his ability both to see the relevance of basic psychological processes as applied to attitude change and to analyze the attitudinal response into separate facets, each of which contributes to the final attitude adopted. His theoretical orientation is concisely summarized in his belief that the "Formulation of the attitude problem in terms of behavior theory . . . requires interest to be focused on the intervening symbolic processes that mediate the acqusition, differentiation, and extinction of attitudinal responses [Hovland, 1951, p. 427]."

CONCLUDING COMMENTS

The work reviewed here provided the background and context for contemporary attitude theory. By 1950, at least three factors converged to affect the subsequent nature of attitude theorizing: most of the psychological foundations of attitude had been theoretically and empirically described, researchers were beginning to augment survey and case history techniques with the precision of the laboratory, and the problems of attitude measurement had ceased being a major issue of contention.

The theoretical formulations summarized in this chapter made early contributions within each of the major classifications identified in Table 1. These pre-1950 contributions have been classified in Table 2. One caution must be observed in any comparison of Tables 1 and 2; no causal interpretation should be made regarding the contribution of early theorists of one category to the development of post-1950 theories in the same category. In some instances direct influence is apparent (e.g., Heider), others had little direct influence (e.g., Allport), and the influence of others cut across several categories (e.g., Lewin).

Research methodology began in the late 1940's and early 1950's to turn to the experimental laboratory for testing hypotheses. Hovland, in agreeing with Lewin's belief that a phenomenon was never fully understood until it could be produced through a change in conditions, was especially vigorous in advocating experimental methodology (Hovland, 1951; Hovland *et al.*, 1949). This emphasis placed requirements on the development of attitude theories which the

TABLE 2
ATTITUDE-THEORETICAL FORMULATIONS DEVELOPED
BETWEEN 1930 AND 1950

Classification	Contributor
Learning-behavior theory	
S-R	Thorndike (1935), Lorge (1936)
	Doob (1947)
Eclectic	Hovland (1948a, 1948b), Hovland *et al.* (1949)
Cognitive integration theory	
Consistency	Heider (1946)
Motivational	Lippmann (1922)
	Lewin (1935, 1951)
	Newcomb (1943)
	M. Sherif & Cantril (1945, 1946, 1947)
	M. B. Smith (1947)
	Asch (1948)
Nonmotivational	Thurstone (1928, 1931)
	Allport (1935)

earlier empirical procedures did not demand. Specificity in preparation of experimental operations led to specificity in hypothesis formation and thence to theory construction. In the main, the theories developed after 1950 have gained in precision but suffered in the breadth of attitudinal processes each incorporates.

Thurstone, and later Likert (1932) and Guttman (1944), provided a rational methodology for the measurement of attitudinal affect. While the relevance of other nonaffective aspects of attitude was clearly recognized (Krech & Crutchfield, 1948; M. B. Smith, 1947) and measurement procedures were available (Abelson, 1955; Lazarsfeld, 1950; Thurstone, 1947) researchers appeared to be content with this single aspect of attitude for their research attention. This emphasis continues yet today, but without the earlier methodological controversy that inhibited substantive research. The bulk of attitude research and, consequently, the theory developed to understand the attitude change process, continues to focus primarily on affect to the detriment of understanding the other characteristics of attitude.

Any historical review is selective in the material it covers and the emphasis it awards the included contributions. It is important, then, to remind the reader what of relevance has not been given detailed exposition. No systematic survey or analysis was attempted here of the variety of definitions proposed for attitude, nor has the technology of measurement been reviewed, nor have the basic empirical phenomena which underlie the topic domain been historically examined, nor have the philosophical backgrounds and differences of each contributor been analyzed. It was decided, rather, to select from the works of each author only those theoretical insights which were of relevance to the process of attitude formation and change.

The development of attitude theory would benefit by theorists moving in the integrative direction of interrelating their formulations with the major alternatives. The theoretical contributions reviewed here, as well as those contributed after 1950, have been directed toward isolating specific psychological processes. In examining the effect on attitudes, the theorist typically made the assumption that all other psychological factors are held constant. What is missing in this approach is a conceptual understanding of the effects on attitude of several, simultaneously engaged psychological processes. There are clearly conditions under which the influence of each process can be heightened, negated, or perhaps even reversed. Indeed, studying the interaction between theoretical processes appears to be the only route by which a comprehensive understanding of attitudes will be attained.

References

Abelson, R. P. A technique and a model for multi-dimensional attitude scaling. *Public Opinion Quarterly, Winter*, 1954-1955, 405-418.

Abelson, R. P. Modes of resolution of belief dilemmas. *Journal of Conflict Resolution*, 1959, 3, 343-352.

Abelson, R. P., Aronson, E., McGuire, W. J., Newcomb, T. M., Rosenberg, M. J., & Tannenbaum, P. H. (Eds.), *Theories of cognitive consistency: A sourcebook.* Chicago: Rand McNally, 1968, in press.

Abelson, R. P., & Rosenberg, M. J. Symbolic psycho-logic: A model of attitudinal cognition. *Behavioral Science*, 1958, 3, 1-13.

Adorno, T., Frenkel-Brunswik, E., Levinson, D., & Sanford, R. *The authoritarian personality.* New York: Harper, 1950.

Allport, G. W. Attitudes. In C. A. Murchison (Ed.), *A handbook of social psychology.* Worcester, Mass.: Clark University Press, 1935. Pp. 798-844.

Anderson, N. H. Primacy effects in personality impression formation using a generalized order effect paradigm. *Journal of Personality and Social Psychology*, 1965, 2, 1-9.

Anderson, N. H. A simple model for information integration. In R. P. Abelson *et al.* (Eds.), *Theories of cognitive consistency: A sourcebook.* Chicago: Rand McNally, 1968, in press.

Asch, S. E. Studies in the principles of judgments and attitudes: II. Determination of judgments by group and by ego standards. *Journal of Social Psychology*, 1940, 12, 433-465.

Asch, S. E. The doctrine of suggestion, prestige and imitation in social psychology. *Psychological Review*, 1948, 55, 250-276.

Asch, S. E. *Social psychology.* Englewood Cliffs, N. J.: Prentice-Hall, 1952.

Bem, D. J. An experimental analysis of self-persuasion. *Journal of Experimental Social Psychology*, 1965, 1, 199-218.

Bem, D. J. Self-perception: An alternative interpretation of cognitive dissonance phenomena. *Psychological Review*, 1967, 74, 183-200.

Brehm, J. W. *A theory of psychological reactance.* New York: Academic Press, 1966.

Brehm, J. W., & Cohen, A. R. *Explorations in cognitive dissonance.* New York: Wiley, 1962.

Brock, T. C. Cognitive restructuring and attitude change. *Journal of Abnormal and Social Psychology*, 1962, 64, 264-271.

Byrne, D., & Clore, G. L. Effectance arousal and attraction. *Journal of Personality and Social Psychology (Monograph)*, 1967, 6, (Whole No. 638).

Campbell, D. T. Social attitudes and other acquired behavioral dispositions. In S. Koch (Ed.), *Psychology: A study of a science.* Vol. 6. New York: McGraw-Hill, 1963. Pp. 94-172.

Cartwright, D., & Harary, F. Structural balance: A generalization of Heider's theory. *Psychological Review*, 1956, 63, 277-293.

Crockett, W. H. Cognitive complexity and impression formation. In B. A. Maher (Ed.), *Progress in experimental personality research.* Vol. 2, New York: Academic Press, 1965. Pp. 47-90.

Deutsch, M., & Krauss, R. M. *Theories in social psychology.* New York: Basic Books, 1965.

Doob, L. The behavior of attitudes. *Psychological Review*, 1947, 54, 135-156.

Edwards, A. L. *Techniques of attitude scale construction.* New York: Appleton, 1957.

Feldman, S. Motivational aspects of attitudinal elements and their place in cognitive interaction. In S. Feldman (Ed.), *Cognitive consistency: Motivational antecedents and behavioral consequences.* New York: Academic Press, 1966. Pp. 75-108.

Feldman, S. The integrative response to a stimulus manifold. In R. P. Abelson *et al.* (Eds.), *Theories of cognitive consistency: A sourcebook.* Chicago: Rand McNally, 1968, in press.

Festinger, L. A theory of social comparison processes. *Human Relations,* 1954, **7,** 117-140.

Festinger, L. *A theory of cognitive dissonance.* Stanford, Calif.: Stanford University Press, 1957.

Fishbein, M. (Ed.), *Readings in attitude theory and measurement.* New York: Wiley, 1967. (a)

Fishbein, M. A behavior theory approach to the relations between beliefs about an object and the attitude toward the object. In M. Fishbein (Ed.), *Readings in attitude theory and measurement.* New York: Wiley, 1967. Pp. 389-400. (b)

Fishbein, M. Attitude and prediction of behavior. In M. Fishbein (Ed.), *Readings in attitude theory and measurement.* New York: Wiley, 1967. Pp. 477-492. (c)

Fleming, D. Attitude: The history of a concept. *Perspectives in American History,* 1967, **1,** 287-365.

Freedman, J. L. Involvement, discrepancy, and change. *Journal of Abnormal and Social Psychology,* 1964, **69,** 290-295.

French, V. V. The structure of sentiments. I. A restatement of the theory of sentiments. *Journal of Personality,* 1947, **15,** 247-282. (a)

French, V. V. The structure of sentiments. II. A preliminary study of sentiments. *Journal of Personality,* 1947, **16,** 78-108. (b)

French, V. V. The structure of sentiments. III. A study of philosophico-religious sentiments. *Journal of Personality,* 1947, **16,** 209-244. (c)

Golightly, C., & Byrne, D. Attitude statements as positive and negative reinforcements. *Science,* 1964, **146,** 798-799.

Greenwald, H. J. The involvement controversy in persuasion research. Unpublished manuscript, Columbia University, 1965.

Guttman, L. A basis for scaling qualitative data. *American Sociological Review,* 1944, **9,** 139-150.

Harvey, O. J. Conceptual systems and attitude change. In C. W. Sherif & M. Sherif (Eds.), *Attitude, ego-involvement and change.* New York: Wiley, 1967. Pp. 201-226.

Heider, F. Attitudes and cognitive organization. *Journal of Psychology,* 1946, **21,** 107-112.

Heider, F. *The psychology of interpersonal relations.* New York: Wiley, 1958.

Helson, H. *Adaptation-level theory.* New York: Harper, 1964.

Hovland, C. I. Social communication. *Proceedings of the American Philosophical Society,* 1948, **92,** 371-375. (a)

Hovland, C. I. Psychology of the communication process. In W. Schramm (Ed.), *Communication in modern society.* Urbana, Ill.: University of Illinois Press, 1948. Pp. 58-65. (b)

Hovland, C. I. Changes in attitude through communication. *Journal of Abnormal and Social Psychology,* 1951, **46,** 424-437.

Hovland, C. I., Janis, I. L., & Kelley, H. H. *Communication and persuasion.* New Haven: Yale University Press, 1953.

Hovland, C. I., Lumsdaine, A., & Sheffield, F. *Experiments on mass communication.* Princeton, N. J.: Princeton University Press, 1949.

Hull, C. *Principles of behavior.* New York: Appleton, 1943.

Insko, C. A. *Theories of attitude change.* New York: Appleton, 1967.

Insko, C. A., & Schopler, J. Triadic consistency: A statement of affective-cognitive-conative consistency. *Psychological Review*, 1967, **74**, 361-376.

Janis, I. Motivational factors in the resolution of decisional conflicts. In M. R. Jones (Ed.), *Nebraska symposium on motivation*. Vol. 7. Lincoln, Neb.: University of Nebraska Press, 1959, Pp. 198-231.

Janis, I., & Gilmore, J. The influence of incentive conditions on the success of role playing in modifying attitudes. *Journal of Personality and Social Psychology*, 1965, **I**, 17-27.

Katz, D. The functional approach to the study of attitudes. *Public Opinion Quarterly*, *1960*, **24**, 163-204.

Katz, D., & Stotland, E. A preliminary statement to a theory of attitude structure and change. In S. Koch (Ed.), *Psychology: A study of a science*. Vol. 3. *Formulations of the person and the social context*. New York: McGraw-Hill, 1959. Pp. 423-475.

Kelman, H. Compliance, identification and internalization: Three processes of attitude change. *Journal of Conflict Resolution*, 1958, **2**, 51-60.

Kerlinger, F. N. Social attitudes and their criterial referents: A structural theory. *Psychological Review*, 1967, **74**, 110-122.

Krech, D., & Crutchfield, R. S. *Theory and problems of social psychology*. New York: McGraw-Hill, 1948.

Latané, B. (Ed.), Studies in social comparison. *Journal of Experimental Social Psychology*, 1966, Supplement 1.

Lazarsfeld, P. F. The logical and mathematical foundation of latent structure analysis. In S. A. Stouffer *et al.* (Eds.), *Measurement and prediction*. Princeton, N. J.: Princeton University Press, 1950. Pp. 362-412.

Lewin, K. *Dynamic theory of personality*. New York: McGraw-Hill, 1935.

Lewin, K. *Field theory in the social sciences*. New York: Harper, 1951.

Lewis, H. B. Studies in the principles of judgments and attitudes: IV. The operation of "prestige suggestion." *Journal of Social Psychology*, 1941, **14**, 229-256.

Likert, R. A. A technique for the measurement of attitudes. *Archives of Psychology*, 1932, **22**, No. 140.

Lindzey, G. *Handbook of social psychology*. Reading, Mass.: Addison-Wesley, 1954.

Lippmann, W. *Public opinion*. New York: Harcourt, Brace, 1922.

Lorge, I. Prestige, suggestion and attitudes. *Journal of Social Psychology*, 1936, **7**, 386-402.

Lott, B. E. Attitude formation: The development of a color-preference response through mediated generalization. *Journal of Abnormal and Social Psychology*, 1955, **50**, 321-326.

McGuire, W. J. A syllogistic analysis of cognitive relationships. In M. J. Rosenberg, C. Hovland, W. McGuire, R. Abelson, & J. Brehm (Eds.), *Attitude organization and change*. New Haven: Yale University Press, 1960. Pp. 65-111.

McGuire, W. J. Inducing resistance to persuasion. In L. Berkowitz (Ed.), *Advances in experimental social psychology*. Vol. 1. New York: Academic Press, 1964. Pp. 191-229.

McGuire, W. J. Attitudes and opinions. *Annual Review of Psychology*, 1966, **17**, 475-514.

McGuire, W. J. Personality and susceptibility to social influence. In E. F. Borgatta, & W. W. Lambert (Eds.), *Handbook of personality theory and research*. Chicago: Rand McNally, 1968, in press.

Merton, R. K. Facts and factitiousness in ethnic opinionnaires. *American Sociological Review*, 1940, **5**, 13-28.

Miller, N. E., & Dollard, J. *Social learning and imitation*. New Haven: Yale University Press, 1941.

Moscovici, S. Attitudes and opinions. *Annual Review of Psychology*, 1963, **14**, 231-260.

Murphy, G., Murply, L. B., & Newcomb, T. M. *Experimental social psychology*. New York: Harper, 1937.

Murray, H. A., & Morgan, C. D. A clinical study of sentiments: I. *Genetic Psychology Monographs*, 1945, **32**, 3-149. (a)

Murray, H. A., & Morgan, C. D. A clinical study of sentiments: II. *Genetic Psychology Monographs*, 1945, **32**, 153-311. (b)

Newcomb, T. M. *Personality and social change*. New York: Holt, 1943.

Newcomb, T. M. An approach to the study of communicative acts. *Psychological Review*, 1953, **60**, 393-404.

Newcomb, T. M. *The acquaintance process*. New York: Holt, 1961.

Osgood, C. E. Cognitive dynamics in the conduct of human affairs. *Public Opinion Quarterly*, 1960, **24**, 341-365.

Osgood, C. E., Suci, G., & Tannenbaum, P. H. *The measurement of meaning*. Urbana, Ill.: University of Illinois Press, 1957.

Osgood, C. E., & Tannenbaum, P. H. The principle of congruity in the prediction of attitude change. *Psychological Review*, 1955, **62**, 42-55.

Ostrom, T. M., & Brock, T. C. A cognitive model of attitudinal involvement. In R. P. Ableson *et al.* (Eds.), *Theories of cognitive consistency: A sourcebook*, Chicago: Rand McNally, 1968, in press.

Peak, H. Attitude and motivation. In M. R. Jones (Ed.), *Nebraska symposium on motivation*. Vol. 3. Lincoln, Neb.: University of Nebraska Press, 1955. Pp. 149-188.

Phillips, J. L. A model for cognitive balance. *Psychological Review*, 1967, **74**, 481-495.

Rhine, R. J. A concept-formation approach to attitude acquisition. *Psychological Review*, 1958, **65**, 362-370.

Rokeach, M. (Ed.) *The open and closed mind*. New York: Basic Books, 1960.

Rokeach, M., & Rothman, G. The principle of belief congruence and the congruity principle as models of cognitive interaction. *Psychological Review*, 1965, **72**, 128-142.

Rosenberg, M. J. Cognitive structure and attitudinal affect. *Journal of Abnormal and Social Psychology*, 1956, **53**, 367-372.

Rosenberg, M. J. An analysis of affective-cognitive consistency. In C. I. Hovland, & M. J. Rosenberg (Eds.), *Attitude organization and change*. New Haven: Yale University Press, 1960. Pp. 15-64.

Rosenberg, M. J., & Abelson, R. P. An analysis of cognitive balancing. In C. I. Hovland & M. J. Rosenberg, (Eds), *Attitude organization and change*. New Haven: Yale University Press, 1960. Pp. 112-163.

Rosenberg, M. J., & Hovland, C. I. Cognitive, affective, and behavioral components of attitudes. In C. I. Hovland, & M. J. Rosenberg, (Eds.), *Attitude organization and change*. New Haven: Yale University Press, 1960, Pp. 1-14.

Sarnoff, I. Psychoanalytic theory and social attitudes. *Public Opinion Quarterly*, 1960, **24**, 251-279.

Schramm, W. *Mass communications*. Urbana, Ill.: University of Illinois Press, 1949.

Schroder, H. M., Driver, M. J., & Streufert, S. *Human information processing*. New York: Holt, 1967.

Scott, W. A. Conceptualizing and measuring structural properties of cognition. In O. J. Harvey (Ed.), *Motivation and social interaction*. New York: Ronald Press, 1963. Pp. 266-288.

Sherif, C. W., Sherif, M., & Nebergall, R. E. *Attitude and attitude change*. Philadelphia: Saunders, 1965.

Sherif, M., & Cantril, H. The psychology of attitudes: I *Psychological Review*, 1945, **52**, 295-319.

Sherif, M., & Cantril, H. The psychology of attitudes: II *Psychological Review*, 1946, **53**, 1-24.

Sherif, M., & Cantril, H. *The psychology of ego-involvements*. New York: Wiley, 1947.

Sherif, M., & Hovland, C. I. *Social judgment*. New Haven: Yale University Press, 1961.

Smith, B. L., Lasswell, H. D., & Casey, R. D. *Propaganda, communication, and public opinion*. Princeton, N. J.: Princeton University Press, 1946.

Smith, M. B. The personal setting of public opinions: A study of attitudes toward Russia. *Public Opinion Quarterly*, 1947, **11**, 507-523.

Smith, M. B. Personal values as determinants of a political attitude. *Journal of Psychology*, 1949, **28**, 477-486.

Smith, M. B. Bruner, J., & White, R. *Opinions and personality*. New York: Wiley, 1956.

Staats, A. W. An outline of an integrated learning theory of attitude formation and function. In M. Fishbein (Ed.), *Readings in attitude theory and measurement*. New York: Wiley, 1967. Pp. 373-376.

Thomas, W. I., & Znaniecki, F. *The Polish peasant in Europe and America*. Vol. 1. Boston: Badger, 1918.

Thorndike, E. L. *The psychology of wants, interests and attitudes*. New York: Appleton, 1935.

Thurstone, L. L. Attitudes can be measured. *American Journal of Sociology*, 1928, **33**, 529-554.

Thurstone, L. L. The measurement of social attitudes. *Journal of Abnormal and Social Psychology*, 1931, **26**, 249-269.

Thurstone, L. L. *Multiple-factor analysis*. Chicago: University of Chicago Press, 1947.

Upshaw, H. S. Own attitude as an anchor in equal-appearing intervals. *Journal of Abnormal and Social Psychology*, 1962, **64**, 85-96.

Upshaw, H. S. The personal reference scale. In L. Berkowitz (Ed.), *Advances in experimental social psychology*. Vol. 4. New York: Academic Press, 1968, in press.

Weiss, R. F. Persuasion and the acquisition of attitude: Models from conditioning and selective learning. *Psychological Reports*, 1962, **11**, 709-732.

Zajonc, R. B. The process of cognitive tuning in communication. *Journal of Abnormal and Social Psychology*, 1960, **61**, 159-167.

PART II: LEARNING-BEHAVIOR THEORY
CONTRIBUTIONS TO ATTITUDE THEORY

2

Social Behaviorism and Human Motivation: Principles of the Attitude-Reinforcer-Discriminative System

ARTHUR W. STAATS
DEPARTMENTS OF PSYCHOLOGY AND EDUCATIONAL PSYCHOLOGY
UNIVERSITY OF HAWAII
HONOLULU, HAWAII

The history of psychology is a history of separatism of various types; for example, learning versus cognitive approaches. Moreover, major efforts within traditional learning approaches have been expended in developing and maintaining separate experimental methods, separate general (philosophical) methodologies, and separate terminologies. This has been very disadvantageous; it is a course that has prevented the development of a believable, comprehensive learning theory of human behavior. Simplistic learning approaches to human behavior, although frequently productive in their own research realm have remained fragmented and vulnerable to criticism in more general considerations—it has been relatively easy to pick an example of behavior that the isolated approach could not handle.

Furthermore, psychology in general, as well as the field of learning, has accepted traditional categories of behavior—even though the categories are actually based upon mentalistic conceptions of bygone times (see Staats, 1967a). Thus, we have categories like problem solving, perception, communication, personality, word meaning, imitation, intelligence, motivation, social interaction, and so on, as though there was in each case a unitary process involved. The investigations of these various types of behavior have proceeded also in isolation from one another—even though it may be suggested that the same principles underlie the various behavioral events.

In view of this state of affairs, the author has attempted to integrate and elaborate the basic principles of learning (classical and instrumental conditioning)—cutting across theoretical separation of principles—as well as the experimental findings from various areas of human learning experimentation *and the observations of the social and behavioral sciences*, to constitute a comprehensive learning theory of human behavior (see Staats, 1961, 1964a, 1966, 1967b, 1968; Staats & Staats, 1963).

The present analysis, which may be considered to be a part of this effort, will have several dominant themes. First, it will suggest that the traditional learning theories have been less than adequate as a basic structure upon which to establish a comprehensive conception of human behavior, including attitudes. It will be indicated that to provide an appropriate basic structure S-R theory has to be elaborated further, not in terms of "explaining" the basic learning principles—the traditional goal of learning theory—but in terms of better abstracting and elaborating the major principles from the mass of experimental results and controversial theories as well as indicating the modes of interaction of classical and instrumental conditioning.

It will also be suggested that in this task the systematist must work in conjunction with broader conceptions of man. Learning principles alone do not constitute a theory of human behavior. While learning principles must be basic in the theoretical structure, they must be employed to develop a general conception. In the realm of attitudes, for example, theories of human motivation derived from naturalistic observations are quite relevant to the task of constructing an adequate theory. In general, the social sciences must be centrally included.

Specifically, "broadening" and integration of learning and attitude theory must include extension into areas involving the same events—whether or not these areas have traditionally been considered within the study of attitudes, or whether the terminology or research methods are the same as those customary in the study of attitudes. The use of different terms and methods are accidents of history which prevent us from seeing commonality in underlying principles. We need theory that shows the common principles and thereby helps unify the study of human behavior. A prominent aspect of this task is to extend attitude theory into applied areas which deal with human problems. It is suggested that much of the social significance of a theory of attitudes lies in its role in a larger conception and in being related to individual and group problems of human behavior.

Finally, an important point, which cuts across these various themes, is that we must study *attitude function* as well as attitude formation and change. It will not be possible to cover these various points in detail, but the discussion will attempt to exemplify these several aspects of the present approach to the study of the principles of formation and function of the attitude system. In addition, implications of the analysis for additional research and theoretical endeavors will be briefly outlined. In sum, *social behaviorism* is characterized herein.

INTEGRATED LEARNING PRINCIPLES

The various results of the already mentioned separatism cannot be dealt with here. However, it is relevant to indicate that theoretical orientations prevalent in learning have prevented us from realizing the various interrelationships between classical and instrumental conditioning. To begin, Hull (1943) did not differentiate between the basic principles of classical and instrumental conditioning. Perhaps because of this Hull did indicate the relationship of conditioned stimulus value and conditioned reinforcement value. Later approaches, although distinguishing the principles better, produced an even less effective basic approach to human learning in other respects. Thus Skinnerian theory is nominally a two-factor (classical-instrumental) learning approach. However, Skinner has overemphasized the separate and independent nature of classical conditioning and operant conditioning. In so doing, he has given a separate terminology to the principles—where quite separate symbols are used for classical and operant conditioning—and has helped prevent the recognition of the interrelationships of the principles (Staats, 1964b, 1966, 1968). Furthermore, he has strongly stressed the precedence and unique importance of operant conditioning theory and has almost entirely neglected classical conditioning in basic research and theory as well as in extensions to complex human behavior. In operation, then, Skinner's approach has been a one-factor learning theory. This is a crucial weakness in constructing a conception of human behavior, as well as in the basic theory itself.

Moreover, Skinner's rejection of the theoretical endeavors of Hull and others, although correct in part in the context of that period, has had the effect of generally suppressing theoretical endeavors in learning. This has prevented elaboration on a theoretical level of the basic learning principles and their interrelationships. Skinner's approach has also rejected detailed stimulus-response theorizing, a crucial drawback which again has retarded theoretical analysis of complex human behavior. The present article cannot deal generally with these topics; however, they will be reflected in the analysis to follow.

In beginning the present analysis and in demonstrating the approach, it is necessary to outline the basic principles to be employed and their interrelationships in a notational system which reflects those interrelationships. First, it may be said that many stimuli have classical *and* instrumental functions. That is, for example, there are stimuli that can function as a ^{UC}S when paired appropriately with a ^{C}S. These stimuli will elicit responses which will be conditioned to the ^{C}S. In addition, however, the same stimulus that functions as a ^{UC}S may also function as an unconditioned reinforcing stimulus or $^{UC\cdot R}S$. That is, the same stimulus when presented following an instrumental response will result in the response becoming stronger on *future* occasions — or remaining strong if it is already in good strength.

There are many such stimuli. Food will serve as a ^{UC}S and elicit the salivary response, among other emotional responses. Food will also serve as a $^{UC\cdot R}S$ and will strengthen instrumental behaviors when presented in a response-contingent manner. Although this is readily apparent, its implications have not been seen, perhaps because of our separatistic traditional theoretical terminology which symbolizes an unconditioned stimulus as ^{UC}S and a primary reinforcer as S^R. Furthermore, in textbooks and lectures the principles are presented separately so the interrelationship is obscured.

This defect in traditional learning theories becomes even more important when the topic of learned or secondary (conditioned) reinforcement is considered (as well as discriminative stimulus control). This topic may *only* clearly be considered when it is realized that stimuli may have multiple functions in classical and instrumental conditioning. That is, it was suggested that food as a stimulus functions as a ^{UC}S and as a reinforcing stimulus $^{UC\cdot R}S$. It may also be suggested that a new stimulus when paired with such a stimulus in a classical conditioning procedure actually acquires both functions. That is, the new stimulus will become a conditioned stimulus and elicit (at least in part) the emotional responses that the unconditioned stimulus elicits. In addition, however, as a consequence of this conditioning the new stimulus will become a conditioned reinforcing stimulus, or $^{C\cdot R}S$. Hull (1943) also suggested that the secondary reinforcing value of a stimulus was due to the fact that it had come to elicit a conditioned response. (It should be realized that the pairing operation may actually occur in many situations. In operant discrimination training, for example, food is paired with a discriminative stimulus. Thus, the discriminative stimulus ^{D}S should come as part of this training to be a $^{C\cdot R}S$. Operant conditioning in general may be said to involve the classical conditioning of reinforcement value since any time a $^{UC\cdot R}S$ — or $^{C\cdot R}S$ — is presented the emotional responses it elicits will be conditioned to any other stimuli that are present.)

It may be noted that it would be expected that higher-order conditioning could also be involved in the formation of conditioned reinforcers. That is, when a conditioned reinforcing stimulus, $^{C \cdot R}S$, is paired with a new stimulus the latter will also become both a ^CS as well as a $^{C \cdot R}S$. This by no means completes the integrated learning analysis. However, it does present several concepts that are of importance to a learning theory of attitudes and human motivation. An additional elaboration of the interaction between classical and instrumental conditioning will be made later. More complete accounts of the author's integrated analysis are given in Staats (1961, 1964a, 1966, 1968) and Staats and Staats (1963). Recent accounts also are beginning to deal with some of the interrelationships between classical and instrumental conditioning (see Miller, 1966; Rescorla & Solomon, 1967; Trapold & Winokur, 1967) in a manner which supports relevant parts of the theoretical formulation.

INTEGRATED LEARNING PRINCIPLES
AND HUMAN MOTIVATION THEORY

The author has already described parts of a learning analysis of the attitudinal system (Staats, 1964a, 1967b, 1968; Staats & Staats, 1963), which will be systematized and extended here. It should be noted that because of traditional categorization schemes and the multiple functions of "motivational stimuli" such stimuli are referred to by different terms such as *emotions, values, instincts, needs, drives, motives, goals, cathexes, reinforcers, urges, utility* (economics), *fetishes, evaluative word meaning, and so on, in addition to the term attitudes. The distinctions set up by demarcating such terms and areas of study constitute artificial barriers to the comprehensive study of human behavior. The present analysis is thus thought to apply to these various terms. It is suggested that the study of attitudes — formation, change, and function — in its broad context is the study of human motivation.*

Generally, the naturalistic observations and conceptions of these various aspects of human motivation stimuli are not couched in terms of empirical principles that are precisely stated and "causative" in the sense that variables are indicated by which to *affect* (or manipulate) human behavior. The laboratory established principles of learning, on the other hand, are relatively precise, detailed, and causative. When the two are combined, based upon the empirical principles, the result is a theory concerned with significant, functional, human behavior, but with the potential for making empirical predictions and producing control of (solutions to) human problems. The present section will present a conception of the human motivational system which will describe the three functions of attitudinal stimuli: (1) the classical conditioning, (2) the reinforcing, and (3) the discriminative controlling functions which such stimuli acquire. The human attitude (motivation) system may be referred to as the attitude-reinforcer-discriminative (A-R-D) system, thus naming the triple functions of the stimuli included in the system. The first two functions will be treated at length initially and later the third.

THE FORMATION AND CHANGE OF THE A-R-D SYSTEM

Many of the theories of the social and behavioral sciences which are based upon naturalistic evidence have recognized that attitudinal stimuli are subject to variation within an individual and between individuals. This has been true even when the concept is of a biological sort, such as Freud's; that is, in his view an investment of body energy is made in the object—giving the object its motivational characteristics. However, while such psychodynamic theories have recognized that objects can change in their motivational functions for a person—in psychoanalytic terms the investment of energy (cathexis) can shift from object to object, increase and decrease, and so on—the means by which these changes occur (or the effects) are not clearly stated in terms of empirical principles. It is suggested that naturalistic observations of long- and short-term shifts in individual and group motivational stimuli, and the like, may be handled in greater detail by the employment of a learning analysis. Moreover, as will be described, when the learning analysis is employed it suggests means by which human behavior can be predicted, measured, and modified.

The important principle for discussing the formation of the individual's A-R-D system is that of classical conditioning—not operant conditioning. That is, as has been described there are stimuli that naturally have functions as unconditioned stimuli (^{UC}S). Food, water, air, sexual stimulation, warmth, and so on, elicit upon presentation positive "emotional" responses (when the organism has been deprived of them). On the other hand, intense tactile, auditory, visual, and chemical stimuli, elicit negative "emotional" responses. When these various stimuli are paired with neutral stimuli, eliciting their particular emotional response, the emotional response is classically conditioned to the neutral stimulus. When a stimulus has come to elicit an emotional response it may be defined as an attitudinal stimulus. This is an important quality that some stimuli can have or acquire—that is, the function of eliciting an emotional or attitudinal response. When a stimulus has acquired this quality, it can be transferred to new stimuli with which it is paired in the process of higher-order conditioning.

Furthermore, it should be remembered that a stimulus that has come to elicit an attitudinal (emotional) response will also function as a reinforcing stimulus. That is, the process of establishing the attitudinal system results in the definition of what stimuli will be reinforcing for the individual.

Thus, it is suggested that the individual's A-R-D system is founded upon the stimuli that originally elicit emotional (attitudinal) responses in him on an unlearned basis, and elaborated by extensive first-order and higher-order classical conditioning. The individual's conditioning history in this respect is infinitely complex and extends over his life history—ample opportunity for a fantastically large number of conditioning trials and all the uniqueness we see in the human attitudinal system. It is also important to note that the A-R-D system differs not only from person to person, but also from small group to small group—by social class, by nation, and by culture. And finally, language plays a central role in the formation and function of individual and group differences in the reinforcer system (see Staats, 1964b, 1967b, 1968).

It should be pointed out that in the naturalistic situation the fact that a classical conditioning process is involved in the establishment of an attitudinal response to a stimulus may be obscured. The presentation of the original attitude stimulus, the $^{UC \cdot R}S$, may be contingent upon some instrumental response, producing instrumental conditioning. The process may thus appear simply as an instrumental conditioning situation even when the more important result is to make a stimulus present in the situation a new conditioned stimulus and consequently a new conditioned reinforcing stimulus ($^{C \cdot R}S$). An example from everyday life may be seen when the parent applies reinforcing verbal stimuli (that elicit positive emotional responses) contingent upon the cooperative play behavior of two siblings. This would have the effect of strengthening the motor responses. In addition, however, the positive attitudinal response elicited in each case by the "social" approval would be conditioned to the other sibling as a social stimulus. In both laboratory and naturalistic (and clinical) situations, the investigator may be misled by the appearance of an instrumental conditioning procedure and fail to realize that a classical conditioning process is just as essentially involved.

It may be added that the principles of classical conditioning are empirical and are known in great detail. As a theory they improve markedly upon the naturalistic concepts of the formation and alteration of attitude stimuli. And, as will be shown, by drawing upon the observations of the clinic and other social and behavioral sciences it is possible to invest the classical conditioning analysis with greater significance. Moreover, a great deal of information about individual and group behavior is given when the nature of the individual's or the group's attitudinal system is known. The principles involved in this case are those of instrumental conditioning, and the account thus begins to deal with the function of attitude stimuli.

THE REINFORCING FUNCTION OF THE A-R-D SYSTEM

Traditionally the study of attitudes has concentrated upon attitude formation and change and the measurement of attitudes. The principles involved in the *function* of attitudes have been assumed, or based upon naturalistic expectations rather than experimentally derived principles. It is suggested, however, that systematic study must be made of the instrumental function of attitude-eliciting stimuli.

In outlining this approach, a short description of the manner in which the attitudinal system determines one's instrumental behaviors will first be given, beginning with an example from the animal laboratory. Let us say that we have two rats of the same genotype. One of them, *rat A*, we subject to training in which a buzzer is presented many times, each time paired with food—in what constitute classical conditioning trials in an instrumental situation (see Zimmerman, 1957). *Rat B* receives experience with the buzzer, but not paired with food. It would be expected that the buzzer would become a positive attitudinal stimulus for *rat A*, but not for *rat B*. Now let us individually place each animal into the same instrumental learning situation involving a lever which when pressed results in the brief sound of the buzzer. We will see that *rat A* will be an enthusiastic learner, he will come to press the bar actively, *rat B* will not. The difference between animals, however, would rest solely upon the fact that for one organism the stimulus had acquired a reinforcer function—would be an attitudinal and thus a motivational stimulus—while for the other it had not.

Using the same analysis, we can see how different behaviors will be formed in children with different A-R-D systems in situations important to child adjustment. Some children are raised in such a manner that some stimuli will elicit attitude responses in them, other children lack the necessary conditioning experience. It has been widely recognized (see, for example, Maccoby & Gibbs, 1954; Rosen, 1956) that differences in the "value" of various events are affected by social class and familial training circumstances. Middle-class children ordinarily are rewarded many times for learning new skills of various kinds. The products (stimuli) resulting from learning new skills (achievements) should thus come to elicit positive attitudes and consequently serve as conditioned reinforcers. It may be added that through similar conditioning experiences the approval of adult "authority" figures can also come to be a strong positive reinforcer for some children.

With these givens it is not difficult to see how child learning, for example, classroom learning and adjustment, may be affected by the A-R-D system. The approval of the teacher and other students and the products of one's own developing skill are the most important sources of reinforcement for "student" behaviors in the traditional classroom. In a manner analogous to our two animals, let us say that two children with differing A-R-D systems are placed in the classroom. For one child, *child A*, the teacher's approval and the child's own achievements are reinforcing, for the other, *child B*, these stimuli are not reinforcing. Let us say that they receive the same treatment in the class, whenever they pay attention to materials the teacher presents and respond in the manner directed they receive the teacher's approval, and their instrumental behaviors produce stimuli that evidence their skill (achievements). Under such a circumstance, *child A*'s attentional and working behaviors will be maintained in good strength and as a result he will continue to develop new skills. *Child B*'s behavior, on the other hand, will not be maintained. His attentional and working behaviors will wane, and other competitive behaviors that are strengthened by stimuli that *are* effective reinforcers will become relatively dominant.

Child A will be seen as interested, motivated, hardworking, and *bright*. Ultimately, he will also measure as very able and bright on class achievement and intelligence tests. *Child B* will be seen as disinterested and dull, possibly also as a behavior problem if problem behaviors are reinforced. He will later also measure this way, and this evidence may be used to support the contention that the child's behavioral failure was due to some personal defect. It may be suggested that many problems of school adjustment which are important for psychology involve deficient or defective A-R-D systems (see Staats & Butterfield, 1965). It may be stated generally that "normal" behavior will only emerge from a situation which has a fixed set of stimuli, supposed to have A-R-D qualities, only when those stimuli actually *do* have those qualities. When normal behavior does not emerge from the situation, we have to scrutinize the A-R-D system of the individual and the A-R-D system in the situation.

Many other examples may be given that involve behaviors important to human adjustment. Let us take two adult males one of whom has because of his conditioning history come to find other males to be strong sex reinforcers—that is, males elicit positive sexual attitudes in him. For this individual, on the other hand, females do not have as strong sexual reinforcing properties. Let us say, also, that the other adult male in this example has an A-R-D system that is just the reverse. These two individuals, placed in the same life situation, will be likely to develop two quite opposite sets of sexual behaviors. Behaviors (and mannerisms) that are successful in attracting and gaining contact with males will be strengthened in the first case. Behaviors that are successful in attracting and gaining contact with females will be strengthened in the second. The same analysis would hold also for other aberrations in sexual behavior. The person for whom children elicit sexual attitudinal responses and have sexual reinforcing value is likely to develop behaviors that are strengthened by sexual contact with children. The person for whom pain and violence are positive sexual reinforcers will be likely to develop instrumental behaviors that culminate in such events.

In addition, certain aspects of neurotic and psychotic behaviors can be considered in terms of deficits and disturbances in the individual's A-R-D system, for example, neurasthenia or simple schizophrenia. Both of these have been described by the author (see Staats & Staats, 1963). Fetishes may also be considered to involve cases where because of the individual's conditioning history an object has come to have strong sex reinforcing value for an individual to an extent that is unusual in comparison to other individuals. It should be noted that these are only examples. Many other abnormal behaviors can be considered in terms of an abnormal A-R-D system and the instrumental conditioning that is consequently effected.

It is important to also add by illustration that the A-R-D system can also suffer impairments because stimuli have come through conditioning to elicit negative attitudinal responses and act as negative reinforcers, thus resulting in behavior disorders. In the area of sex behavior, for example, aberrant behaviors will be produced if the stimuli that must become positive attitudinal stimuli and sex reinforcers are instead, through conditioning, made into negative reinforcers. When this occurs, of course, behavior that takes the individual away from the stimuli will be strengthened. This will make it impossible for the individual to acquire the instrumental behaviors necessary to obtain the reinforcement that otherwise would be available.

This is the same principle that is involved in phobias, irrational fears, anxieties, and so on. That is, while the presence of a phobia (where a stimulus inappropriately elicits a negative attitudinal response) may be of importance in and of itself because of the unpleasant quality of negative emotional responses, or because of an effect upon health, it is important to note that the effect upon the individual's adjustive instrumental behaviors may be of even greater importance. For example, a strong negative attitude to being outdoors will result in the behavior of staying inside. When one is forced (by one's classical conditioning history and instrumental behavior principles) to remain indoors, various types of social interactions are ruled out, one's occupational success may be ruled out, sexual reinforcement may suffer, and so on. The individual's poor life adjustment in which lessened positive reinforcement occurs, and increased negative reinforcement, may result in further unfortunate development of the A-R-D system and thus additional problems.

It should also be indicated that groups of people can differ from each other in their A-R-D systems. Following the above analysis this would result in different types of behavior coming to be dominant in the group. That is, for example, if a group has a reinforcement system in which success in competition is a strong positive reinforcer, then this will serve to make behaviors that culminate in such success dominant in that culture. If success in competition is less positive, or even negative, then fewer examples of such instrumental behaviors will develop. Much description in sociology and anthropology can be considered in terms of differences in the A-R-D system between groups, subgroups, cultures, and so on. Many times it is important to the treatment of social problems to describe the A-R-D system of subgroups in our own society. Through this type of description, an understanding may be gained of the causes of undesirable behaviors, and possibilities of prevention and treatment may be suggested by the analysis. Thus, many of the aspects of problem behaviors of the children we now call culturally deprived arise from social conditions that prevent the development of an A-R-D system that is appropriate for the conditions to which they are subjected. This has, of course, been true for American Negroes, in various ways. For example, when the social situation prevents the positive attitudinal stimuli of "success" from being paired with the stimuli of hard work, acquiring skills, intellectual achievement, educational status, and so on, these latter *stimuli* will not acquire positive attitudinal value and thus reinforcement value. In addition when a group within the larger group has been discriminated against in various aversive ways, this will also constitute negative attitudinal conditioning for the individuals involved. By verbal means, involving the principles of classical conditioning of meaning and attitudes (see Staats, 1966, 1964b, 1968; Staats & Staats, 1958), this conditioning can be passed to other individuals. When there is a consistent aversive experience of a subgroup culture presented by members of the larger group, the reinforcement system of the subgroup will come to include strong negative attitudes toward members of the larger group. This will affect the extent to which members of the larger group can serve as positive social reinforcers of the behavior of members of the subgroup. For example, the member of the subgroup who interacts with a member of the larger group in a learning situation—such as the case where the member of the larger group is a supervisor, therapist, or a teacher—will respond "atypically" if the member of the larger group elicits negative attitudinal responses and, as will be described, thus controls avoidance and oppositional behaviors.

The applications of the learning theory of human attitudes to problems of human behavior, and to a general conception of human behavior, cannot be exhausted in this paper. The preceding discussion attempts only to indicate some of the potentialities and, by the examples chosen, to indicate that the realm of attitude study is concerned with various types of human behavior—from theoretical to applied areas—even though the behaviors are not traditionally included in the study of attitudes. In order to spell out some of the additional implications of the concept of the A-R-D system, the straightforward learning principles require additional elaboration—the concern of the next two sections.

THE HIERARCHICAL NATURE OF THE A-R-D SYSTEM AND ITS FUNCTIONS.

Additional conceptions within psychology and the other social and behavioral sciences can be seen to be related to the learning theory of attitudes (human motivation). Maslow (1954), as one example, has suggested that one's needs (or in the present terms one's attitudes and reinforcers) are ordered in terms of strength. When the strongest "needs" are satisfied, then the next strongest becomes prepotent, and so on. Another example of a social science principle which lends itself to a hierarchical conception concerns the law of diminishing (marginal or extra) utility, from economics (Samuelson, 1958, p. 430). This states that "the more the individual has of some given commodity [in the present terms, a reinforcer], the *less* satisfaction (or utility) he would obtain from an additional unit of it" (Ulmer, 1959, p. 319).

The present concept of the A-R-D system may be elaborated by characterizing the system's hierarchical nature, and by outlining some of the laboratory principles that would be expected to be involved, again utilizing naturalistic observations and conceptions. To begin, it may be suggested that the A-R-D system is a system because the elements in the system have modes of "interaction," one of which is involved in the hierarchical nature of the system. At any moment in time the various stimuli in the individual's system would be expected to have a *relative* reinforcing intensity. Relative as well as absolute strength would have an important affect upon the individual's or group's behavior.

Let us say, for example, that two individuals have a stimulus in each of their "reinforcer systems" that has precisely the same reinforcing value, *reinforcer A*. Let us also say, however, that for one individual there are no stronger reinforcers in his system; while for the other individual there is another stimulus, *reinforcer B*, that is an even stronger reinforcer. Now let the individuals be placed in a situation in which both reinforcers are available; but one reinforcer is presented contingent upon one instrumental behavior and the other reinforcer is presented contingent upon an incompatible behavior. Under these circumstances the two individuals will develop different behaviors. The individual with the reinforcer system in which *reinforcer B* is the most "dominant" reinforcer will develop most dominantly the behavior that is followed by that reinforcer. The other individual, with the system in which *reinforcer A* is relatively stronger will develop predominantly the other behavior. It is thus suggested that it is not only the absolute value of reinforcers that determines individual and group differences in behavior, but also the relative values of the various reinforcers in the A-R-D system.

One corollary should be added here. It appears that there are subsystems within the major system. That is, there are classes of reinforcers that are related. Take sex reinforcers as an example. It may be suggested that there are many different individual sex reinforcers which constitute a class, and probably there are subclasses within the class. Certainly, food reinforcers constitute a class of the A-R-D system (with subclasses also). When one is deprived of food, as an example, it would be expected that the whole class would be increased in reinforcing value. If the strongest food reinforcer in the hierarchy was not available, then the next strongest would be the dominant available reinforcer. The model would suggest that a relatively weak member of a class of reinforcers could be raised into a position of relative dominance in the total system through deprivation of stronger members of its class. A man deprived of potable fluids might be more affected by some brackish water than by a usually stronger reinforcer in some other class of reinforcers, such as sexual reinforcers, food reinforcers, social approval reinforcers, and so on.

Several other specifications may be indicated here in elaborating the conception. The relative strengths of the reinforcers in the system may be changed by first-order or higher-order classical conditioning experiences. This conditioning may be of the usual variety or it may involve incompatible conditioning; that is, a stimulus that has come to elicit one attitudinal response will no longer do so (or not to the same extent) when an incompatible emotional response is conditioned to the stimulus. This has been called counterconditioning. In addition, the relative strengths of reinforcers in an individual motivational system may be changed by extinction procedures. These two processes may require a number of conditioning (or extinction) trials in any case and thus may develop slowly. Also, once a stimulus has come to elicit an attitudinal response and thus be a reinforcer, it will remain so unless further conditioning or extinction procedures produce a change.

In addition to these enduring and slowly acquired processes of change in the relative (and absolute) strength of reinforcers in the motivational system, there are also operations that can change the system more rapidly, usually with a less permanent effect. That is, deprivation operations also increase the reinforcing strength of a positive reinforcing stimulus in an absolute sense. Satiation, on the other hand, decreases the strength of a reinforcing stimulus. In both cases the operation can be expected to change also the relative dominance of reinforcers in the system. When the condition of deprivation or satiation is returned to the starting point, however, the reinforcers will regain their former relative position—the changes produced directly follow the deprivation-satiation variations.

The manner in which groups and individuals can vary in behavior because different stimuli are effective in their A-R-D systems has already been discussed. A few examples will be given here where the relative (hierarchical) ordering of the A-R-D system is affected by deprivation-satiation variations, producing variations in behavior. As an example, adult social reinforcement may occur in small portions for the housewife with several small children. As a result of this deprivation this class of social stimuli may increase in reinforcement value to a far greater extent than is the case with her husband. He, being satiated on social reinforcers because of his work situation, finds spending evenings at home more reinforcing; she finds social events more reinforcing. As another example, deprivation of sex reinforcers would be expected to increase the reinforcing value of this class of stimuli, at the expense of other reinforcers in the individual's system. For the adolescent, under this type of deprivation, other reinforcers may be relatively weak and the behavior maintained by those reinforcers — study, reading, family activities — may weaken.

Deprivation-satiation also causes attitudinal differences in social groups. While experiencing less deprivation for sex reinforcers (Kinsey. et al, 1948), the lower economic classes on the other hand suffer much more deprivation of material reinforcers such as money, fine clothes, cars, and so on, as well as more deprivation of social reinforcers such as prestige, social approval, and so on. Juvenile delinquency and criminality have been considered by the author in terms of a partial statement of this principle (Staats & Staats, 1963); this and several other aspects of the present approach recently have been employed in another analysis of criminal behavior (Burgess & Akers, 1966).

It is important to indicate that deprivation may also affect the A-R-D system, and thus behavior, in another way that does not emerge from consideration of laboratory learning principles. For example, when a prisoner is deprived of contact with the opposite sex, the general class of sex reinforcers will increase in relative strength. As a consequence, reinforcers of lesser value in the class, but which are more accessible, such as homosexual contact, will be relatively stronger and may instrumentally condition behavior that would be unlikely to occur without the deprivation. It should be emphasized that in this way each instance of a homosexual act constitutes a whole series of classical conditioning trials since a sexual act extends over a considerable length of time. The homosexual conditioning experience would be expected to increase the sexual attitudinal value of the class of social stimulus involved — members of the same sex — thus further altering the structure of the A-R-D system on a more permanent basis.

RULES OF APPLICATION OF REINFORCERS AND THE A-R-D SYSTEM

It was said in introducing the present paper that the straightforward statement of learning principles does not constitute a theory of human behavior — even when the principles have been demonstrated with simple human behaviors. It is necessary to extend the basic principles into the realms of human behavior of interest to the behavioral and social sciences. In doing this the naturalistic observations and the concepts they have yielded must exert a prominent influence in the theory construction task. New principles not suggested in the laboratory may be expected to emerge from extending the laboratory principles in the analysis of the complex circumstances of human life. Examples of this have already been presented in the preceding analyses, but it will help to elaborate this methodological suggestion by more pointed examples of the ways that basic principles alone are inadequate. As one illustration, the relationship between the basic principles may not be seen in the laboratory because one is concerned about isolating the principles and studying them independently. The relationship of the principles, on the other hand, may be very important when dealing with complex human behavior. The relationship between the attitudinal-reinforcing value of a stimulus and its discriminative stimulus value, yet to be discussed, is such an example.

It is also the case that effects which are difficult to produce in the laboratory because of limited numbers of conditioning trials, and the like, may take place readily and importantly in real life where conditioning opportunities may be unlimited. The principle of higher-order conditioning is such an example. Furthermore, certain conditions or principles may be an irrelevant part of laboratory manipulation and yet be very significant when the principles or conditions are extended on a theoretical and empirical level to the study of man. The hierarchical nature of the reinforcement system and the principles involved, unlike the case on the human level, are not crucial in the animal laboratory. The present section will be concerned with describing another such case which is relevant to the present theory.

To begin, in the laboratory there is a certain "rule" in existence when the principle of reinforcement is studied. The rule involves what behavior the investigator elects to reinforce and in what manner (e.g., schedule of reinforcement). In the rat he will reinforce bar pressing behavior, or running down a runway, or turning in one direction in a T-maze; in the pidgeon he will reinforce pecking a key, or a key of a certain color, and so on. The behavior is selected for various practical reasons relevant to laboratory work; to be specificable objectively, naturally occurring, simple enough to be treated as a unit, of limited duration enabling repeated trials, and so on.

This aspect of the principle of reinforcement which has only practical importance in the basic study involves in the study of human organization some of the most significant matters. Independently of what attitudinal stimuli serve as reinforcers for a particular group or culture, there can be differences between groups in the rules by which the reinforcers are applied. The ways that groups differ in this respect, the ways that these differences develop and change, and the effects that are produced on human behavior may be seen as primary topics for scientific and professional areas concerned with man. A few examples indicating the importance of the rules of applying reinforcers will be made.

As one illustration, in our society some of the stimuli that have a good deal of reinforcing value are titles, positions, status roles; social and personal attention, acclaim, and respect; money, fine clothes, expensive cars, and houses; and various honors and awards. In our society, there are also rules (not necessarily formal or explicit) for the application of these stimuli. That is, they are delivered contingent upon some kinds of behavior but not upon others. Thus, large amounts of these stimuli are delivered contingent upon exceptionally skilled baseball, football, acting, dancing, or comic behaviors, among others. Relatively small amounts are delivered contingent upon the behaviors of skilled manual work, studying, unskilled manual work, nursing, and many others.

These characteristics of our reinforcing system and its rules of application to, continue with the example, have an effect upon the manner in which behavior in our society is shaped. Consider thus, a boy who has two classes of skilled behaviors: one a set of intellectual skills consisting of knowledge and well-developed study and scholarly work habits and the other consisting of some form of fine athletic prowess. Let us say that either behavior could be developed to "championship" caliber. Now, in a situation in which the societal rule is that the larger amount of reinforcement is made contingent upon the one behavior, this behavior will be strengthened, and as must be the case, at the expense of the other to the extent that the behaviors are incompatible. In our society, of course, many of the strongest reinforcers are more apt to be more liberally applied to athletic rather than scholarly behavior.

When groups are considered, it would also be expected that the reinforcer system and its rules of application will determine the types of behaviors that are dominant. A society that has a differing set of reinforcers and rules will evidence different behavior over the group of people exposed to that set of conditions. A society, for example, whose reinforcers are made contingent upon scholarly behaviors to a larger extent than another society will create stronger behaviors of that type, in a greater number of people, than will the other society. In general, many of the different cultural, national, class, and familial behaviors that have been observed in sociology, anthropology, clinical and social psychology, and other behavioral sciences, can be considered to involve this aspect of human motivation—the A-R-D system and its *rules of application*.

It should be indicated that sometimes the rule specifies a particular *behavior-social stimulus-reinforcement* relationship. Thus sexual behavior and sexual reinforcement occur in all societies. However the rules regulate the type of behavior and the type of social stimulus. Thus, in our culture, sexual behavior will be reinforced, but only in certain situations, with certain people. People such as siblings, parents, children, same sex partners, unwilling partners, and so on are excluded. We also have many examples of cultures and subcultures with markedly different rules, for example, the ancient Greek, Roman, Hawaiian, and Egyptian cultures, homosexual groups, marital "switching" clubs, and so on.

It may be added that there are rules also for the application of negative reinforcers as well as positive, and these can differ for families, subcultures, and cultures. For example, a family has rules by which certain behaviors are punished. So does a group or a society. Many rules concerning the application of negative reinforcers when the behavior or social stimulus involved is inappropriate are made explicit in the form of legal or religious laws. Certain behavior-social stimulus-reinforcement relationships are relatively likely to be heavily controlled by laws, as occurs in the area of sex. These rules may also be called mores, values, or norms in the social sciences.

The experimental, social, or clinical psychologist who is interested in human behavior must go to the social and behavioral sciences and their naturalistic observations of man for information concerning these important matters. It may be suggested, however, that the concepts and the principles of the basic science serve as the theory within which to understand and extend the naturalistic observations and concepts. Thus, the theory of human behavior does not emerge from the basic laboratory principles themselves (as some philosophies of psychology would imply, for example, Skinner's "experimental analysis of behavior" methodology), nor from the naturalistic observations themselves.

THE "GOAL" [DISCRIMINATIVE] FUNCTION OF THE A-R-D SYSTEM

There is a third aspect of a learning theory of attitudes and human motivation that also involves a principle that does not emerge from the laboratory, but which has antecedents in the naturalistic observations and concepts of clinical psychology and other social sciences. The author has in part described this principle elsewhere (Staats, 1964a, 1967b, 1968; Staats & Staats, 1963). The analysis requires an integration of the principles of classical conditioning, conditioned reinforcement, and discriminative stimulus control. The analysis provides the principles with which to treat the *D aspect* of the A-R-D system.

The laboratory study of the principle of reinforcement has been largely concerned with the reinforcing effect of reinforcing stimuli. It should be noted that the effect of a reinforcing stimulus occurs when it is presented *after* some response—and the effect involves strengthening *future* occurrences of that behavior. The reinforcing function of a stimulus is not defined by the ability of the stimulus to control (or bring on) instrumental behavior. The traditional learning theories did not explicitly make this point. Consequently, many investigators have not understood this definition clearly or followed it in their research with humans. Thus, it is not uncommon to see a study in which the reinforcing value of a stimulus is increased by the experimental manipulation; but the effect is measured by the increase in the instrumental behavior the stimulus *elicits*, not by an increase in its reinforcing function. Although the stimulus has never been presented as a reinforcer, contingent upon the behavior studied, the effect is erroneously discussed as if it was due to the reinforcing action of the stimulus. (see Bandura, Ross & Ross, 1963, as an example, as described below).

This is an easy confusion, however, for there has not been an appreciation by laboratory investigators of how conditioned stimulus and reinforcing value are inextricably intertwined with discriminative stimulus value when studying or treating complex human behavior. Clinical and social theories, while at times recognizing the multiple functions of motivational stimuli, have not clearly defined the functions or indicated the operating principles. Newcomb (1950, p. 80) and Klineberg (1954, p. 76), as examples, discuss motives as including states of *drive*, as well as *directing* behavior toward some goal. Norms and values play the same role in sociology—referring to control of behavior and to satisfaction—and these functions are ordinarily not clearly distinguished (Johnson, 1960, p. 50). Freud, as another example, posited that an instinct has both an aim and a particular behavior for attaining the object that satisfies the aim and reduces the tension of the instinct.

In the laboratory, on the other hand, the several functions of stimuli have been clearly seen, but the relationship has not been adequately stipulated. (Hull suggested that the concept of motivation, or drive, had both an "energizing" and "guiding" function—and the concept of anticipatory goal response is also relevant—but the learning theory was not developed to serve as a basis for a theory of human motivation, or human behavior in general, and the theory serves poorly in this role. Skinner has not treated the interacting function of stimuli.) This appears to be another case where an amalgamation of the laboratory and social-clinical theories is required to deal adequately with human behavior.

Actually, the analysis of the "rewarding" and "goal" functions of reinforcing stimuli is complex. It may be reduced for a summary account, however. To begin, the sensory stimuli of an object or event that also has a reinforcing quality are likely to come to control behaviors that approach or avoid the stimuli. As an example, when a child sees the food stimulus, if he crawls toward the stimulus (but not away from it) this response is followed by obtaining the stimulus — which is a reinforcement. This process fulfills the requirements for making a stimulus a discriminative stimulus; that is, a stimulus in the presence of which a response is reinforced will come to control the response.

This brief analysis must be expanded in human behavior in several directions. First, the child will learn a large class of "striving" behaviors that will come under the discriminative control of such reinforcing stimuli; for example, crawling toward, walking toward, running toward, climbing over and around obstacles, reaching and grabbing for, fighting and struggling for, asking, begging, and crying for, working for, wheedling for, arguing for, flattering for, being ingratiating for, being respectful for, as well as competing for in various ways.

In addition, the child's class of striving behaviors will come under the discriminative control of a large number of different reinforcing stimuli on the basis of his experience with those, or similar, stimuli. Thus, in the child's conditioning history a wide variety of stimulus objects that are reinforcers will come to control responses that result in obtaining those objects.

Furthermore, through various mediated generalization mechanisms stimulus objects with which the individual has *previously had no direct conditioning experience* will have the goal (discriminative) value immediately. This may take place through language, as one example. That is, after the word "food" has come to be a conditioned reinforcer (through classical conditioning) and also a discriminative stimulus for striving behavior, a new stimulus that is labeled by the word "food" will thereby immediately gain discriminative control. It may also be suggested, although the complete mediated generalization analysis will not be given here, that any stimulus that elicits a positive emotional or attitudinal response (any reinforcing stimulus) will also have, to that extent, discriminative stimulus value, the first time the stimulus is contacted. The principle is again that of mediated generalization.

(It should be noted that although a stimulus will tend to control a wide number of striving responses, whether or not a response occurs will also be a function of other controlling stimuli that are present in the situation. For example, although a reinforcing stimulus may control reaching for and asking for behavior, the latter will be more likely to occur when there is another person present. As another example, a stimulus object that is labeled food will not control striving behavior if it elicits a negative emotional response because of its visual characteristics.)

At any rate, it is suggested that the strength of the discriminative stimulus value will vary, in part, as a function of manipulation of the reinforcing value of the stimulus. Thus, the discriminative value of the stimulus will increase or decrease according to *classical conditioning variables* as well as *deprivation-satiation* conditions.

The preceding analysis was made only for positive reinforcing stimuli. However, an analogous analysis can be made for negative reinforcing stimuli. Because of their effects on behavior, negative reinforcing stimuli come to control striving away from or striving against behaviors, which would include a broad class of responses ranging from running away from, through fighting, avoiding, arguing with, insulting, voting against, rating negatively, and so on.

It should be noted that in contrast to the laboratory situation, it is usually the discriminative control of instrumental behaviors that social and behavioral science investigators use to index motivational stimuli. The social psychologist, clinician, sociologist, or anthropologist, for example, ordinarily observes what people strive for (verbally or otherwise) when he studies attitudes or motivation. This is why he has so generally introduced the concept of goal-directed behavior (which while correct in certain respects is usually also teleological) and has frequently glossed over the principles of classical conditioning and reinforcement. The social theorist, or clinical theorist, does not see whether the receipt of a stimulus elicits an emotional response or strengthens future occurrences of an instrumental behavior. In fact it would ordinarily be impossible to do so in view of the complexity of many human behaviors studied or treated, the infrequency of their occurrence, and so on. It is suggested that these variations in the principles of the laboratory worker and those of the social scientist have prevented their integration into a productive relationship in this important realm of study.

IMPLICATIONS, RESEARCH EXTENSIONS, AND APPLICATIONS

One of the primary considerations of the present theory is its applicability to the concerns of various fields of the study of complex human behavior. It is felt that it is necessary to produce theory in the realm of human behavior that has significance ranging from basic laboratory research, through data and theory of importance to the social sciences, to fields concerned with the actual solution of human problems. In part the analysis has been conducted to indicate that the study of attitudes does not demarcate an area that is separate in principle from the study of many other aspects of human behavior considered under various terms. These points may be further elaborated by indicating examples of the extensions of the theory to various areas of research and application.

Basic Research in the A-R-D System

This section will describe a few of the experiments which underlie the theory of the formation and instrumental functions of attitude stimuli, and then indicate some of the extensions which the theory suggests. First, the present author and associates (Staats, Staats, & Crawford, 1962) have shown that a stimulus, in this case a word, will come to elicit emotional responses according to the principles of classical conditioning. In this experiment the ^CS was paired with the aversive ^{UC}S (electric shock and loud noise). As a consequence of the conditioning, emotional responses (as measured by the galvanic skin response) were conditioned to the ^CS. Furthermore, the subjects who had been so conditioned indicated that the word had acquired a negative attitudinal value for them by rating the word as more unpleasant than did control subjects. Another important finding was that the intensity of the conditioned emotional response was positively related to the intensity of the rated negative attitudes — suggesting again that the same process is responsible for the physiological emotional conditioning and the attitudinal rating. These findings, which have been replicated by Maltzman, Raskin, Gould, and Johnson (1965), substantiate the present analysis of attitude formation as classical conditioning. The findings also indicate that *attitudinal ratings* can be used to index emotional, or attitudinal, conditioning.

To continue, however, once a stimulus has come to elicit an attitudinal response it should be capable of making other stimuli into attitudinal stimuli, according to the principle of higher-order conditioning. This has been shown in a number of studies conducted by the author and his associates. In one study, for example, national names (like

Dutch) were used as to-be-conditioned stimuli and were paired a number of times with previously conditioned words employed as ^{UC}S words that would elicit either a positive or negative attitudinal response. Examples of positive ^{UC}S words are *beauty, gift, happy, healthy,* and so on. Examples of negative ^{UC}S words are *sour, agony, disgusting, dirty.* The national name was paired only one time with a particular ^{UC}S, but many times with words which elicited the same attitudinal response. As expected, the national name paired with words eliciting a negative attitudinal response came to be rated as unpleasant; the reverse occurred when the conditioning was in the opposite direction (Staats & Staats, 1958). Later studies by the author and associates demonstrated that (a) the strength of the effect is a function of the number of conditioning trials (Staats & Staats, 1959); (b) the conditioning of the attitudinal response to a word will generalize to its synonyms (Staats, Staats, & Heard, 1959); and (c) the strength of the effect is a function of the ratio of reinforcement employed (C. K. Staats, Staats, and Heard, 1960); all of which follow expectations the author derived from the basic conditioning principles.

These studies apply to the *formation* of attitudes. However, the present theory suggests that attitudinal stimuli should *function* according to the principles of instrumental conditioning. An experimental hypothesis derived from this theory would be that attitudinal stimuli presented contingent upon a motor behavior should increase the strength of that motor behavior. Finley and Staats (1967) have tested this hypothesis in a study in which children were to make one of two alternative motor responses whenever a light appeared before them. Each emission of one of the two responses was followed by a positive attitudinal stimulus for one group of subjects, a negative attitudinal stimulus for another group, and a neutral stimulus for a third group.

Three groups of sixth grade children were used: positive attitudinal words presented contingent upon the motor response strengthened the response, negative attitudinal words weakened the response, neutral words had a neutral effect. The result showed that words that are ^CS and elicit an attitudinal response, which can thus be used to classically condition attitudes to new stimuli, will also function as reinforcing stimuli in the learning of instrumental behaviors.

While specific studies have not been set up to test the discriminative (controlling) function of attitudinal stimuli, there are a number of studies in the literature of social psychology that support the present analysis — even though the studies sprang from different theoretical standpoints. For example, Bandura *et al.* (1963) conducted an experiment in which one of two adults was paired with "positive attitude stimuli" in the presence of an observing child. This, according to the present theory, should have increased the reinforcing value of that adult and thus the discriminative stimulus value of that adult for a large class of striving-for behaviors, including imitational behaviors. The results showed this to be the case for imitational behavior. (Bandura *et al.*, however, following Mowrer's 1960 learning theory, interpreted their results in straightforward reinforcement terms, which is incorrect. That is, the child's imitational behavior in the study was not strengthened by response-contingent reinforcement, it was elicited or controlled by the adult. See Staats, 1968, for additional discussion of this point.)

The results of Lott and Lott (1960) may also be interpreted in the present terms. That is, children who had been paired with rewards were later selected more frequently as someone to be a companion on a trip. Again, it may be suggested, making the children positive attitudinal stimuli through classical conditioning had the effect of controlling a class of striving-for behaviors, one of which was the sociometric choice. (See Staats, 1964a, pp. 330-336, for a more complete analysis.)

The manner of statement of the theory, it may be suggested, as well as its integration into various areas of study, provides a basis from which to project research that should be conducted. Thus, for example, there is a host of research that should be conducted to demonstrate and to explore further the interrelationship of classical and instrumental conditioning in the study and measurement of attitudinal stimuli. Such research might test (1) the effects of schedules of reinforcement on the strength of instrumental conditioning employing attitudinal stimuli such as words, and (2) the possibility that the intensity of the rating of attitudinal significance of a word is related to the strength of the word's reinforcing value, discriminative stimulus value, and the word's ability to produce intense classical conditioning. It would also be important to create attitudinal stimuli (words and other stimuli) in the laboratory on the basis of simple and higher-order classical conditioning and then test the classical conditioning and instrumental functions the attitudinal stimuli should then have.

SOCIAL INTERACTION AND THE A-R-D SYSTEM[1]

It is expected that the A-R-D qualities of a person would help determine his effect upon other people in various ways usually considered under the terms leadership, imitation, social power, identification, obedience, persuasion, communication, and so on. A whole area of study of social interaction can also be derived from the analysis. That is, it should be possible to manipulate the attitudinal value of a social stimulus (a person) and then test changes in the value

---

[1] An addendum to this section will be found on p. 389.

of the social stimulus as an ^{UC}S, as a reinforcing stimulus, and as a controlling discriminative stimulus. Thus, the positive attitudinal value of the person could be changed through classical conditioning procedures in which the person is paired with positive attitudinal stimuli. Then the effects of the person would be expected to change. People or other stimuli (messages, for example) paired with this person should acquire more attitudinal value according to classical conditioning principles. Also when this person reinforces someone else's instrumental behaviors (for example, in the type of task used by Gewirtz and Baer, 1958) the effect of the classical conditioning should make the person a strong reinforcer. Moreover, the person who through classical conditioning has acquired positive attitudinal value should as a consequence also acquire controlling value for a large class of striving-for behaviors for the person so conditioned. The person who elicits the positive attitude should as a consequence be more imitated, more followed, and more effective in persuasion. He should be voted for more, rated higher on sociometric scales, be helped and rewarded more, and so on.

It should be noted that the positive attitudinal value of a person could be altered in various ways: by pairing the individual with positive attitudinal stimulus objects or events, or words labeling those objects and events; by naming the individual with a positive attitudinal title (such as doctor) or label (such as brilliant); by extinction procedures; as well as through deprivation. With respect to the latter, Gewirtz and Baer (1958) found that the reinforcement value of a person for children increased when the children were deprived of people. It would be expected from the present theory that such deprivation would also raise the attitudinal value of the person for classical conditioning processes as well as the person's discriminative controlling value for the various striving-for behaviors.

The above expectations should also hold for negative attitudinal social stimuli. Increase in the intensity of the attitude would be expected to change the person's effect on other people in terms of the person's reinforcing value, discriminative stimulus value, and his efficacy in the classical conditioning process.

One further point may be made regarding such research. The present theory makes a number of suggestions that should also be studied in the basic laboratory. For example, it was suggested that the hierarchical nature of the reinforcer system is important in determining behavior, and also that deprivation would affect the hierarchical nature of the system. Additional research should be conducted to specify these principles, and the other aspects of the interaction of classical and instrumental conditioning.

PERSONALITY THEORY, ASSESSMENT, AND THE A-R-D SYSTEM

It is suggested that a major task of developing a personality theory that has its basis in the principles and methods of general psychology is to describe the formation and function of the A-R-D system in various areas of human behavior in combination with the observations of the social and behavioral sciences and with clinical and abnormal psychology. Thus, for example, we must make specific analyses of types of psychopathology in terms of abnormalities in the A-R-D system. This must be done on a broad basis, including various diagnostic categories, and in detail which includes description of the development of the "abnormal" system. Suggestions have been made in the present paper and in other analyses of the author (Staats, 1964a, 1967b, 1968; Staats & Butterfield, 1965; Staats, Minke, Goodwin, & Landeen, 1967; Staats & Staats, 1963), but complete and detailed coverage is necessary. The descriptions of abnormal and clinical psychology provide some of the data which is necessary to begin such a project, as do the data of social psychology and other social and behavioral sciences. As part of this it is also necessary to begin to specify what an appropriate (normal) A-R-D system should consist of in our society and to indicate the conditions necessary to produce this basic feature of human learning. (Additional research for social psychology, sociology, and anthropology which would contribute to this task will be mentioned in a later section.)

In addition, there is the problem of assessing this important determinant of human behavior, the motivational system. The author has suggested that certain types of psychological tests actually "assess the reinforcers that are effective for an individual or a group" (Staats & Staats, 1963, p. 305), although the tests were not constructed on the basis of this rationale, or in many cases on the basis of any rationale. (This will be elaborated to include the three functions of such stimuli.) Examples may be given from interest inventories and inventories of values, attitudes, needs, and so on. For example, more than half the items on the Strong Vocational Interest Blank (Strong, 1952) ask the subject to state whether he likes, dislikes, or is indifferent to various occupations, school subjects, amusements, activities, and characteristics and roles of people.

It is suggested that other tests of attitudes, values, interests, personality and so on also assess the various functions of the A-R-D system. The present theory provides an analysis of what such test items actually are. That is, a test item in which a stimulus object, event, person, behavior, or what have you is listed and the individual responds by indicating *like, dislike,* or *indifference* in any of a variety of ways may be considered in the following terms. The verbal test stimulus elicits an attitudinal response (because it has been paired with the actual emotional stimulus, for example) which makes the test stimulus both a conditioned stimulus as well as a reinforcing stimulus. As a consequence of these functions the stimulus will also be a discriminative stimulus controlling either a class of striving-for or a class of striving-away from behaviors, as the case may be, including the verbal behaviors of checking or writing *like* or *dislike,* and so on. It is the discriminative function of the stimulus that is being measured, however, not the other two functions. *It is suggested that it is because all three stimulus functions are related in the manner described, that the three functions can be assessed from observations only of the discriminative stimulus value.*

Research in this area should be conducted to test the theory that such items on tests do indeed measure conditioned stimulus value and reinforcing stimulus value, as well as discriminative stimulus value. Thus, for example, one experimental hypothesis would be that people who indicate on an inventory positive attitudes (or interests, needs, and so on) for certain stimulus objects, events, or activities should be reinforced more strongly by those stimuli or their verbal labels in an instrumental conditioning situation (such as that used by Finley and Staats, 1967). In addition, the words on such a test (or the actual stimuli) should also serve better in a classical conditioning situation such as has been described herein. Thus, a person who tested as having positive attitudes toward sports and sports figures should be classically conditioned to positive attitudes toward a stimulus which is paired with words labeling sports events and the names of prominent sportsmen, whereas a person with negative attitudes toward the same stimuli would be conditioned in a negative direction from the same experience. This type of research would relate the field of psychological measurement to the basic field of psychology.

It has been suggested by more recent investigators that traditional measuring instruments should be discarded in favor of direct reinforcement procedures (see Patterson 1967); that the reinforcing value of a stimulus should be directly assessed by seeing whether it functions as a reinforcer and will strengthen a motor behavior — rather than by seeing how the person responds to a verbal item. It should be noted that on the basis of the present analysis, however, it should be equally possible to assess the reinforcing value of a stimulus by assessing any of its three stimulus functions, that of a ^{C}S, that of a $^{C \cdot R}S$, or that of a discriminative stimulus (as in rating the item). The present analysis thus provides a behavioral rationale for the use of tests, and indicates that verbal test items are just as behaviorally appropriate as a direct operant conditioning procedure. The only criteria for the selection of method would be resolved by economy of time and effort, transparency of method, and so on.

The study by Finley and Staats (1967) showed that attitudinal rating scales did index the reinforcing properties of words, as did the operant conditioning methods later used, or as do traditional test items. It is thus suggested that this rating type of item could be used effectively in inventories which assess motivational variables. That is, the amount of reading per item is markedly curtailed over many traditional types of items so that time spent on an item is brief. In addition, it is possible by choice of the polar adjectives used to anchor the scale to make items that are less transparent than *like* or *dislike;* for example, *fair-unfair, healthy-sick, strong-weak, rough-smooth, relaxed-tense, brave-cowardly, calm-agitated, ugly-handsome,* and so on—all of which measure attitudes (Osgood & Suci, 1955) and would thus be expected to indicate reinforcing (attitudinal) value. (This is not to say that ratings, verbal items, or indeed instrumental conditioning assessment of attitudinal value will always produce the same result as if the stimulus had occurred in the person's life situation, since stimulus variables different than those in the life situation can exert control in the testing situation.)

Finally, it is suggested that the learning analysis of human motivation provides a theoretical structure within which various types of personality tests could be more systematically developed and related to one another. When this is done the field of testing (in this area at any rate) would be tied in with the basic science so that the developments of each would be of concern to the other—the essential ingredient for breaking down the basic and applied schism.

APPLIED ATTITUDE CHANGE AND THE A-R-D SYSTEM: BEHAVIOR THERAPY AND BEHAVIOR MODIFICATION

It has already been suggested herein that the larger field of attitude study is the investigation of the A-R-D systems of individuals and groups. This includes the manner in which the system functions. Thus, as one example, it has been suggested that many individual and social problems occur when the A-R-D system of the individual or the subgroup does not coincide with the A-R-D system functioning in the society or social institution. This may be seen readily in the social institution of education. Other problems fall into such applied areas of study as clinical treatment, juvenile delinquency, and so on. It is further suggested that the attitude theory meets one of its demands for verification and generality in its ability to provide a theoretical framework within which to consider and deal with such problems. Moreover, such applied areas offer facilities within which to develop the principles of the study of attitudes.

Thus, a few brief examples will be outlined to indicate the relevance of considering areas of psychological treatment as arenas of applied attitude change or manipulation. This is done (1) to indicate the generality of the present theory, (2) to suggest greater integration among presently isolated fields of psychology, (3) to improve research and treatment in the applied areas, as well as (4) to improve research and theory in the study of attitudes.

The areas of behavior modification and behavior therapy lend themselves readily to consideration as examples of applied attitude change (and, moreover, the lack of conceptualization in these fields calls for theoretical endeavor). To begin, it is suggested that behavior therapy (aversion therapy, counter conditioning, desensitization, and so on) involves changing the value of some of the attitudinal stimuli in the individual's system through classical conditioning principles. Thus, a person with a phobia (strong negative attitude) for certain stimuli will through conditioning procedures come to respond less intensely to these stimuli. Or, conversely, a person with unusual or unusually strong positive attitudinal responses to stimuli, alcohol for the alcoholic, same sex social stimuli for the homosexual, fetish stimuli for the fetishist, and so on—will be changed in a negative direction through the classical conditioning procedures of behavior therapy. Actually, simply recognizing that behavior therapy in large part consists of changing the value of attitudinal stimuli of various kinds opens a large area of research for the attitude theorist. In the present case, however, it is suggested that significant contributions can also be made by the attitude theory to understanding more fully the process of behavior therapy.

For example, Breger and McGaugh (1965) asked—correctly so, in an article that included less well-founded criticisms—if a neurosis consists solely of specific symptoms, how do behavior therapists account for the *general* results of their specific treatments. To illustrate the criticism, and indicate how the present theory provides the answer, let us use Raymonds's case (1960) of the patient treated by aversive conditioning to reduce his sexual attraction by baby carriages and women's handbags. After the counter-conditioning (aversive) treatment he no longer approached these objects. Moreover, the treatment generalized—the patient's sexual relationship with his wife improved. When the conception of the A-R-D system is applied to this case, the generalization of the treatment can be expected. That is, the fetish objects and the wife may be seen as sexual stimuli in the patient's hierarchical A-R-D system. Thus, it would be predicted that lowering the value of the fetish objects would raise the relative value of other stimuli in the system—in this case the wife—in the three functions of A-R-D stimuli, thus increasing his sexual activity.

It should be indicated that without a sophisticated understanding of the principles of the A-R-D system, and assessment of the individual's A-R-D system, the behavior therapy treatment could easily be symtomatic and result in further pathology. That is, if the next strongest reinforcer in the patient's sexual reinforcing system had been people of the same sex (or some other "abnormal" social stimulus), rather than the patient's wife, lowering the attitudinal value of the fetish objects as reinforcers could have resulted in homosexual behavior becoming more dominant, which might even be less desirable than the original problem. This example indicates the need for relating a sophisticated learning conception of the A-R-D system to the field of behavior therapy—including knowledge of the relationship of conditioned stimulus, discriminative stimulus, and reinforcer stimulus value. *For while behavior therapy changes conditioned stimulus value in the controlled treatment procedure, its results depend upon the change of discriminative stimulus and reinforcing value in the natural and unmonitored conditions of the patient's life circumstances.* (See Staats, in press, for further clinical analyses.)

A similar situation exists in the area of behavior modification. It is suggested that behavior modification involves the use of an artificial reinforcement system suited to the patient for whom the reinforcement system in his life situation is functionally inadequate. Because of the lack of theoretical analysis in this field, however, various possibilities for manipulating the reinforcer system have not been recognized. For example, the fact that the treatment also results in classical conditioning that *changes* the patient's attitude is not realized; thus the potential for changing the individual's A-R-D system is not exploited. While behavior therapy has been concerned with the classical conditioning of attitudes and leaves the other learning concomitants uncontrolled, behavior modification manipulates response contingent reinforcement and neglects investigation of the classical conditioning of attitudes that results the effects of this conditioning. The major point here again, however, is that the attitude theory and clinical treatment concern the same principles and the same types of events. Psychologists interested in the study of attitudes should be concerned about the extension and test of their methods, principles, and theories in the context of clinical treatment. While it is not possible to go into these matters now in a manner that is in any way complete, it is suggested that other problems of human behavior also provide the same natural laboratories for the development of attitude theories. Again, however, relating the fields of attitude theory and clinical treatment by founding them on the same basic principles would make the affairs of each have a common interest dissolving the basic-applied schism.

THE A-R-D SYSTEMS OF SOCIETIES AND SOCIAL INSTITUTIONS: SOCIOLOGICAL AND CROSS-CULTURAL RESEARCH

For some time there has been a waning enthusiasm for the use of psychoanalytic theory in the study of differences between cultures. Cross-cultural studies have tended to become more strictly empirical because of the paucity of theoretical principles that appear to have generality across various peoples (Guthrie, 1966).

However, basic psychological principles should be evident with different cultures and groups within a culture, although the particular stimulus and response events may vary. Moreover, it is felt that a theory of attitudes (or human motivation in general) should be based upon principles that have that type of generality.

In the present case, the principles in the human motivation theory should be useful as a structure within which to study and compare peoples (cultures) as well as institutions and groups. It is suggested that a society or social institution may be described, and compared to others, in terms of its A-R-D system. This would involve observation of the stimulus objects, events, activities, behaviors, positions in society, and so on, which elicit positive attitudes, which thus serve as positive reinforcers and discriminative stimuli. The hierarchical aspects of the A-R-D system should also vary over groups and cultures. Moreover, the rules for application of the reinforcers to specific behaviors should also vary. Each of these variations would in terms of the present theory be expected to be a determinant of the behavior of the members of the group and thus of the character of the group. As already suggested, the conjunction or disjunction of the A-R-D systems of the social institution and the individual must also be studied for the social problems produced.

It should be noted that in the present context of principles, experimental research should also be derivable from the analysis. That is the description of the various aspects of the group's A-R-D system would constitute a set of hypotheses concerning the behaviors that the (conjunctive) members of the group should display. These hypotheses could then be tested by observing whether or not the behaviors occur as predicted. It is suggested that such studies could make objective and scientifically interesting cross-cultural comparisons and the study of national (or group) character (about which there has also been waning interest because the endeavor has not been tied into a meaningful theoretical-research structure [Hoebel, 1967]).

It should also be possible to introduce controlled experimental study into sociological and anthropological research. For example, the type of research previously described in the *Basic Research on the A-R-D System* and the *Social Interaction and the A-R-D System sections* could be conducted on peoples in different groups and cultures in a comparative way. Thus, it could be seen in controlled experimentation whether a name with positive attitudinal value when paired with a person will better control imitational behavior, perhaps using the type of procedure Bandura *et al.* demonstrated. The other types of study outlined in that preceding section could also be conducted across cultures. In this manner the principles of learning and the motivational theory would be tested for generality and a general conception of human behavior extended and developed.

In the present author's view it is incumbent upon the theory of attitudes to be stated in terms that produce research, but in addition the theory must eventually link up with conceptions concerned with man's general behavior. In this way a unified, comprehensive, theoretical structure will result. This general endeavor should range from the basic learning principles of the animal laboratory to the most significant aspects of complex human behavior. It is the purpose of the present paper to indicate some of the lines of this general theory and its methodology, to sketch the outlines of a sub-theory of human motivation developed within the general approach, and to indicate some of the areas which can be unified and researched by means of the theory of motivation.

The author has chosen the label "social behaviorism" to typify the general approach. This is done to indicate that a new approach to learning theory is involved, where the purpose is to develop a basic learning theory especially for the treatment of human behavior. This is in distinction to the traditional learning theories which were constructed to "explain" the facts of the animal laboratory (see Staats, 1968). In addition, the label of "social behaviorism" is intended to indicate the method of using the observations and concepts of the social and behavioral sciences, the clinic, psychological measurement, and so on to elaborate the learning theory as a conception of human behavior. The present analysis by no means encompasses the areas of concern to the general conception. However, it does indicate the general lines of the approach as well as demonstrate its utility for extension into the areas described.

References

Bandura, A., Ross, D., & Ross, S. A comparative test of the status envy, social power, and the secondary reinforcement theories of identification learning. *Journal of Abnormal and Social Psychology*, 1963, 67, 527-534.

Breger, L., & McGaugh, J. L. Critique and reformulation of "Learning-theory approaches to psychotherapy and neurosis." *Psychological Bulletin*, 1965, 63, 338-358.

Burgess, R. L., & Akers, R. L. A differential association-reinforcement theory of criminal behavior. *Sociological Problems*, 1966, 14, 128-147.

Finley, J. R., & Staats, A. W. Evaluative meaning words as reinforcing stimuli. *Journal of Verbal Learning and Verbal Behavior*, 1967, 6, 193-197.

Gewirtz, L. L., & Baer, D. M. Deprivation and satiation of social reinforcers as drive conditions. *Journal of Abnormal and Social Psychology*, 1958, 57, 165-172.

Guthrie, G. The cultural origin of personality differences. Paper presented at the meeting of the Hawaiian Psychological Association, Honolulu, Hawaii, December, 1966.

Hoebel, E. A. Anthropological perspectives on national character. *Annals of the American Academy of Political and Social Science*, 1967, 370, 1-7.

Hull, C. E. *Principles of behavior*. New York: Appleton, 1943.

Johnson, H. M. *Sociology: A systematic introduction*. New York: Harcourt, 1960.

Kinsey, A. C., Pomeroy, W. B., & Martin, C. E. *Sexual behavior in the human male*. Philadelphia: Saunders, 1948.

Klineberg, O. *Social psychology*. New York: Holt, 1954.

Lott, B. E., & Lott, A. J. The formation of positive attitudes toward group members. *Journal of Abnormal and Social Psychology*, 1960, 61, 297-300.

Maccoby, E. E., & Gibbs, P. K. Methods of child-rearing in two social classes. In W. E. Martin and C. B. Stendler (Eds.), *Readings in child development*. New York: Harcourt, 1954.

Maltzman, I., Raskin, D. C., Gould, J., & Johnson, O. Individual differences in the orienting reflex and semantic conditioning and generalization under different UCS intensities. Paper presented at the annual meetings of the Western Psychological Association, Honolulu, June, 1965.

Maslow, A. H. *Motivation and personality*. New York: Harper, 1954.

Miller, N. E. Experiments relevant to learning theory and psychopathology. Proceedings of the 18th International Congress of Psychology, Moscow, 1966.

Newcomb, T. M. *Social psychology*. New York: Holt, 1950.

Osgood, C. E., & Suci, G. J. Factor analysis of meaning. *Journal of Experimental Psychology*, 1955, 50, 325-338.

Patterson, G. R. Prediction of victimization from an instrumental conditioning procedure. *Journal of Consulting Psychology*, 1967, 31, 147-152.

Raymond, M. J. Case of fetishism treated by aversion therapy. In H. J. Eysenck (Ed.), *Behavior therapy and the neuroses*. Oxford: Pergamon Press, 1960.

Rescorla, R. A., and Solomon, R. L. Two-process learning theory: Relationships between Pavlovian conditioning and instrumental learning. *Psychological Review*, 1967, 74, 151-182.

Rosen, B. C. The achievement syndrome: A psychocultural dimension of social stratification. *American Sociological Review*, 1956, **21**, 203-211.

Samuelson, P. A. *Economics: An introductory analysis.* (4th ed.). New York: McGraw-Hill, 1958.

Staats, A. W. Verbal habit, families, concepts, and the operant conditioning of word classes. *Psychological Review*, 1961, **68**, 190-204.

Staats, A. W. (Ed.) *Human learning.* New York: Holt, 1964. (a)

Staats, A. W. Conditioned stimuli, conditioned reinforces, and word meaning. In A. W. Staats (Ed.), *Human learning.* New York: Holt, 1964. Pp. **ccc–ccc**. (b).

Staats, A. W. A case in and a strategy for the extension of learning principles to the problems of human behavior. In L. Krasner and L. P. Ullman (Eds.) *Research in behavior modification.* New York: Holt, 1965, 121-144.

Staats, A. W. An integrated-functional learning approach to complex human behavior. In B. Kleinmuntz (Ed.), *Problem solving: Research, method, and theory.* New York: Wiley, 1966. Pp. 259-339.

Staats, A. W. Categories and underlying processes, or representative behavior samples and S-R analyses: Opposing strategies. Paper presented at the annual meetings of the American Psychological Association, Washington, D.C., September, 1967. (a)

Staats, A. W. An outline of an integrated learning theory and of attitude formation and function. In M. Fishbein, (Ed.), *Readings in attitude theory and measurement.* New York: Wiley, 1967. (b)

Staats, A. W. *Learning, language, and cognition.* New York: Holt, 1968.

Staats, A. W. Social Behaviorism, Human Motivation, and the Conditioning Therapies. In Maher, B. (Ed.), *Progress in Experimental Personality Research*, 1969, **5**. New York: Academic Press, in press.

Staats, A. W., and Butterfield, W. H. Treatment of nonreading in a culturally-deprived juvenile delinquent: An application of reinforcement principles. *Child Development*, 1965, **36**, 925-942.

Staats, A. W., Minke, K. A., Goodwin, W., and Landeen, J. Cognitive behavior modification: "Motivated learning" reading treatment with subprofessional therapy-technicians. *Behavior Research and Therapy*, 1967, **5**, 283-299.

Staats, A. W., and Staats, C. K. Attitudes established by classical conditioning. *Journal of Abnormal and Social Psychology*, 1958, **57**, 37-40.

Staats, A. W., and Staats, C. K. Effect of number of trials on the language conditioning of meaning. *Journal of General Psychology*, 1959, **61**, 211-223.

Staats, A. W., and Staats, C. K. *Complex human behavior.* New York: Holt, 1963.

Staats, A. W., Staats, C. K., and Crawford, H. L. First-order conditioning of meaning and the parallel conditioning of a GSR. *Journal of General Psychology*, 1962, **67**, 159-167.

Staats, A. W., Staats, C. K., and Heard, W. G. Language conditioning of meaning to meaning using a semantic generalization paradigm. *Journal of Experimental Psychology*, 1959, **57**, 187-192.

Staats, C. K., Staats, A. W., and Heard, W. G. Attitude development and ratio of reinforcement. *Sociometry*, 1960, **23**, 338-350.

Strong, E. K., Jr. *Vocational interest blank for men: Manual.* Stanford, Calif.: Stanford University Press, 1952.

Trapold, M. A., and Winokur, S. Transfer from classical conditioning and extinction to acquisition, extinction, and stimulus generalization of a positively reinforced instrumental response. *Journal of Experimental Psychology*, 1967, **73**, 517-525.

Ulmer, M. J. *Economics: Theory and practice.* Boston: Houghton, Mifflin, 1959.

Zimmerman, D. W. Durable secondary reinforcement: Method and theory. *Psychological Review*, 1957, **64**, 373-383.

3

A Learning Theory
Approach to Interpersonal Attitudes [1]

ALBERT J. LOTT AND BERNICE E. LOTT
DEPARTMENT OF PSYCHOLOGY
UNIVERSITY OF KENTUCKY
LEXINGTON, KENTUCKY

The research discussed in this paper constitutes a systematic test of a learning theory analysis of interpersonal attraction. In this approach, hypotheses relevant to both the development and consequences of positive attitudes toward persons have been derived from broad principles of behavior, as formulated primarily by Hull and Spence. By defining interpersonal attraction in S-R terms we are able to place this concept within a large nomological net in which other concepts have already been linked theoretically and empirically, and which provides a basis for derivations specific to the investigation of social behavior.

To be attracted to, or to like, another is construed within our framework as having a positive attitude toward another, and a positive attitude is defined, following Doob (1947), as an implicit, anticipatory goal response $(r_g\text{-}s_g)$ having both cue and drive properties. It is the $r_g\text{-}s_g$ and the conditions which influence its evocation and strength, on the one hand, and its motivational and overt response consequences, on the other hand, that provide the theoretical bridge between S-R learn-

[1] The preparation of this chapter has been supported by a grant (GS-1438) from the National Science Foundation, Division of Social Sciences. Some portions of the paper were presented earlier at a symposium on "Interpersonal Attraction" held at the Southwestern Psychological Association meetings in Arlington, Texas, April, 1966.

ing theory and an understanding of the social phenomenon of liking. The core idea of the present approach is that learning to like a particular stimulus person is essentially learning to anticipate reward when that person is present or, in Mowrer's terms (1960), a liked person is one to whom "hope," the conditionable component of the reaction to positive reinforcement, has been conditioned. Subsequently, the liked person (or some representation of him) can raise general drive level in the liker, in proportion to the degree of liking (or strength of r_g-s_g), and can function as a secondary reward. Liking can also mediate between the stimulus person evoking this implicit response and a variety of overt acts. Thus, we are interested specifically in (a) the conditions under which positive attitudes toward persons may be learned; (b) the overt responses which are typically conditioned to positive attitudes and from which the latter may be inferred; and (c) the consequences which liking has for interpersonal and other behaviors.

The terms interpersonal attraction and liking are used here interchangeably and neither term is considered more general than the other. A single stimulus person may, of course, come to evoke both positive and negative (hence ambivalent) attitudes of differing or equal strengths, depending upon the history of association with him. Our analysis at present deals only with the conditions under which positive interpersonal attitudes may develop and the consequences which follow for behavior.

THE LEARNING OF POSITIVE INTERPERSONAL ATTITUDES

The primary proposition relevant to the learning of liking is that if a person is rewarded in the presence of another, a positive attitude toward that other will be formed. This rests upon the following assumptions (Lott & Lott, 1960, p. 298):

1. Persons may be conceptualized as discriminable stimuli to which responses may be learned.
2. A person who experiences reinforcement or reward for some behavior will react to the reward, i.e., will perform some observable or covert goal response (R_G or r_g).
3. This response to reward will become conditioned, like any other response, to all discriminable stimuli present at the time of reinforcement.
4. A person . . . who is present at the time that Individual X, for example, is rewarded thus becomes able in a later situation to evoke R_G, or, what is more likely, its fractional and anticipatory component, r_g-s_g. This latter response, which Hull has called "expectative" (1952, Ch. 5), was earlier interpreted by Doob (1947) as the underlying mechanism of an attitude.

The concept of goal response (R_G) implies not just consummatory activity but the more complex combination of evaluative, verbal, autonomic, and central reactions which are only partially overt but which we assume human beings reliably make to rewarding objects or situations. When a child, for example, receives praise, the R_G will almost certainly include a smile of pleasure. When any individual is rewarded, positive affect is assumed to accompany such observable responses as a laugh, an exclamation, physical approach to the goal, etc. In addition, although the anticipatory goal response has generally been interpreted as a peripheral response, the present use of the r_g-s_g mechanism treats it as a theoretical concept. As such, as others have pointed out (Black, 1965; Miller, 1963), neither its nature nor locus of occurrence requires explicit specification (at least, at the moment).

An anticipatory goal response (r_g-s_g) will become conditioned to a discriminable stimulus person (S_P) who is consistently present when an instrumental response (R_X) is reinforced and a positive attitude will thus be acquired. It should be clear that no instrumental or other direct relationship between the S_P and the reward is implied nor considered necessary. The sufficient condition for the formation of a positive attitude toward S_P is merely his consistent presence during receipt of reward.

ANTECEDENT CONDITIONS

Reward

The primary hypothesis stated above has been tested and substantiated in several experiments. In our first study (Lott & Lott, 1960), 16 same-sex groups of three children each played a noncompetitive board game ("Rocket Ship") during which some children were rewarded for success and others were not. Each play group was composed of children from the same third or fifth grade classroom who had not chosen each other on either of two sociometric tests previously administered by their teacher. Four types of play groups were used which differed only in the number of children who were rewarded during the game (zero, one, two, or all) although Ss in every group were told that any number of members could win. The between group variations in number of winners were introduced to approximate natural conditions and thus avoid having the children feel that the game was rigged since it was expected that the Ss would talk to one another about the game as they returned to their classroom.

The game was played in two sessions by each group (once in the morning and once in the afternoon) and reward was defined as the accumulation by an S (over both sessions) of 4 plastic cars for 4 (out of a possible 6) successful landings of his rocket ship on a planet target. Shortly before the close of the school day, approximately 1 hour after the last group had played the game, the classroom teacher administered the dependent measure in the form of a sociometric test requiring each child to choose two from his class for a "vacation on a nearby star out in space." Those children who had been rewarded during the game made significantly more choices of play-group members (who had been present when they obtained reward) than did children who had not been rewarded during the game.

The independent variable in the above study was simply reward versus no reward, administered to each S in an all-or-none manner; the 4 prizes which constituted the reward condition were earned gradually over two play sessions but were given to the winners all at once at the very end of the game. The purpose of a second study (James & Lott, 1964) was to test the effect of additional variations in reward frequency, since it follows from the theoretical model that the strength of positive attitudes toward previously neutral persons should be an increasing function of the frequency with which goal responses have been made in their presence. Essentially the same procedure was followed in this experiment as in the first except that children won 6, 3, or 0 nickels for successful planet landings and two dependent measures were used, sociometric choice and ranking of classmates. The findings of the first experiment were replicated in that significantly more of the Ss in the 6-reward condition chose fellow group members subsequent to the game experience (and ranked them higher than they did nonplay-group member classmates) than did children who had received either 3 or 0 nickels. There was no reliable difference between the latter two conditions. That the receipt of 3, out of a possible 6 rewards, was equivalent (in its effectiveness as measured in this study) to the receipt of 0 rewards raises an important question regarding the definition of reward for human subjects, under conditions where relevant drives are assumed to operate but are neither manipulated nor premeasured. We shall have occasion to deal with this question again in a later portion of this paper.

Additional support for our primary proposition, that the receipt of reward in the presence of a previously neutral person is a sufficient condition for the development of a positive attitude toward that person, was obtained from a study conducted in a semicontrolled, natural-appearing classroom setting (Lott & Lott, 1964). Fourth and fifth graders were divided into 8 same-sex groups of 8 children per group on the basis of sociometric data obtained from a test in which each child rated all others of the same sex in his class on a 5-point liking scale. Ss placed in the same group were ones who had relatively neutral attitudes toward one another. Each group was given a special 30-minute lesson in first aid by an attractive, new female teacher who systematically rewarded only even-numbered subjects by recognizing, positively responding to, and maintaining eye contact with them. Odd-numbered children were primarily ignored or, if necessary, responded to critically. As predicted, rewarded Ss increased their rating of fellow group members, both other rewarded children and nonrewarded children, more than did nonrewarded Ss. These differences are significant (by the Mann-Whitney U test, one-tailed) for ratings made of rewarded children ($p < .001$), for ratings made of the nonrewarded children ($p < .05$), and for ratings made of all group members taken together ($p < .001$). The relevant data are shown in Fig. 1.

The changes in mean ratings from pre- to posttest made by both the rewarded and nonrewarded Ss of other rewarded and nonrewarded group members were reliable changes (as evaluated by the Wilcoxon test). All the Ss, in other words, tended to rate their fellow group members higher after their joint experience in the special first aid class than they had before, which may be attributed to the fact that these children had been singled out for special treatment and the lesson was taught by a very pleasant teacher. The general experience was certainly conducive to producing a Hawthorne effect as is suggested by the uniformly high posttest ratings made of the teacher and the lesson. Nevertheless, the rewarded children increased their ratings of fellow members even more, and significantly so, than the nonrewarded children. Thus, differential treatment by the special teacher (validated independently by two observers) for a period as short as 30 minutes succeeded in producing differential changes in the liking of classmates.

It is also of interest that the nonrewarded Ss, as can be seen in Fig. 1, increased their liking for other nonrewarded classmates more than they did for the rewarded Ss ($p = .01$, two-tailed Wilcoxon test), but the rewarded children increased their liking equally for the other children present in the group, regardless of the type of treatment the others had received.

Delay of reward

A variable which should affect the strength of association between a previously neutral stimulus and an anticipatory goal response, apart

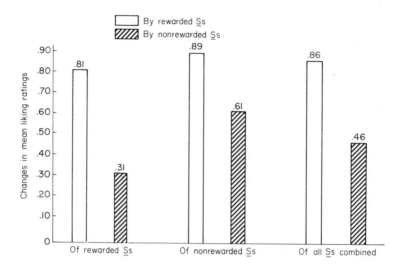

FIG. 1. Changes from pre- to posttest in mean liking ratings of group members following differential reward by teacher.

from the number of rewards obtained in the presence of that stimulus, is the length of time between the ending of the reward-producing response and the actual receipt of that reward. This expectation follows from Hull's proposal that ". . . the greater the delay in reinforcement, the weaker will be the generalized r_G, the weaker the s_G, and consequently the weaker the secondary reinforcement . . . [1952, p. 128]," and from rat studies (Jenkins, 1950; Logan, 1952) which report data supporting this proposition. A recently completed experiment (Lott, Aponte, Lott, & McGinley, in press, related delay of reinforcement to the development of liking by obtaining supportive evidence for the hypothesis that attraction to a previously neutral person will be greater when that person has been associated with immediate, rather than delayed reward.

Thirty-two first-grade children (16 of each sex) performed a simple task in the alternate presence of two adult assistants. One assistant (Mr. I) was consistently associated with immediate reward contingent upon S's task completion while the other (Mr. D) was consistently associated with a 10-second delay in reward. Each subject experienced both conditions, performing the same task in the presence of each of the assistants in a predetermined order counterbalanced over

Ss. To control for possible differences in initial likability of the assistants, each served as Mr. I for half the Ss and as Mr. D for the other half.

Each S participated in the experiment individually. He was first shown a table containing assorted toys and instructed to choose one which he could then keep if he played the game well. The toy chosen was then hung prominently in the middle of the apparatus so it would be in full view of S as he carried out the experimental tasks. S was instructed by E to fill a 15-hole form board with marbles ". . . as fast as you can." The assistant for a given trial gave the "ready," "start," and "stop" signals (the latter, after all the holes were filled); these constituted all of each assistant's verbal acts. No eye contact was maintained with a subject and each assistant's face was relatively impassive.

After a completed trial E, who sat behind the apparatus and could be heard but not seen by S, administered either a delayed or immediate reward, in the form of a dried bean ejected down a chute. S had been instructed to put his beans in a Pyrex graduated cylinder and had been told that he would be given the toy he had chosen when the cylinder was filled up to a red line. Twenty-eight trials were given, broken into 7 blocks of 4 trials each, 2 under delayed and 2 under immediate reward conditions.

On completion of trial 28, an S had enough beans to fill the cylinder to the red line; he was told he had done well and given his toy. Both assistants left the room and E administered the dependent measures of liking. Each S was shown 9 in. × 11 in. photos of Mr. I and Mr. D to be certain he was evaluating the proper individual. The measures used and their order of presentation were as follows: (a) "Which helper did you like the best?" S then signified his answer by pointing to one of the photos (only the backs of which faced E who had first shuffled them) and giving the helper's name. (b) "If you were going to play another game, which helper would you choose to play with?" (c) A 15-step rating scale was given to S for each helper with instructions to put ". . . an X on the step that shows how much you like him." (d) A semantic differential test was administered verbally, following a procedure suggested by Donahoe (1961).

The differences between Ss' ratings of Mr. I and Mr. D on the step-rating scale and the semantic differential were evaluated by the Wilcoxon matched-pairs, signed-ranks test. Both measures showed clearly that the assistant associated with immediate reward was liked significantly more than the assistant associated with delayed reward (p < .005). On the simple "like best" question, Mr. I was chosen by

63% and Mr. D by 37% of the Ss ($p = .07$, one-tailed). The "play another game with" question proved insensitive to the independent variable; 50% of the Ss chose each helper.

A control group of 16 first graders was run under the same procedure as the experimental Ss except that each S experienced, randomly, *both* immediate and delayed reward in the presence of each assistant. Under these conditions none of the dependent measures yielded significant differences in liking of the two helpers. These data together with those obtained from the experimental Ss provide strong support for our hypothesis.

Vicarious Reward

Vicarious experiences have been demonstrated to be effective in the acquisition of instrumental responses (e.g., Bruning, 1965) as well as in classical conditioning (Bandura & Rosenthal, 1966; Berger, 1962). Theoretically, it should be the case that secondary reward stimuli, also, can be established on a vicarious basis by, as Bandura and Rosenthal (1966) noted, "observing others experiencing positive reinforcement in contiguous association with discriminative stimuli."

While this is not the place to speculate at length on the processes which underlie learning by vicarious experience, we suggest that perhaps observing or inferring goal response behavior on the part of another person tends to evoke $r_g\text{-}s_g$'s in the observer. When this occurs, the observer's response may be called empathic. The likelihood of an empathic response should be a positive function of the degree to which the model is liked by the observer, either because of past goal attainment in the presence of the model or through the operation of primary stimulus generalization if the model is overtly similar to (or described as similar to) either the observer himself or persons the observer likes. If the model is disliked, or is similar to disliked others, the result may well be envy rather than empathy when the model is observed obtaining reward; that is, the evocation of $r_g\text{-}s_g$ in the observer will be interfered with by competing responses which define dislike.[2]

---

[2] An analysis of the conditions under which persons learn to dislike one another and the consequences of such negative interpersonal attitudes is currently in progress. Dislike, we believe, can be understood as anticipation of punishment or frustration, and is evoked by a stimulus previously associated with, or otherwise related to, such noxious experience. Dislike can thus be defined in Amsel's terms as $r_f - s_f$ or $r_p - s_p$ (1962); it should tend to evoke avoidance responses and function in the same way as anxiety.

Under conditions of positive or neutral relationship between the observer and a rewarded model, r_g-s_g's evoked in the observer should be conditionable to discriminable stimuli which are consistently present, and these stimuli will, consequently, become more attractive to the observer than they were before. Since the r_g-s_g evoked in the observer as he watches a model obtain reward is probably of lesser strength than the goal response made by the rewarded person, consequent increases in attraction to any stimuli which have been present should be less for the observer than for the rewarded model.

To demonstrate the influence of vicarious reward on the development of interpersonal liking, an investigation employing 360 third-grade children was conducted (Lott, Lott, & Matthews, 1967). Sixty same sex groups of six children each played Bingo games under conditions in which winning and losing of games was experimentally controlled.

In a preexperimental phase of the study potential subjects were tested to identify pairs of same-sex friends. Ss were chosen for the experiment in the following way: a pair of children who liked each other very much was selected from each of three different classrooms so that each pair was unacquainted with the children in the other pairs. When members of a group were assembled in the experimental room, name tags were pinned prominently on each child and the Ss were introduced to one another. E showed the children a display of toys and explained that Ss would be able to obtain one of them if they won at the games they were going to play and that the toy they could choose would depend on the number of games they won.

The experimental room was arranged so that the two friends in each pair sat next to one another at desks in a semicircle around E's desk. Ss were told that they were going to play Bingo but that only 3 children could actually play. It was explained that one child from each pair would be a Player and the other a Helper (determined by E's assistant who flipped a coin for each pair of Ss). Helpers were told that they would get to play a different game on another day soon, and that on this occasion their job was only to make sure that their partners did not miss any of the Bingo numbers which E was going to call. It was emphasized that only Players, not Helpers, would receive prizes for winning the games. Players were told that each time they won a game they would receive a white chip which could later be used like money to buy one of the toys they had seen; the greater the number of chips, the better the toy which could be obtained.

Four Bingo games were played and manipulated in such a way that E could control the pattern of rewards in each group. Twenty groups of each of the following 3 types were run in a random order: 4-0-0, where one Player won all 4 games and the other Players won none; 3-1-0, where one Player won 3 games, another won 1 game, and the third won none; and 2-2-0, where two Players won 2 games each and the third won none. Determination of winners and losers in each group was by chance and depended upon the desks at which the pairs of Ss had seated themselves. After completion of the games, E asked each Player how many chips he had accumulated and then led each Player-Helper pair to the toy display where the Player chose his prize. The desks were then rearranged in a large circle so that all the Ss were relatively far from one another but could still clearly see each other's name tags. All Ss, both Players and Helpers, were given a "secret fold-er" which contained the dependent variable measures, in a pre-arranged order. First, each S rated every other group member on the same type of 15-step rating scale as had previously been administered in the classrooms. After the scales were collected E read aloud, while Ss read silently, three questions designed to tap incidental learning.[3] This was followed by 3 questions aimed at obtaining a gross estimate of each child's emotional reactions to winning and losing. The questions asked were: "How did you feel when you or your partner won?," which was to be answered by very happy, happy, alright, or didn't care; "How did you feel when you or your partner lost?", which was to be answered by very sad, sad, alright, or didn't care; and the Helpers were asked if they thought they might "get to play with the toy" that their partner had won, or might have won.

The two principal predictions were that (a) Players who were re-warded by winning 4 games in the 4-0-0 situation or 2 games in the 2-2-0 groups would like the others present (both Players and Helpers) more than Players who won no games; in the 3-1-0 groups the Player who won 3 games was expected to end up liking the others reliably more than the Player who won 1 game and both to differ from the Player who won none. (b) Helpers whose partners were rewarded would like the others present reliably more than Helpers of nonre-warded partners, although these differences were expected to be smaller than the differences between rewarded and nonrewarded Players. That portion of the study concerned with the first prediction was intended to replicate previous work, but within the particular group contexts of different reward patterns which were included to approximate natural conditions. The second prediction is entirely

---

[3]Space limitations preclude discussion of this phase of the experiment.

new and extends our basic paradigm to test the influence of vicarious reinforcement on the development of liking.

An additional prediction was that the degree of expressed "happiness" by winning Players and their Helpers would be positively related to their liking of group members while the degree of expressed "sadness" by losing Players and their Helpers would be negatively related. This hypothesis is based upon the assumption that the strength of a goal response, which includes an affective component, should influence the strength of the implicit r_g-s_g and hence the strength of the association between the anticipatory goal response and a neutral stimulus. It follows then that the degree of satisfaction experienced during goal attainment should be related to the subsequent attraction for fellow group members.

To test the hypotheses, a score was obtained for each S by averaging his postmeasure ratings of all members of his Bingo group (excluding the rating of his partner), subtracting this from the mean rating he had previously given to his same-sex classmates (not including his partner), and multiplying by 10. Scores on the rating scale of liking ranged from very high liking (1) to very low liking (15). The mean rating of classmates was used as a baseline to correct for individual differences in rating style because some Ss tended to rate higher or lower than others. The range of these adjusted scores was +58 to −92. Figure 2 presents the mean of these scores for the rewarded and nonrewarded Players and their Helpers in the three different reward-pattern Bingo groups. Positive scores indicate greater average liking of group members after the games than of same-sex classmates, and the higher the score, the greater the relative liking of group members. Negative scores, on the other hand, mean that Bingo group members were liked less than same-sex classmates.

All differences were evaluated by the Mann Whitney U test (one-tailed). As predicted, in the 4-0-0 groups the Players who won 4 games liked their fellow group members more than those who won 0 games ($p = .07$); similarly, the liking scores of Helpers of 4-game winning partners were significantly higher than those of Helpers who observed nonrewarded partners ($p = .007$). On the other hand, there were no reliable differences between the 4-game winning Players and their Helpers nor between the 0-game winning Players and their Helpers. In the 3-1-0 condition, winning 1 out of 4 games was apparently far more effective than winning 3 games for both Players and their Helpers. Among the former, the liking scores of 1-game winners were greater than those of both 3-game and 0-game winners ($p = .01$),

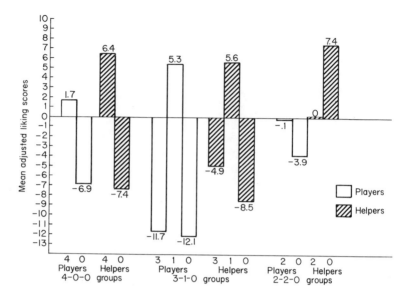

FIG. 2.   Mean liking of other group members, relative to liking of same-sex class-mates, by rewarded and nonrewarded Players and their Helpers.

while among the Helpers the liking scores of those who observed 1-game winning partners reliably exceeded those of Helpers of 0-game winners ($p = .025$) but not those of Helpers of the 3-game winners. There was no significant difference between 3-game and 0-game winning Players, nor between the Helpers of 3-game and 0-game winners. As was true of the 4-0-0 condition, here, too, Players and Helpers reacted similarly to the reward manipulations and did not differ from each other in the 3-, 1-, or 0- categories. Only in the 2-2-0 condition were there no significant differences between rewarded and nonrewarded Players or their Helpers[4], and again there were no Player-Helper differences.

These results, taken together, can be said to provide additional support for the influence of direct reward on the formation of positive attitudes toward persons present at the time reward is received. In addition, the data provide substantial evidence that positive attitudes can also be developed under conditions where an individual experiences

---

[4]The Helpers of 0-game winners ended up liking fellow group members more than the Helpers of 2-game winners. Since this finding was opposite to the prediction, it was evaluated by a two-tailed test and the probability level was found to be $p = .10$.

only vicarious reward. Although the Helpers in this investigation were instructed to check their partner-Players for errors, they were clearly not active participants in the games: they were not given Bingo cards; they did not place markers on numbers; they received no chip when their partner won a game; they were not able to choose prizes; and they received no prizes.

Further confirmation of the effectiveness of both the direct and vicarious reward experiences in influencing attitude formation comes from the obtained relation between the liking scores and Ss' self-reports of how they felt about their own or their partner's wins and losses. On the question relevant for winners, Ss were divided into those who said they were very happy and those who said happy, alright, or didn't care. (This division was dictated by the obtained frequencies.) As predicted, for six of the eight relevant subgroups (4-, 3-, 2-, and 1- game winning Players and their respective Helpers) the median liking score of Ss who said they were very happy when they or their partners won was greater than the median liking score of Ss who gave other answers ($p = .06$, Sign Test). On the question relevant to losers, Ss in each subgroup were divided into those who said they were very sad or sad when they or their partners lost and those who said they felt alright or didn't care. There were 6 subgroups of Ss who experienced losing only (the 0-game winning Players and their Helpers in the 4-0-0, 3-1-0, and 2-2-0 conditions). All of these supported the hypothesis, i.e., the median liking score of Ss who reported feeling very sad or sad was lower than that of the other Ss. This is a highly significant finding ($p = .02$, Sign Test). On the other hand, the median scores of Ss in the 6 subgroups of Ss who experienced both winning and losing (3-, 2-, 1- game winning Players and their Helpers) showed no reliable association with responses to the "losing" question.

The above data from the self-report questions, taken together with the findings that directly or vicariously winning 1 game out of 4 was more effective than winning 3 out of 4 and that Ss who won 2 games and lost 2 games out of 4 did not differ from those who won 0 games, indicate that what is crucial in defining a reinforcing state of affairs is the subject's reaction to a reward stimulus. This can be illustrated by data obtained on the 3-game and 1-game winning Players. All of these Ss received a prize at the end of the games, in contrast to the 0-game winners, but it had been pointed out to the Ss that the more games they won, the better the prize they could have and one would assume that winning 3 games would provide more opportunities for the making of goal responses than the winning of one game. The data suggest, however, that this assumption is questionable and that perhaps the goal response to having "just made it" (receiving a prize on the basis of only one chip or one game won) was extremely strong, while the 3-game winners may have experienced great disappointment at not having won them all. That this interpretation has some merit is indicated by responses to the question regarding how Ss had felt when they lost games. Ten of the 20 3-game winning Players, or 50% said they had felt "very sad" or "sad" compared with only 6 of the 20, or 30%, of the 1-game winning Players. This difference is especially interesting in light of the fact that 3-game winners lost only one game while 1-game winners lost three.

The problem of defining reward for human Ss was recognized in attempting to interpret the findings of a previously mentioned study on reward frequency (James & Lott, 1964) and has been discussed by other investigators (e.g., Kagan, 1967; Walters, 1968). What would seem to be required is some independent validation of the rewarding properties of a stimulus for the subject sample used, apart from the results obtained on measures of the dependent variable.

Other Antecedent Conditions

It is expected that any variable which influences the strength of r_g-s_g will also affect the probability that (and the speed with which) a previously neutral stimulus will come to evoke that r_g-s_g. Black (1965), in a paper concerned with incentive motivation [the Hullian construct K which, according to Spence (1956), summarizes the motivational consequences of r_g-s_g], has noted that the strength of r_g-s_g will be an increasing function of the frequency with which the goal response has been elicited in the presence of the stimulus, and of the duration of the goal response, determined primarily by the magnitude of reward. Further, the strength of r_g-s_g should reflect the vigor of the goal response and hence any variable which contributes to this latter characteristic should similarly affect the implicit component. Black has reasoned that the vigor of a goal response should vary directly with drive level and therefore, that procedures employed to vary D, like time of deprivation, should also vary K, or the strength of r_g-s_g.

What are the implications of this for research on interpersonal attraction? Very simply, any variable which increases incentive motivation should also increase the attractiveness of the stimulus-person who is consistently present when the goal response is made. If Black is correct in his view that K varies as a function of drive level, then the anticipatory goal response, or positive attitude, which is conditioned to the stimulus-person should be greater when the rewarded individual's drive, relevant to a particular class of reinforcing stimuli, is high. We intend to test this derivation in investigations with children using a variety of rewards (adult approval, attention, food, money, and the opportunity to explore novel situations) under conditions of assumed natural deprivation, using poor or culturally deprived children, and also under conditions of manipulated deprivation and satiation. We anticipate interesting problems with naturally deprived children since, in this case, motivation for approval, for example, may never have been acquired and hence the associated drive would be low rather than high. In any case, we will test the following hypothesis: liking for a person consistently present during reinforcement will vary as a function of the inferred drive level of the child who receives drive-relevant reward contingent upon some instrumental response.

We have not meant to imply in the preceding pages that the consistent receipt of reward in the presence of a discriminable other person is the only condition under which liking for that person may be learned, but rather that this condition is a sufficient one. Obviously people also learn to like others who reward them directly. A very sizable body of research on the relationship between interpersonal attraction and reinforcement has been directed to demonstrating that person A will like person B to the extent that B provides, or is perceived as the source of, reinforcement for A in the form of primary gratification or secondary rewards such as approval, agreement, similarity, and so on. A review of much of this recent literature (Lott & Lott, 1965) indicated that liking of a person is generally conceded to be some function of the rewards which stem from interaction or anticipated interaction with him. We would predict that a person who is consistently the direct source of one's gratification will come to evoke a stronger positive attitude than a person who is merely consistently present. This follows from the greater temporal and spatial contiguity of a reward source to the reward and from the assumed greater likelihood that persons will attend to or orient toward a reward source more than to other stimuli. Where a previously neutral stimulus person is the *source* of reinforcement something like a "double shot" of reward value should be conditioned to him. Our concern thus far has been with the more general "single-shot" condition.

It is also predictable, from the principles of primary stimulus generalization and mediated generalization, that an individual will respond positively to, i.e., will like, persons who are either physically similar to, or who call forth the same language or other response as, another person whom he has previously learned to associate with reward.

MEASURES OF LIKING

Once a positive attitude toward another person has been reliably established it is generally detectable by others, in a variety of situations, by particular overt responses which the liker makes in the presence of the liked person or some symbolic representation of him. Research in this area has generally reflected insufficient concern with the measurement of the behavior from which liking must be inferred. Cook and Selltiz (1964) have noted this same deficiency in attitude research in general. It is clearly desirable to make inferences from a large variety of measures which sample the broad class of behaviors which people have learned to perform in the actual or symbolic presence of persons to whom they are attracted. When a number of conceptually derived measurements converge, greater confidence can be placed in the operation of the implicit theoretical variable which is assumed to mediate the overt behavior and in terms of which experimental results are interpreted. Because of such considerations we are currently testing a number of measuring devices which should reflect differences in interpersonal attraction. Our intent is to validate measures which vary from direct self-disclosure techniques to more oblique or unobtrusive measures such as recently discussed by Webb, Campbell, Schwartz, and Sechrest (1966).

With regard to self-report measures, we have used both choice of individuals for a specific criterion activity (the sociometric question) and rating scales of liking. Further down on the dimension of "direct-indirect," as a characteristic of the measuring device, is the semantic differential technique which we made use of in the delay study discussed earlier.

Doob (1947) noted that attitudes may help to orient an individual, that an attitude's cue properties may be part of a general set that leads a person to attend to certain external stimuli rather than others, and that therefore, attitude-relevant stimuli should be more salient than stimuli which are attitudinally neutral. It may be the case that the r_g-s_g mechanism serves to lower perceptual thresholds for the stimulus to which it has been conditioned because such a stimulus has acquired additional affective meaning (Mowrer, 1960) or because its intensity has been increased (Kimble, 1961). We have predicted, for example, that under conditions of stereoscopic binocular rivalry (Engel, 1956), a photograph of a liked person will predominate over a photograph of a neutral person of equal familiarity. A trend in support of this hypothesis has recently been obtained in our laboratory by Beran (1968) utilizing a sample of first year law students. We plan also to compare other perceptual measures, such as speed of recognition of tachistoscopically presented photos of persons and speed of recognition of photos under impoverished stimulus conditions (i.e., blurred or dimly illuminated pictures), with rating scale data, and we predict superior recognition of liked as compared with neutral persons under conditions where the stimulus persons are equally familiar to the subject.

At present, data are also being obtained on several other indirect measures, two of which have been suggested by work of Nunnally, Duchnowski, and Parker (1965). They reported use of a "Looking Box" which requires the S to push a button to make a stimulus visible in a window of the box for a short period of time. The light illuminating the stimulus shuts off automatically and if the S wishes to view the stimulus again, he has to push an appropriate button. Nunnally *et al.* found that nonsense syllables which had been associated with rewards were viewed longer than those not previously paired with rewards. Our Ss are being asked to view photos of classmates and playgroup members who differ in their attractiveness to the Ss. We are also adapting the "Treasure Hunt" technique reported by Nunnally and his colleagues. Their Ss were presented with identical white boxes on top of which a nonsense syllable was printed. Some of the syllables had previously been associated with rewards and others had not. Ss, under instruction to find the box which had money hidden under it, looked more frequently under the boxes which had a nonsense syllable previously paired with reward than under the other boxes. We have substituted photos of children, differing in the degree to which they are liked, for the nonsense syllables.

CONSEQUENCES OF LIKING

Liked Persons as Secondary Reinforcers

The choice of dependent measures of interpersonal attraction is intimately related to theoretical expectations of the consequences which liking a person has for the behavior of the liker. Hull proposed (1952, Ch. 5) that the secondary reinforcing property of a stimulus depends upon that stimulus being able to evoke an "expectative" response or an anticipation of reward, namely r_g-s_g. A liked person, then, in evoking a positive attitude should thus be able to function as a secondary reinforcer.

If this is the case then the presence of a liked person, or his approval of certain acts, should serve to strengthen, maintain, or otherwise shape behavior of an individual who is attracted to him. Data relevant to this general hypothesis were obtained in a study with college students (Lott & Lott, 1961). Fifteen natural, preexisting groups of 6 to 10 members each discussed for 30 minutes a college-relevant problem in a semicontrolled laboratory situation. Following the discussion, anonymous opinions were obtained on the issue and results directly opposite to the actual findings were reported to the group as the dominant group opinion. A second opinion scale was administered after a musical interlude described to the Ss as a period of silent contemplation of the issue. The percentage of group members who changed their opinion in the direction of the contrived information was taken as the measure of conformity within each group. This measure of conformity was positively and significantly correlated with the cohesiveness level of the group—cohesiveness was defined and measured in terms of mutual interpersonal attraction among group members. This had been predicted on the basis of the secondary reinforcing properties of liked persons; the greater the liking for fellow group members, the more likely is it that their opinions will be adopted.

We are currently testing the additional hypothesis that if a liked person is presented contingent upon a response, then that response will be strengthened or its acquisition facilitated. Byrne and his associates (Byrne, Young, & Griffitt, 1966; Golightly & Byrne, 1964) have shown that presentation of statements which conform to a subject's attitudes can reinforce a discrimination response. The suggestion which follows from our model is that actual or symbolic presentation of people who are highly liked by subjects can function similarly and act as particularly powerful reinforcements. It is well known that conditioned reinforcers like parents, especially mothers, serve to strengthen new behavior on the part of their children simply by their presence. It makes theoretical sense to expect that other highly liked persons can function similarly.

LIKED PERSONS AS MOTIVATORS

In addition to its relevance for secondary reinforcement, the r_g-s_g mechanism is also assumed to have drive properties (Doob, 1947). On this basis we have hypothesized that the behavior of individuals who like each other will reflect greater drive in one another's presence than the behavior of individuals who are affectively neutral toward each other. Support for this hypothesis has already been obtained in two experiments. In one, which also related interpersonal attraction to conformity behavior and was discussed above (Lott & Lott, 1961), frequency of communication during a specific 30-minute discussion session was found to be positively and significantly correlated with the degree of intermember liking within natural college groups. Within-group communication was taken to indicate the level of generalized drive of the group members.

A second experiment (Lott & Lott, 1966) tested the prediction that children who like each other more will perform better on a learning task in one another's presence than children working on the same task in the presence of those they like less. Since performance, or the reaction potential of learned behavior, is postulated to be a positive function of drive (Hull, 1951, Ch. 14), and since attitudes are presumed to have drive value, better individual performance on the learning tasks was expected in high than in low cohesive groups. Two levels of cohesiveness, defined in terms of mutual intermember attraction, were created by placing children in groups on the basis of preratings made of one another by same-sex classmates.

Fourth and fifth grade children served as Ss. Working in the presence of 2 or 3 highly liked or less liked classmates (i.e., in high or low cohesive groups), each S learned a list of Spanish equivalents for English words. IQ levels of the Ss were taken into account when forming the groups so that there were four experimental conditions: high cohesiveness-high IQ, low cohesiveness-high IQ, high cohesiveness-low IQ, and low cohesiveness-low IQ. On measures of acquisition, retention over a one week period, subsequent relearning by means of a different study procedure, and finally, the learning of a second similar task, it was found that high IQ children (especially girls) performed better in the presence of highly liked classmates than in the presence of less liked classmates, as predicted. For the low IQ Ss however, there were no reliable differences, but children in low cohesive groups tended to do slightly better than those in high cohesive groups, opposite to the prediction. Results obtained on a time measure for the first learning task are in line with the learning data: high cohesive groups were significantly faster in completing the specified study procedure than low cohesive groups within the high IQ sample, while within the low IQ sample low cohesive groups worked faster than high cohesive groups (although this latter difference was not statistically reliable). Posthoc considerations of the data led to the interpretation that the experimental tasks were difficult or complex for the low IQ children in our sample and that for such children the increment in drive produced by the presence of liked others served to decrease learning efficiency because high drive strengthens competing incorrect responses as well as correct ones (e.g., Farber & Spence, 1953; Taylor 1956). For the high IQ children, on the other hand, the tasks were relatively simple as demonstrated by the consistent and significant superiority of high over low IQ children on all the tasks. In the case of high IQ children, and especially the girls, increased drive level improved task performance.

Because the experimental conditions of this investigation are similar in important respects to those generally employed in investigations of social facilitation, our data have significance for this particular area of concern within social psychology. In an excellent critique of the social facilitation literature, Zajonc (1965) concluded that:

> It would appear that the emission of well-learned responses is facilitated by the presence of spectators, while the acquisition of new responses is impaired .

In explanation of this empirical generalization Zajonc suggested, further, that:

> [an] audience enhances the emission of dominant responses. If the dominant responses are the correct ones, . . . the presence of an audience will be of benefit to the individual. But if they are mostly wrong, . . . then these wrong responses will be enhanced in the presence of an audience, and the emission of correct responses will be postponed or prevented.

The presence of others, in other words, is hypothesized as increasing a person's "general arousal or drive level." Our investigation distinguished between two kinds of others, highly liked and less liked, and our findings regarding the performance of Ss for whom the tasks were easy indicate that performance is superior in the presence of the highly liked as compared with the less liked coactors. Thus, our findings support Zajonc's hypothesis, but suggest that social facilitation must be analyzed not only in terms of the nature of the responses required of the subject in a particular task but also in terms of the attitudinal relationship between the performer and his audience or his coactors.

Data relevant to these considerations should soon be forthcoming from a study in which Ss work in pairs which differ in their degree of mutual attraction, ranging from like very much to neutral to dislike, on verbal tasks of two levels of complexity. Exploratory work with a simple finger maze has already yielded positive results in the comparison of high like and neutral S pairs.

SUMMARY

This paper has presented a learning theory approach to interpersonal attraction which utilizes general behavior principles to specify the conditions under which persons will learn to like one another and the consequences of liking for subsequent behavior. The central idea is that liking or attraction can be most effectively analyzed when defined in terms of positive attitudes toward persons, where attitudes are further defined in S-R terms. Hypotheses derived from the theoretical model and investigations designed to test them have been described and discussed.

References

Amsel, A. Frustrative nonreward in partial reinforcement and discrimination learning: Some recent history and a theoretical extension. *Psychological Review*, 1962, **69**, 306-328.

Bandura, A., & Rosenthal, T. L. Vicarious classical conditioning as a function of arousal level. *Journal of Personality and Social Psychology*, 1966, 3, 54-62.

Beran, L. The influence of interpersonal attraction on binocular resolution. Unpublished master's thesis, University of Kentucky, 1968.

Berger, S. Conditioning through vicarious instigation. *Psychological Review*, 1962, **69**, 450-466.

Black, R. On the combination of drive and incentive motivation. *Psychological Review*, 1965, **72**, 310-317.

Bruning, J. L. Direct and vicarious effects of a shift in magnitude of reward on performance. *Journal of Personality and Social Psychology*, 1965, **2**, 278-282.

Byrne, D., Young, R. K., & Griffitt, W. The reinforcement properties of attitude statements. *Journal of Experimental Research in Personality*, 1966, **1**, 266-276.

Cook, S., & Selltiz, C. A multiple-indicator approach to attitude measurement. *Psychological Bulletin*, 1964, **62**, 36-55.

Donahoe, J. W. Changes in meaning as a function of age. *Journal of Genetic Psychology*, 1961, **99**, 23-28.

Doob, L. W. The behavior of attitudes. *Psychological Review*, 1947, **54**, 135-156.

Engel, E. The role of content in binocular resolution. *American Journal of Psychology*, 1956, **69**, 87-91.

Farber, I. E., & Spence, K. W. Complex learning and conditioning as a function of anxiety. *Journal of Experimental Psychology*, 1953, **45**, 120-125.

Golightly, C., & Byrne, D. Attitude statements as positive and negative reinforcements. *Science*, 1964, **146**, 798-799.

Hull, C. L. *Essentials of behavior*. New Haven: Yale University Press, 1951.

Hull, C. L. *A behavior system*. New Haven: Yale University Press, 1952.

James, G., & Lott, A. J. Reward frequency and the formation of positive attitudes toward group members. *Journal of Social Psychology*, 1964, **62**, 111-115.

Jenkins, W. O. A temporal gradient of derived reinforcement. *American Journal of Psychology*, 1950, **63**, 237-243.

Kagan, J. On the need for relativism. *American Psychologist*, 1967, **22**, 131-142.

Kimble, G. A. *Hilgard and Marquis' conditioning and learning.* (2nd ed.) New York: Appleton, 1961.

Logan, F. A. The role of delay of reinforcement in determining reaction potential. *Journal of Experimental Psychology*, 1952, **43**, 393-399.

Lott, A. J., Aponte, J. F., Lott, B. E., & McGinley, W. H. The effect of delayed reward on the development of positive attitudes toward persons. *Journal of Experimental Social Psychology*, in press.

Lott, A. J., & Lott, B. E. Group cohesiveness, communication level, and conformity. *Journal of Abnormal and Social Psychology*, 1961, **62**, 408-412.

Lott, A. J., & Lott, B. E. *Influence of classroom group cohesiveness on learning and adherence to standards.* Cooperative Research Project No. 1700. Lexington: Kentucky Research Foundation, 1964. (Mimeo)

Lott, A. J., & Lott, B. E. Group cohesiveness as interpersonal attraction: A review of relationships with antecedent and consequent variables. *Psychological Bulletin*, 1965, **64**, 259-309.

Lott, A. J., & Lott, B. E. Group cohesiveness and individual learning. *Journal of Educational Psychology*, 1966, **57**, 61-73.

Lott, A. J., Lott, B. E., & Matthews, G. Interpersonal attraction as a function of vicarious reward. Unpublished manuscript, 1967.

Lott, B. E., & Lott, A. J. The formation of positive attitudes toward group members. *Journal of Abnormal and Social Psychology*, 1960, **61**, 297-300.

Miller, N. E. Some reflections on the law of effect produce a new alternative to drive reduction. In M. R. Jones (Ed.), *Nebraska symposium on motivation.* Lincoln: University of Nebraska Press, 1963. Pp. 65-112.

Mowrer, O. H. *Learning theory and behavior.* New York: Wiley, 1960.

Nunnally, J. C., Duchnowski, A. J., & Parker, R. K. Association of neutral objects with rewards: Effect on verbal evaluation, reward expectancy, and selective attention. *Journal of Personality and Social Psychology*, 1965, **1**, 270-274.

Spence, K. W. *Behavior theory and conditioning.* New Haven: Yale University Press, 1956.

Taylor, J. A. Drive theory and manifest anxiety. *Psychological Bulletin*, 1956, **53**, 303-320.

Walters, R. Some conditions facilitating the occurrence of imitative behavior. In E. C. Simmel, R. A. Hoppe, & G. A. Milton (Eds.), *Social facilitation and imitative behavior.* Boston: Allyn & Bacon, 1968. Pp. 7-30.

Webb, E. J., Campbell, D. T., Schwartz, R. D., & Sechrest, L. *Unobtrusive measures: Nonreactive research in the social sciences.* Chicago: Rand McNally, 1966.

Zajonc, R. B. Social facilitation. *Science*, 1965, **149**, 269-274.

4

A "Spread of Effect" in Attitude Formation

RALPH L. ROSNOW[1]
DEPARTMENT OF PSYCHOLOGY
TEMPLE UNIVERSITY
PHILADELPHIA, PENNSYLVANIA

Over the years researchers have repeatedly demonstrated the potency in behavior modification of such primary reinforcements as food and water and such symbolic, or secondary, reinforcements as praise and reproof, agreement and disagreement, approval and disapproval. In fact, one of the foundations of our educational system is the assumption that grades and social approval and disapproval, by virtue of their acquired potency as symbolic reinforcements, are effective and reliable tools for shaping students' behavior (e.g., Staats & Staats, 1964). The same assumption provides a rationale for many of our legal and social practices.

If symbolic reinforcements can condition behavior, and if, as is often assumed, attitudes are simply learned predispositions to verbal and action behavior (Doob, 1947), might not symbolic reinforcements condition attitudes as well? For example, can program mood shape viewers' attitudes toward the products advertised in television commercials? Can a learning theory analysis of the persuasion process predict the effect on opinion change of varying the order of presentation of persuasive communications? Can telling a debater that he has won increase his belief in the viewpoint he advocated in the debate?

[1]Preparation of this chapter was supported by a grant (GS-1733) to the author from the National Science Foundation. I thank the following colleagues for their helpful comments and criticisms: Barry Collins, George Gitter, Herbert Greenwald, Robert Lana, and Robert Weiss.

Can rewarding a child while he is in the presence of other children influence his attitude toward the others? Can experiencing a reinforcing event at about the same time as having been exposed to successive opposing arguments on a controversial issue shape one's attitude toward the issue?

There is evidence to suggest that the answer to all of these questions is yes. Investigators at the Schwerin Research Corporation have consistently found that television programs can shape viewers' attitudes toward the products advertised in the commercials. Receptivity, they suggest, is complexly related to the usual audience factors as well as program mood and commercial content. Hence, an advertisement for an analgesic would probably fare better than a food commercial in the middle time slot of a tense adult drama, because the analgesic symbolizes a means for reducing tension.[2] McGuire (1957) has shown that a learning theory analysis can predict the effect on opinion change of varying the order of presentation of persuasive communications. Viewing the receipt of each communication as a separate conditioning trial on which the source was a conditioned stimulus for inducing receptivity, McGuire was able to heighten persuasiveness by placing the more desirable, or "rewarding," communication first. Scott (1957, 1959) has found that telling a debater that he has won can increase his belief in the viewpoint he advocated in the debate. Scott (1957) had pairs of University of Colorado undergraduates defend positions diametrically opposite to their beliefs; he evaluated the quality of the presentations by means of a rigged audience vote. Winners, he found, changed their opinions in the direction of debate significantly more than either losers or nondebaters.[3] Lott and Lott (1960; see also their chapter in this volume) have found that rewarding a child while he is in the presence of other

[2]The Schwerin findings are summarized in their *Bulletin*, 1960, 8, No. 8, 1–5 and in their *Fact sheet on program-commercial compatibility*, 1962, October.

[3]Somewhat analagous effects as regards attitude modification by means of verbal or social reinforcement of counterattitudinal advocacy have been demonstrated by Bostrom, Vlandis, and Rosenbaum (1961), Buckhout and Rosenberg (1966), Goldstein and McGinnies (1964), Sarbin and Allen (1964), and Wallace (1966). Other investigators have explored the relationship between the magnitude of reinforcements presented prior to a counterattitudinal response and subsequent opinion change, notably Festinger and Carlsmith (1959), Rosenberg (1965), and Carlsmith, Collins, and Helmreich (1966). Their results form the basis of an interesting controversy which finds cognitive dissonance theory predicting an inverse relationship between magnitude of reward and opinion change, and reinforcement theory predicting just the opposite (see Rosnow & Robinson, 1967, pp. 297 ff.).

children can influence his attitude toward the others. Groups of children played a game, where the object was to land cardboard rocket ships on planetary objectives. One effect of winning the game was to reinforce the winner's positive attitudes of other children in the group. In a similar vein, our research, which follows, suggests that experiencing a reinforcing event at about the same time as having been exposed to successive opposing arguments on a controversial issue can shape one's attitude toward the issue.

RATIONALE AND HYPOTHESES

The initial impetus for our research was provided by the *spread of effect*, the proposition that a reinforcement can influence both the stimulus-response connections which immediately precede it as well as those which occur immediately after the reinforcement. Thorndike (1933a, 1933b) introduced the notion of a positive spread of effect, or gradient of reward, in a monograph published in 1933. In it, he interpreted the results from a series of thirteen experiments as evidence for his assertion that the bolstering effect of a reward, or "satisfying state of affairs," could spread forward and backward in time, "spreading its influence out upon the connections of the system, and influencing one most, its nearest neighbors next most, and so on" (Thorndike, 1933a, p. 67). It was these results that, Thorndike contended, provided conclusive support for his earlier (Thorndike, 1911) law of effect. The parallel assertion of a negative spread of effect, or gradient of punishment, was not advanced until several years later when Tilton (1939, 1945), a former student of Thorndike, succeeded in plotting a spread of effect on either side of a punished response. Almost immediately the subject became shrouded in controversy and heated debate. Both methodological complications in the Thorndike and Tilton experiments were enumerated, as were alternative hypotheses propounded for Thorndike's diffusion explanation of the empirical phenomenon. Since that literature is reviewed elsewhere (Hilgard, 1956; Marx, 1956; Postman, 1963), it will suffice here simply to note that, although debate continues concerning the spread of effect and Thorndike's law (cf. Greenwald, 1966; Marx, 1967; Postman, 1966), it is generally conceded, as Postman (1963, p. 397) concludes, that "the basic propositions of Thorndike's theory have weathered with considerable success both theoretical critiques and attempts at experimental refutation."

Several years ago my associates and I began to use the empirical spread of effect in a heuristic sense as a model to generate hypotheses concerning the temporal forward (*proactive*) and temporal backward (*retroactive*) effects of rewarding or punishing events on the reaction to persuasive communication which occurs at about the same time as the events. In this research we have assumed that if attitudes are learned mediating responses (Doob, 1947), then opinion change must be accompanied by a concomitant change in some aspect of the corresponding attitude.[4] Using as reinforcers such obviously pleasant or noxious events as verbal approval or disapproval, increased grades or surprise exams, we hypothesized that contiguity between a rewarding event and a two-sided communication would facilitate the tendency to respond in the direction of whichever side was closer in time to the reward. We also hypothesized that contiguity between a punishing event and a two-sided persuasive communication would weaken or suppress that tendency, with the observable effect of the stronger response being in the direction of whichever side was farther from the reinforcement.

EXPERIMENTAL PROCEDURE

Though there were some minor variations which will be noted as the individual experiments are described, a fairly standard procedure was used throughout this research. (See Table 1.) Several days after their opinions were measured, subjects experienced a rewarding (A1, A2) or punishing event (A3, A4) just before (A2, A4) or after (A1, A3) they were exposed to a two-sided persuasive communication, following which their opinions once again were measured.[5] By *two-sided communication*, we mean a message which contained equipollent pro and con arguments on the same controversial issue (cf. Wrench, 1964). With this type of stimulus, it was reasoned that the subjects would be unlikely to conclude that either side was endorsed by the communicator, and thus would not be influenced

---

[4]"Opinion" can simply be thought of here as a verbal response. "Attitude," however, is conceptualized as a three-dimensional construct whose components reflect affective, cognitive, and action behavior (*cf.* Rosnow & Robinson, 1967, xv−xvi). In the present context opinion is primarily related to the affective and cognitive components of attitude.

[5]The one major departure from this design was Rosnow (1966a), in which a two-sided communication both preceded and followed the reinforcement.

TABLE 1
PROTOTYPE DESIGN AND PREDICTIONS[a]

(A1)		(A2)		(A3)		(A4)	
Pretest Opinionnaire							
Several Days							
		Rewarding event				Punishing event	
(B1)	(B2)	(B1)	(B2)	(B1)	(B2)	(B1)	(B2)
Pro	Con	Pro	Con	Pro	Con	Pro	Con
Con	Pro	Con	Pro	Con	Pro	Con	Pro
Rewarding event				Punishing event			
Posttest Opinionnaire							
Recency		Primacy		Primacy		Recency	

[a]To test for primacy and recency, a subtraction-difference procedure was used where pretest scores were subtracted from their respective posttest scores, the resulting gain score for the con-first sequence (B2) then subtracted from the gain score for the pro-first sequence (B1). The difference-between-gain scores was then tested against the null hypothesis using the t statistic. If the final difference was positive, primacy was indicated; if the difference was negative, recency. Since the direction of difference was predicted in all cases, one-tailed tests were used throughout.

by that demand characteristic when responding to the communication. In this research the juxtaposition of the arguments was always counterbalanced, some of the subjects receiving pro arguments and then con (B1), others receiving con arguments first (B2).

The data were analyzed using a subtraction-difference procedure, described by Lana (1961), which identifies primacy and recency effects. *Primacy* refers to the case where opinions are influenced more by the arguments presented first; *recency*, where opinions are influenced more by the arguments presented last. Based on the general hypothesis derived from the spread of effect that opinion change would be in the direction of whichever arguments were closer in time to a rewarding event or farther from a punishing event, primacy was predicted if a two-sided communication either followed a reward (A2) or preceded a punishment (A3). Recency was predicted if a two-sided communication either preceded a reward (A1) or followed a punishment (A4).

EXPERIMENTAL DATA

Two experiments were conducted to test these hypotheses. In both experiments the subjects were male and female, nonvolunteer, third- and fourth-year high school students. The same communication was used in both experiments, a 4-minute-long, two-sided persuasive communication which debated the issue of the United States' use of nuclear weapons.

The design of one experiment (Rosnow & Russell, 1963) corresponded exactly to the prototype design as depicted in the left-hand columns in Table 1 (Treatments A1 and A2). The 78 subjects in this experiment were told by their instructor that an exam on which they had done poorly was unfair and, therefore, their grades would be discounted. This "rewarding" event either followed (A1) or preceded (A2) the experimenter's reading to the subjects the two-sided persuasive communication.

The other experiment (Rosnow, 1965) corresponded exactly to the design depicted in the right-hand columns in Table 1 (A3 and A4). Again, reinforcement and communication were administered by different people. The "punishing" event was a surprise quiz on a fictitious homework assignment and their instructor's justifying the quiz by telling the 84 students that he was disappointed in the quality of their work and planned to test them "just to see how much you really know." The punishing event either followed (A3) or preceded (A4) the experimenter's reading of the nuclear weapons communication to the subjects.

The results of the two experiments are shown in Table 2. Only the retroactive effects were obtained as predicted. Opinions tended to change in the direction of whichever arguments were closer in time to a subsequent reward or farther from a subsequent punishment, thus implying not the spread of effect that was hypothesized, but rather a simple delayed reinforcement effect (e.g., Hull, 1943, pp. 135 ff.).

Two possible explanations of our failure to find proactive effects occurred to us. One alternative concerned the fact that the two-sided communication was not an instantaneous stimulus and, therefore, a temporal lag had to exist between the onset of the communication and the subject's reaction to it. When the communication preceded the reinforcing event, reaction to the communication led directly into the reinforcement. However, when the communication followed the reinforcing event, the delay in reaction time may have exceeded the

TABLE 2
The Influence of Satisfying and Dissatisfying Events as Reinforcers of Opinion Change[a]

Effects	(A1) Reward after		(A2) Reward before		(A3) Punishment after		(A4) Punishment before	
	(B1) Pro first	(B2) Con first	(B1) Pro first	(B2) Con first	(B1) Pro first	(B2) Con first	(B1) Pro first	(B2) Con first
Pre	15.1[b]	14.3	15.2	13.9	15.5	14.0	15.0	15.0
Post	14.6	14.8	14.6	13.8	16.0	13.4	15.1	15.2
Gain	−.5	+.5	−.6	−.1	+.5	−.6	+.1	+.2
	(18)[c]	(18)	(21)	(21)	(17)	(17)	(25)	(25)
Prediction	Recency		Primacy		Primacy		Recency	
Obtained difference	−1.0[d]		−.5		+1.1[d]		−.1	
	(Recency)		(Recency)		(Primacy)		(Recency)	

[a] Data for A1 and A2 from Rosnow and Russell (1963), and for A3 and A4 from Rosnow (1965).

[b] Summed opinion scores could range from five, or a highly unfavorable attitude toward the use of nuclear weapons, to a highly favorable 25, a score of 15 being neutral.

[c] Numbers in parentheses indicate size of sample on which cell means are based.

[d] $p < .05$, one-tailed.

time delay that would be optimum to link the reaction to the communication with the reaction to the reinforcement due to decay in the reinforcement gradient. It followed that the likelihood of finding proactive effects would be increased either (a) by reducing the interval between the two reactions or (b) by decelerating the rate of decay of the reinforcement gradient.

An alternative explanation was that some other variable may unwittingly have been introduced which altered the probabilities of occurrence of the effects of the intentionally manipulated variables. For example, Lana (1961) has shown that subjects who are familiar with a topic tend to be influenced more by arguments they hear first and that subjects unfamiliar with a topic tend to be influenced more by arguments heard last. If more subjects in Rosnow (1965) than in Rosnow and Russell (1963) were already familiar with the topic prior to their exposure to the communication, then this would account for the tendency toward primacy in the former study and the tendency toward recency in the latter. One could test this hypothesis by simultaneously manipulating the implied complementary and competing interactions.

These various alternatives were pursued in the experiments that are described next.

REDUCING THE TIME LAG

The first alternative, that of reducing the interval between the reactions to the reinforcement and the communication (see also Weiss' chapter in this volume), was explored by Rosnow (1966a) using a procedure modified after the active participation procedure of Janis and King (1954) and reinforcements patterned after Scott (1957).

The volunteer subjects in this experiment were male and female Boston University undergraduates. The general procedure consisted of the subject's extemporaneously arguing aloud in defense of four pro- and four anti-civil defense statements (e.g., "A very large civil defense program actually increases the chance of a deadly atomic attack, because we would be spending defense money where it doesn't do any good."). A counterbalanced, before-after design was used, in which approximately half of the subjects defended the statements in the order pro-pro-con-con-con-con-pro-pro, and the other half defended them in the order con-con-pro-pro-pro-pro-con-con. Opinions toward each of the eight civil defense statements were obtained two weeks before the treatment, immediately after the treatment, and again two and one-half weeks later.

On the pretense that he was helping the experimenter to gather arguments for a subsequent propaganda study, the subject was instructed to argue to the best of his ability in favor of each statement as it was presented to him and that he would later be told how well he had performed. Precisely 45 seconds was allowed for each statement's defense. To induce personal involvement and thereby to increase his motivation, a tape recorder and microphone were in view to impress the subject that a permanent record was being made of his arguments. The spread of effect hypotheses were tested using four counterbalanced experimental groups. In two of the groups a reward in the form of verbal approval was interpolated between the fourth and fifth arguments (e.g., pro-pro-con-con-Reward-con-con-pro-pro). The same procedure was followed in two other experimental groups, except that punishment (viz. disapproval) was substituted for reward. The reinforcement procedure consisted of the experimenter's interrupting the subject after his fourth defense and stating that his arguments were either better or worse than average, the reinforcement being administered independent of the actual quality of the subject's performance. Immediately after the reinforcement, the subject was instructed to resume defending the statements. Two control groups were employed in which counterbalanced defenses took place without reinforcement.

A summary of the results obtained in the four experimental groups is contained in Table 3. To determine the proactive and retroactive effects of the reinforcements, the subtraction-difference procedure was computed separately on responses to the four opinionnaire items which corresponded to the four statements defended prior to the reinforcement (A1 and A3) and then on responses to the four opinionnaire items which corresponded to the four statements which followed the reinforcement (A2 and A4). Persistency of the effects was determined by subtracting initial opinion scores from scores on the delayed posttest opinionnaire.

The strongest support for the spread of effect hypotheses was provided by the immediate posttest. Opinions changed, as predicted, in the direction of whichever arguments were closer in time to the rewarding stimulus (approval) or farther from the punishing stimulus (disapproval). Although three out of four delayed effects were also in the predicted direction, only the proactive effect of the reward was significant at the .05 level. Following Miller and Campbell (1959), that retention is causally related to opinion change, perhaps

TABLE 3

THE EFFECTS OF VERBAL APPROVAL AND DISAPPROVAL AS REINFORCERS OF OPINION CHANGE[a]

Effects	(A1) Reward after		(A2) Reward before		(A3) Punishment after		(A4) Punishment before	
	(B1) Pro first	(B2) Con first	(B1) Pro first	(B2) Con first	(B1) Pro first	(B2) Con first	(B1) Pro first	(B2) Con first
Immediate								
Gain	−.6 (11)[b]	+3.2 (12)	+2.9 (12)	−1.1 (11)	+1.5 (12)	−5.0 (10)	−3.7 (10)	+3.2 (12)
Prediction	Recency		Primacy		Primacy		Recency	
Obtained difference	−3.8[c] (Recency)		+4.0[c] (Primacy)		+6.5[c] (Primacy)		−6.9[c] (Recency)	
After 17 days								
Gain	−1.7 (9)	+1.1 (11)	+2.0 (11)	−3.8 (9)	+1.0 (7)	−2.0 (9)	0 (9)	−.1 (7)
Prediction	Recency		Primacy		Primacy		Recency	
Obtained difference	−2.8 (Recency)		+5.8[c] (Primacy)		+3.0 (Primacy)		+.1 (Primacy)	

[a]Data from Rosnow (1966a).

[b]Numbers in parentheses indicate size of sample on which cell means are based.

[c]$p < .05$, one-tailed.

the weak delayed effects were due to subjects having forgotten the message.[6]

The subtraction-difference procedure was also computed on the difference-between-gain scores of the control groups, first on the counterbalanced responses to the initial four statements and then on the final four statements. None of the immediate or delayed effects for direction in the control groups was significant, the most powerful effect failing to achieve even the .10 level.

DECELERATING THE DECAY OF REINFORCEMENT

As an alternative to reducing the time interval between reinforcement and communication, it was proposed that proactive effects might also be revealed if the rate of decay of the reinforcement were impeded. That is, by prolonging the reinforcer's potency, it might be possible to link the reaction to the reinforcement with the subsequent reaction to a two-sided communication which was contiguous with the reinforcement. This might be accomplished by using a stimulus whose reinforcement was released over an extended period, i.e., a kind of "continuous action reagent." By analogy, the principle underlying the continuous action cold tablet is to release its medication a little at a time, thereby maintaining its potency for an extended period. Similarly, a continuous action social reagent would release its reinforcement a little at a time, thereby prolonging the potency of the reinforcement. For example, intermittently feeding small amounts of a desirable food to a hungry organism or providing small amounts of water for a thirsty organism might suffice as a sustained positive reinforcement.[7] Food and water, however, are primary reinforcements, and the problem here is the diffusion of symbolic reinforcements.

Golightly and Byrne's discovery (1964) of the positive and negative reinforcing properties of consonant and dissonant attitude statements suggested a solution to this problem. They employed a simple dis-

---

[6]The relationship between retention and opinion change is discussed in detail by Greenwald (this volume).

[7]The "eating-while-reading" studies of Janis and his students (Dabbs & Janis, 1965; Janis, Kaye, & Kirschner, 1965) are roughly illustrative of this principle. Janis, Kaye, and Kirschner gave hungry Yale undergraduates soda pop and peanuts to eat at the same time that the students were engaged in reading a series of one-sided persuasive communications. Eating while reading resulted in more opinion change in the direction of the communications than was produced in a reading-only control—results which McGuire (1966, p. 482) summarizes as showing "that things go better with coke."

crimination task to test the proposition that short consonant and dissonant attitude statements could be used in the same way as traditional verbal rewards and punishments to reinforce learning. Statements with which their subjects strongly agreed were positive reinforcers;[8] those with which they strongly disagreed were negative reinforcers. These findings raised the interesting possibility that a one-sided communication consisting entirely of opinion-supporting statements (*consonant communication*), or a one-sided communication consisting entirely of opinion-attacking statements (*dissonant communication*), could suffice as a sustained symbolic reinforcement.

This idea provided the rationale for a study by Corrozi and Rosnow (1968), although no attempt was made to test whether or not the rate of decay of the reinforcement was actually impeded using such a technique. The design of the study corresponded exactly to that shown in Table 1. The sample consisted of eight classes of male and female high school juniors and seniors. Two weeks after their instructors had administered an opinionnaire containing items about the artist Pablo Picasso, the experimenter read to each of the eight groups a 700-word, two-sided communication containing pro and con arguments about Picasso. As shown in Table 1, the juxtaposition of the pro and con arguments was counterbalanced. Four classes received the pro arguments first (B1); the other four received the con arguments first (B2). Following Golightly and Byrne, the rewarding and punishing events were consonant and dissonant communications which either preceded or followed the two-sided communication.[9] The posttest opinionnaire was administered immediately thereafter.

The results are summarized in Table 4. Three out of four predictions were strongly supported, the fourth failing to reach the .05 level of significance. Both the proactive and the retroactive effects of the consonant communication, or "reward," were in the predicted direction and were significant at the .05 level. The proactive effect

---

[8]This finding is also evidence for the assumption in Weiss' opinion change model (1962) of the positively reinforcing property of opinion-supporting arguments (see also his chapter in this volume). The Golightly and Byrne findings have since been replicated by Byrne, Young, and Griffitt (1966).

[9]The consonant and dissonant communications were just over 200 words in length and consisted entirely of opinion-supporting or opinion-attacking statements. The dissonant communication advocated a longer school week of six 9-hour days, while the consonant communication took the position that the school week was already long enough. Another class of 20 students was found to agree strongly with the consonant communication and to disagree with the dissonant communication ($t = 9.94$, $df = 18$, $p < .05$).

TABLE 4
THE INFLUENCE OF CONSONANT AND DISSONANT STATEMENTS AS REINFORCERS OF OPINION CHANGE[a]

Effects	(A1) Reward after		(A2) Reward before		(A3) Punishment after		(A4) Punishment before	
	(B1) Pro first	(B2) Con first	(B1) Pro first	(B2) Con first	(B1) Pro first	(B2) Con first	(B1) Pro first	(B2) Con first
Pre	18.1[b]	16.2	17.2	17.3	17.0	17.1	17.4	15.3
Post	17.6	18.1	18.0	16.5	17.5	16.8	15.5	16.6
Gain	-.5	+1.9	+.8	-.8	+.5	-.3	-1.9	+1.3
	(19)[c]	(19)	(19)	(19)	(19)	(19)	(19)	(19)
Prediction	Recency		Primacy		Primacy		Recency	
Obtained difference	-2.4[d]		+1.6[d]		+.8		-3.2[d]	
	(Recency)		(Primacy)		(Primacy)		(Recency)	

[a] Data from Corrozi and Rosnow (1968).
[b] Summed opinion scores could range from five, or a highly unfavorable opinion of Picasso, to a highly favorable 25, a score of 15 being neutral.
[c] Numbers in parentheses indicate size of sample on which cell means are based.
[d] $p < .05$, one-tailed.

of the dissonant communication, or "punishment," was also in the predicted direction ($p < .05$). Only the retroactive effect of the dissonant communication failed to achieve the specified level of significance.

COMPLEMENTARY AND COMPETING VARIABLES

As an alternative to reducing the time lag or decelerating the decay of reinforcement, it also was implied that the likelihood of finding the hypothesized effects might further be increased if complementary primacy and recency variables were manipulated at the same time. The reasoning here was that two primacy variables, by their complementary interaction (or perhaps by their summation), would have a greater likelihood of producing primacy than could be expected from the competing interaction of a primacy with a recency variable. In order to test this proposition two primacy and two recency variables were selected (cf. Rosnow, 1966b), and a situation was concocted in which the various interactions could occur.

Based on Lana's finding (1961), noted earlier, concerning the influence of familiarity in primacy-recency the following hypotheses were derived:

a. Primacy would occur if a two-sided communication on a familiar topic were immediately preceded by a rewarding event.

b. Recency would occur if a two-sided communication on an unfamiliar topic were immediately followed by a rewarding event.

c. There would be no effect if (1) a two-sided communication on a familiar topic were immediately followed by a rewarding event, or (2) a two-sided communication on an unfamiliar topic were immediately preceded by a rewarding event.

Rosnow and Lana (1965) tested these hypotheses using high school students as subjects and following the procedure of Rosnow and Russell (1963), i.e., rewarding the students by discounting poor grades. Familiarity with the topic, civil defense, was determined by means of an information questionnaire administered along with the pretest opinionnaire. High and low familiarity subgroups were formed on the basis of a median split of scores on the information questionnaire.

The results are summarized in Table 5. As predicted, primacy resulted when the rewarding event immediately preceded the two-sided communication for subjects who were familiar with the topic. Also as predicted, recency resulted when the rewarding event

TABLE 5

The Influence on Opinion of Complementary and Competing Variables[a]

Effects	(A1) Reward after				(A2) Reward before			
	(B1) High familiarity		(B2) Low familiarity		(B1) High familiarity		(B2) Low familiarity	
	(C1) Pro first	(C2) Con first	(C1) Pro first	(C2) Con first	(C1) Pro first	(C2) Con first	(C1) Pro first	(C2) Con first
Pre	20.1[b]	20.4	21.0	19.8	20.2	20.0	19.6	19.4
Post	18.5	18.6	17.9	18.3	19.6	18.4	17.2	16.7
Gain	-1.6	-1.8	-3.1	-1.5	-.6	-1.6	-2.4	-2.7
	(10)[c]	(10)	(10)	(10)	(10)	(10)	(10)	(10)
Prediction	No effect		Recency		Primacy		No effect	
Obtained difference	+.2		-1.6[d]		+1.0[d]		+.3	
	(Primacy)		(Recency)		(Primacy)		(Primacy)	

[a] Data from Rosnow and Lana (1965).

[b] Summed opinion scores could range from five, or a highly unfavorable attitude toward civil defense, to a highly favorable 25, a score of 15 being neutral.

[c] Numbers in parentheses indicate size of sample on which cell means are based.

[d] $p < .05$, one-tailed.

immediately followed the two-sided communication for subjects who were not highly familiar with the topic. Only negligible effects resulted when high familiarity interacted with the retroactive reinforcement or when low familiarity interacted with the proactive reinforcement.[10]

GENERAL CONCLUSIONS

The question was raised if experiencing a reinforcing event at about the same time as having been exposed to successive opposing arguments on a controversial issue could shape one's attitude toward the issue. This research suggests that it can.

Assuming that attitudes are learned mediating responses, it followed that opinion change would be accompanied by a concomitant change in some aspect of the corresponding attitude. Using as rewards or punishments such obviously pleasant or noxious stimuli as verbal approval or disapproval, increased grades or surprise exams, opinion-supporting or opinion-attacking arguments, our finding was that opinions tended to change in the direction of arguments that occurred closer in time to a reward or farther from a punishment. Presumably contiguity between such rewards and an argument served to strengthen the tendency to respond in the direction of the argument, while punishment weakened that tendency. The findings also suggest that several extraneous factors may affect that relationship with the likelihood of producing a proactive diffusion of effect possibly increasing (a) the shorter the time interval between the reactions to the reinforcement and the argument, (b)

---

[10]It must be noted, however, that Rosnow, Holz, and Levin (1966), following a similar rationale, failed to produce the order effects which would be expected from a complementary interaction of a retroactive reward or punishment with the familiarity variable. They suggest that an *enculturated response*, defined as a "normative pattern of behavior acquired through socialization," may have interacted with the reinforcement and familiarity variables in a manner so as to cancel the expected effects. In their study, the two-sided communication was comprised of prosecution and defense arguments from an actual bigamy trial. Thus, the enculturated response hypothesis was based on the notion, inherent in the American system of jurisprudence, that an individual is presumed innocent until proved guilty. This would imply a stronger overall tendency to vote innocent rather than guilty, but, in regard to the bigamy issue, a greater leniency toward the male defendant by male than by female judges.

the slower the rate of decay of the reinforcement, or (c) if complementary variables interact.

The impetus for this research was provided by the spread of effect, the empirical phenomenon having been used in a heuristic sense as a model to generate opinion change hypotheses. However, there may well be inadequacies with such a model which might not apply to an alternative explanation in terms of a more orthodox reinforcement, or conditioning by contiguity, model. For example, the spread of effect has traditionally referred to a situation of responding to serially presented stimuli of a less complex nature than the successive opposing arguments used here. Thus, Thorndike's original stimuli were series of uncompleted statements, words, geometric forms, or nonsense syllables. Also, the types of responses to those stimuli were simpler than the yielding response implied here. Perhaps a more serious problem is that most of the empirical gradients of effect that have thus far been reported are aftergradients, leading some investigators to hedge on the possibility that the foregradient may yet prove to be entirely artifactual. Because the decidedly less controversial conditioning model skirts these objections, it could in the long run prove to be a more parsimonious interpretation of the results. The time intervals here are well within the bounds of obtained conditioning effects with animals in laboratory settings, and, since our rewards and punishments were noncontingent on specific responses, it may be argued that this situation roughly corresponds to a classical conditioning paradigm. One is still left, of course, with the problem of explaining the proactive effects—perhaps as a kind of "backward conditioning."

Finally, when conditions such as those manipulated here occur outside the laboratory one might speculate concerning their impact on attitude formation. It is possible that their effect may often be inadvertent, differentially strengthening or weakening tendencies to respond to bits of information from the stream of information to which we, in this age of mass communication, are almost continuously subjected. The grand effect may not be unlike Schramm's conception of the impact of the mass media:

> . . . [these conditions] are like drops of calcareous water falling from the roof of a cave upon an ancient stalagmite. Sometimes an especially big drop leaves an especially large deposit, in such a position that it can be seen and actually appears to change the shape of the stalagmite. Usually the residue of each new drop simply merges with the older deposits, and the structure grows, almost imperceptibly, in the direction of the source of supply [Schramm, 1949, p. 397].

References

Bostrom, R., Vlandis, J., & Rosenbaum, M. Grades as reinforcing contingencies and attitude change. *Journal of Educational Psychology*, 1961, **52**, 112-115.

Buckhout, R., & Rosenberg, M. J. Verbal reinforcement and attitude change. *Psychological Reports*, 1966, **18**, 691-694.

Byrne, D., Young, R. K., & Griffitt, W. The reinforcement properties of attitude statements. *Journal of Experimental Research in Personality*, 1966, **1**, 266-276.

Carlsmith, J. M., Collins, B. E., & Helmreich, R. L. Studies in forced compliance: I. The effect of pressure for compliance on attitude change produced by face-to-face role playing and anonymous essay writing. *Journal of Personality and Social Psychology*, 1966, **4**, 1-13.

Corrozi, J. F., & Rosnow, R. L. Consonant and dissonant communications as positive and negative reinforcements in opinion change. *Journal of Personality and Social Psychology*, 1968, **8**, 27-30.

Dabbs, J. M., & Janis, I. L. Why does eating while reading facilitate opinion change?— An experimental inquiry. *Journal of Experimental Social Psychology*, 1965, **1**, 133-144.

Doob, L. W. The behavior of attitudes. *Psychological Review*, 1947, **54**, 135-156.

Festinger, L., & Carlsmith, J. M. Cognitive consequences of forced compliance. *Journal of Abnormal and Social Psychology*, 1959, **58**, 203-210.

Goldstein, I., & McGinnies, E. Compliance and attitude change under conditions of differential social reinforcement. *Journal of Abnormal and Social Psychology*, 1964, **68**, 567-570.

Golightly, C. A., & Byrne, D. Attitude statements as positive and negative reinforcements. *Science*, 1964, **146**, 798-799.

Greenwald, A. G. Nuttin's neglected critique of the law of effect. *Psychological Bulletin*, 1966, **65**, 199-205.

Hilgard, E. R. *Theories of learning.* New York: Appleton, 1956.

Hull, C. L. *Principles of behavior.* New York: Appleton, 1943.

Janis, I. L., Kaye, D., & Kirschner, P. Facilitating effects of "eating-while-reading" on responsiveness to persuasive communications. *Journal of Personality and Social Psychology*, 1965, **1**, 181-186.

Janis, I. L., & King, B. The influence of role-playing on opinion-change. *Journal of Abnormal and Social Psychology*, 1954, **49**, 211-218.

Lana, R. E. Familiarity and the order of presentation of persuasive communications. *Journal of Abnormal and Social Psychology*, 1961, **62**, 573-577.

Lott, B. E., & Lott, A. J. The formation of positive attitudes toward group members. *Journal of Abnormal and Social Psychology*, 1960, **61**, 297-300.

Marx, M. Spread of effect: A critical review. *Genetic Psychology Monographs*, 1956, **53**, 119-186.

Marx, M. Analysis of the spread of effect: A comparison of Thorndike and Nuttin. *Psychological Bulletin*, 1967, **67**, 413-415.

McGuire, W. J. Order of presentation as a factor in "conditioning" persuasiveness. In C. I. Hovland *et al., The order of presentation in persuasion.* New Haven: Yale University Press, 1957. Pp. 98-114.

McGuire, W. J. Attitudes and opinions. *Annual Review of Psychology*, 1966, **17**, 475-514.

Miller, N., & Campbell, D. T. Recency and primacy as a function of the timing of speeches and measurements. *Journal of Abnormal and Social Psychology*, 1959, **59**, 1-9.

Postman, L. Rewards and punishments in human learning. In L. Postman (Ed.), *Psychology in the making*. New York: Knopf, 1963. Pp. 331-401.

Postman, L. Reply to Greenwald. *Psychological Bulletin*, 1966, **65**, 383-388.

Rosenberg, M. J. When dissonance fails: On eliminating evaluation apprehension from attitude measurement. *Journal of Personality and Social Psychology*, 1965, **1**, 28-42.

Rosnow, R. L. A delay-of-reinforcement effect in persuasive communication? *Journal of Social Psychology*, 1965, **67**, 39-43.

Rosnow, R. L. "Conditioning" the direction of opinion change in persuasive communication. *Journal of Social Psychology*, 1966, **69**, 291-303. (a)

Rosnow, R. L. Whatever happened to the "law of primacy"? *Journal of Communication*, 1966, **16**, 10-31. (b)

Rosnow, R. L., Holz, R. F., & Levin, J. Differential effects of complementary and competing variables in primacy-recency. *Journal of Social Psychology*, 1966, **69**, 135-147.

Rosnow, R. L., & Lana, R. E. Complementary and competing-order effects in opinion change. *Journal of Social Psychology*, 1965, **66**, 201-207.

Rosnow, R. L., & Robinson, E. J. (Eds.). *Experiments in persuasion*. New York: Academic Press, 1967.

Rosnow, R. L., & Russell, G. Spread of effect of reinforcement in persuasive communication. *Psychological Reports*, 1963, **12**, 731-735.

Sarbin, T. R., & Allen, V. L. Role enactment, audience feedback, and attitude change. *Sociometry*, 1964, **27**, 183-193.

Schramm, W. The effects of mass communications: A review. *Journalism Quarterly*, 1949, **26**, 397-409.

Scott, W. A. Attitude change through reward of verbal behavior. *Journal of Abnormal and Social Psychology*, 1957, **55**, 72-75.

Scott, W. A. Attitude change by response reinforcement: Replication and extension. *Sociometry*, 1959, **22**, 328-335.

Staats, A. W., & Staats, C. K. *Complex human behavior: A systematic extension of learning principles*. New York: Holt, 1964.

Thorndike, E. L. *Animal intelligence*. New York: Macmillan, 1911.

Thorndike, E. L. An experimental study of rewards. *Teachers College Contributions to Education*, 1933, No. 580. (a)

Thorndike, E. L. A proof of the law of effect. *Science*, 1933, **77**, 173-175. (b)

Tilton, J. W. The effect of "right" and "wrong" upon the learning of nonsense syllables in multiple choice arrangement. *Journal of Educational Psychology*, 1939, **30**, 95-115.

Tilton, J. W. Gradients of effect. *Journal of Genetic Psychology*, 1945, **66**, 3-19.

Wallace, J. Role reward and dissonance reduction. *Journal of Personality and Social Psychology*, 1966, **3**, 305-312.

Weiss, R. F. Persuasion and the acquisition of attitudes: Models from conditioning and selective learning. *Psychological Reports*, 1962, **11**, 709-732.

Wrench, D. F. The perception of two-sided messages. *Human Relations*, 1964, **17**, 227-233.

5

An Extension of Hullian Learning
Theory to Persuasive Communication[1]

ROBERT FRANK WEISS

DEPARTMENT OF PSYCHOLOGY
UNIVERSITY OF OKLAHOMA
NORMAN, OKLAHOMA

INTRODUCTION

As knowledge of attitude change processes has grown, a wide variety of theoretical analyses has been developed to integrate portions of this knowledge, to guide further research, or to solve "classical" problems of attitude change research. Several of these theoretical analyses have employed learning principles as a model for attitude change processes (e.g., Bugelski & Hersen, 1966; Carriero, 1967; Cervin, 1955; Doob, 1947; Hildum & Brown, 1956; Janis, 1957; Krasner, Knowles, & Ullmann, 1965; Lott, 1955; McGuire, 1957; Miller & Campbell, 1959; Radtke, 1967; Razran, 1938, 1954; Rhine, 1958; Rosnow, 1966; Scott, 1957; Staats & Staats, 1958; Tannenbaum & Gengel, 1966; Weiss, 1962; see also the chapters by Lott and Lott, Rosnow, and Staats in this volume). A consideration of these analyses makes it abundantly clear that a variety of fruitful analogies may be drawn between learning and attitude formation, rather than there being one uniquely correct approach. In this chapter, the general approach which Neal Miller (1959) has called "extension of liberalized S-R theory" is employed to develop a theory of the effects of certain

[1]This investigation was supported in part by Grants MH-04523 and MH-12402 from the National Institute of Mental Health.

aspects of persuasion on the learning and motivation of attitudes. Hull-Miller-Spence learning theory (e.g., Hull, 1943, 1952; Logan, 1959; Miller & Dollard, 1941; K. W. Spence, 1956, 1960) is used as a model for persuasion situations corresponding to instrumental reward conditioning, selective learning, and classical conditioning.

Hullian learning theory (abbreviated frequently hereafter simply as "learning theory") has been developed primarily to predict individual behavior in highly controlled experimental situations. Learning theory has, nevertheless, been extended not only to attitude change, but to numerous other social processes, with a considerable measure of success (e.g., Dollard & Miller, 1950; Miller & Dollard, 1941; Weiss, 1963; Wheeler, 1966; Whiting & Child, 1953; Wolpe, 1958). The explanatory power of learning theory stems, in part, from two sources. First, Hullian theory includes a number of principles which may be combined in a determinate manner. Principles which may seem relatively trivial when taken singly become powerful explanatory tools when the manner of their interaction can be specified. Second, Hullian theory is quantitative, with the usual advantages that attend scientific quantification.

TECHNIQUE OF THEORY CONSTRUCTION

The use of a model in theory construction typically involves the specification of a dictionary of analogies (rules of correspondence) which relate the variables of the model to the variables of the data area to be explained and predicted. Once this is done, the relations holding among the variables of the model must, theoretically, also hold between the corresponding (analogous) variables in the data area to be explained (e.g., Campbell, 1920; Lachman, 1960; Nagel, 1961; Oppenheimer, 1956). The systematic use of learning theory as a model for attitude change makes it possible to take full advantage of the two characteristics of learning theory mentioned above: combination of principles in a determinate manner and quantitative specification. For example, there are a number of principles regarding the effects of delay of reward on measures of instrumental conditioning, which may be stated informally as (1) the delay of reward gradient is decreasing and negatively accelerated in shape; (2) delay of reward and number of trials combine multiplicatively; and (3) delay of reward and drive combine additively. If a social variable is to be theoretically analogous to delay of reward, its effects on appropriate dependent measures must show that (1) this social variable gradient is decreasing and negatively accelerated in shape; (2) this social variable and number of trials combine multiplicatively; and (3) this social variable and drive combine additively.

The above material illustrates the development of an analogy between learning and social *independent* variables. The analogy does not have testable implications until analogies between learning and social *dependent* variables are also developed. Moreover, it is necessary to clearly specify *what kind of learning situation* the social conditions are analogous to; approach-avoidance conflict, instrumental reward conditioning, selective learning, etc., differ sharply in certain regards.

Models and Translations

The theories developed here are not "mere translations of one behavioral science language into another," since the theories generate hypotheses which are often not in the existing literature. A "mere translation" would require, for example, that the hypotheses concerning the previous paragraph's social variable already exist in the literature of persuasion research, before they could be merely translated into statements about delay of reinforcement and number of trials.

Analogy and Reduction

Nowhere in this essay is it proposed that social behavior represents a "distinct higher level of phenomena which can only be fully explained by reducing it to a lower level of phenomena such as conditioning." Nor is this dubious philosophical program implicit in our intentions. Rather, the intention has been to use the relatively well-understood as a model for that which is presently less well-understood. The programmatic assumptions involved are commonplaces of scientific method: well-constructed models and analogies help to stimulate and guide research and to integrate broad ranges of knowledge through an underlying set of common principles.

The Nature of Reinforcement

The theories developed here are not concerned with the ultimate nature of reinforcement: an empirical law-of-effect position is taken throughout. The drive-reduction hypothesis is not essential to Hull-Miller-Spence learning theory. The theory predicts and explains in the same manner without reference to this particular conception of the nature of reinforcement (Dollard & Miller, 1950; Miller, 1959; K. W. Spence, 1956).

TOPICS AND ORGANIZATION

The theory is concerned with such familiar variables of persuasion research as source credibility and role playing, such commonsensical variables as argument strength and repetition of persuasive communication, as well as several novel variables which are less immediately obvious. The theory is essentially concerned with attitude formation rather than attitude reversal. As would be expected, the questions asked are sometimes quite different from those asked in research which does not stem from learning theory.

The remainder of the chapter will be concerned with the effects of opinion-supporting arguments and opinion-eliciting arguments in communication situations corresponding to fundamental types of learning conditions. The next section will discuss the effects of opinion-supporting arguments in explicit conclusion-drawing situations analogous to instrumental reward conditioning and selective learning, while a second section will discuss the effects of opinion-eliciting arguments in an implicit conclusion-drawing situation analogous to classical conditioning.

INSTRUMENTAL LEARNING OF ATTITUDES

PRIMARY CONCEPTS

In terms of the empirical law of effect, an event which follows a response and increases the strength of that response on the next trial is called a reinforcer. Responses as different as saying plural nouns or running down an alley may be reinforced by events as diverse as an experimenter's "mm-hmm" or lab chow pellets. In this research Ss read aloud persuasive communications designed so that the opinion to be learned is followed by an opinion-supporting argument. (The argument consists of information supporting the opinion, and specifically excludes repetitions of the opinion.) It seems reasonable to expect that an opinion which is followed by a convincing argument will be strengthened more than an unsupported opinion. Such an argument would then function as a reinforcer of the opinion response and might perhaps exhibit other functional properties of reinforcers. One such property is the inverse relationship between delay of reinforcement and response strength, and a logical development of the paradigm outlined above indicates that the delay of argument (time interval between the opinion response and the reinforcing argument) may be regarded as analogous to delay of reinforcement.

Figure 1 summarizes the paradigm: the visual cues from the communication (including the sight of the written opinion statement) are analogous to the visual and response-produced cues from running a straight alley; the opinion is analogous to the instrumental running response to be learned; the argument is analogous to reinforcement; delay of argument is analogous to delay of reinforcement; and the entire sequence is analogous to a reinforced trial. The situation includes not only an instrumental response (the opinion response), but also a goal response (stating the argument). In this sense then, the persuasion sequence outlined here may be said to conform to the paradigm of instrumental reward conditioning.

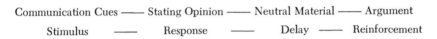

FIG. 1. Correspondences between an instrumental conditioning trial and a persuasion trial.

Some writers associate instrumental conditioning with "voluntary" behavior and classical conditioning with "involuntary" behavior. Therefore, they would find intuitively unappealing the fact that the instrumental opinion response is guided here by a written communication rather than being freely emitted by S. The paradigm outlined above, however, emphasizes the fact that in instrumental conditioning "the aim of the experimenter is to arrange for the occurrence of but a single response or response chain which is followed by reinforcement" and that the experimenter therefore attempts to "maximize from the first the occurrence of this to-be-learned response and to minimize the occurrence of competing responses. In the maze type of instrumental situation the likelihood of competing responses occurring is reduced by having but a single straight-ahead alley instead of a number of alternative ones [K. W. Spence, 1956, pp. 37-38]." The persuasive communication is intended to be analogous to such a straight alley. Both rats and sophomores can flatly refuse to "run the alley," but very few of either species do.

INDEPENDENT VARIABLES: RULES OF CORRESPONDENCE

The ideas just developed are systematically expanded in this section. The first two columns of Table 1 (items 1–10) summarize the rules of correspondence (analogies) assumed among the independent variables of instrumental conditioning and the independent variables of persuasive communication.

Acquisition and Extinction Trials

The persuasion sequence shown in Fig. 1 (communication cues – opinion response – argument) is analogous to a reinforced trial in instrumental reward conditioning. Repetition of this sequence thus corresponds to an increasing number of reinforced trials (Table 1, No. 1), and the interval between such repetitions corresponds to the intertrial interval (No. 2). Each repetition of a persuasion trial also automatically includes a presentation of the argument (reinforcement) which it would be conventional in Hullian theory to also count separately as number of reinforcements (No. 3). While the argument functions as a reinforcer of the opinion response, it is virtually certain that other such reinforcers (e.g., pleasing the experimenter) are available in this situation. Thus presentation of the communications with the argument omitted probably cannot be regarded as a completely unreinforced (extinction) trial.

Delay of Reinforcement

As previously noted, the time interval between the opinion response and the reinforcing argument is analogous to delay of reinforcement (No. 4). The length of a response (e.g., a short alley versus a long one) is often considered to affect response strength through within-chain delay of reinforcement. It is possible that a short opinion to be learned may correspond to a short alley and a long opinion to a long alley (No. 5), although the manipulation of this variable poses intricate theoretical problems (Weiss, 1962).

Magnitude of Reinforcement and Goal Response

Two persuasion variables may be regarded as analogous to magnitude of reinforcement. The strength of the reinforcing argument (as determined by its content and phrasing) is directly analogous to

TABLE 1

RULES OF CORRESPONDENCE RELATING THE VARIABLES IN
INSTRUMENTAL REWARD LEARNING AND PERSUASIVE COMMUNICATION[a]

Persuasion	Learning	Hullian construct	Function relating variable to construct
1. Number of persuasion trials	Number of reinforced trials	H	Increasing, negatively accelerated
2. Interval between persuasion trials	Intertrial interval	I	Decreasing
3. Number of exposures to argument	Number of reinforcements	K	Increasing, negatively accelerated
4. Delay of argument	Delay of reinforcement	K	Decreasing, negatively accelerated
5. Length of opinion statement	Length of response chain (within-chain delay)	K	Decreasing, negatively accelerated
6. Strength of argument	Magnitude of reinforcement	K	Increasing, negatively accelerated
7. Source credibility	Magnitude of reinforcement	K	Increasing, negatively accelerated
8. Activeness of participation in argument	Vigor of goal response	K	Increasing
9. Activeness of participation in statement of opinion	Response generalization	H	Decreasing
10. Stimulus change	Stimulus change, stimulus generalization	H	Decreasing, negatively accelerated
11. Speed (1/latency) of agreement	Speed (1/latency)	$\bar{E}$	Increasing, linear
12. Percent choice, opinion$_1$ vs. opinion$_2$	Percent choice R$_1$ versus R$_2$	$\bar{E}_1, \bar{E}_2,$ L, O	Complex

[a]Relation to Hullian constructs also shown.

magnitude of reinforcement (No. 6).[2] Source credibility, a familiar variable in persuasion research (e.g., Hovland & Mandell, 1952; Hovland & Weiss, 1951; W. Weiss, 1967), can also be employed in research guided by the present theory. The credibility of the source of an argument affects the power of the argument to convincingly support (reinforce) the opinion response, and is therefore analogous to magnitude of reinforcement (No. 7).[3]

The instrumental persuasion situation includes both an instrumental response (the opinion response) and a goal response (stating the argument). An analogy to a conditioning variable, vigor of goal response, is clearly suggested by the role-playing studies of Janis and King (1954) and King and Janis (1956). Stating the argument aloud with feeling and expression would correspond to a goal response of relatively high vigor, while passive listening to a statement of the argument would represent a goal response of low vigor (No. 8).

Generalization Variables

Another variable of interest is also suggested by the role-playing experiments. These studies did not separate activeness of participation in the statement of the argument (the goal response) from active-

---

[2]Argument content should be understood as including not only "logical proofs" but also pleasant consequences (McGuire, 1957), etc. The content or phrasing which will make an argument strong or weak depends on the audience addressed, and it would often, therefore, be advisable to obtain judgments of argument strength from a sample comparable to the experimental sample. In a *parametric* study it would be necessary to scale judgments of the several arguments employed by an equal-intervals method, in order to determine the true shape of the function. A multidimensional scaling of arguments would probably reveal several dimensions of content and phrasing which could then be experimentally manipulated. It is clear that additional arguments known to Ss would affect argument strength and that choice of topics for a communication would necessarily be guided by this consideration. By the same token the number of different arguments included in a communication would also affect attitude strength, though the manner of combination of these arguments would depend on the compatibility of the goal (argument) responses based on them (e.g., Beier, 1958; Logan, Beier, & Ellis, 1955).

[3]This reinforcement magnitude interpretation is in partial disagreement with the stimulus-generalization interpretation of Hovland, Janis, and Kelley (1953). It should be noted, however, that the hypothesis advanced in this paper is concerned with the source of the argument, and that where the credibility of the source of the entire communication is varied (as in the experiments cited above) a more complex analysis may possibly be required. Parametric studies of source credibility raise problems similar to those encountered in studying argument strength (see footnote 2). The "consensus technique" (Weiss, 1967a; Weiss *et al.*, 1964, 1968b; this chapter, p. 137), however, permits parametric study of source credibility without requiring a multidimensional scaling of sources.

ness of participation in the statement of the opinion (the instrumental response). This latter variable may correspond in part to a trials variable, upon the hypothesis that a passive listening group does not practice the opinion response as thoroughly as an active statement group. It is possible, however, that the entire effect of such a variable would depend on the relation of the response learned in training (overt or covert statement of opinion) to the response required in the opinion testing situation, i.e., to response generalization (No. 9).

Change in stimulus conditions from training to testing (stimulus generalization) is also applicable to the persuasion situation. Since the opinion response is conditioned to the stimuli of the communication, similarities in wording between the communication and the opinion-testing situation are of particular importance (No. 10).

Borrowed Variables

There are also a number of learning variables and analogs of learning variables which may be taken from their normal context and borrowed without modification for use in connection with this theory. Prominent among these are drive variables such as manifest anxiety (e.g., J. T. Spence & Spence, 1966; Taylor, 1953), the Cervin emotionality scale (e.g., Cervin, 1955), time stress (e.g., Castaneda & Palermo, 1955; Clark, 1962), social facilitation (Zajonc & Sales, 1966), and, under certain circumstances, induced anxiety (e.g., Leventhal, Singer, & Jones, 1965; K. W. Spence & Goldstein, 1961). In addition to these drive variables, the introversion-extroversion variables governing the rate of development of excitation and inhibition (e.g., Eysenck, 1965; Franks, 1957) should be mentioned. While such borrowed variables do not occupy a necessary place in the structure of analogy developed here, there is no harm in seeing whether they can enrich the present theory by continuing to function "correctly" outside their original research context.

DEPENDENT VARIABLES: RULES OF CORRESPONDENCE

In the two preceding sections we have specified the kind of learning situation (instrumental reward conditioning) to which our persuasion situation is analogous, and we have developed a dictionary of analogies between learning and persuasion independent variables. These analogies do not have testable implications until analogies between learning and persuasion dependent variables are also developed.

Instrumental Conditioning

In attitude change research, attitude strength has typically been measured by amplitude of agreement with an opinion statement. That is to say, Ss are usually asked how much they agree or disagree. In the Hullian theory of instrumental reward conditioning, speed (1/latency) and resistance to extinction are the measures of response strength (excitatory potential). Amplitude is related to excitatory potential only in some forms of classical conditioning. In the instrumental conditioning of attitudes, the appropriate measures of attitude strength would then be, not amplitude of agreement, but speed of agreement and opinion resistance to extinction. Of these two measures, only speed (Table 1, No. 11) is employed, in the light of previous discussion indicating that the situation does not include a clear analog of extinction.

An attitude measuring apparatus assessed each S's speed of agreement after S had been exposed to persuasive communication. A statement of the opinion (preceded by buffers) was projected on a screen and S signified his agreement (if he agreed) by moving a lever toward the statement. When the opinion statement was projected on the screen, an electric timer automatically began to measure latency of agreement (to .01 second). When the lever was moved ¼ in., a photobeam silently stopped the timer (speed = 1/latency). An equally good measure of latency was the time from the projection of the opinion statement until the lever had been moved the full distance (14 in.) toward the screen. The timing equipment was not visible to the Ss, who did not know they were being timed. If an S did not respond within 45 seconds, his speed of agreement was considered to be zero. Ss who did not agree did not move the lever.

Selective Learning

Learning theory treats selective learning as an extension of instrumental reward conditioning. Each S learns two instrumental reward conditioned responses, which are differentially reinforced. The relative strengths of the two responses may then be assessed by presenting both alternatives simultaneously and allowing S to choose between them. The dependent variable is percent choice. Typically, the number of trials for each response is controlled by forced trials in which S is presented with only one of the alternatives: e.g., the right arm of the T-maze is closed off and S can only go to the left. Selective learning of attitudes is treated as an extension of instrumental attitude conditioning, employing the same persuasive communications. Each S learns two separate and unrelated instrumental reward conditioned attitudes, which are differentially reinforced through exposure to two persuasive communications. Each exposure to a communication constitutes a "forced trial." (Communications presenting pro and con arguments relevant to a single opinion lie outside the bounds of this theory—they more nearly resemble approach-avoidance conflict.) The relative strength of the two opinions is assessed by presenting both alternatives simultaneously, and then requiring S to choose between them. After exposure to the persuasive communications, Ss were tested with the attitude-measuring apparatus described above, with the difference being that the two attitude statements were presented simultaneously, one on each of two screens. S chose the opinion with which he most agreed by moving the lever toward one of the statements (Table 1, No. 12).

20. The British House of Lords should be reorganized.

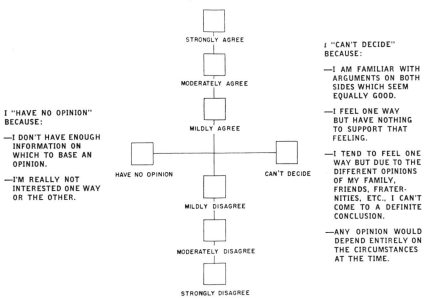

FIG. 2. An item from a paper and pencil test used to screen Ss or opinions in order to meet the theoretical requirement regarding the initial state of the attitude response. An S who neither agreed nor disagreed could check either "no opinion" or "can't decide" but not both. These two zero points were intended to differentiate between Ss who were neutral because they had two or more conflicting opinion responses and those who were neutral because they had no previously learned opinion. In the studies conducted so far, only "no opinion" Ss were used, though Ss who "mildly agree" are acceptable in principle. (From Weiss, Rawson & Pasamanick, 1963.)

EXPERIMENTAL PROCEDURE

While there are essential differences of detail among the experiments, the following procedure is typical. The Ss were undergraduate students, 60 Ss in each experimental condition. In order to study attitude "conditioning" rather than "habit reversal" all Ss selected had no initial opinion, as measured by a questionnaire 2−8 weeks before the experiment (Fig. 2). The experiment was represented to the Ss as a study of "speech patterns and decision-making." Speech patterns were ostensibly assessed by instructing the S to read several short passages into the microphone of a clearly visible tape recorder "with as much expression and conviction as possible." The last of these passages was the persuasive communication. One-trial Ss read each passage once and two-trial Ss read each passage two times. Except in the selective learning experiment, each S was exposed to only one persuasive communication. As a further contribution to the deception, after completing half the reading, the Ss listened to a recording of "effective public speakers" and were instructed to "listen as carefully as you can and note each person's distinct speaking characteristics and style of presentation." The attitude measuring apparatus assessed each S's speed of agreement immediately after S had been exposed to the persuasive communication. A statement of the attitude (preceded by 14 buffers) was projected on a screen and S signified his agreement (if he agreed) by moving a lever toward the statement, as described in detail in "dependent variables," above. The timing equipment was not visible or audible to Ss who did not know they were being timed (according to interviews with 75 Ss) regardless of whether they accepted the official cover of a "decision-making task." There was also a no-persuasion control condition which differed from the experimental conditions only in the omission of the persuasive communication from the several readings.

PREDICTIONS AND RESULTS

Rules of correspondence have been assumed between the variables of instrumental learning and the variables of persuasive communication. Once such rules of correspondence are assumed, the functional relationships holding among the learning variables in the learning theory model should also hold among the corresponding persuasion variables. The left column of Fig. 3 shows the *learning* relationships predicted by Hullian learning theory and typically found in learning research (e.g., Hull, 1951, 1952; Logan, 1959; K. W. Spence, 1956). To the right of each learning relationship is shown the results of the writer's experiments on the corresponding persuasion variables. To the extent that each right-hand persuasion figure resembles its learning model on the left, the theory predicts correctly. The systematic use of learning theory as a model for attitude change makes it possible to take full advantage of two characteristics of learning theory mentioned in the introduction: combination of principles in a determinate manner and quantitative specification. Determinate combination of principles permits us to predict that a persuasion variable will be analogous to a learning variable not only in its *main effect* but also in the pattern of its *interactions* with other variables. Quantitative specification permits, among other things, the prediction of curve shapes rather than limiting the analogy to greater-than, less-than comparisons.

Instrumental Conditioning: Delay of Argument

Figure 3A shows speed as a negatively accelerated decreasing function of delay of reinforcement (e.g., Hull, 1951; Logan, 1960; Perin, 1943). Figure 3A' shows the same relationship between the corresponding persuasion variables: speed of agreement is a negatively accelerated decreasing function of delay of argument (Weiss, 1967b). Other experiments in which only two levels of delay are compared also demonstrate a delay of argument effect. Weiss, Buchanan, and Pasamanick (1965) found that speed of agreement was faster for a group persuaded with a 4-second delay than for a group persuaded with a 20-second delay, and Weiss (1967b) found that speed was faster for zero delay than for 2.8-second delay (Fig. 3B').

Instrumental Conditioning: Interaction of Delay with Trials

Figure 3B shows how delay of reinforcement and number of conditioning trials combine multiplicatively (diverging curves) to determine speed (e.g., Hull, 1951; Perin, 1943). Figure 3B' shows the same relationship between the corresponding persuasion variables: delay of argument and number of persuasion trials combine multiplicatively to determine speed of agreement (Weiss, 1967b).

Selective Learning: Delay of Argument

When Ss have learned two responses, one reinforced with a short delay and the other with a long delay, the Ss will tend to choose the response which was reinforced with the shorter delay (e.g., Loess, 1952; Logan, 1952; K. W. Spence, 1956; also Lipsitt & Castaneda, 1958). An analogous result was found in persuasive communication.

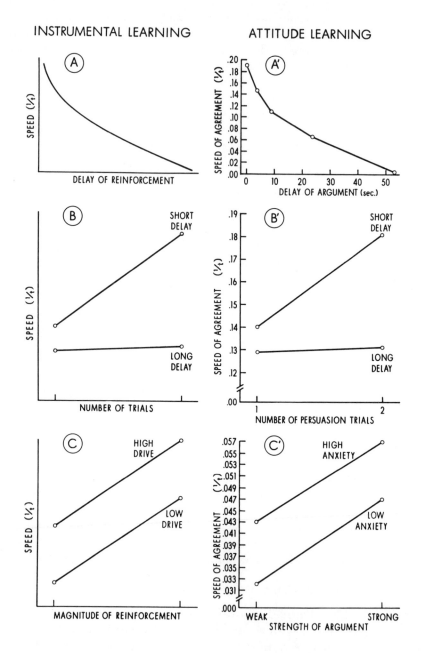

Fig. 3.   Learning model and persuasion results.

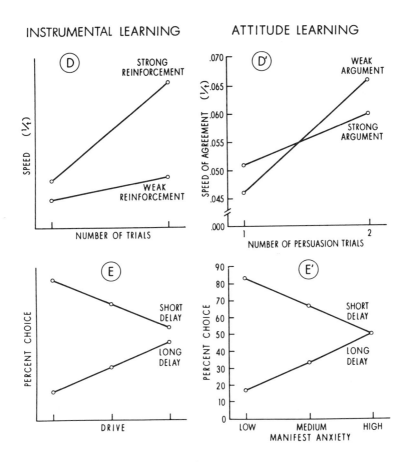

INSTRUMENTAL LEARNING   ATTITUDE LEARNING

FIG. 3 (*continued*)

When Ss were persuaded on two opinions, one reinforced with a short delay of argument and one reinforced with a long delay, the Ss tended to choose the opinion which was persuaded with the shorter delay (Fig. 3E') (Weiss, Rawson, & Pasamanick, 1963).

Selective Learning: Interaction of Delay with Drive

A little-known aspect of Hullian theory is that, under certain circumstances, it predicts that discrimination at *low* drive will be superior to discrimination at high drive (Fig. 3E).

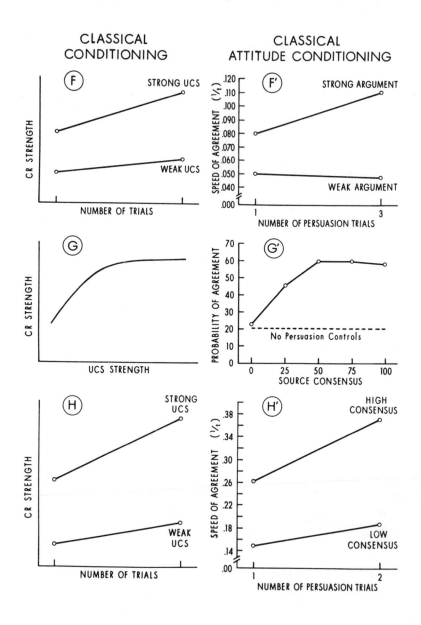

FIG. 3 (continued)

"The implications of the theory are that there will be an inverse relation between performance (per cent choice of short delay) and drive level under conditions which keep the reaction potentials in the low range. These conditions may be specified as low initial habit strengths of the two competing responses, the early stages of selective learning and low ranges of drive level. Thus, it would be expected that a differential in favor of lower drive groups would tend to be present in the early stages of training and at low absolute levels of drive [K. W. Spence, 1956, p. 217]."

These conditions for keeping excitatory potentials in the low range were met in an experiment by Weiss *et al.* (1963). Figure 3E' shows the relationships between the corresponding persuasion variables: as predicted, S's tendency to choose the opinion learned with short delay of argument was greater at lower levels of manifest anxiety than at higher levels of manifest anxiety.

Instrumental Conditioning: Drive

In contrast with the various effects of drive in selective learning, one of which has just been discussed, the effect of drive in conditioning is always to increase speed (Fig. 3C) (e.g., K. W. Spence, 1956; Yamaguchi, 1951). Figure 3C' shows an analogous effect in persuasive communication: speed of agreement is faster for the two high manifest anxiety groups than for the two low anxiety groups (Fig. 3C') (Weiss *et al.*, 1963).

Instrumental Conditioning: Argument Strength

Speed is an increasing function of magnitude of reinforcement (e.g., Crespi, 1942; Hull, 1951; Zeaman, 1949), as shown in Figs. 3C and 3D. The same relationship is shown between the corresponding persuasion variables in Fig. 3C': speed of agreement is faster for the two groups reinforced with a strong argument than it is for the two groups reinforced with a weak argument (Weiss *et al.*, 1963). In another experiment, however, no significant effect of argument strength was found (Fig. 3D') (Weiss & Pasamanick, 1964).

Instrumental Conditioning: Interaction of Argument Strength and Drive

Figure 3C shows how magnitude of reinforcement and drive combine additively (parallel curves) to determine speed (e.g., Black, 1965; K. W. Spence, 1956; Weiss, 1960). Figure 3C' shows the same relationship between the corresponding learning variables: argument strength and drive combine additively to determine speed of agreement.

Instrumental Conditioning: Number of Persuasion Trials

Speed is an increasing function of the number of reinforced trials, as shown in Figs. 3B and 3D. The same relationship was found between the corresponding persuasion variables: speed of agreement was faster for Ss who were exposed to the persuasive communication twice than it was for Ss who were exposed only once (Figs. 3B' and 3D') (Weiss, 1967b; Weiss & Pasamanick, 1964; Weiss & Weiss, 1968).

Alternative Procedure for Deriving above Predictions

In Hullian theory the independent and dependent variables are linked to a system of theoretical constructs (intervening variables). The system of theoretical constructs permits the prediction of a multiplicity of relationships among the several independent and dependent variables. In the social extensions of learning theory discussed here, the linkages of the independent and dependent variables to the theoretical constructs follow automatically once the analogizing has been done. No additional assumptions are required. For example, in instrumental conditioning, the theoretical construct K is a negatively accelerated decreasing function of delay of reinforcement. The same relationship holds for the corresponding persuasion variable: K is a negatively accelerated decreasing function of delay of argument. Thus, the persuasion variables may be substituted for the corresponding learning variables in the equations of learning theory (Table 1, No. 4).

The relationships among the variables of persuasive communication and the constructs of learning theory are shown in Table 1 and Fig. 4 (with the same numbering of variables in Table 1 and Fig. 4). At the top of Fig. 4 are shown the independent variables, and at the bottom the dependent variables, while the equation inside the rectangle represents the theoretical constructs and the relationships among them.[4] The arrows leading into the rectangle represent the relationships between the independent variables and the theoretical constructs, and these relationships are specified in summary form in Table 1 (items 1−10). The arrow leading out of the rectangle represents the relationships between the final construct, E, and the dependent variables (Table 1, items 11−12). The theoretical con-

---

[4]The oscillatory and threshold intervening variables have been omitted in the interests of simplicity, since these constructs function identically in persuasion theory and learning theory. K. W. Spence (1956) has suggested that the effects of (nonchaining) delay of reinforcement are mediated by an inhibitory variable. For reasons which need not be detailed here, this paper follows K. W. Spence's earlier (1954) formulation in which delay effects are mediated by K.

structs include drive (D), incentive motivation (K), habit strength (H) and inhibitory potential (I) which combine to determine effective excitatory potential (E) in the manner specified by the equation inside the rectangle (Logan, 1959; K. W. Spence, 1954, 1956). It can be seen, therefore, that increases in those independent variables of which H, D, and K are increasing functions will increase excitatory potential (E) (Table 1, items 1, 3, and 6−8, also borrowed drive variables such as manifest anxiety) and that increments in independent variables of which H, D, and K are decreasing functions will decrease E (No. 4, 5, 9, 10). Increasing inhibitory potential (I) also decreases E (No. 2). The equation indicates, moreover, that the effects of the six incentive (K) variables combine additively with the effects of the drive (D) and inhibitory (I) variables. The incentive and drive variables both interact multiplicatively, however, with the effects of habit (H) variables such as number of persuasion trials. Increases in E increase speed linearly (No. 11). In selective learning, the opinion response with the greater momentary $\bar{E}$ will be the opinion chosen (No. 12).

Derivations may be carried out in the regular learning manner (e.g., Hull, 1943; Logan, 1959; K. W. Spence, 1956). As an abbreviated example: (a) K is a decreasing function of delay of argument; (b) K is one of the variables determining $\bar{E}$; (c) speed of agreement is a linear function of $\bar{E}$; and therefore (d) speed of agreement is a negatively

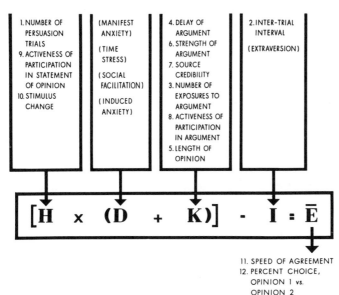

FIG. 4. Substitution of persuasion variables for corresponding learning variables in the Hullian theory of instrumental reward learning.

accelerated decreasing function of delay of argument. Where it seems advantageous, the persuasion variables may be substituted for the corresponding learning variables in other devices of learning theory (so that one could entertain the notion of fractional anticipatory argument responses) and in learning theories other than the Hullian.

INITIAL AND BOUNDARY CONDITIONS

Any theory is intended to apply only within a limited range of conditions. "Ideally all such limitations should be stated explicitly by the theorist although, in practice, he may not have recognized some of these and may not yet be ready to specify others [Logan, 1959]." Since the theory of persuasion developed here is based on analogies with learning research and theory, some of the most essential initial and boundary conditions are also based on analogies with learning. Some points have already been made, since definitions of the instrumental conditioning and selective learning persuasion situations are, in effect, statements of initial and boundary conditions.

Initial State of the Attitude Response

In instrumental conditioning the aim of the experimenter is to "limit the investigation to the study of the strengthening of a single response," and the experimenter therefore attempts "to minimize the occurrence of competing responses [K. W. Spence, 1956, p. 38]." In instrumental attitude conditioning, opinions competing with the to-be-learned opinion must also be minimized. It is therefore necessary to limit the experiment either to the strengthening of an opinion which S already holds, or to the establishment of a learned opinion in Ss who have (approximately) no previously learned opinion on a given topic (see Fig. 2). If Ss were to be persuaded against their initial opinion, this would constitute, not conditioning, but habit reversal. This distinction is essential, since the same independent variables may have diametrically opposite effects in the two situations. For example, increasing drive improves performance in conditioning and impairs a habit reversal. When more than one habit is involved, all responses are increased in strength by an increment in drive, but the response with the greatest habit is the one most strengthened, because of the multiplicative relation between D and H (e.g., Kendler & Lachman, 1958; see also Carment, 1961; Cervin, 1955; Cottrell & Wack, 1967; J. T. Spence & Spence, 1966; Zajonc & Sales, 1966).

Boundary Conditions of Delay

One boundary condition was discovered in the course of research (Weiss *et al.*, 1965). The neutral material which was inserted between the opinion statement and the argument was read aloud by Ss, and delay of argument was regulated either by interrupting Ss after the appropriate interval (5 and 20 seconds) or without interruption by the use of neutral material designed to last the appropriate interval (mean delay = 4 and 20 seconds). Speed of agreement was an increasing function of delay with the interruption method and a decreasing function of delay with the noninterruption method. This effect is explicable in terms of the notion that interruption is punitive, either because it has been associated with incorrectness and inadequacy of performance in most Ss' learning history, or for even more fundamental reasons (Mandler & Watson, 1966). The interruption method thus confounds a true delay of argument effect with a relatively powerful delay of punishment (interruption) effect operating in the opposite direction.

In delay of argument studies, care has also been taken to conceal the relationship between opinion statement and argument. If this relationship is immediately obvious to a delayed-argument S as he reads the communications, then delay is effectively zero. The communications were constructed so that, when opinion statement and argument were separated by a brief intervening passage, it was not obvious that they formed a single message. The theory should be regarded as applying only to research in which the content of the argument and the conditions under which the argument is administered (e.g., delay) do not differ greatly from one persuasion trial to the next.

CLASSICAL CONDITIONING OF ATTITUDES

Primary Concepts

A persuasive communication may explicitly state the opinion to be learned, or it may merely imply an opinion, leaving it to the S to draw the unstated conclusion (e.g., Hovland & Mandell, 1952). In the instrumental conditioning of attitudes, the opinion to be learned is explicitly stated in the communication. In the classical conditioning of attitudes the opinion to be learned is merely implied by the communication, and S is left to draw the unstated conclusion for himself. In this theory the communication-element which implies the opinion is called an opinion-eliciting argument. The technique for the construction of opinion-eliciting arguments is adapted from the work of McGuire (1960a,b,c). The opinion to be learned is the conclusion of a syllogism. The communication includes the premises of the syllogism (the opinion-eliciting argument), but not the conclusion. The dependent variable is S's belief in the conclusion of the syllogism.

Research based on this classical conditioning model requires persuasive communications which incorporate two elements: (1) the *opinion-eliciting argument* (syllogism premises); and (2) the *cue statement*, two (neutral) words which immediately precede the opinion-eliciting argument and will later constitute part of the test used to measure attitude acquisition. The cue statement precedes the opinion-eliciting argument, so that a subject listening to (or reading) the communication will first hear the cue statement, followed by the opinion-eliciting argument (syllogism premises), and then draw the conclusion implied by the argument. This sequence of events may be regarded as analogous to the sequence: conditioned stimulus (CS), unconditioned stimulus (UCS), unconditioned response (UR) (Fig. 5). The cue statement is the conditioned stimulus, and the opinion-eliciting argument is the unconditioned stimulus which elicits the implied opinion—the unconditioned response. Through repetition of the sequence the implied opinion (UR) becomes conditioned to the cue statement (CS) and thus becomes a conditioned opinion (CR) as shown in Fig. 5.[5]

INDEPENDENT VARIABLES: RULES OF CORRESPONDENCE

The ideas just developed are systematically expanded in this section. The first two columns of Table 2 (items 1–10) summarize the rules of correspondence assumed among the independent variables

---

[5]This basic analogy fits the classical defense conditioning and classical reward conditioning paradigms about equally well. In the discussion which follows, the defense conditioning paradigm will be favored, partly because of hunch, partly because defense conditioning provides a somewhat better understood model, and partly because of the surreptitious influence of consistency-dissonance theories which suggest that opinion-eliciting arguments should be drive-inducing (e.g., McGuire, 1960b, 1960c). In any case, the analogies between the independent variables in conditioning and persuasion (Table 2, Columns 1–2) constitute the heart of the theory, the other formulations (e.g., Fig. 7) are more provisional.

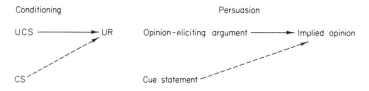

FIG. 5. Corresponding paradigms for classical conditioning and persuasive communication. (From Weiss, Weiss & Chalupa, 1967.)

of classical conditioning and the independent variables of persuasive communication.

Acquisition and Extinction Trials

Each exposure to the complete communication consists of a paired presentation of the cue statement (CS) and the argument (UCS), and hence represents a reinforced trial (Table 2, No. 1). A persuasion trial on which the cue statement is not followed by the opinion-eliciting argument therefore represents an unreinforced (extinction or partial reinforcement) trial (No. 3).

UCS-Strength

If the opinion-eliciting argument is analogous to the UCS, then the power of the opinion-eliciting argument to convincingly imply an opinion is analogous to the strength of the UCS (No. 5). The credibility of the source of the argument affects the power of the argument to convincingly imply the opinion and, hence, also corresponds to UCS strength (No. 6).

CS Variables and Stimulus Generalization

According to our basic paradigm, the cue statement is analogous to the conditioned stimulus in classical conditioning. A change in the cue statement, from persuasion to testing, should then correspond to CS-change and operate through a stimulus generalization mechanism (No. 8). The physical intensity (e.g., brightness) of the cue statement and, perhaps, the distinctiveness or vividness of the cue statement correspond to CS-intensity (No. 9). The time interval between the beginning of the cue statement (CS) and the opinion-eliciting argument (UCS) is analogous to the CS-UCS interval. This analog of CS-UCS interval may be varied either by varying the length of the cue statement (delayed conditioning) or, more appropriately, by interposing some neutral material between the cue statement and the argument (trace conditioning) (No. 10).

TABLE 2
RULES OF CORRESPONDENCE RELATING THE VARIABLES IN
CLASSICAL CONDITIONING AND PERSUASIVE COMMUNICATION[a]

Persuasion	Classical conditioning	Hullian construct	Function relating variable to construct
1. Number of persuasion trials	Number of reinforced trials	H	Increasing, negatively accelerated
2. Interval between persuasion trials	Intertrial interval	I	Decreasing
3. Number of exposures to cue statement alone	Number of unreinforced trials	I	Increasing
4. Number of exposures to argument alone	Number of exposures to UCS without CS	D	Increasing
5. Argument strength	UCS Strength	D	Increasing, negatively accelerated
6. Source credibility	UCS Strength	D	Increasing, negatively accelerated
7. Length of argument	UCS Duration	H	Decreasing
8. Cue statement change	CS-Change (stimulus generalization)	H	Decreasing, negatively accelerated
9. Cue statement intensity or vividness	CS-Intensity	H, I	Complex
10. Cue statement– Argument interval	CS-UCS Interval	H, I	Complex
11. Speed (1/latency) of agreement	Speed (1/latency)	$\overline{E}$	Increasing, normal-ogive
12. Probability of agreement	Probability	$\overline{E}$	Increasing, normal-ogive
13. Calculated excitatory potential	Calculated excitatory potential	$\overline{E}$	Linear
14. Amplitude of agreement	Amplitude	$\overline{E}$	–
15. Magnitude of agreement	Magnitude	$\overline{E}$	–
16. Number of exposures to cue statement alone until opinion is extinguished	Number of trials to extinction	$\overline{E}$	Increasing, linear?

[a]Relation to Hullian constructs also shown.

Borrowed Variables

As in instrumental attitude conditioning, learning variables or analogs of learning variables, such as score on the manifest anxiety scale, may be borrowed without modification in order to determine whether they can enrich the present theory by continuing to function correctly outside their original research context or boundary conditions.

DEPENDENT VARIABLES: RULES OF CORRESPONDENCE

In the two preceding sections we have specified the kind of learning situation (classical conditioning) to which our persuasion situation is analogous, and we have developed a dictionary of analogies between learning and persuasion independent variables. These analogies do not have testable implications until analogies between learning and persuasion dependent variables are also developed. In classical conditioning research, amplitude, probability, latency, and resistance to extinction have all been used as dependent variables. In research guided by Hullian theory, the strength of the intervening variable determining all such measures, excitatory potential ($\bar{E}$), may be directly calculated from probability data according to procedures detailed by Hull (1943).

An analog of latency (or its reciprocal, speed) is already familiar from the discussion of instrumental attitude conditioning. Latency of agreement has been measured in classical attitude conditioning (Table 2, No. 11) with only a slight modification of the instrumental apparatus. The cue statement was projected on the screen, and below it was projected the opinion conditioned through persuasive communication. The cue statement was the two words which had immediately preceded the opinion-eliciting argument in the persuasive communication. The Ss were instructed to first look at the top (cue statement), next the bottom (opinion), and then to signify their agreement (if they agreed) by moving a lever toward the opinion. Latency was measured from the projection of the statement until the movement of the lever, just as in instrumental attitude conditioning. This procedure also affords a measure of probability of agreement, corresponding to probability in classical conditioning. If an S has been exposed to four persuasive communications and agrees with three, his probability of agreement is 75 % (No. 12).

Figure 6 shows a linear relationship between speed and probability of agreement. In separate analyses covering single versus repeated exposures to persuasive communication and reading aloud versus listening to the persuasive communication, the linear trend was

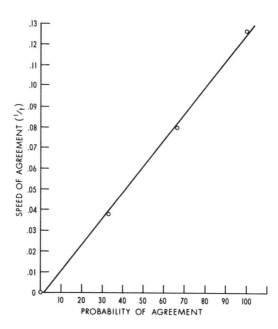

FIG. 6.   Linear relationship between speed of agreement and probability of agreement in classical attitude conditioning.

always significant well beyond the .001 level and always accounted for more than 99% of the between variance. The nonlinear (quadratic and cubic) residuals were nonsignificant and negligible in the amount of variance explained (Weiss, 1968).

Excitatory potential ($\overline{E}$) may be directly calculated from the probability data, following the normal integral procedure specified by Hull (1943) (No. 13). Hull's calculational procedure yields an increasing normal-ogive relationship between probability and excitatory potential. Since speed of agreement was found to be linearly related to probability of agreement in classical attitude conditioning, it too bears an ogival relationship to excitatory potential.

Hull (1943, 1952) limited his treatment of amplitude to responses under the control of the autonomic nervous system, and Spence (1956) did not employ amplitude measures in his eyelid studies, but for pragmatic rather than basic theoretical reasons. Our rejection of amplitude measures also had a pragmatic basis. Amplitude of agreement may be measured by allowing S to indicate how strongly he agrees (if he agrees) by moving the lever along a graduated scale of agreement (No. 14). These amplitude measures did not bear any consistent relationship to excitatory potential, much less the specifically linear relationship specified in Hullian theory (e.g., Hull, 1952). A further indication of the low construct validity of the amplitude measure was its failure to vary with the independent variables in the required manner (Weiss, 1968; Weiss & Weiss, 1968).[6]

Resistance to extinction has not been studied, but could, in principle, be measured by repeatedly presenting the cue statement unaccompanied by the argument and determining through repeated testings when S ceases to agree (No. 16). The dependent variables actually employed in this research were then speed, probability, and calculated excitatory potential, all of which functioned similarly, with speed proving to be the most discriminating.

EXPERIMENTAL PROCEDURE

While there are essential differences of detail among the experiments, the following procedure is typical. The Ss were undergraduates. The design was a 2×2 factorial with 40 Ss in each of the four cells. There were two levels of number of persuasion trials (1 versus 3 readings of the persuasive communications) and two levels of strength of argument. There was also a no-persuasion control group ($N = 40$) which was exposed to the same buffer communications as the experimental groups, but not to the persuasive communications.

Under the impression that he was participating in a study of "speech patterns and decision-making" each experimental S read three persuasive communications and three buffers into a tape recorder. One-trial Ss read each communication once and 3-trial Ss read each communication three times. There were two reading sessions within the 30 to 50 minute experimental period, each immediately followed by attitude measurement. The first reading session covered two persuasive communications and one buffer, and the second, one persuasive and one buffer.

In order to study "conditioning" rather than "habit reversal" the persuasive communications were directed at fictitious opinion topics, on which 96−98% of a sample of 100 similar undergraduates had no initial opinion. These were: (1) the Bonda Fossil was a bird, (2) the Kopaks are descended from the ancient Mongols, and (3) Bayzin was

---

[6]The amplitude measuring procedure also affords an acceptable measure of probability of agreement, an excessively variable magnitude (Humphreys, 1943) measure (No. 15), and a useless measure of decision time which behaves quite differently from the latency measure described above.

considerate of his troops. The Bayzin communication concerned a (fictitious) thirteenth century Turkish general. The premises (argued with different strength for the two argument conditions) were (1) Great generals are considerate of their troops, and (2) Bayzin was a great general.

The attitude measuring apparatus assessed each S's probability and latency of agreement with the opinion after S had been exposed to persuasive communication. The cue statement was projected on a screen, and below it was projected the opinion conditioned through persuasive communication (e.g., cue statement: "Asia Minor"; opinion: "Bayzin was considerate of his troops"). Each S was instructed to look first at the top (cue statement), next the bottom (opinion) and then to signify his agreement (if he agreed) by moving a lever toward the opinion. Latency was measured automatically from the projection of the statement until the movement of the lever, just as in instrumental conditioning. (Most other details also follow instrumental procedure, where applicable; e.g., in deception of Ss.) Mean speeds were computed for each S from his three latency scores.

PREDICTIONS AND RESULTS

Rules of correspondence have been assumed between the variables of classical conditioning and the variables of persuasive communication. Theoretically, the functional relationships between the conditioning variables should also hold between the corresponding persuasion variables. As before, the left column of Fig. 3 shows the learning relationships predicted by Hullian theory and typically found in learning research. To the right of each learning relationship is shown the results of the writer's experiments on the corresponding persuasion variables.

Number of Persuasion Trials

Conditioned response strength is an increasing function of the number of conditioning trials (Fig. 3F). The same relationship was found between the corresponding persuasion variables: speed of agreement was faster for Ss who were exposed to the persuasive communication three times than it was for Ss exposed only once (Fig. 3F') (Weiss et al., 1968a; Weiss & Weiss, 1968).

Argument Strength

Conditioned response strength is an increasing function of UCS strength (Ross & Spence, 1960; Spence & Platt, 1966), as shown in

Fig. 3F. Figure 3F' shows an analogous relationship in persuasive communication: speed of agreement is faster for the two groups persuaded with a strong argument than it is for the two groups persuaded with a weak argument (Weiss *et al.*, 1968a).

Interaction of Argument Strength and Trials

Figure 3F shows how UCS strength and number of conditioning trials combine multiplicatively (diverging curves) to determine CR strength (e.g., K. W. Spence, 1956; K. W. Spence & Platt, 1966). Figure 3F' shows an analogous relationship in persuasive communication: argument strength and number of persuasion trials combine multiplicatively (diverging curves) to determine speed of agreement (Weiss *et al.*, 1968a).

Source Credibility

In credibility research the source has typically been individual: a low-credibility person or publication constitutes one experimental condition and a high-credibility person or publication constitutes the other. If the source were a group (eyewitnesses, experts, newspapers, co-religionists) it would be possible to vary the degree of consensus among the group source (0, 25, 50, 75, 100% of the experts). This aspect of credibility, which may be called source consensus, is simple to vary quantitatively. Figure 3G shows conditioned response strength as an increasing negatively accelerated function of UCS strength (Ross & Spence, 1960; K. W. Spence & Platt, 1966). Figure 3G' shows the same relationship between the corresponding persuasion variables: probability of agreement is a negatively accelerated increasing function of source consensus (Weiss, Weiss, & Chalupa, 1968b). Other experiments in which only two levels of consensus are compared also demonstrate consensus effects (Weiss, 1967a; Weiss *et al.*, 1964; also our unpublished data in Fig. 3H').

Interaction of Source Credibility and Trials

Figure 3H shows how UCS strength and number of conditioning trials combine multiplicatively (diverging curves) to determine CR strength (e.g., K. W. Spence, 1956; K. W. Spence & Platt, 1966). Figure 3H' shows an analogous relationship in preliminary data from a current study of persuasive communication: source consensus and number of exposures to persuasive communication appear to combine multiplicatively to determine speed of agreement. Unlike other data reported here, this result was not statistically significant at the time this chapter was written.

Alternative Procedures for Deriving above Predictions

Once the assumptions of correspondence among persuasion variables and conditioning variables have been made, it requires no additional assumptions to substitute persuasion variables for the corresponding conditioning variables in the equations of learning theory. The relationships among the variables of persuasive communication and the constructs of learning theory are shown in Table 2 and Fig. 7 (with the same numbering of variables in Table 2 and Fig. 7). At the top of Fig. 7 are shown the independent variables, and at the bottom the dependent variables, while the equation inside the rectangle represents the theoretical constructs and the relationships among them.[7] The arrows leading into the rectangle represent the relationships between the independent variables and the theoretical constructs, and these relationships are specified in summary form in Table 2 (items 1 − 10). The arrow leading out of the rectangle represents the relationships between the final construct, $\bar{E}$, and the dependent variables (Nos. 11, 12, 13, 16). The theoretical constructs include drive (D), habit strength (H), and inhibitory potential (I) which combine to determine effective excitatory potential $(\bar{E})$ in the manner specified by the equation inside the rectangle (Logan, 1954, 1959; K. W. Spence, 1956, 1960; J. T. Spence & Spence, 1966). It can be seen, therefore, that increases in those independent variables of which H and D are increasing functions will increase excitatory potential $(\bar{E})$ (Table 2, items 1, 4, 5, 6; also borrowed drive variables such as manifest anxiety) and that increments in independent variables of which H and D are decreasing functions will decrease $\bar{E}$ (Nos. 7 and 8). Increasing inhibitory potential (I) also decreases $\bar{E}$ (Nos. 2 and 3). The equation indicates, moreover, that the drive

---

[7]While UCS strength has been shown to affect both drive (D) and habit (H) in eyelid conditioning (K. W. Spence, Haggard, & Ross, 1958; Trapold & Spence, 1960), the procedures for separating these effects are inappropriate to research in persuasive communication. The differentiation of these two effects of UCS strength is most essential in accounting for switches in UCS strength from one series of trials to another, whereas the present theory is restricted to constant conditions of argument strength across trials. This restriction permits a simplification in which the analogs of UCS strength may be regarded as affecting only D.

The effects of CS-intensity variables may be handled either through a stimulus dynamism construct (Grice & Hunter, 1964; Hull, 1952) or through the stimulus generalization of H and I, as shown (Logan, 1954; Perkins, 1953). Length of argument corresponds to UCS duration. Providing that argument length can be increased without also increasing argument strength, argument length effects may be attributed to H (Dufort, 1967).

variables interact multiplicatively with the effects of habit (*H*) variables, such as number of persuasion trials, to determine $\bar{E}$. Increases in $\bar{E}$ increase the dependent measures of opinion response strength (Nos. 11, 12, 13, 16).

Derivations may be carried out in the regular learning manner (e.g., Hull, 1943; Logan, 1959; K. W. Spence, 1956). As an abbreviated example: (a) *H* is an increasing function of number of exposures to persuasive communication; (b) *D* is an increasing function of argument strength; (c) *H* and *D* combine multiplicatively ($D \times H$) to determine $\bar{E}$; (d) speed of agreement is a linear function of $\bar{E}$; therefore (e) number of exposures and argument strength combine multiplicatively to determine speed of agreement. Where it seems advantageous, the persuasion variables may be substituted for the corresponding learning variables in other devices of learning theory and in learning theories other than the Hullian.

INITIAL AND BOUNDARY CONDITIONS

Because of a strong "sleeper effect" of source credibility (Hovland & Weiss, 1951), we found it important to have opinion measurement follow each persuasive communication as closely as possible in credibility studies. Most other necessary points have already been

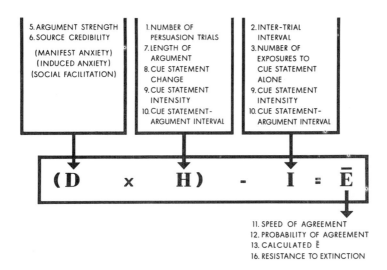

FIG. 7. Substitution of persuasion variables for corresponding conditioning variables in the Hullian theory of classical defense conditioning.

made, since the definition of the classical attitude conditioning situation is, in effect, a statement of initial and boundary conditions. Contrasts between the instrumental and classical attitude conditioning situations serve to emphasize some of these defining boundary conditions. The differences between instrumental and classical conditioning of attitudes thus include the distinction between explicit (instrumental) and implicit (classical) conclusion-drawing, and the distinction between opinion-supporting (instrumental) and opinion-eliciting (syllogism premises, classical) arguments. There are also similarities between the two conditioning situations. Classical conditioning, like instrumental conditioning, represents the study of the strengthening of a single response tendency. Consequently, the assumptions regarding initial opinion, etc., made in connection with the discussion of instrumental persuasion also apply here.

SUMMARY

Employing the general approach which Neal Miller (1959) has called "extension of liberalized S-R theory," a theory of the effects of certain aspects of persuasive communication upon the learning and motivation of attitudes was developed. The results of eleven experiments designed to test the theory were reported. Hull-Miller-Spence learning theory was used as a model for persuasion situations analogous to instrumental reward conditioning, selective learning, and classical conditioning. Systematic analogies (rules of correspondence) were drawn between learning independent variables and such persuasion independent variables as source credibility, delay of argument and number of persuasion trials. Analogies were also drawn between learning dependent variables and such persuasion dependent variables as speed of agreement and forced-choice behavior. Once such rules of correspondence are assumed, the functional relationships holding among the learning variables in the learning theory model should also hold among the corresponding persuasion variables. In general, the relations among the persuasion variables were found to be isomorphic with the relations among the corresponding learning variables. Thus, for example, delay of argument in persuasion was considered to be analogous to delay of reinforcement in instrumental conditioning and selective learning. As in selective learning, our subjects learned to choose the opinion response which had been "reinforced" with the shorter delay. In attitude "conditioning," a delay of argument gradient of the same shape as a delay of reinforcement gradient was discovered. Again, as in conditioning, delay combined multiplicatively with the number of persuasion "trials" to determine attitude strength. Results of other experiments also supported the theory.

References

Beier, E. M. Effects of trial-to-trial variation in magnitude of reward upon an instrumental running response. Unpublished doctoral dissertation, Yale University, 1958.

Black, R. W. On the combination of drive and incentive motivation. *Psychological Review*, 1965, **72**, 310-317.

Bugelski, B. R. & Hersen, M. Conditioning acceptance or rejection of information. *Journal of Experimental Psychology*, 1966, **71**, 619-623.

Campbell, N. R. *Physics, the elements*. Cambridge, England: Cambridge University Press, 1920.

Carment, D. W. Ascendent-submissive behaviour in pairs of human subjects as a function of their emotional responsiveness and opinion-strength. *Canadian Journal of Psychology*, 1961, **15**, 45-51.

Carriero, J. N. The conditioning of negative attitudes to unfamiliar items of information. *Journal of Verbal Learning and Verbal Behavior*, 1967, **6**, 128-135.

Castaneda, A., & Palermo, D. S. Psychomotor performance as a function of amount of training and stress. *Journal of Experimental Psychology*, 1955, **50**, 175-179.

Cervin, V. Experimental investigation of behaviour in social situations. I. Behaviour under opposition. *Canadian Journal of Psychology*, 1955, **9**, 107-116.

Clark, R. E. The role of drive (time stress) in complex learning: An emphasis on prelearning phenomena. *Journal of Experimental Psychology*, 1962, **63**, 57-61.

Cottrell, N. B., & Wack, D. L. Energizing effects of cognitive dissonance upon dominant and subordinate responses. *Journal of Personality and Social Psychology*, 1967, **6**, 132-138.

Crespi, L. P. Quantitative variation of incentive and performance in the white rat. *American Journal of Psychology*, 1942, **55**, 467-517.

Dollard, J., & Miller, N. E. *Personality and psychotherapy*. New York: McGraw-Hill, 1950.

Doob, L. W. The behavior of attitudes. *Psychological Review*, 1947, **54**, 135-156.

Dufort, R. H. Eyelid conditioning as a function of UCS duration with drive equated. *Journal of Experimental Psychology*, 1967, **74**, 321-323.

Eysenck, H. J. Extraversion and the acquisition of eyeblink and GSR conditioned responses. *Psychological Bulletin*, 1965, **63**, 258-270.

Franks, C. M. Personality factors and the rate of conditioning. *British Journal of Psychology*, 1957, **48**, 119-126.

Grice, G. R., & Hunter, J. J. Stimulus intensity effects depend on the type of experimental design. *Psychological Review*, 1964, **71**, 247-256.

Hildum, D. C., & Brown, R. W. Verbal reinforcement and interviewer bias. *Journal of Abnormal and Social Psychology*, 1956, **53**, 108-111.

Hovland, C. I., Janis, I. L., & Kelley, H. H. *Communication and persuasion.* New Haven: Yale University Press, 1953.

Hovland, C. I., & Mandell, W. An experimental comparison of conclusion-drawing by the communicator and by the audience. *Journal of Abnormal and Social Psychology,* 1952, **47**, 581-588.

Hovland, C. I., & Weiss, W. The influence of source credibility on communication effectiveness. *Public Opinion Quarterly,* 1951, **15**, 635-650.

Hull, C. L. *Principles of behavior.* New York: Appleton, 1943.

Hull, C. L. *Essentials of behavior.* New Haven: Yale University Press, 1951.

Hull, C. L. *A behavior system.* New Haven: Yale University Press, 1952.

Humphreys, L. G. Measures of strength of conditioned eyelid responses. *Journal of General Psychology,* 1943, **29**, 101-111.

Janis, I. L. Motivational effects of different sequential arrangements of conflicting arguments: A theoretical analysis. In C. I. Hovland (Ed.), *The order of presentation in persuasion.* New Haven: Yale University Press, 1957. Pp. 170-186.

Janis, I. L., & King, B. T. The influence of role-playing in opinion change. *Journal of Abnormal and Social Psychology,* 1954, **49**, 211-218.

Kendler, H. H., & Lachman, R. Habit reversal as a function of schedule of reinforcement and drive strength. *Journal of Experimental Psychology,* 1958, **55**, 584-591.

King, B. T., & Janis, I. L. Comparison of the effectiveness of improvised vs. non-improvised role-playing in producing opinion change. *Human Relations,* 1956, **9**, 177-186.

Krasner, L., Knowles, J. B., & Ullmann, L. P. Effect of verbal conditioning of attitudes on subsequent motor performance. *Journal of Personality and Social Psychology,* 1965, **1**, 407-412.

Lachman, R. The model in theory construction. *Psychological Review,* 1960, **67**, 113-129.

Leventhal, H., Singer, R., & Jones, S. Effects of fear and specificity of recommendation upon attitudes and behavior. *Journal of Personality and Social Psychology,* 1965, **2**, 20-29.

Lipsitt, L., & Castaneda, A. Effects of delayed reward on choice behavior and response speeds in children. *Journal of Comparative and Physiological Psychology,* 1958, **51**, 57-65.

Loess, H. B. The effect of variation of motivational level and changes in motivational level on performance in learning. Unpublished doctoral dissertation, State University of Iowa, 1952.

Logan, F. A. The role of delay of reinforcement in determining reaction potential. *Journal of Experimental Psychology,* 1952, **43**, 393-399.

Logan, F. A. A note on stimulus intensity dynamism. *Psychological Review,* 1954, **61**, 77-80.

Logan, F. A. The Hull-Spence approach. In S. Koch (Ed.), *Psychology: A study of a science.* Vol. 2. *General systematic formulations, learning, and special processes.* New York: McGraw-Hill, 1959. Pp. 293-358.

Logan, F. A. *Incentive.* New Haven: Yale University Press, 1960.

Logan, F. A., Beier, E., & Ellis, R. A. The effect of varied reinforcement on speed of locomotion. *Journal of Experimental Psychology,* 1955, **49**, 260-266.

Lott (née Eisman), B. J. Attitude formation: The development of a color preference response through mediated generalization. *Journal of Abnormal and Social Psychology,* 1955, **50**, 321-326.

Mandler, G., & Watson, D. L. Anxiety and the interruption of behavior. In C. D. Spielberger (Ed.), *Anxiety and behavior*. New York: Academic Press, 1966. P. 263-290.

McGuire, W. J. Order of presentation as a factor in "conditioning" persuasiveness. In C. I. Hovland (Ed.), *The order of presentation in persuasion*. New Haven: Yale University Press, 1957. Pp. 98-114.

McGuire, W. J. A syllogistic analysis of cognitive relationships. In C. I. Hovland, and M. J. Rosenberg (Eds.), *Attitude organization and change*. New Haven: Yale University Press, 1960. Pp. 65-111. (a)

McGuire, W. J. Cognitive consistency and attitude change. *Journal of Abnormal and Social Psychology*, 1960, **60**, 345-353. (b)

McGuire, W. J. Direct and indirect effects of dissonance-producing messages. *Journal of Abnormal and Social Psychology*, 1960, **60**, 354-358. (c)

Miller, N., & Campbell, D. T. Recency and primacy in persuasion as a function of the timing of speeches and measurements. *Journal of Abnormal and Social Psychology*, 1959, **59**, 1-9.

Miller, N. E. Extensions of liberalized S-R theory. In S. Koch (Ed.), *Psychology: A study of a science*. Vol. 2. *General systematic formulations, learning, and special processes*. New York: McGraw-Hill, 1959. Pp. 196-292.

Miller, N. E., & Dollard, J. *Social learning and imitation*. New Haven: Yale University Press, 1941.

Nagel, E. *The structure of science*. New York: Harcourt, Brace, & World, 1961.

Oppenheimer, R. Analogy in science. *American Psychologist*, 1956, **11**, 127-135.

Perin, C. T. A quantitative investigation of the delay of reinforcement gradient. *Journal of Experimental Psychology*, 1943, **32**, 37-51.

Perkins, C. C., Jr. The relation between conditioned stimulus intensity and response strength. *Journal of Experimental Psychology*, 1953, **46**, 225-231.

Radtke, R. C. Effects of verbally mediated drive on a motor response and evaluative ratings. *Journal of Experimental Psychology*, 1967, **73**, 22-27.

Razran, G. Conditioning away social bias by the luncheon technique. *Psychological Bulletin*, 1938, **35**, 693.

Razran, G. The conditioned evocation of attitudes. *Journal of Experimental Psychology*, 1954, **48**, 278-282.

Rhine, R. J. A concept-formation approach to attitude acquisition. *Psychological Review*, 1958, **65**, 362-370.

Rosnow, R. L. "Conditioning" the direction of opinion change in persuasive communication. *Journal of Social Psychology*, 1966, **69**, 291-303.

Ross, L. E., & Spence, K. W. Eyelid conditioning performance under partial reinforcement as a function of UCS intensity. *Journal of Experimental Psychology*, 1960, **59**, 379-382.

Scott, W. A. Attitude change through reward of verbal behavior. *Journal of Abnormal and Social Psychology*, 1957, **55**, 72-75.

Spence, J. T., & Spence, K. W. The motivational components of manifest anxiety: Drive and drive stimuli. In C. D. Spielberger (Ed.), *Anxiety and behavior*. New York: Academic Press, 1966. Pp. 291-326.

Spence, K. W. Current interpretation of learning data and some recent developments in stimulus-response theory. In D. K. Adams *et al.*, *Learning theory, personality theory, and clinical research*. (The Kentucky Symposium) New York: Wiley, 1954. Pp. 1-21.

Spence, K. W. *Behavior theory and conditioning*. New Haven: Yale University Press, 1956.

Spence, K. W. *Behavior theory and learning.* Englewood Cliffs, N. J.: Prentice-Hall, 1960.

Spence, K. W., & Goldstein, H. Eyelid conditioning performance as a function of emotion-producing instructions. *Journal of Experimental Psychology,* 1961, **62,** 291-294.

Spence, K. W., Haggard, D. F., & Ross, L. E. UCS intensity and associative (habit) strength of the eyelid CR. *Journal of Experimental Psychology,* 1958, **55,** 404-411.

Spence, K. W., & Platt, J. R. UCS intensity and performance in eyelid conditioning. *Psychological Bulletin,* 1966, **65,** 1-10.

Staats, A. W., & Staats, C. K. Attitudes established by classical conditioning. *Journal of Abnormal and Social Psychology,* 1958, **57,** 37-40.

Tannenbaum, P. H. & Gengel, R. W. Generalization of attitude change through congruity principle relationships. *Journal of Personality and Social Psychology,* 1966, **3,** 299-304.

Taylor, J. A. A personality scale of manifest anxiety. *Journal of Abnormal and Social Psychology,* 1953, **48,** 285-290.

Trapold, M. A., & Spence, K. W. Performance changes in eyelid conditioning as related to the motivational and reinforcing properties of the UCS. *Journal of Experimental Psychology,* 1960, **59,** 209-213.

Weiss, R. F. Deprivation and reward magnitude effects on speed throughout the goal gradient. *Journal of Experimental Psychology,* 1960, **60,** 384-390.

Weiss, R. F. Persuasion and the acquisition of attitudes: Models from conditioning and selective learning. *Psychological Reports,* 1962, **11,** 709-732.

Weiss, R. F. Defection from social movements and subsequent recruitment to new movements. *Sociometry,* 1963, **26,** 1-20.

Weiss, R. F. Consensus technique for the variation of source credibility. *Psychological Reports,* 1967, **20,** 1159-1162. (a)

Weiss, R. F. A delay of argument gradient in the instrumental conditioning of attitudes. *Psychonomic Science,* 1967, **8,** 457-458. (b)

Weiss, R. F. Latency, amplitude and probability measures of conditioned attitude strength. Unpublished study, 1968.

Weiss, R. F., Buchanan, W. & Pasamanick, B. Social consensus in persuasive communication. *Psychological Reports,* 1964, **14,** 95-98.

Weiss, R. F., Buchanan, W., & Pasamanick, B. Delay of reinforcement and delay of punishment in persuasive communication. *Psychological Reports,* 1965, **16,** 576.

Weiss, R. F., Chalupa, L. M., Gorman, B. S., & Goodman, N. Classical conditioning of attitudes as a function of number of persuasion trials and argument (UCS) strength. *Psychonomic Science,* 1968, **11,** 59-60.

Weiss, R. F., & Pasamanick, B. Number of exposures to persuasive communication in the instrumental conditioning of attitudes. *Journal of Social Psychology,* 1964, **63,** 373-382.

Weiss, R. F., Rawson, H. E., & Pasamanick, B. Argument strength, delay of argument, and anxiety in the "conditioning" and "selective learning" of attitudes. *Journal of Abnormal and Social Psychology,* 1963, **67,** 157-165.

Weiss, R. F., & Weiss, J. J. Repetition of persuasive communication. Unpublished study, 1968.

Weiss, R. F., Weiss, J. J., & Chalupa, L. M. Classical conditioning of attitudes as a function of source consensus. *Psychonomic Science,* 1968, **9,** 465-466. (b)

Weiss, W. Communicator effectiveness in relation to the strength of the communication. *Psychological Reports,* 1967, **20,** 1037-1038.

Wheeler, L. Toward a theory of behavioral contagion. *Psychological Review*, 1966, **73**, 179-192.

Whiting, J. W. M., & Child, I. L. *Child training and personality*. New Haven: Yale University Press, 1953.

Wolpe, J. *Psychotherapy by reciprocal inhibition*. Stanford, Calif.: Stanford University Press, 1958.

Yamaguchi, H. G. Drive (D) as a function of hours of hunger (h). *Journal of Experimental Psychology*, 1951, **42**, 108-117.

Zajonc, R. B., & Sales, S. M. Social facilitation of dominant and subordinate responses. *Journal of Experimental Social Psychology*, 1966, **2**, 160-168.

Zeaman, D. Response latency as a function of the amount of reinforcement. *Journal of Experimental Psychology*, 1949, **39**, 466-83.

6

Cognitive Learning, Cognitive Response to Persuasion, and Attitude Change[1]

ANTHONY G. GREENWALD

DEPARTMENT OF PSYCHOLOGY
OHIO STATE UNIVERSITY
COLUMBUS, OHIO

It is a common assumption that the effectiveness of a persuasive communication is, at least in part, a function of the extent to which its content is learned and retained by its audience. This assumed learning-persuasion relation is based on a reasonable analogy between the persuasive communication and an informational communication such as a classroom lecture. In the lecture, it is by definition of the educational situation that retention of content is taken as a measure of effectiveness. In the persuasion situation, however, the essential criterion of effectiveness is *acceptance* of content. It remains an empirical question to determine whether acceptance of a persuasive communication is related to retention of its content.

The hypothesis that acceptance of a communication is, in some part, a function of learning or retention of its content has received explicit endorsement by a number of attitude researchers and theorists (e.g., Hovland, Janis, & Kelley, 1953; McGuire, this volume; Miller

[1]Preparation of this report and the research reported here were supported in large part by grants from the National Science Foundation (GS-1601) and the Mershon Social Sciences Program at Ohio State University. The author is particularly indebted to Rosita Daskal Albert, Dallas Cullen, Robert Love, and Joseph Sakumura who have participated actively in various phases of the research reported here. A condensed version of this chapter was presented at the American Psychological Association symposium, "Alternatives to consistency theory in the study of attitude change," Washington, D.C., September, 1967.

& Campbell, 1959; Watts & McGuire, 1964) and has aroused no published opposition. Indeed, this *cognitive learning model* of persuasion is most reasonable. It is widely accepted that cognitions bearing on the object of an attitude form a major component of the structure of the attitude toward that object (see, for example, Campbell, 1947; Katz & Stotland, 1959; Krech, Crutchfield, & Ballachey, 1962; Rokeach, 1960; Smith, Bruner, & White, 1956). Since the individual is not born with his cognitions, but acquires them, there seems to be no reasonable alternative to the assumption that cognitions bearing on attitude objects are learned. Further, the most obvious source of such cognitions is the wealth of persuasive messages to which one is exposed via the public communications media as well as through face-to-face communications.

In light of the overpowering reasonableness of the persuasion-as-a-function-of-retention hypothesis, it is rather surprising how unsupporting the research evidence is. A few studies have directly examined the relation between the learning and attitudinal effects of persuasive communications (Insko, 1964; Miller & Campbell, 1959; Watts & McGuire, 1964). These studies have generally found that both communication retention and persuasion diminish with increasing time between communication and posttest, consistent with the hypothesis that retention is necessary for persuasion. On the other hand, these same studies have found only weak and variable correlations between communication retention and persuasion among subjects tested at the same posttest interval, suggesting that the relation between retention and persuasion is not a necessary one. In a conceptually relevant study on impression formation, Anderson and Hubert (1963) have concluded that there are separate memory systems for retention of a set of person-descriptive adjectives and of the person-impression derived from them; their results thus also suggest little or no necessary relation between a communication's retention and its effectiveness. Additionally, in a number of studies scattered throughout the attitude literature (and reviewed in Hovland *et al.*, 1953), variables shown to affect opinion demonstrably — such as credibility, fear arousal, and organization of arguments — have not been found to have corresponding effects on retention of communicated arguments. Such negative findings on retention measures have typically been used to counter any possible interpretation for obtained attitude change differences in terms of unintentionally induced differences in attention to or retention of communication content. In sum, the research evidence must be interpreted as uncongenial to the hypothesis that persuasion is a function of retention of persuasive arguments. (In partial reviews of the relevant literature, Insko, 1967, and McGuire, 1968, reach similar conclusions.)

It must be concluded that either (a) learning of attitude-relevant cognitions (i.e., persuasive arguments) is unrelated to attitude formation and change; or (b) persuasive communications can induce attitude change without necessarily providing the cognitive content on which the attitude is based. The first conclusion carries the implication that learned cognitions are not fundamental to the structure of attitudes. Rather than accept this conclusion, which runs counter to most conceptions of attitude, it seemed worth some effort to explore sources other than persuasive communications as possible origins of learned attitudinal cognitions.

COGNITIVE RESPONSES TO PERSUASION

There is, of course, an important extracommunication source of cognitive content in the persuasion situation: the cognitive reactions of the communication recipient to incoming persuasive information. When a person receives a communication and is faced with the decision of accepting or rejecting the persuasion, he may be expected to attempt to relate the new information to his existing attitudes, knowledge, feelings, etc. In the course of doing this, he likely rehearses substantial cognitive content beyond that of the persuasive message itself. The present hypothesis is, then, that rehearsal and learning of cognitive responses to persuasion may provide a basis for explaining persisting effects of communications in terms of cognitive learning. The learning of cognitive response content may, indeed, be more fundamental to persuasion than is the learning of communication content.

This hypothesis is not a new one. The following passages from previous works indicate views bearing the essence of the present hypothesis.

> . . . there is reason to expect that those audience members who are already opposed to the point of view being presented may be distracted [from the content of a communication] by "rehearsing" their own arguments while the topic is being presented and will be antagonized by the omission of the arguments on their side [Hovland, Lumsdaine, & Sheffield, 1949, p. 201].

> When exposed to [a persuasive communication], a member of the audience is assumed to react with at least two distinct responses. He thinks of his own [opinion], and also of the [opinion] suggested by the communicator. . . . Merely thinking about the new opinion along with the old would not, in itself,

lead to opinion change. The individual could *memorize* the content of the [new opinion] while his opinion remained unchanged. Practice, which is so important for memorizing verbal material in educational or training situations, is not sufficient for bringing about the *acceptance* of a new opinion [Hovland *et al.*, 1953, p. 11].

It was hypothesized that conformity in the communication situation will increase attitude change to the extent to which implicit *supporting* responses are produced, and decrease attitude change to the extent to which implicit *interfering* responses are produced....

By supporting response is meant any implicit response made by the individual (usually a self-verbalization), which provides arguments in favor of the overt response he makes; which produces further motivations in the direction of the overt response; or which relates the overt response to other stimulus situations. By interfering response is meant any implicit response made by the individual which provides motivation against the overt response he makes; which limits the stimulus situations to which the overt response is applicable; or which is generally irrelevant (such as aggressive or distracting responses) [Kelman, 1953, p. 187, 211].

Despite a number of speculations similar to the ones just cited, there has been no direct experimental exploration of the role of cognitive responses in persuasion, and, in fact, there is not much research that is even relevant. The research on active participation in the communication process (e.g., Hovland *et al.*, 1953, Ch. 7) comes closest to being relevant. Elsewhere, isolated experiments (e.g., Brock, 1967; Janis & Terwilliger, 1962; Kelman, 1953) have explored *dependent* variables approximating the present conception of cognitive responses to persuasion. Research in which cognitive responses to persuasion are employed as *independent* variables in experimental persuasion situations is particularly needed. Before proceeding to a consideration of evidence collected in the author's laboratory, it will be useful to state the present hypothesis with some precision.

It is proposed that the persuasion situation is usefully regarded as a complex stimulus that evokes in the recipient a complex cognitive response. The essential dimensions of the recipient's cognitive response are, at the least, (a) response content, i.e., degree of acceptance versus rejection of the position advocated in the communication, and (b) intensity, or vigor, of response. The latter dimension, as well as other possible dimensions of cognitive response, will not be considered further in this chapter. The essential components of the persuasion situation as a stimulus—that is, as determinant of the cognitive response content—are setting, source, and communication content. An additional major set of determinants of the cognitive response content is the set of characteristics brought by the recipient to the persuasion situation, including his existing repertory of attitude-relevant cognitions as well as personality traits and group memberships.

As in many other treatments of persuasion, the cognitive response analysis assumes that attitude change can be achieved by the modification, through learning, of the recipient's repertory of attitude-relevant cognitions. Such modification might include strengthening of existing cognitions as well as introduction of new ones. The present emphasis on the mediating role of the recipient's own cognitive responses to persuasion may be formulated as an assertion that cognitive modification of attitudes requires active (not necessarily overt) rehearsal of attitude-relevant cognitions at a time when the attitude object or opinion issue is salient. Thus the effects of persuasive communications might range from persuasion—when the recipient rehearses content supporting the advocated position—to boomerang—when the recipient rehearses content opposing the advocated position.

As a consequence of the present emphasis on the recipient's rehearsal of his own responses to persuasion, it is assumed that learning of communication content does *not* play an essential role in mediating the effects of persuasive communications. The present formulation, therefore, is capable of maintaining an analysis of persuasion effects in terms of cognitive learning while being compatible with findings indicating no necessary relation between communication retention and persuasion.

It is possible to formulate the cognitive response analysis in terms of an analogy to the classical conditioning paradigm. In this analogy, the persuasion situation corresponds to the unconditioned stimulus in that it has a response evocation capacity; that is, it influences the content of the recipient's cognitive response. As an analog of the unconditioned response, the cognitive response becomes transferred to the attitude object, which is analogous to the conditioned stimulus of the classical paradigm. While this analogy may be decidedly useful, especially in relating the present analysis to other treatments that have invoked the classical conditioning model (see the chapters by Staats and Weiss in this volume), it would be inappropriate currently to regard the model as more than a possibly suggestive analogy. A point of difficulty that would arise if the model is taken literally, for example, would concern the nature of the conditioned response in persuasion; it would be unnecessarily cumbersome, at this stage, to incorporate in the present analysis an analogy to the conditioning model's assumption that conditioned responses are either fractional components of unconditioned responses or preparatory adjustments to unconditioned stimuli.

STUDIES OF COGNITIVE LEARNING AND ATTITUDE CHANGE

The cognitive response analysis of persuasion has guided a series of experiments conducted at Ohio State University. While the primary focus of this research has concerned the properties and functions of recipients' cognitive responses in persuasion situations, a secondary focus has been on the role of communication content in persuasion. The present section is devoted largely to the findings of completed portions of this research program. The first two subsections deal with experiments in which communication content learning and cognitive response rehearsal have been employed as manipulated independent variables, enabling conclusions about their causal involvement in persuasion. The next two subsections are concerned with experiments in which retention of communicated arguments and occurrence and retention of cognitive responses have been observed as dependent variables; from these experiments it is possible to draw conclusions about the determinants and correlates of cognitive response content and of retention of cognitive responses and communication content. A final subsection provides a brief review of literature on variables influencing the retention of communicated persuasive arguments.

It is to be emphasized that the research program described here is very much in progress. At appropriate points below, the nature of planned and in-progress research will be indicated; these comments will serve, perhaps, more to indicate the author's awareness of questions that remain to be answered than to enlighten the reader.

ATTITUDE CHANGE AND LEARNING OF COMMUNICATION CONTENT

Previous studies of the relationship between communication retention and opinion change have tested this relationship correlationally — subjects received a communication and were subsequently tested for both retention of content and acceptance of the viewpoint of the communication. With the assistance of Rosita Albert and Dallas Cullen, the author conducted a study (unpublished) in which communication retention was a manipulated independent variable, with opinion as the dependent variable. Such a design, it may be noted, is more appropriate to drawing a conclusion about the causal role of communication learning in attitude change than is a correlational design.

The experiment employed three communications concerning United States foreign aid policy. One of these consisted of 6 brief arguments favoring foreign aid, 1 of 6 arguments opposing foreign aid, while the third was composed of all 12 of these arguments and did not draw either a favorable or unfavorable conclusion. For each communication, a group of subjects was asked to rehearse the individual arguments contained in it, in preparation for a subsequent retention test; in addition to these three groups, two other groups received the 12-argument communication, and, after briefly reading it once, in entirety, were asked to rehearse only 6 arguments that had been underlined. For one of these groups, the 6 underlined arguments were those favoring foreign aid, while for the other group the 6 opposing foreign aid were underlined. Subjects were tested for opinion on the issue and then for retention of *all* arguments in their communications (not just rehearsed ones) immediately following the learning task and again, unexpectedly, after a 1-week interval.

For the group receiving the one-sided pro-foreign aid message ($N = 16$), an average of 3.7 (out of 6) arguments were retained for the immediate retention test and 3.1 for the unexpected retention test one week later. The corresponding means for the group receiving the one-sided anti-message ($N = 20$) were 3.6 arguments retained immediately and 2.4 after a week. Since these two groups differed significantly from each other in opinion in the directions advocated in their communications, both immediately ($F = 9.50$, $df = 1, 34$, $p < .01$) and after a week ($F = 7.03$, $p < .02$), these data were consistent with the hypothesis that communication learning and persuasion are related. Among subjects receiving the two-sided communications, those assigned to learn pro arguments ($N = 18$) retained substantially more pro than con arguments ($p < .001$, for each testing); the reverse was true, as expected, for those ($N = 19$) asked to rehearse con arguments ($p < .001$, for each testing); and those asked to learn both sets ($N = 18$) retained approximately equal numbers of each.

The effectiveness of the partial learning assignments for the two-sided communications can be indicated by the fact that subjects retained an average of 3.0 assigned arguments compared to 0.3 nonassigned ones on the immediate retention test; for the delayed retention test, the corresponding means were 1.8 assigned and 0.3 nonassigned arguments. If there is, indeed, a causal relation between argument learning and persuasion, these manipulated differences in retention should have produced corresponding differences in opinion.

However, there were no opinion differences among the three groups receiving two-sided communications, either immediately ($F < 1$, $df = 2, 52$) or after a week ($F < 1$).

It must be concluded that learning of communication content is not a sufficient condition, and perhaps not even a necessary condition, for persuasion. That is, learned arguments supporting one side of the foreign aid issue were ineffective when, at the time of learning, subjects were made aware that credible opposing arguments were available — even though the opposing arguments were poorly retained. This finding stands in contrast with those of studies demonstrating across-cell correlations between learning and persuasion (e.g., Insko, 1964; Miller & Campbell, 1959; Watts & McGuire, 1964). The lack of opinion differences between conditions with decided retention differences in the present study suggests that such previously obtained across-cell correlations should not be interpreted in terms of a causal relation between communication retention and persuasion.

ACCEPTANCE AND RECALL OF IMPROVISED ARGUMENTS

If, as is presently supposed, attitudes change in the direction of cognitive content rehearsed during a persuasion situation, then procedures that manipulate the content of the recipient's cognitive responses should have persuasive effect. A traditional persuasion procedure that may be viewed as a manipulation of cognitive response content is the improvised role-playing procedure in which a subject is asked to deliver a persuasive message supporting a position initially unacceptable to him. The majority of research evidence indicates that role playing produces greater persuasion toward the unacceptable position than does passive receipt of a persuasive communication (cf. Insko, 1967, p. 222). Such results are quite compatible with the present point that a communication recipient's rehearsal of his *own* arguments may be more important in persuasion than is his rehearsal of arguments contained in a communication to which he is exposed. However, some commentators feel that the currently available evidence on role playing is equivocal (see McGuire, 1966, p. 498). Because of this empirical uncertainty, the present research program included an experiment intended to assess the effect of improvised role playing on both acceptance and retention of arguments.

In this experiment (Greenwald & Albert, 1968), each subject improvised five arguments in response to an assignment to advocate either specialized (career preparatory) or general (liberal arts) undergraduate education. Improvisation was obtained in response to five neutrally worded questions that could be answered with an argument supporting either viewpoint. Assignment to positions was random with approximately 90 subjects being assigned to each side. In addition to being exposed to their own improvised arguments supporting one side of the issue, subjects carefully read and studied—for about the same amount of time they had spent improvising—a set of arguments supporting the opposite side that was actually written by another subject in the study. Since each subject's improvisations served once as an improvised set of arguments and once as an externally originated set (for a different subject), this procedure served to equate quality of arguments for the two sets over the sample of subjects, although not necessarily for each subject. After a 20-minute irrelevant task, the subjects were tested for opinion on the general-specialized education issue and were then asked to recall as many arguments as they could of those to which they had been exposed—both their own and the ones that had been improvised by another subject.

Figure 1 gives the opinion and retention results for this study. It may be seen that subjects arrived at opinions consistent, on the average, with the position to which they had been assigned. The opinion difference between the two groups was statistically significant ($F = 7.42$, $df = 1$, 177, $p < .01$). A more powerful effect was obtained with the retention measure, with subjects tending to recall much more of their own improvised arguments than they did of those improvised by another subject ($F = 168.10$, $df = 1,777$, $p < .001$). A supplementary finding was that subjects tended to rate their own arguments as more original than the other's ($p < .001$), indicating that, other things being equal, one tends to evaluate his own thoughts more favorably than others'. In summary, these results demonstrated that the subject's rehearsal of his own cognitions and externally originated cognitions of comparable quality tended to result in attitude change in the direction of the content of the subject's own cognitions. These results support the general trend of findings in the role-playing literature. More importantly for present purposes, they add force to the hypothesis that the recipient's rehearsal of his own cognitive responses plays an important role in persuasion.

It should be noted that the Greenwald-Albert experiment does not provide an explanation of the special efficacy of the recipient's own improvised arguments. It could be that subjects' increased retention of their own arguments was responsible for the observed attitude effect; however, alternative explanations are possible in terms of

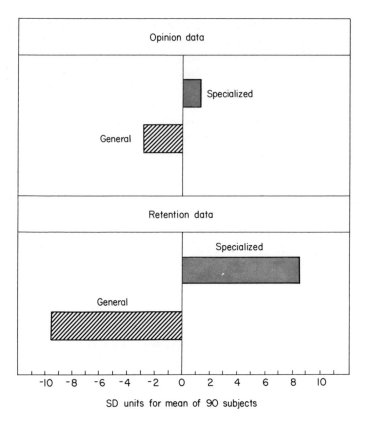

FIG. 1.   Opinion and retention as a function of position assigned for improvisation. (Bars are labeled with the assigned position. Positive scores on the opinion measure represent favorableness to specialized education; positive scores on the retention measure represent greater recall of arguments favoring specialized education than of ones favoring general education.) (Greenwald & Albert, 1968.)

perception of the self as the source of arguments or in terms of subjects' ability to generate arguments particularly effective in regard to their own attitude structure (cf. Hovland *et al.*, 1953, pp. 233-237). A series of experiments designed to select among these explanations will be conducted in the near future as part of the present research program.

CONTENT AND CORRELATES OF COGNITIVE RESPONSES TO PERSUASION

A series of experiments conducted by Dallas Cullen, under the author's supervision, explored the content of subjects' thoughts relevant to the topic of a persuasive communication that they had just received. The communication, on the issue of general versus specialized undergraduate education, advocated the view that college education should be directed specifically at career preparation (that is, should be specialized). It was assumed that cognitive effects of the communication could be assessed by comparing the issue-relevant thoughts of subjects who received this communication with thoughts on the same issue expressed by control subjects who had received a communication on a different topic.

The subjects in this series of experiments were Ohio State University introductory psychology students who participated in classroom size groups. Four separate experiments were conducted with only minor variations in procedure. The basic procedure for Experiment I included an introduction to the issue of general versus specialized education consisting mainly of a definition of the alternative positions. Then a communication of about 250 words containing 12 distinct arguments supporting specialized undergraduate education was administered in printed form. Control subjects, at this time, read a communication concerning instructional television. Next, all subjects (including controls) were asked to "collect their thoughts" on the issue of general versus specialized undergraduate education by listing thoughts that were:

> . . . pertinent to forming and expressing an opinion on the issue of general versus specialized education. These thoughts may consist of (a) information favorable to one or the other viewpoint; (b) personal values of yours that are favorable to one or the other viewpoint; (c) features of either viewpoint that you perceive as good; (d) features of either viewpoint that you perceive as bad or harmful; and (e) any other thoughts you feel to be pertinent.
>
> In writing down these thoughts, please separate your thoughts into individual ideas to be written down separately. An "individual idea" is one that, to the best of your judgment, expresses only a *single* fact, value, good or bad feature, or thought.

Following this "thought-listing" procedure, subjects completed a brief questionnaire of four Likert-type items measuring opinion on the general-specialized education issue. Finally, subjects were instructed to look back at the thoughts they had listed concerning general and specialized education and to judge, for each individual thought, whether it was favorable to general or specialized education and how favorable it was, on a three-point scale of slightly favorable (1), moderately favorable (2), and very favorable (3).

Experiment II added an opinion pretest to the basic procedure; it consisted of the four Likert-type items also used as the opinion posttest.

For Experiment III, subjects were given an additional judgment task, at the end of the experiment, in regard to their listed thoughts. They were to assign each thought to one of three categories: (a) those having their source in the experimental materials (the introductory definitions and the persuasive communication); (b) modifications of the experimental materials (such as illustrations of, qualifications of, and reactions to communicated arguments); and (c) ideas not traceable to the experimental materials. These three categories are to be identified here, respectively, as (a) externally originated, (b) recipient-modified, and (c) recipient-generated cognitions. The aim of Experiment III was to compare subject coding of listed-thought responses into these three categories with independent coding by judges; no control group was employed.

In the last experiment in this series, two different communication conditions were employed. One (group IVA) employed the same communication used in the previous experiments while the other (group IVB) was modified by adding material acknowledging opposing arguments (ones favoring general education) and refuting them where possible (cf. Hovland *et al.*, 1949, Ch. 8). Subjects in Experiment IV also performed the additional categorization of their listed thoughts that had been requested of subjects in Experiment III.

For Experiments I, II, and III the classification of thoughts into externally originated, recipient-modified, and recipient-generated categories was performed by judges who were able to agree on these classifications for 85% of their judgments. This extent of agreement was not considered entirely satisfactory, especially when it was found, in Experiment III, that judges' classifications agreed with subjects' classifications for only 62% of judgments (chance agreement would be 33%). Since subjects were able to perform the judging task with relative ease, it was decided that it would be most satisfactory to use subject self-scoring for subsequent groups.

The data for the four experiments were first examined in terms of the quantities of thoughts as distributed among the three categories — externally originated, recipient-modified, and recipient-generated. These data are given in Fig. 2. Judges' categorizations were used for Experiments I and II; for Experiments III and IV, subjects' own categorizations were used. The most significant feature of the data summarized in Fig. 2 is that the recipient-generated category accounted for the majority of thoughts listed by communication-receiving subjects — despite the fact that their thoughts were tapped

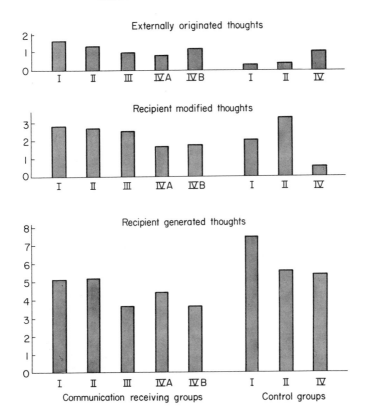

FIG. 2.   Mean quantities of listed thoughts in three categories. (Numbers of subjects are as follows: communication-receiving groups: I (48), II (48), III (68), IVA (26), IVB (28); control groups: I (16), II (16), IV (13).) (Greenwald & Cullen, unpublished data.)

immediately after reading a communication containing a dozen distinct relevant thoughts that could have been listed.[2]

Subjects' judgments of the position supported by each of their listed thoughts were used to calculate an index summarizing the thoughts' content on the general-specialized education issue. It will be recalled that each thought was weighted according to its degree of support for the position it supported. The index was calculated by subtracting the sum of weights for thoughts favoring general education

[2]The quantities of listed thoughts in the externally originated and recipient-modified categories for control groups were greater than zero because control subjects could and did list or react to material contained in introductory definitions of the concepts of general and specialized education.

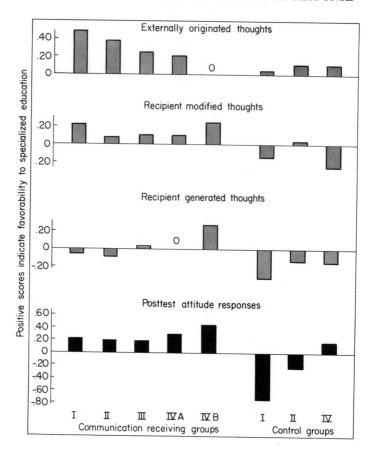

FIG. 3. Mean directional content of listed thoughts in three categories and mean posttest attitude responses. (The extreme scores on the three category indexes are +1.00 and −1.00; for the posttest attitude responses, the extremes are +2.50 and −2.50.) (Greenwald & Cullen, unpublished data.)

from the sum for those favoring specialized education, then dividing this difference by the sum of weights for all thoughts. This calculation was done separately for thoughts in each of the three categories —externally originated, recipient-modified, and recipient-generated. Figure 3 gives the mean values of these *directional content indexes* for the various groups in the present series of experiments. For comparison, the mean posttest opinion questionnaire responses are given at the bottom of Fig. 3. The effects of the communications can be seen in the generally more positive index values and posttest opinion scores for communication groups than for controls. The significance levels for these comparisons, combining over Experiments I, II, and IV (no control group was used in Experiment III) were: externally originated category, $p < .02$; recipient-modified category, $p < .02$; recipient-generated category, $p < .07$; and posttest opinion, $p < .001$ (all one-tailed).

It may be noted that the communication received by subjects in group IVB—which differed from the others in that it acknowledged opposing arguments—produced the most favorable posttest opinion questionnaire responses and the most positive responses in the recipient-generated category, while producing the least positive responses in the externally originated category. This pattern of findings is suggestive of the importance of recipient-generated cognitions, relative to externally originated ones, in persuasion.

Figure 4 gives for each group the correlations with posttest opinion for the three category directional content indexes as well as for one based on all thoughts combined. It may be noted that the correlations involving the recipient-generated category index were quite high relative to those for the externally originated category. This suggests, once more, the importance of recipient-generated cognitions in the recipient's attitude structure.[3]

The correlations with posttest opinion for the recipient-generated category index and for the index based on all thoughts combined were sufficiently high to suggest that the thought-listing procedure used in the present experiments might be very useful as a *measure* of opinion. A very desirable aspect of the thought-listing procedure is that it is applicable to virtually any attitude issue without necessity for time consuming scaling and item selection procedures. Research currently underway, being conducted by Cullen, is exploring the reliability, validity, and sensitivity-to-change properties of the thought-listing procedure in comparison with more traditional attitude scaling procedures. (See experiment reported on pp. 163–165 for an illustration of the use of the thought-listing procedure as an opinion measure.)

Table 1 gives the additional correlational data that were obtained

---

[3]Split-half reliability of the externally originated category index (.74) was actually slightly higher than that for the recipient-generated category (.68), which indicates that the difference between correlation magnitudes could not be attributed to relative unreliability of the externally originated category index. However, it must be noted that the externally originated material was nearly uniformly favorable to the specialized education position; thus, it is possible that range restriction for the externally originated category index was responsible, in part, for the low-magnitude correlations obtained between externally originated thought content and posttest opinion.

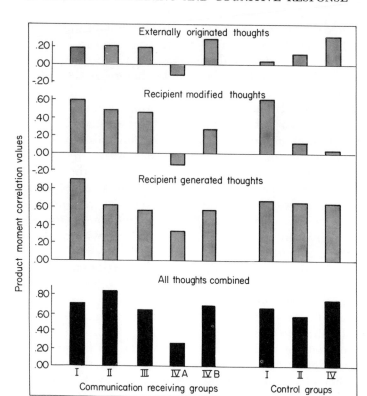

FIG. 4. Correlations with posttest attitude for four listed thought directional content indexes. (Greenwald & Cullen, unpublished data.)

TABLE 1

CORRELATIONS OF LISTED THOUGHT CONTENT
INDEXES WITH PRETEST AND POSTTEST ATTITUDE MEASURES[a]

| | Correlations with | |
Content index	Pretest attitude	Posttest attitude[b]
Externally originated thoughts	.20	.06
Recipient-modified thoughts	.56[c]	−.02
Recipient-generated thoughts	.52[c]	.39[c]
All thoughts combined	.71[c]	.65[c]

[a]Experiment II Data; $N = 48$.

[b]Pretest attitude has been partialed out of correlations with posttest attitude.

[c]$p < .01$.

from Experiment II by virtue of the use of a pretest opinion measure. On the left side of the table, it may be seen that pretest opinion was positively correlated with all of the directional content indexes, indicating that pretest opinion was an important determinant of the content of cognitions rehearsed in response to the persuasion situation. On the right side of the table, correlations between the category directional content indexes and posttest opinion are given, with pretest opinion partialed out. Significant positive correlations were obtained only for the recipient-generated category index and for the one based on all thoughts combined—again suggesting the importance of recipient-generated cognitions in persuasion, relative to externally originated ones.

In summary, Cullen's experiments provided a variety of evidence indicating important involvement of cognitive responses to persuasion in attitude structure. These findings, especially those for recipient-generated cognitive responses, were consistent with the present hypothesis that rehearsal of cognitive responses to persuasive communications is an essential mediator of cognitive attitude change.

PERSUASION AND RETENTION OF COGNITIVE RESPONSES

The preceding series of experiments examined attitude-relevant cognitions that were recorded shortly after the receipt of a persuasive communication. Robert Love's master's thesis research (in preparation), conducted under the author's direction, examined recipient's cognitions *during* a persuasive communication situation. The aim of this experiment was chiefly to assess correlations of persuasion effectiveness with retention of communication content and retention of cognitive response content, observed immediately following and one week after the initial communication situation.

Love's sample was divided into two groups, one receiving a persuasive communication on admitting Puerto Rico as the fifty-first state ($N = 33$), the other receiving a communication advocating popular election of the Secretary of State ($N = 35$); both communications were adapted with minor modifications from ones used by Watts and McGuire (1964). Subjects first received an opinion pretest (Likert-type), following which the appropriate communication was administered in printed form. Each communication presented three main supporting arguments in separate paragraphs: following each paragraph, four blank lines were provided for the subject to write a one-sentence reaction to the main point of the paragraph (the main point was underlined in the printed communication). This procedure served to obtain a sample of cognitive responses rehearsed during the persuasion situation.[4] After the communication, subjects' opinions were again assessed, this time using the thought-listing procedure (see p. 157), following which subjects were given an unexpected test for recall of (a) the three main points of the communication and (b) the reactions that had been written following each. The same subjects were recruited for an ostensibly different experiment, one week later, at which time the opinion posttest and the recall test were unexpectedly readministered.

The data were analyzed for partial correlations (pretest partialed out) of posttest opinion with (a) the content of cognitive reactions to the communication (number of favorable minus number of unfavorable reactions), (b) retention of the main arguments of the communication (number of arguments recalled; maximum $= 3$), and (c) retention of cognitive reactions (number of favorable minus number of unfavorable reactions recalled). These correlational results are given in Table 2. It is apparent that the best predictor of the effect of the communications was the measure of content of the cognitive reactions that were written during the communication exposure (average of 4 r's $= .52$); the next best predictor was the retention index for the cognitive reactions (average of 4 r's $= .30$); decidedly the poorest predictor was the retention measure for the persuasive communication itself (average of 4 r's $= .03$). These results strongly support the present contention that cognitive responses to persuasion are important in mediating persuasion effects while retention of communication content is not.

Supplementary data were obtained from subjects' classifications of the thoughts they had listed for the opinion posttests into the categories of (a) having originated in the persuasive message, (b) having originated in written reactions to the persuasive message, and (c) traceable to neither of these sources. Subjects' written reactions were most often represented in their listed thoughts (mean number $= 2.26$),

---

[4]Note that this procedure explicitly encouraged rehearsal of recipients' cognitive responses in that subjects were instructed to produce thoughts and to spend time writing their thoughts. This removes the present experimental situation a bit from the type of communication situation involving only a one-way transmission from source to recipient. However, this was unavoidable in the interests of obtaining usable information about the content of recipients' cognitions during persuasion. Moreover, the situation was analogous to another important type of persuasion situation in which source and recipient are in face-to-face confrontation, the source typically being interrupted by the recipient's reactions to the communication.

TABLE 2

PARTIAL CORRELATIONS OF COGNITIVE REACTION AND RETENTION MEASURES
WITH IMMEDIATE AND DELAYED POSTTEST OPINION

	Communication topic			
	Puerto Rico $(N=33)$		Secretary of State $(N=35)$	
Predictors of posttest opinion	Immediate opinion posttest	Delayed opinion posttest	Immediate opinion posttest	Delayed opinion posttest
1. Content of cognitive reactions during communication	.47[a]	.52[a]	.59[a]	.48[a]
2. Retention of communication content				
Immediate	−.12	−	.19	−
Delayed	−	.15	−	−.09
3. Retention of cognitive reaction content				
Immediate	.22	−	.23	−
Delayed	−	.45[a]	−	.30[b]

Note: These data are from a master's thesis by Robert E. Love (in preparation). Pretest opinion was partialed out of the correlations reported in this table.
[a] p < .01, one-tailed.
[b] p < .05, one-tailed.

while the communication content was least often represented (mean number = 1.21). (An average of 1.90 thoughts was traceable to neither source.) These findings lend further support to the conclusion that cognitive responses to the communications were more significant in providing content for cognitive attitude change than were the communications themselves.

THE COGNITIVE LEARNING PROCESS IN PERSUASION

The chief theoretical aim of this chapter has been to establish the basis for useful analysis of attitude change as a cognitive learning process. To do this, it was necessary to focus on cognitive responses rehearsed during persuasion situations. Specific learning-theoretical topics, such as the roles of incentives, reinforcers, and conditions of practice, have been ignored for the moment.

At present, knowledge concerning the determinants of learning of attitude-relevant cognitions is quite limited. Certainly, much is known theoretically about verbal learning, including learning of meaningful material (see McGeoch & Irion, 1952; Woodworth & Schlosberg, 1954). However, the particular variables involved in attitude-relevant learning—for example, covert rehearsal, preexisting attitudes, prior familiarity with information, and comprehension of persuasive messages—are not well understood in learning-theoretical terms. Number of presentations of a persuasive argument is about the only variable that is unequivocally established as a determinant of argument retention (see, for example, Greenwald & Sakumura, 1968; Jones & Kohler, 1958; Levine & Murphy, 1943; Waly & Cook, 1966). Until quite recently, another widely accepted principle of learning of persuasive arguments was that audiences would selectively attend to and remember information consonant with their pre-existing attitudes. Several studies had demonstrated effects of this nature (e.g., Jones & Kohler, 1958; Levine & Murphy, 1943). Recent attempts to replicate this phenomenon (Greenwald & Sakumura, 1968; Waly & Cook, 1966) have met with absolutely no success, so that the phenomenon of selective learning of attitude-consonant information must currently be regarded as of dubious validity.

Other determinants of attitude-relevant learning that have been implicated by empirical research are information utility (Jones & Aneshansel, 1956) and novelty (Greenwald & Sakumura, 1968). Since utility and novelty are variables known to increase attention to persuasive information,[5] it appears likely that their effects on learning of persuasive arguments may be mediated by these attentional effects rather than by any direct role in the learning process.

The findings of the studies just mentioned, and of other relevant studies not cited here, do not require the supposition that any variable other than duration of exposure (i.e., attention) to persuasive information is a determinant of information learning (cf. Cooper & Pantle, 1967). It seems likely also that comprehension of information is a determinant of retention (see Fitzgerald & Ausubel, 1963); however, minimal evidence is available concerning this relationship. Additionally, conditions of practice, particularly distribution of practice over time, should be expected to affect learning of persuasive information in much the same manner that they affect learning of other verbal material; again, little pertinent evidence is available, although the literature concerned with primacy and recency effects in persuasion (see Rosnow's chapter in this volume, and references;

---

[5]Brock, T. C., Albert, S. M., & Becker, L. A. Familiarity, utility and supportiveness as determinants of information receptivity. (in preparation)

also Anderson & Hubert, 1963) may be interpreted in terms of the conditions-of-practice variable.

The effects of rewards and punishments occurring in the persuasion situation are certainly relevant to theoretical interpretations of cognitive learning. However, although effects of rewards and punishments on attitude measures have frequently been demonstrated, the processes underlying such effects are poorly understood. Competing explanations in terms of classical conditioning, instrumental learning, dissonance reduction (Brehm & Cohen, 1962), and attention mechanisms (Janis & Gilmore, 1965), all can be justified by appeal to portions of the relevant literature. (The reader will find extensive discussion of reward and punishment effects, interpreted in terms of conditioning processes, in the chapters by Lott and Lott, Rosnow, Staats, and Weiss in this volume.)

The procedure of having subjects actively rehearse their own persuasive arguments was found by Greenwald and Albert (1968; also summarized earlier in this chapter) to produce substantial enhancement of argument retention as well as noticeable self-persuasion. At the moment, it is unknown whether these effects were due to enhanced original attention to the improvised arguments or to other factors. Nonetheless, the focus on learning of persuasive arguments actively rehearsed in a persuasion situation has provided the basis for presently reasserting the importance of cognitive learning in persuasion. Thus, the study of determinants of persuasive-argument learning—a problem area in which, to summarize the present brief literature review, current ignorance is considerable—can be justified not only as an interesting exercise in learning theory, but in terms of its practical value in interpreting the basis for effective and durable persuasion.

CONCLUSION—COGNITIVE PROCESS, COGNITIVE LEARNING, AND ATTITUDE CHANGE

The present program of research set out to establish the legitimacy of a conception of attitude change through persuasive communication as, at least in part, a cognitive learning process. In the course of doing this, the obtained experimental evidence repeatedly indicated that the effects of persuasive communications are strongly mediated by the content of attitude-relevant cognitions elicited (and thus rehearsed and learned) during the persuasion situation. The analysis of determinants of cognitive response content may very well require explanatory principles outside the scope of the learning principles with which the present research was concerned. There is, however, no lack of theories in the cognitive integration area that might be applied to the analysis of determinants of cognitive response content. Cognitive consistency theories, for example, can be used to predict that cognitive responses to persuasion will be consistent with pre-existing attitude-relevant cognitions. The assimilation-contrast approach (Sherif & Hovland, 1961) predicts that the individual reacts with favorable cognitions to persuasive statements within his latitude of acceptance and with unfavorable cognitions to statements outside his latitude of acceptance. Reactance theory (see Brehm's chapter in this volume) predicts that unfavorable cognitive reactions will occur in persuasive situations of a coercive nature. Brock's commodity analysis (see his chapter in this volume) predicts favorability of cognitive reaction to persuasive information to be a decreasing function of the perceived availability of the information. Functional analyses of attitude change (Katz, 1960; Sarnoff, 1960; see also Baron's chapter in this volume) provide more complex principles that might be used to predict cognitive reactions to persuasion given knowledge about the motivational basis of existing attitude structures.

In light of these observations, it would appear fruitful to approach the study of persuasive communication effectiveness with a combination of cognitive process theory and learning theory. The effects of independent variable manipulations in persuasion situations, such as credibility, organization of arguments, communication medium, etc., could be studied simultaneously in terms of their effects on the content of cognitive responses to persuasion and on learning of persuasive information. Existing data, noted at the outset of this chapter, suggest that most of the traditional independent variables of persuasion do *not* significantly affect retention of persuasive information. (Their effects on attitude presumably are mediated strictly through their effects on cognitive responses to persuasion.) The absence of retention effects of "traditional" persuasion variables may, however, only reflect the fact that attitude change researchers have been more interested in manipulating variables that affect *acceptance* of persuasive information than ones that affect attention to and retention of persuasive information. In the combined application of cognitive integration theory and learning theory to persuasion, cognitive integration theory should offer an account of the processes involved in acceptance of persuasion while learning theory should seek to account for persistence of induced changes through learning and retention processes. Neither of these areas of theory, when considered alone, can currently be expected to provide a complete account of the processes by which attitudes are formed or lastingly changed in response to persuasive communications.

References

Anderson, N. H., & Hubert, S. Effects of concomitant verbal recall on order effects in personality impression formation. *Journal of Verbal Learning and Verbal Behavior,* 1963, **2**, 379-391.

Brehm, J. W., & Cohen, A. R. *Explorations in cognitive dissonance.* New York: Wiley, 1962.

Brock, T. C. Communication discrepancy and intent to persuade as determinants of counterargument production. *Journal of Experimental Social Psychology,* 1967, **3**, 296-309.

Campbell, D. T. The generality of a social attitude. Unpublished doctoral dissertation, University of California, Berkeley, 1947.

Cooper, Elaine H., & Pantle, A. J. The total-time hypothesis in verbal learning. *Psychological Bulletin,* 1967, **68**, 221-234.

Fitzgerald, D., & Ausubel, D. P. Cognitive versus affective factors in the learning and retention of controversial material. *Journal of Educational Psychology,* 1963, **54**, 73-84.

Greenwald, A. G. An amended learning model of persuasion. Paper read at American Psychological Association, Washington, D. C., September 1967.

Greenwald, A. G., & Albert, Rosita D. Acceptance and recall of improvised arguments. *Journal of Personality and Social Psychology,* 1968, 8, 31-34.

Greenwald, A. G., Albert, Rosita D., & Cullen, Dallas M. Persuasion as a function of communication content learning. Unpublished manuscript, Ohio State Univ., 1968.

Greenwald, A. G., & Sakumura, J. S. Attitude and selective learning: Where are the phenomena of yesteryear? *Journal of Personality and Social Psychology,* 1967, **7**, 387-397.

Hovland, C. I., Janis, I. L., & Kelley, H. H. *Communication and persuasion.* New Haven: Yale University Press, 1953.

Hovland, C. I., Lumsdaine, A. A., & Sheffield, F. D. *Experiments on mass communication.* Princeton, N. J.: Princeton University Press, 1949.

Insko, C. A. Primacy versus recency in persuasion as a function of the timing of arguments and measures. *Journal of Abnormal and Social Psychology,* 1964, **69**, 381-391.

Insko, C. A. *Theories of attitude change.* New York: Appleton, 1967.

Janis, I. L., & Gilmore, J. B. The influence of incentive conditions on the success of role playing in modifying attitudes. *Journal of Personality and Social Psychology,* 1965, **1**, 17-27.

Janis, I. L. & Terwilliger, R. F. An experimental study of psychological resistances to fear-arousing communications. *Journal of Abnormal and Social Psychology,* 1962, **65**, 403-410.

Jones, E. E., & Aneshansel, J. The learning and utilization of contravaluant material. *Journal of Abnormal and Social Psychology,* 1956, **53**, 27-33.

Jones, E. E., & Kohler, R. The effects of plausibility on the learning of controversial statements. *Journal of Abnormal and Social Psychology,* 1958, **57**, 315-320.

Katz, D. The functional approach to the study of attitudes. *Public Opinion Quarterly*, 1960, **24**, 163-204.

Katz, D., & Stotland, E. A preliminary statement to a theory of attitude structure and change. In S. Koch (Ed.), *Psychology: A study of a science.* Vol. 3. New York: McGraw-Hill, 1959. Pp. 423-475.

Kelman, H. C. Attitude change as a function of response restriction. *Human Relations*, 1953, **6**, 185-214.

Krech, D., Crutchfield, R. S., & Ballachey, E. L. *Individual in society.* New York: McGraw-Hill, 1962.

Levine, J. M., & Murphy, G. The learning and forgetting of controversial material. *Journal of Abnormal and Social Psychology*, 1943, **38**, 507-517.

McGeoch, J. A., & Irion, A. L. *The psychology of human learning.* New York: Longmans Green, 1952.

McGuire, W. J. Attitudes and opinions. *Annual Review of Psychology*, 1966, **17**, 475-514.

McGuire, W. J. Nature of attitudes and attitude change. In G. Lindzey & E. Aronson (Eds.), *Handbook of social psychology.* (2nd ed.) Reading, Mass.: Addison-Wesley, 1968, in press.

Miller, N., & Campbell, D. T. Recency and primacy in persuasion as a function of the timing of speeches and measurements. *Journal of Abnormal and Social Psychology*, 1959, **59**, 1-9.

Rokeach, M. *Open and closed mind.* New York: Basic Books, 1960.

Sarnoff, I. Psychoanalytic theory and social attitudes. *Public Opinion Quarterly*, 1960, **24**, 251-279.

Sherif, M., & Hovland, C. I. *Social judgment.* New Haven: Yale University Press, 1961.

Smith, M. B., Bruner, J. S., & White, R. W. *Opinions and personality.* New York: Wiley, 1956.

Waly, P., & Cook, S. W. Attitude as a determinant of learning and memory: A failure to confirm. *Journal of Personality and Social Psychology*, 1966, **4**, 280-288.

Watts, W. A., & McGuire, W. J. Persistency of induced opinion change and retention of the inducing message contents. *Journal of Abnormal and Social Psychology*, 1964, **68**, 233-241.

Woodworth, R. S., & Schlosberg, H. *Experimental psychology.* (Rev. ed.) New York: Holt, 1954.

7

Personality and Attitude Change:
An Information-Processing Theory

WILLIAM J. MC GUIRE
DEPARTMENT OF PSYCHOLOGY
UNIVERSITY OF CALIFORNIA, SAN DIEGO
LA JOLLA, CALIFORNIA

THE NATURE OF A SYSTEMS THEORY

A scientific theory is a packed down synopsis of obtained relationships. It is when knowledge obtains this form that the information gained through experimental investigation becomes, not just the joy of the individual researchers who make up the invisible college in the area, but a lasting heritage of the broader scientific and public circles in which the invisible college exists and is sustained. While the isolated experiment may be the hope and the despair of the scientist who conducts it, its results are seldom inspiring to the outside reader. Only when the results of numerous individual studies are brought into conjunction with one another does a general theoretical housing emerge that makes the numerous individual studies seem worthwhile to the outside observer. The individual study, isolated from any such broader theoretical contacts, sometimes even elicits the ridicule of the layman, whether we mean here the alert member of the general public, the scoffing legislator at the annual hearing of a subcommittee on research appropriations, or even the members of one's own discipline whose work falls under another rubric.

It seems to me that social psychology is currently going through a phase in which the packing down and distilling of broad areas of knowledge is somewhat out of favor. Two other styles of work seem to be more in fashion today. An appreciable number of productive work-

171

ers focus on a very narrow series of accumulative experiments (on topics such as the effect of adjective combinations on impression formation or the effects of varying payoff matrices on cooperative choices in prisoner's dilemma games.) This is indeed cumulative research as one hopes for in science, but it tells all but the initiates more about the phenomenon under investigation than they really want to know. A second currently fashionable style of work, more comprehensible to the outsider, but also tending to arouse the puritanical indignation of some (McGuire, 1967; Ring, 1967), involves moving around rapidly by applying a clever theoretical notion to one area after another in a series of demonstration experiments. These and other styles of research do contribute to the general scientific enterprise and we suspect that each researcher is most productive when allowed to do the kind of work he feels to be most stimulating. Hence, we would be satisfied to see those who resonate with the current fashions continue such work styles. We are advocating that the currently neglected enterprise of broader theorizing be added to, rather than replace, these other worthwhile aspects of the total scientific endeavor. Indeed, broader theorizing is possible only when the more focused and specific workers actively pursue their experimentation.

Theoretical housings of the type we have in mind here might be called "systems" theorizing. They are designed for middle range problem areas (such as the topic on which we focused in this chapter, personality factors in attitude change) which would probably be considered uncomfortably broad by the straight-line experimenter and esoterically narrow by the nonexpert. The systems theorist tries to weave together the specific lines of research and the isolated experiments to formulate a theoretical housing that will subsume and give coherence to the reliable information we currently have about relationships in the given area and will suggest new relationships for further investigation. A notable example of systems theorizing is Hullian Behavior Theory which was formulated to subsume a variety of accepted empirical relationships in the area of simple human and animal learning. Hull's formulation happens to be a partial progenitor of the learning theory formulations presented in several chapters of this book and so serves conveniently here to depict several characteristics of the approach. Systems theorizing involves asserting a series of postulates that can generate the observed relationships in the area. They can be derived from various sources, including inductions from common sense observations of the natural world, analyses of the results of experiments conducted under refined laboratory conditions, creative inspiration based on analogy, functional analysis, etc. These postulates tend to be logically independent of one another; the main thing they have in common is that each bears on the area for which the theoretical housing is being developed and is felt to account for some of the variance in the behavior of interest. In Hullian Behavioristics, these postulates have to do with frequency of reinforcement, drive level, stimulus generalization, work inhibition, conditioned inhibition, etc., as they affect performance. The purpose of assembling such a set of postulates is to systematize and clarify existing knowledge and to generate new, testable hypotheses to extend that knowledge. Developing and testing a systems theory presents a number of difficult problems owing to the unrelatedness and open-endedness of the list of fundamental postulates. Since one can start with any set of postulates and enlarge the set indefinitely, such a theory is potentially nonparsimonious, inelegant, and untestable. It is hard to ascertain whether adding a postulate produces any considerable increase in explanatory power or is simply redundant with the previous assumptions. Any empirical embarrassment which the theory encounters in principle can be removed by the addition of a new postulate. There seems to be an inherent danger in this indefinite salvageability of a systems theory. We can make it suffice as a product simulation of the behavior with which we deal by shoring up any initial list of postulates (which might provide an inadequate process simulation) by the endless addition of new assumptions that lead us further and further into a misunderstanding of the processes involved.

A number of expedients can be taken to minimize these inherent dangers in systems theorizing, some appropriate at the stage of theory formulating and others at the stage of theory testing. In the theory formulating stage, one takes into consideration that not all the possible postulates are equally important to the theory. They differ in attractiveness in a number of regards — including relevance to the phenomenon being described, extent to which we are confident in their validity on the basis of experimental data or on other grounds, their independence of the other postulates in the system, etc. In constructing a systems theory it is useful to take such information into account. An appropriate procedure is the one which Hull happened to use, namely, a functional analysis. This involves examining the demands which the environment in which he evolved puts on the person in the behavioral area that the the the theory is supposed to cover (see McGuire, 1968a, for a fuller discussion of this heuristic). The problem is one of teasing out the essential survival problems in this area and assuming that the human operates on principles that allow him to cope with these problems in an economical fashion. (Admittedly, this heuristic assumes that the human has evolved with an optimal solution.) As the most fundamental postulates purportedly describing how humans function in the area, the theorist selects the principles which would best allow a person to cope with the fundamental survival problem in the area or utilize the most valuable survival opportunity. To such primary postulates, the theorist adds secondary and tertiary ones which serve as correctives to prevent excessive operation on the principles embodied in the primary postulates or as refinements allow the differential operation of these fundamental principles depending upon the particular situation. In our systems theory to handle personality factors and attitude change, we followed this heuristic strategy. We viewed the basic survival opportunity as openness to useful information and guidance from other people, with a necessary corrective of critical evaluation and useful refinements having to do with situational specificity.

While such caution during the theory-construction phase somewhat minimizes the peril that this type of theorizing will lead us further and further into a blind alley, any carefulness during the theory formulation, however sophisticated, only lessens rather than eliminates the danger. It is always possible by the addition of new postulates to the system to "save the appearances," if we may use that Hellenic expression. Our anxieties to assure testability are partly mitigated by confidence that the esthetic needs of scientists will not allow such a post factum salvaging to proceed indefinitely. If the multiplication of assumptions proceeded endlessly, the theoretical structure in which we seek to house the obtained relationships in the area would become so unesthetic that the theoretical approach will finally be abandoned, if not by the theory's progenitor himself, at least by the young people entering the area, with less investment in and imprinting on the old paradigm. Also, another testing consideration limits the endless multiplication of assumptions. As each new postulate is added to the system to account for observed empirical discrepancies from the old deductions, the addition adds multiple new predictions in terms of interaction effects with many of the old postulates. Hence, many possible postulates whose addition would yield a main effect to account for a particular observed discrepancy would have to be rejected immediately because they also yield interaction predictions which are disconfirmed by existing, or easily obtainable data. It is this consideration that leads us, in our systems theorizing regarding personality factors in attitude change, to stress the importance of interaction predictions.

In this section we shall first describe the existing body of knowledge about personality and attitude change relationships on which we built the present systems theory and then outline the theory itself. The first topic involves marking out the subject matter area to which the theory is meant to apply and sketching briefly the state of our knowledge in that area at the time the theory was formulated. The second topic, depicting the theory itself, involves describing the three postulates and two corollaries that make up the core of the predictive system.

THE STATE OF THE QUESTION

Scope of Our Theory

The terms "personality" and "attitude change" are both used in a broad sense in the current discussion, so that the present theory covers a fairly wide area. By personality we have in mind any variable on which people differ, including capacity variables like intelligence, demographic variables like age and sex, and dynamic characteristics like anxiety and self-esteem. Some would consider the latter as most appropriately called personality variables. Hence, considering the intended scope of the present theory we might more appropriately refer to "individual difference factors" rather than "personality factors" in attitude change. Since the experimental data in terms of which we shall discuss the theory here deal with dynamic factors like self-esteem and anxiety, we cautiously used the narrower term in our present chapter title. However, the theory is intended to apply equally well to any individual difference characteristic (and indeed, to other kinds of independent variables) as they affect attitude change.

The applicability of the theory is also rather general on the dependent variable side. While we have used attitude change in the title, the theory is meant to apply to all social influence situations whether they involve suggestion, conformity, persuasion, etc., and whether the target measure is cognitions, affect, gross behavior, etc. The theory is designed to account for the relationships between any individual difference characteristic and susceptibility to social influence in any situation. Hence, the theory applies to how individual difference characteristics will be related to hypnotic or waking suggestibility (as in Hull's [1933] body sway inductions); and to conformity to authority or group consensus (as in the Sherif [1935] or Asch [1956] conformity situations); and to mass media persuasibility (as in Hovland's [1954] communication situations).

We have argued elsewhere (McGuire, 1968a) that the relationship of personality characteristics to susceptibility in any one of these types of social influence situations cannot be directly generalized to the others. It might seem at first glance that if this contention of specificity is valid, one should study personality correlates separately in each type of influencibility situation. However, we think that the specificity is an attraction, rather than a deterrent to studying several of the situations in conjunction. Under these circumstances we think that the more inclusive study yields a whole which is greater than the sum of the parts. While each type of situation studied in isolation gives us certain information about personality relationships to influencibility, when studied in conjunction we have the further dividend of obtaining information on interaction effects also. These interaction effects indicate more clearly the nature of the underlying processes in each of the influence situations. Hence, in constructing the present systems theory, as well as in testing it, we are attempting to account for the relationships of any type of individual difference characteristic to susceptibility in any type of influence situation. Due to this fairly broad scope, it is inevitable that the theory will be fairly complex, with a variety of orthogonal postulates. It also follows that the appropriate experimental designs will be rather complicated so as to yield information on higher order interaction effects.

State of the Empirical Knowledge

Scientific researchers are very diverse as regards their attitudes toward the antiquity and popularity of their area of study. At one extreme, there are the numerous researchers given to regarding their work as created ex nihilo, a brave new area of study not even thought of until their investigations began. These researchers often seem to be reinventing the wheel and as having to recapitulate phylogeny due to their failure to recognize that there is an already existing scholarly foundation on which they might build. At the opposite extreme, also well occupied, are those who tend to regard their current research as the culmination of a straight-line evolution that the science has been pursuing since its birth. To the outsider, these parochial imperialists present the same spectacle as does Father Knickerbocker as he depicts human history as a rather slow moving preparation for the founding of the City of New York. The first group experiences anxieties if the specter of related past work is raised to threaten their feelings of originality. Those at the latter extreme suffer separation anxiety unless they can establish that their work is in the mainstream of their discipline's development and so focused on its perennial problems. At the risk of seeming to be in the latter group, we claim that susceptibility to social influence is the oldest individual difference variable as well as the oldest topic in social psychology to receive scientific attention.

Susceptibility to social influence was first investigated in its special aspect of suggestibility. The famous controversy between the schools of Nancy and Paris over the generality of suggestibility (which brought into confrontation Liébeault and Bernheim against Charcot and Janet) is a well-known incident in the history of psychology and psychiatry. That this controversy is of venerable age (as experimental psychology goes) is illustrated by the fact that Binet published several volumes of investigation in support of the Paris School before he turned his attention to the measurement of individual differences in intelligence, for which he is now somewhat better known.

Even if the claim of absolute antiquity is somewhat exaggerated, it seems undeniable (McGuire, 1968a) that interest in this topic of influencibility developed early and has continued unabated. As a result of this long interest there is a vast literature on the topic and a considerable body of experimental results regarding personality-susceptibility relationships (McGuire, 1968a, b). This literature consists largely of reports of isolated experiments, done to test ad hoc hypotheses rather than to test the implications of a general theory. These studies generally disregarded all but a few earlier studies done in the area. As a result, the conditions of the various experiments differ widely as regards the subjects used, the types of influence inductions employed, the effects measured, etc. Not surprisingly, the results of the separate experiments do not neatly supplement one another, and where they are relevant to one another, they seem mutually contradictory as frequently as they replicate or extend one another.

We can illustrate this confused state of affairs by adverting to a single personality variable, that of self-esteem. This choice is hardly an atypical one since this variable and anxiety constitute the two most popular individual difference characteristics that have been studied for their attitude change relationships. The untidy nature of the corpus of results can be illustrated without our going back to Paris at the turn of the century. The past dozen years of progress will suffice to show the upward and onward movement of this confusion. In 1954 the answer regarding the relationship between self-esteem and influencibility seemed simple if somewhat ambiguous. In that year, Janis (1954) found a negative relationship between self-esteem and influencibility. At about the same time McGuire and Ryan (1955) found a positive relationship between these two variables. In general, a fairly simple if unclear picture was indicated such that influencibility either increased or decreased with increasing self-esteem. A dozen years later, the answer regarding this relationship seemed less simple but no less ambiguous. Cox and Bauer (1964) found an inverted-U-shaped nonmonotonic relationship between influencibility and attitude change. Simultaneously, Silverman (1964) found a nonmonotonic relationship of upright-U shape. Hence, it now appeared that self-esteem is nonmonotonically related to influencibility with the maximum, or perhaps minimum, influencibility occuring at intermediate ranges of self-esteem. It is from this nettle of confusion that we hope to pluck the flower of truth.

To save the appearances of so complex a set of results as this, the reader should not expect a simple theory. Hence in anticipation of our ponderous theoretical apparatus of three postulates and two corollaries, we appeal to the unembarrassed assertion by Irving Sarnoff (personal communication) that, "If you are describing a pretzel shaped universe, you may have to use pretzel shaped hypotheses." Indeed, the systems theory that we present here is only part of the longer story developed elsewhere (McGuire, 1968a). And it must be admitted that even that broader and more complex theory does not suffice to subsume the Silverman upright-U relationship mentioned above, though it will handle the other three types of relationships just cited. Our embarassment at not being able to work Silverman's results into the theory is somewhat lessened by our impression that it is an extremely rare finding and that Silverman himself has subsequently reported the exact opposite nonmonotonic relationship more in accord with Cox and Bauer's finding as well as the present theory (Silverman, Ford, & Morganti, 1966). Nevertheless, it would be well to keep in mind that there do exist some obtained relationships that are wildly discrepant from what even our complex and eclectic theory can handle.

POSTULATES FOR A SYSTEMS THEORY OF PERSONALITY-INFLUENCIBILITY RELATIONSHIP

While it is an advantage of systems theorizing that it can select its postulates eclectically, we have already indicated some reasons why this selection should be disciplined by a general orientation lest the system become unwieldly, untidy, and untestable. Behind the formulation we are presenting here lies a general Markov chain, information-processing conceptualization of the social influence process. We shall first describe this general conceptualization and then present the three postulates and two corollaries to which it gives rise.

The General Conceptualization of Social Influence Processes

We follow M. Brewster Smith (1965) by maintaining that research on attitude change derives from four broad approaches: information-processing theory, perceptual theory, consistency theory, and functional theory. Our present formulation about personality relationships in the attitude change area falls quite clearly under the information-processing rubric (which elsewhere we have called the "learning theory" approach), and so we shall here confine our discussion to it. We have discussed both it and the other three theoretical approaches more fully elsewhere (McGuire, 1968a, b). Use of the information-processing approach involves predicting how an independent variable will be related to attitude change by analysis of that variable's likely effect on learning the contents of the social influence communication. The guiding idea here is that an essential problem in a social influence situation is adequate reception of the persuasive message. At a minimum, it is assumed that the extent to which a person is influenced by a message will be positively related to the extent to which he attends to and comprehends its persuasive content. Use of this approach, then, involves predicting how any independent variable in the communication situation (such as order of presentation, source credibility, level of fear appeal, receiver's self-esteem, time since message receipt, etc.) will be related to attitude change by analyzing that variable's likely impact on learning the message contents. Hence, if there is a primacy effect in learning, then one is predicted also as regards opinion change; if there is a negatively decelerated decay in retention of message content, a like function is predicted as regards the persistence of induced attitude change, etc. A version of this rather simple-minded depiction of the attitude change process lies behind the present theory.

The guiding idea of our information-processing conceptualization is actually somewhat more elaborate than the impoverished learning theory approach just depicted. The social influence process is visualized as a six-step Markov chain. That is, for attitude change to be induced, there must occur six successive steps, each dependent on the previous step as a necessary but not sufficient condition. First of all, there is only a certain probability that a persuasive message will actually be communicated; factors affecting this variable are studied mainly by people who work in the mass communication and content analysis areas. There is then some conditional probability that the subject will adequately attend to such a message if it is presented. Given that he attends adequately, there is only some probability that he will sufficiently comprehend the arguments and conclusions being urged in the message. It is usually hard in practice to distinguish operationally between these second and third steps of attention and comprehension. We can, however, measure them jointly by administering a reading comprehension test that measures how well the person can report the message content, as compared with a control subject who has not been exposed to the message. His score on this test of recall provides a measure of how well he attended to and also comprehended the contents, without clarifying whether failures of recall were due to inadequate attention, inadequate comprehension, or both. Perhaps new techniques (such as pupil dilation) will someday allow us to get a direct measure of attention and thus allow us to tease out the relative contribution of these two mediators. At the present stage of applying this model, we make no attempt to separate the second and third processes empirically.

To continue our depiction of the six-step process beyond this third stage of comprehension, it can then be said that given adequate message comprehension, there is only some probability that the person will yield to and be convinced by the arguments which he has heard. The typical one-session laboratory experiment on attitude change usually measures the process only up to this fourth step, by introducing immediately a postcommunication opinionnaire to measure the extent to which the person actually agrees with the conclusion argued. This agreement level, as compared to his precommunication level of agreement or the agreement level of a control group who has not heard the communication, indicates the attitude change produced by the message. A fifth step must be considered when, in most natural environment research and some laboratory experimentation on attitude change, impact is measured only after some time has passed. Even where the person immediately yielded to the arguments, there is only some probability that he will retain his newly adopted position until the delayed measure is made. Furthermore, the measure of attitude change impact often involves some gross behavior (such as buying, voting, contributing, etc.) which has only a certain probability of occurrence, even given that the ideological yielding is retained, which introduces a sixth step into the total process.

In our present development of this six-step formulation into a systems theory for personality relationships in the attitude change area, we shall adopt some simplifications that facilitate exposition and experimentation without being intrinsic shortcomings in the formulation. One simplification is that we shall not here discuss the last two steps in the chain, retention and derivative overt behavior. Rather, we shall adopt the experimental conveniences of analyzing the persuasion process only as far as the yielding step; that is, we shall measure the attitude change impact in terms of opinionnaire responses obtained shortly after the presentation of the persuasive communication. A second simplification, the reasons for which were indicated above,

is that we will not try to measure separately the attention and comprehension steps, but rather measure them jointly by the score obtained
on an immediate test of retention of message contents. A third simplification, again conventionally adopted for experimental convenience,
is that we shall not allow the first step, message presentation, to be a
variable under the subject's control. Rather, we shall use the standard
laboratory technique of presenting standard persuasive communications to some groups while presenting none or other standard messages to other groups. This abbreviated systems theory of the attitude
change process constitutes the motivation behind the several postulates regarding personality-influencibility to which we now turn.

Postulate I: The Multiple-Mediation Assumption

Our first postulate simply makes explicit the common sense essence
of the information-processing approach: that any personality characteristic (or indeed any independent variable in the communication
situation) can affect attitude change by having an impact on any one or
more of the mediational steps just outlined. Thus, if we ask what is the
relationship between self-esteem and influencibility, we can find an
adequate answer only by analyzing the likely impact of self-esteem on
each of the mediators, including the attention to and comprehension
of the message, as well as the yielding to what is comprehended. The
necessity for making this point explicit derives from the fact that in
most conventional thinking about personality-influencibility relationships, there is an overemphasis on the mediational role of yielding.

This overemphasis on the yielding mediator can be illustrated anec-
dotally by asking a layman to conjecture regarding the relationship
between intelligence and persuasibility. He is likely to suggest that
the more intelligent people tend to be less persuasible. When pushed
to account for this prediction, he suggests that the more intelligent
person tends to be less yielding to social influence attempts since he
has more information to bolster his initial opinion and is better able to
see the flaws in the arguments used in the persuasive message; moreover, the highly intelligent person is typically more confident in himself and more willing to maintain a position discrepant from peer or
authority sources. It will be noted that all of these explanatory concepts have to do with the yielding mediator and overlook completely
the reception mediator. That is, they disregard the impact of intelligence on attention to and comprehension of the message. But while
the yielding mediator indicates a negative relationship between intelligence and persuasibility, it seems reasonable to conjecture a posi-

tive relationship between the two on the basis of the reception mediator. The more intelligent person tends to have more interest in the outside world and thus be more attentive to persuasive messages; he will be better able to understand the conclusion being urged and the relevance of the arguments presented. This failure to take into consideration this mediational role of reception makes it difficult to account for certain obtained results. For example, U.S. Army personnel in World War II tended to be more influenced by the "Why We Fight" films to the extent that they were better educated (Hovland, Lumsdaine, & Sheffield, 1949). This type of result becomes more comprehensible when we realize that even these open "propaganda" films had sufficient subtlety so that the superior receptive capacity of the more intelligent soldiers made them more vulnerable to being influenced than did their superior critical ability protect them from influence via the yielding mediator. In general, postulate I calls our attention to the fact that to predict how a characteristic like intelligence is related to influencibility we must consider the impact on the reception as well as yielding mediator.

Postulate II: The Compensatory Assumption

If our first postulate simply made explicit a common sense analysis, our second postulate might seem by contrast to be outrageously arbitrary. It asserts that the mutually opposite operation of the two mediators, reception and yielding, as was just described in the case of intelligence, is typical of personality-influencibility relationships. That is, any personality characteristic which has a positive relationship to reception, tends to be negatively related to yielding, and vice versa. We are assuming here that nature is deliciously equitable so that any characteristic which makes an individual vulnerable to social influence through one of the mediators tends to protect him from influence via another.

Since we posit this compensatory principle as an initial postulate, technically we do not have to justify it except by demonstrating its usefulness in yielding valid predictions. Yet its apparent arbitrariness moves us to argue that such a dynamic equilibrium situation is made plausible by considerations of engineering efficiency, by the data available in the literature, and by esthetic speculations that border on the theological. Since these justifications are discussed more fully elsewhere (McGuire, 1968a), we shall not review them here. Our position on this point is rather analogous to that of Neal Miller regarding the assumption in his conflict theory that the avoidance gradient is steeper than that for approach. One presents reasonable arguments based on data or considerations of efficiency why this state of affairs should widely obtain. But if delayed too long by an obstinate critic, one adopts the fall-back position that this state of affairs may not be universal, but that one's exposition will deal only with situations in which the posited conditions do obtain. We shall simply state here that we think the compensatory principle holds very generally; but that in any case we are simply dealing with personality-influencibility relationships in which it does hold. More specifically, we maintain that it does hold in the case of the two most frequently studied personality variables in attitude change research, anxiety and self-esteem, on which the empirical work discussed here has been focused. Anxiety, for example, is assumed to be negatively related to the reception and positively to the yielding mediator; while self-esteem is assumed to have the opposite relationships (see McGuire, 1968a, for a fuller discussion of these assumptions).

Two corollaries can be derived from this compensatory principle. The first corollary is that, because of the compensatory contributions of the two mediators, the overall relationshp between the personality variable and attitude change will tend to be nonmonotonic, with maximum influencibility found at some intermediate level of the personality characteristic. It can be shown that when such a compensatory, dynamic equilibrium situation obtains as regards the mediators, the overall relationship will tend to be of this inverted-U shape under a wide range of parametric conditions. This type of model has appeared in many areas of psychological research and so will be familiar to many readers. The algebraic considerations and the empirical basis for this model in the personality-influencibility area have been presented elsewhere (McGuire, 1963, 1968a) so that we shall here simply state the corollary without seeking to justify it.

The second corollary following from the compensatory principle has to do with the interaction between chronic and acute variations in personality characteristics. We refer here to the person's chronic level on a personality variable, such as his natural persisting level of anxiety, as compared with his acute level on this variable produced by a momentary situational or experimental manipulation of his anxiety by exposing him to frightening conditions. This second corollary states that an experimental manipulation of acute anxiety (or any other personality characteristic) will have an effect on influencibility that depends upon the person's chronic level on that variable. More specifically, raising one's acute anxiety by some fear induction (or his self-esteem by an experience of success) will tend to increase the person's influencibility, if he is chronically quite low on these variables, and will tend to decrease his influencibility, if he is chronically high on them. That this corollary would follow from the compensatory postulate and its nonmonotonic corollary can be grasped if one visualizes the inverted-U shaped curve, with the chronically low person lying to the left of the inflection point and the chronically high near or to the right of this point. If the laboratory induction adds a fixed increment to the chronic level this interaction effect would follow.

A parenthetical caution is in order regarding this second corollary as it bears on the acute versus chronic question. We regard it as valid as far as it goes, but also as inadequate in portraying the true complexity of the relationship between the acute and the chronic variations in a personality characteristic. This corollary considers the two types of variation as essentially equivalent and additive. In the fuller depiction of the systems theory which we present elsewhere (McGuire, 1968a), we deal with a fourth postulate, not considered in the present chapter, which complicates the picture described here. Specifically, it assumes that the person's chronic natural level on a given personality characteristic is imbedded in a matrix of related traits which help him to cope with the problems to which this chronic level exposes him. The situationally induced, acute level of the variable constitutes a "purer" manifestation of the characteristic, without the imbeddedness in compensatory traits. We shall do no more here than caution the reader that this second corollary should not be taken as the whole story regarding the personality-influencibility relationship that one would find with acute as compared with chronic variations in the characteristic.

Postulate III: The Situational Weighting Assumption

The operationalists among us tend to reach for our guns when we come upon a theory that predicts nonmonotonic relationships. Such a formulation, when put forward in an area as qualitative and unspecific regarding its parameters as is typical in psychological work, can be the last refuge of scoundrels, because it is able to account for almost any obtained relationship. If the data indicate a positive relationship between the independent and the dependent variables, the theorist can say that the sampled range of the independent variable was to the left of the inverted-U inflection point; if a negative relationship is obtained, he can say it lay to the right; if no relationship is found, he can say that his two conditions lay on opposite sides of the inflection point. So many different outcomes would be in accord with such a theory, that its scientific status is threatened by the difficulty of specifying any outcome that would disconfirm it. The third postulate attempts to tie down the theory somewhat, by specifying some of the parameters at least in an ordinal sense, so that certain outcomes, particularly as regards interaction effects, would be embarrassing to the theory. Postulate III asserts that the precise shape and location of the inverted-U relationship between individual difference characteristics and susceptibility to social influence will vary with specifiable aspects of the communication situation.

This third postulate capitalizes on our having sufficient knowledge of some social influence situations so that we can specify systematic differences among them as regards the extent to which the several mediators contribute to the convariance between the personality characteristic and the attitude change effect. Some social influence situations allow much more individual difference variance as regards the mediational role of attention and comprehension of the persuasive materials than do others. For example, the typical suggestion situation entails a very repetitive message such as a three minute recital to the effect that "you are falling back, back . . ." which seems so clearcut that any normal college sophomore presumably can grasp the gist of it. Hence, a personality variable's relationship to receptivity would be unimportant in determining its relationship to susceptibility to such suggestion. In suggestion situations the personality variable's relationship to the yielding mediator carries most of the weight in establishing its relationship to attitude change. A much different reception weighting would obtain in many of the laboratory and field persuasion situations which involve argumentative messages of greater subtlety. For example, a persuasive message designed to enhance the attractiveness of a product or a politician via a mass media or in face-to-face presentation typically allows for much more variance in message reception. Illustrative would be the World War II "Why We Fight" films of the U.S. Army which were mentioned above. With these moderately complex messages, the personality variable's relationship to attention and comprehension will have some important weight in determining its ultimate relationship to attitude change. The audiences of the mass media, and even the subjects in laboratory research on attitude change, tend to have little intrinsic interest in the topics discussed in the persuasive message so that their attention to and learning of its contents tend to be rather precarious. Hence, one can expect considerable individual difference variance in message comprehension even when the communication situation might seem relatively simple to academicians.

Just as we can design the social influence situation so as to vary the reception mediator's weight in determining the personality-influencibility relationship, so we can select situations so as to manipulate the variance due to the yielding mediator. For example, some topics are so culturally defined as "matters of fact" that almost any college soph- omore will be inclined to yield completely to the persuasive message in so far as he understands it. The exposition of a scientific theory, as presented by a physics instructor to the college sophomore, would constitute such a situation. Here we would expect that the relation- ship of a personality characteristic to the amount of attitude change achieved by such a lecture would be mediated almost entirely by that characteristic's relationship to the reception mediator. On the other hand, there are situations dealing with matters of taste, such as the relative attractiveness of two motion pictures, in which we would expect considerable individual difference variance in the yielding mediator. In these latter cases, the personality characteristic's ulti- mate relationship to attitude change would be much affected by its relationship to the yielding mediator.

In this discussion of the situational weighting postulate, we have been fairly programmatic and qualitative. Elsewhere (McGuire, 1968a) we have argued that it would not be prohibitively difficult to obtain a more exact analysis of the contributions of the several media- tors to the attitude change variance in a variety of social influence situ- ations. Until such an analysis has been achieved, we can at least make certain types of interaction predictions; for example, when we con- trast simple and unambiguous conformity situations with more subtle argumentative persuasion situations, as described above. The recep- tion mediator can be assumed to play a larger role in determining the personality-influencibility relationship in the latter situation. We can, therefore, predict that the relationship of a variable like intelligence to attitude change will be predictably different in one of the situations as compared to the other. Specifically, the level of intelligence which produces maximum influencibility will be higher in the latter situa- tion than in the former. The strategy in the research discussed below is to derive from the theory predictions regarding these situation-per- sonality interaction effects as regards attitude change.

General Strategy for Testing the Theory

The generic concept imbedded in the theory we have been display- ing here is that a personality characteristic over its whole range will exhibit a nonmonotonic relationship to influencibility. Further, a whole family of these inverted-U functions are derivable, such that the vertical and horizontal displacement of the inflection point (the level of the personality characteristic at which maximal attitude change occurs) varies from situation to situation in predictable ways in accord with the absolute and relative weightings of the variance mediated by the reception and the yielding processes. Predictions from the theory can be tested in terms of within and between experimental comparisons from research already reported in the literature, as we have attempted to demonstrate elsewhere (McGuire, 1968 a,b). In this chapter we will evaluate the theoretical formulation in terms of two experiments designed specifically to test its derivations. These two studies were designed to test predictions regarding an overall non-monotonic function, situational differences in the location of this function and interactions between chronic and acute variations of the personality characteristic. In the next section these two experiments and their implications for the present formulation will be discussed.

TWO EXPERIMENTS DESIGNED TO TEST THE SYSTEMS THEORY

A systems theory is developed to some extent inductively by the sequential addition of postulates that can account increasingly well for the obtained empirical relationships in an area. There is also, of course, an a priori deductive process in inferring the additional postulate. Studies designed to test the adequacy of the present systems theory in accounting for personality-influencibility relationships can also be used in the theory-formulating enterprise to suggest new hypotheses required to make the formulation valid. The two studies that will be described in this section can be viewed as serving this double function. These two experiments, one by Millman (1965) utilizing anxiety as the personality characteristic, and the other by Nisbett and Gordon (1967) focusing on self-esteem, were parallel in many regards; but while each study employed its personality characteristic to test similar predictions, there were certain differences in the two designs in that they were intended to supplement one another to some extent. Each involved essentially the same three-variable orthogonal design, which included acute variations of the personality characteristic, chronic variations of it, and variations in the situational weighting of the reception mediator. There were, however, a number of differences in experimental tactics between the two studies, introduced either for convenience or to allow testing of slightly different nuances of the theory. The two studies were done simultaneously and therefore did not allow the accumulation of sophistication that would have resulted from one study being built on the experience of the other. Although they were done simultaneously and are similar in design, we shall describe them separately and successively for clarity and exposition.

SUSAN MILLMAN'S ANXIETY STUDY

Predictions

The Millman experiment was designed to test some of the implications of the present systems theory as applied to anxiety by McGuire (1961, 1963). According to this formulation, the overall relationship between the person's anxiety level while he is being exposed to a persuasive message and the message's attitude change impact will be nonmonotonic, provided we accept the assumptions (McGuire, 1968a) that anxiety is negatively related to the reception mediator and positively to the yielding mediator.

Since the theory leaves the precise parameters unspecified, any outcome (except perhaps the appearance of a full right-side-up U-shaped function) between the two variables could be handled by the theory. Hence, to facilitate the opportunity for disconfirmation, interaction predictions were made along the lines suggested by corollary 2 and postulate III. That is, it was predicted that an experimentally manipulated increase in acute anxiety would add less to the persuasibility of those already high in chronic anxiety than to those who operated on lower levels of chronic anxiety. Furthermore, it was predicted that increases in the anxiety level would have less beneficial effects on attitude change with hard to comprehend messages as compared to easy ones. The study was also designed to tease out three components of the momentary anxiety level: the person's chronic anxiety level, the anxiety produced by the contents of the message, and situationally induced anxiety from manipulations irrelevant to the communication topic. It had been hoped that the relationships of these various anxiety variables to the two mediators could be adequately studied. Unfortunately, practical considerations made it necessary to curtail some aspects of this research prematurely so that the results are not completely satisfactory in those regards. Another aspect of the experiment which we record here that is far from ideal is that the manipulation seems to have been unsuccessful with one of the two issues used so that the results reported below deal with only half of the obtained data. Further details on these points are discussed by Millman (1965).

It should be understood that our criticism does not imply that the two experiments reported here are poor compared to other research on personality-influencibility relationships. On the contrary, we regard these two experiments as far above the average of those reported in the literature. The shortcomings in this general body of research include: poor measures of the dependent, independent and intervening variables; inadequate manipulations; small sample size; sampling a too-narrow range on the personality variable; designs, etc. All of these have troubled us ever since we grappled in detail with this problem in the McGuire and Ryan study (1955). These inadequacies seem to us responsible for the unusually conflicting body of results in this area. We resolved at that early date not to publish personally any empirical results in this personality-influencibility area until we could undertake a study of sufficient scope that would add comprehension rather than confusion to the area. It did not seem appropriate to impose the same stringent demands on the published research of our students or on our own informally circulated work. We do not believe that the time and place to be silent and to speak out is the same for every man or every form of discourse.

Method

The aspects of the Millman study that we shall describe here involved presenting 48 college students with a tape recorded discussion of a scholarly nature which argued that the population of China would soon reach a high figure (in excess of what most college students would spontaneously estimate without having been exposed to a persuasive recording). Half the students heard the tape recorded discussion under good technical conditions; the other half heard it overrecorded with noise that made comprehension somewhat difficult. This difference represented the high versus low comprehensibility variations.

Each of the other two independent variables involved the subject's anxiety. One of these involved his chronic anxiety level, as given by his score on a shortened version of the Taylor Manifest Anxiety Scale, adjusted post factum for social desirability. On the basis of these adjusted chronic anxiety scores (obtained prior to the experimental manipulations), the subjects were partitioned by a median split into high and low chronic anxiety subgroups. Orthogonally to this chronic anxiety variation, the person's acute anxiety was manipulated by fear arousing conditions having nothing to do with the message topic. Half of the subjects were told that they would subsequently be performing at the task in a moderately warm and humid room (the acute low anxiety condition) and the other half were told that they would be subsequently performing while receiving severe electric shocks (the acute high anxiety condition). Hence, the experiment as we shall describe it here consisted of a $2 \times 2 \times 2$ design.

The study was presented to the subjects as a test of verbal comprehension under different stress conditions. He was told that he would first be given a test of aural comprehension under ordinary learning conditions and then under a high stress condition. The low acute group were told that the stress condition would involve working in a warm room; and the high acute group, that it would involve taking the test while being exposed to severe electric shock. The various personality tests which the subjects were given were explained as being means of determining what kinds of people are most affected by stress. No mention was made that the subject's opinions regarding the topics of the messages would be measured or that the hypotheses dealt with influencibility. After the acute anxiety level was manipulated by the description of the low or high threat condition described above, the subjects were presented with tape recorded messages which were supposedly the comprehension test materials but actually were the persuasive inductions. After he had heard the tape recorded dialogue under "normal" conditions, the subject's comprehension of the contents was measured as was his own opinion regarding the point at issue, namely, the likely population of China in coming years. Comprehension was measured by eight multiple choice items; and opinion change was assessed by the before-after change score on a six-item opinionnaire. The experiment was terminated when these measures were obtained; that is, the subjects were not asked actually to perform under the stress conditions whose description constituted the acute anxiety manipulation. The true purpose of the experiment was then revealed to the subjects and the nature and reasons for the deceits employed were explained to them. They were asked not to discuss the experiment with others.

Results

The checks on the manipulations indicated that the three independent variables were successfully varied as intended. However, this was the case only for the "China" issue that yielded the results we report here, and not for a second "mental illness" issue. Hence there is some slight danger that these results represent a post factum capitalization on chance differences. Less worrisome is the fact that on some of the anxiety manipulation checks, the intended differences did not appear at a statistically significant level (Millman, 1965). This is probably due, at least in part, to the fact that this study was designed as a methodological tour de force as regards measures of anxiety. Inevitably, the broad net that was cast in selecting indicatiors resulted in some of them not yielding significant differences.

As regards the mediating variable of message comprehension, the situational manipulation of comprehensibility, not surprisingly, had a significant effect. The message heard in the low comprehensible condition (with a noisy overrecording) produced significantly lower scores than the message heard under the better auditory clarity conditions. The acute anxiety manipulation also had a significant effect on message comprehensibility, with those under the high threat condition learning the contents better than did those anticipating only the mildly stressful treatment. Chronic anxiety level had only a trivial relationship to message comprehension. The interaction between chronic and acute anxiety was also insignificant though one might have expected such an interaction on the basis of the Taylor-Spence theorizing.

A quite different picture emerges as regards the opinion change dependent variable. Persons in the high anxiety condition showed slightly more opinion change than those in the low with both the chronic and acute variations, but neither difference reached the conventional level of statistical significance. The present theory made no predictions about such main effects. Most interesting for the present theory was that there was a sizeable interaction between these two variables in the predicted direction. Those chronically low in anxiety showed more opinion change under induced high threat than low; while those chronically high in anxiety showed depressed attitude change when they were exposed to high threat. This is the kind of relationship one would expect on the basis of Postulate II and its corollaries, which imply that if the person is chronically low in anxiety, an induced fright will tend to raise his anxiety to the optimal intermediate level; while if he is chronically high, the fear arousing induction will tend to raise his anxiety beyond the optimal.

Unfortunately for the theory, or at least for the testing of it in this situation, the attempted message comprehensibility variation was not successful in producing a significant difference in opinion change. Hence, there was no opportunity to test for the predictions of situational-personality interaction which could be derived on the basis of Postulate III. Furthermore, as in most attitude change research (McGuire, 1966, 1968b), the gross measures of message comprehension and of attitude change showed only a trivial relationship. Indeed the effects of the independent variables on the two measures, learning and attitude change, tended to be maddeningly reciprocal as regards what was significant: those variables that were significantly related to one of these measures tended to be unrelated to the other.

THE NISBETT-GORDON SELF-ESTEEM STUDY

The Nisbett and Gordon study essentially paralleled that of Susan Millman, except that self-esteem played the role in their study which anxiety played in hers. They used a three-variable orthogonal design including chronic and acute variations in self-esteem and high versus low message complexity. The resources in their study were, however, invested somewhat differently than in hers in that they employed more subjects and used a more drastic manipulation of message complexity but omitted the direct measure of the reception mediator and utilized their subjects in groups rather than individually.

Method

In this study, as in the Millman study, college students served as the subjects and the research was represented as concerned with their comprehension of the materials presented, without mention of any interest in their persuasibility. We shall provide here a somewhat simplified account of the experimental conditions, a fuller description being conveniently available elsewhere (Nisbett and Gordon, 1967). The chronic and acute self-esteem independent variables were manipulated along the lines of a contemporaneous study done in our laboratory (Conlon, 1965). Chronic self-esteem was measured by a self-report scale derived from the MMPI with numerous adaptations by McGuire and Ryan (1955). Acute self-esteem was manipulated by administering to the subjects a pseudo-test of intelligence one week before the presentation of the persuasive material, and then telling the subject, just prior to that presentation, his purported score on the intelligence test. Half the subjects, chosen at random, were given information indicating that they had done extremely well on this supposed intelligence test (the acute high self-esteem group) and the remainder were given information which suggested that they had done very poorly (the acute low self-esteem group). Immediately after this false feedback, the persuasive materials were presented.

The persuasive messages were of two types, one rather sparse of content, which was designed to allow but little variation in the reception mediator. As the social influence situation designed to allow relatively little variance as regards reception, a conformity induction was employed in which positions regarding health practices were clearly stated in one sentence and the subjects were given norms which indicated the clearcut consensus of health authorities regarding these practices. (The critical items for measuring conformity effects were two practices on which the position represented as the authority viewpoint was quite discrepant from those which college students ordinarily endorsed.) The second type of social influence situation, allowing for more variance in the reception mediator, involved presenting subjects with lengthy, semitechnical passages arguing for a stand on certain health practices that were quite at variance with those ordinarily espoused by college students. After presentation of these two types of social influence inductions, the subjects were given an opinionnaire which constituted an after-only measure of their opinions on these several health issues involved in the design. The session was then ended with a revelation that the intelligence test scores which they had been given were completely fictitious and of the other critical aspects of the experiment.

Results

Although the experimenters received a strong clinical impression that the false feedback of intelligence test scores at the beginning of the second persuasion session made a considerable impression upon the subjects, the check on this success-failure manipulation did not show a conventionally significant difference in self-esteem. On all three checks on this manipulation, the difference was in the appropriate direction, but none of the differences attained the .05 level of significance. In view of this indifferent success of the acute self-esteem manipulation, the relationship of this variable to opinion change must be interpreted with some caution.

Because in the Nisbett-Gordon study it was feasible to employ considerably more subjects than in the Millman study reported above, the sample was partitioned into more than two levels as regards chronic self-esteem. The results as regards chronic self-esteem and influencibility are quite in keeping with the systems theory outlined in the previous section, and the assumptions (McGuire, 1968a) that self-esteem is positively related to the reception mediator and negatively to the yielding mediator. In the low reception variance, conformity situation, the inverted-U shaped nonmonotonic relationship is plainly shown between chronic self-esteem and attitude change. In the high reception variance, persuasion condition, where we would expect the inflection point to occur at much higher levels of self-esteem, the relationship between chronic self-esteem and persuasibility is an increasing one throughout the entire range of self-esteem sampled. These results are in line with what one would be led to expect on the basis of Postulate III. It should be noted that the positive relationship between self-esteem and persuasibility found here tends to confirm that found by McGuire and Ryan (1955) and to reverse the Janis (1954) finding and the "common sense" prediction one makes when one commits the common fallacy of ignoring the role of the reception mediator.

The results as regards the acute self-esteem variable are much less supportive of the theory, as might be expected in view of the indifferent success of its manipulation. There was no main effect of acute self-esteem on attitude change in either the social influence situation involving low reception variance or in that involving high reception variance. Furthermore, there is no significant interaction between chronic and acute self-esteem variables such as is required by corollary 2. In fact, such evidence on this interaction as can be deduced from the data suggests that the shape of the relationship is the reverse of that derivable from the model, such that a success experience may increase the influencibility of those low in chronic self-esteem more than that of the chronic highs.

EMPIRICAL STATUS OF THE THEORY

Neither the Millman (1965) nor the Nisbett and Gordon (1967) experiments have provided anything like a thorough and definitive test of the systems theory which has been partially presented here and discussed more fully elsewhere (McGuire, 1968a). The inadequacy of the two studies in this regard is manifest even though these studies were more elaborately designed and more carefully done than most of the research in the personality-influencibility area and were planned specifically to test the theory. Even less definitive are those studies in the literature which were designed independently of the present theory, although some of the individual studies, such as those reported by Gelfand (1962) and by Silverman (1964), confront the theory almost as effectively as the two studies described here that were designed explicitly for that purpose. Also, some cross-experimental comparisons of results (such as between the Janis [1954] and the McGuire and Ryan [1955] studies) can also be nicely ordered by the theory.

A number of deficiencies can be specified in the previous personality-persuasibility research (and, as indicated above, the two studies described here are not entirely free from these defects) as regards an adequate test of the systems theory developed here. The manipulations of the personality variables are often inadequate (or at least are inadequately detected by the checks on the manipulation). The subject populations have tended to be so narrow that the chronic variation represented in the sample tends to be too small and too atypical to leave us confident that a sufficiently wide range of the variable has been tapped to allow the nonmonotonic overall relationship to appear. The complex interactions between the chronic and acute variations on a given personality dimension, as suggested by corollary 2 of Postulate III and by Postulate IV of the fuller treatment of this systems theory (McGuire, 1968a) remains to be investigated, or even to be adequately specified theoretically.

Still other deficiencies in the empirical research stand in the way of an adequate testing of the systems theory that we have been developing. Refined measures of the mediating processes are lacking. A direct measure has been attempted only for the reception mediator, and measures of content learning have been rather inadequate in all but a few carefully designed attitude change studies (Watts and McGuire, 1964; see also Greenwald's chapter in this volume). Direct measures of the yielding variable have been neglected altogether, though proposals in this regard have been made (McGuire, 1961, 1968a). We also need a more sophisticated understanding of the relationship between purported proximal dependent variables (such as reception) and the more distal ones (such as opinion change) which they are supposedly mediating as regards relationship to the independent variable. Aspects of this almost metascientific question have been explored elsewhere (McGuire, 1969).

In general, it seems to us that the adequate testing of a systems theory requires a more than usually elaborate empirical effort. The characteristics of such elaborate experimentation include: multivariable orthogonal designs; wide ranges on the independent variables; direct measures of the mediating processes as well as the distal dependent variable, and covariance analyses that will determine the relationship between the independent and the dependent variable with and without adjustment of the several mediators. Research of this scope is currently under way in our laboratory.

References

Asch, S. E. Studies of independence and conformity: A minority of one against a unanimous majority. *Psychological Monographs*, 1956, **70**(9, Whole No. 416).

Conlon, E. T. Performance as determined by expectation of success or failure. Ph.D. dissertation, Columbia University, 1965.

Cox, D. F., and Bauer, R. A. Self-confidence and persuasibility in women. *Public Opinion Quarterly*, 1964, **28**, 453-466.

Gelfand, D. M. The influence of self-esteem on the rate of verbal conditioning and social watching behavior. *Journal of Abnormal and Social Psychology*, 1962, **65**, 259-265.

Hovland, C. I. Effects of the mass media of communication. In G. Lindzey (Ed.), *Handbook of social psychology*. Reading, Mass: Addison-Wesley, 1954. Pp. 1062-1103.

Hovland, C. I., Lumsdaine, A. A., and Sheffield, F. D. *Experiments on mass communications*. Princeton, N. J.: Princeton University Press, 1949.

Hull, C. L. *Hypnosis and suggestibility*. New York: Appleton, 1933.

Janis, I. L. Personality correlates of susceptibility to persuasion. *Journal of Personality*, 1954, **22**, 504-518.

McGuire, W. J. *Correlates of persuasibility and of immunizibility against persuasion.* (Proposal to the National Science Foundation) Urbana, Ill.: University of Illinois, 1961.

McGuire, W. J. *Effectiveness of fear appeals in advertising.* New York: Advertising Research Foundation, 1963.

McGuire, W. J. Attitudes and opinions. *Annual Review of Psychology*, 1966, **17**, 475-514.

McGuire, W. J. Some impending reorientations in social psychology. *Journal of Experimental Social Psychology*, 1967, **3**, 124-139.

McGuire, W. J. Personality and susceptibility to social influence. In E. F. Borgatta and W. W. Lambert (Eds.), *Handbook of personality theory and research.* Chicago: Rand McNally, 1968, in press. (a)

McGuire, W. J. Attitudes and attitude change. In G. Lindzey and E. Aronson (Eds.), *Handbook of social psychology*. (2nd ed.) Reading, Mass: Addison-Wesley, 1968, Vol. 3, in press. (b)

McGuire, W. J. The learning theory approach to attitude change. In C. McClintock (Ed.), *Experimental social psychology*. New York: Holt, 1969, in preparation.

McGuire, W. J., and Ryan, J. Receptivity as a mediator of personality-persuasibility relationships. Minneapolis: University of Minnesota, Laboratory for Research in Social Relations, 1955. (Mimeo)

Millman, S. The relationship between anxiety, learning and opinion change. Ph.D. dissertation, Columbia University, 1965.

Nisbett, R. E., and Gordon, A. Self-esteem and susceptibility to social influence. *Journal of Personality and Social Psychology*, 1967, **5**, 268-276.

Ring, K. Experimental social psychology: Some sober questions about some frivolous values. *Journal of Experimental Social Psychology*, 1967, **3**, 113-123.

Sherif, M. A study of some social factors in perception. *Archives of Psychology, New York* 1935, No. 187.

Silverman, I. Differential effects of ego threat upon persuasibility for high and low self-esteem subjects. *Journal of Abnormal and Social Psychology*, 1964, **69**, 567-572.

Silverman, I., Ford, L. H., and Morganti, J. B. Inter-related effects of social desirability, sex, self-esteem and complexity of argument on persuasibility. *Journal of Personality*, 1966, **34**, 555-568.

Smith, M. B. Attitude change. In *Encyclopedia of the social sciences*, 1968, in press. (Mimeo, 1965.)

Watts, W. A., and McGuire, W. J. Persistence of induced opinion change and retention of inducing message content. *Journal of Abnormal and Social Psychology*, 1964, **68**, 233-241.

8

Attitudes as Self-Descriptions: Another Look at the Attitude-Behavior Link[1]

DARYL J. BEM

DEPARTMENT OF PSYCHOLOGY
CARNEGIE-MELLON UNIVERSITY
PITTSBURGH, PENNSYLVANIA

An attitude is an individual's self-description of his affinities for and aversions to some identifiable aspect of his environment. This is not, of course, one of the definitions advanced in the social-psychological literature on attitudes, but it is the definition that an unreconstructed behaviorist would offer after perusing that literature carefully. For no matter what conceptual definition of an attitude an author advances in the introduction to an article, its operational metamorphosis into a subject's self-descriptive statement appears to be a fairly predictable feature of the method section.

Even reconstructed behaviorists, who equate attitudes with internal mediating responses, are found, in their methods sections, plying their subjects with pencil, paper, and Semantic Differential, an instrument that theoretically taps verbal descriptions of internal "affective" responses (e.g., Fishbein, 1967; Osgood, Suci, & Tannenbaum, 1957; Staats & Staats, 1958). The so-named "cognitive" component of an attitude is ordinarily equated with self-descriptive

[1]Preparation of this article was supported by National Science Foundation Grant GS 1452 for the study of "Self-Awareness and Self-Control." The study on brown bread consumption could not have been conducted without the invaluable aid of Harlan L. Lane, David M. Carlson, William Sheppard, Father Secondo Sarpieri, Tom J. Nelson, and the kitchen staff of the St. Louis Home for Exceptional Boys, Chelsea, Michigan. Sandra L. Bem made valuable comments on the conceptual treatment of self-instruction.

belief statements, and we typically assess the "behavioral" component of an attitude by inquiring of our subjects whether they have quit smoking since our experimental manipulation or if they would rather fight than switch. It is our subjects who observe their affect, their cognitions, their smoking, fighting, or switching; and, operationally, it is their descriptions of those observations which comprise their attitudes.

It is true, of course, that investigators sometimes employ physiological measures, disguised or indirect indices, and even behavioral observations in attitude research, but these are typically treated as supplementary variables whose relations to the "real" attitudes — that is, subjects' self-descriptions — are considered empirical matters, if not the goal of the research itself. Even when these variables are to be equated definitionally with attitudes, they are almost always validated against the self-descriptive measure first to ascertain that they are, in fact, indices of the "real" attitudes. (See Campbell, 1950, and McGuire, 1966, for reviews.) Self-descriptions thus remain the ultimate operational criterion of the "real" attitude. Why not, then, our conceptual definition?

This suggestion is not meant to be facetious, for we should like to propose here that viewing attitudes as self-descriptions in their own right has heuristic value for re-examining the classical problem of the relationships between attitudes and behaviors. In particular, we should like to suggest specific mechanisms through which attitudes can function as both independent and dependent variables in the attitude-behavior link. For our purposes, then, an attitude *is* an individual's self-description of his affinities for and aversions to some identifiable aspect of his environment.

ATTITUDES AS DESCRIPTIONS OF INTERNAL STATES

In general terms, it would appear that individuals learn to describe stimuli in their environment through some process of discrimination training. Further, it would appear that such descriptions can and do generalize along several dimensions to similar stimuli with which an individual has had no direct previous encounter. Although linguistic skills may modify and facilitate this procedure in ways which are not entirely understood, the basic paradigm would still appear to hold. Presumably, too, this basic paradigm applies as well to stimuli that are located in the individual's private internal environment. In training a child to describe pain, for example, the socializing community, at some point, must teach him the correct descriptive responses when the appropriate private stimuli are impinging upon him. Or, as Skinner (1953, 1957) suggests, self-descriptions of some internal stimuli can be learned through metaphor or stimulus generalization. The child may learn to describe "butterflies in the stomach" without explicit discrimination training.

Attitude statements may have a similar basis. Thus, the ability of individuals to respond reliably on instruments like the Semantic Differential may have been acquired because the internal "affective" responses have been paired with external stimuli for which the individual already possesses a set of descriptors or because the internal responses share common attributes with such external stimuli. The mediational theories which underlie the use of the Semantic Differential propose mechanisms by which "affective" responses get hooked up to stimulus objects, but they have remained mute about the process by which the individual can respond verbally to these internal responses.

Skinner (1953, 1957), however, has analyzed the limited resources available to the community for training its members to respond differentially to their internal states and has concluded that such "self-knowledge" would necessarily suffer from inevitable inadequacies, a conclusion which now has some experimental support. For example, Osgood et al. (1957) report that responses on the Semantic Differential can be factor analyzed into a very small number of factors, factors which appear to have extensive cross-cultural generality as well. This finding is consistent with the hypothesis that an individual is unable to make more than a small number of independent discriminations among stimuli that have never been publicly available to his socializing community.

It also appears that the internal stimulus control of an individual's self-descriptions can be easily overridden by external sources of control. For example, Valins (1966) was able to manipulate attitudes toward stimulus pictures of seminude females by giving his male subjects false auditory feedback which they could interpret as their heartbeat. In general, private stimuli may play a smaller role than the individual himself suspects. For example, by manipulating the external cues of the situation, Schachter and Singer (1962) were able to evoke self-descriptions of emotional states as disparate as euphoria and anger from subjects in whom operationally identical states of physiological arousal had been induced. It appears that these subjects utilized internal stimuli only to make the gross discrimination that they were emotional, but that the more subtle discrimination of *which* emotion they were experiencing was under the control of external cues.

If, in fact, discriminations of internal stimuli are as fragile and as gross as these considerations suggest, then we must look to other sources of information to which the individual can turn to arrive at his highly differentiated sets of attitudes. One potential source of information resides in his beliefs, the "cognitive" component of his attitude. Fishbein (1967) has proposed an extended behavioral model of attitude formation which incorporates beliefs into the attitude formation process, and some consistency theorists have proposed mechanisms that could provide a cognitive base for attitudinal description. These models also have the virtue of clarifying ways in which attitude change can occur when beliefs are changed through persuasive techniques.

Attitudes, then, can be viewed as self-descriptions which are partially based on the individual's observations of his internal "affective" responses and his beliefs or "cognitive" responses. Some such process is usually just assumed rather than made explicit when attitudes are measured. The heuristic value of making the process explicit becomes clearer when we consider the "behavioral" component of attitudes. It is to this source of attitudinal self-description that we now turn.

ATTITUDES AS DESCRIPTIONS OF BEHAVIOR

It was mentioned earlier that the socializing community could teach a child to describe pain by providing him with the correct verbal response at the critical time when the appropriate private stimuli are impinging upon him. But, the community itself must necessarily identify the "critical time" on the basis of observable stimuli or responses and implicitly assume that the private stimuli are, in fact, accompanying these public events. This suggests the possibility that many of the self-descriptive statements that appear to be exclusively under the discriminative control of private stimuli may, in fact, still be partially controlled by the same accompanying events used by the socializing community itself to infer the individual's inner states. To put this into the present context, an individual's attitudes and the attitudes that an outside observer would attribute to him may be functionally similar in that both are partial "inferences" from the same evidence: the public behaviors and accompanying cues upon which the socializing community has relied in training him to make such self-descriptive statements in the first place. For convenience, we shall term this hypothesis the interpersonal model of self-perception. To illustrate, when the answer to the question, "Do you like brown bread?" is "I guess I do, I'm always eating it," it seems clear that the individual's own overt behavior is the source of his attitude. Indeed, his reply is functionally equivalent to the reply his wife might give for him: "I guess he does, he is always eating it." Only to the extent that "brown bread" elicits strongly conditioned internal responses, might he have additional evidence, not currently available to his wife, on which to base his self-descriptive statement.

This analysis does not imply, of course, that the individual will always explicitly identify the evidence upon which his attitudes are based—as is the case in this example—nor is it necessarily true that he *could* verbalize the basis of his inference if asked to do so. As Heider (1958) has said in connection with interpersonal perception, "Attributions may not be experienced as interpretations at all, but rather as intrinsic to the original stimuli [p. 256]." Our interpersonal model of self-perception, then, similarly does not require that a chain of inference be a part of the individual's phenomenology when he states his attitudes.

Evidence for the self-perception model has been marshaled indirectly, by reinterpreting studies conducted within the framework of cognitive dissonance theory (Festinger, 1957) and directly through laboratory experimentation (Bandler, Madaras & Bem, in press; Bem, 1965, 1966, 1967). We shall here present only an abbreviated description of some of these studies.[2]

ATTITUDES AS A FUNCTION OF FORCED-COMPLIANCE

A number of studies have been conducted within cognitive dissonance theory which employ the forced-compliance paradigm. In these experiments, an individual is induced to engage in some behavior that would imply his endorsement of a particular set of beliefs or attitudes. Following his behavior, his belief or attitude is assessed to see if it is a function of the behavior in which he has engaged and of the manipulated stimulus conditions under which it was evoked. The most widely cited study of this type was conducted by Festinger

---

[2]A more complete presentation of the data presented in the following section as well as an explicit comparison between dissonance theory and the present formulation will be found in Bem (1967).

and Carlsmith (1959). In their experiment, 60 undergraduates were randomly assigned to one of three experimental conditions. In the $1 condition, the subject was first required to perform long repetitive laboratory tasks in an individual experimental session. He was then hired by the experimenter as an "assistant" and paid $1 to tell a waiting fellow student (a stooge) that the tasks were enjoyable and interesting. In the $20 condition, each subject was hired for $20 to do the same thing. Control subjects simply engaged in the repetitive tasks. After the experiment, each subject indicated how much he had enjoyed the tasks. The results show that the subjects paid $1 evaluated the tasks as significantly more enjoyable than did subjects who had been paid $20. The $20 subjects did not express attitudes significantly different from those expressed by the control subjects.

To interpret these findings within the self-perception framework, consider the viewpoint of an outside observer who hears the individual making favorable statements about the tasks to a fellow student, and who further knows that the individual was paid $1 ($20) to do so. This hypothetical observer is then asked to state the actual attitude of the individual he has heard. An outside observer would almost certainly judge a $20 communicator to be under the control of the reinforcement contingencies of the money and not at all under the discriminative control of the tasks he appears to be describing. That is, the $20 communicator is not credible in that his statements cannot be used as a guide for inferring his actual attitudes. Hence, the observer could conclude that the individual found such repetitive tasks dull and boring in spite of what he has said. Although the behavior of a $1 communicator might also appear to be partially controlled by the payoff, an outside observer would be more likely to judge him to be expressing his actual attitudes and hence, would infer the communicator's attitude from the content of the communication itself. He would thus judge this individual to be favorable toward the tasks. If one now places our hypothetical observer and the communicator into the same skin, the findings obtained by Festinger and Carlsmith are the result. The final attitudes are thus viewed as a set of self-judgments made by the individual about his own behavior in the light of the contextual constraints in which it appears to be occurring.

This analysis of the findings was tested by actually having outside observers attempt to infer the attitude of a subject in the original study. Conceptually, this replicated the Festinger-Carlsmith experiment with the single exception that the observer and the observed were no longer the same individual. More precisely, this provided a *simulation* of the Festinger-Carlsmith experiment, a test of the hypothesis that self-judgments and interpersonal judgments are "outputs" of the same "program." Like a computer simulation, then, a successful replication of the inverse functional relation between amount of compensation and the final attitude statement would provide a sufficiency test, a plausibility demonstration, of the process that we propose lies behind the phenomenon.

Seventy-five college undergraduates participated in the simulation, 25 subjects each in a $1, a $20, or a control condition. All subjects listened to a tape recording which described a college sophomore named Bob Downing, who had participated in an experiment involving two motor tasks. The tasks were described in detail, but non-evaluatively; the alleged purpose of the experiment was also described. At this point, the control subjects were asked to evaluate Bob's attitudes toward the tasks. The experimental subjects were further told that Bob had accepted an offer of $1 ($20) to go into the waiting room and tell the next subject that the tasks had been enjoyable. The subjects then listened to a brief conversation which they were told was an actual recording of Bob and the girl subject who was in the waiting room. In sum, the situation attempted to duplicate on tape the situation actually experienced by Festinger and Carlsmith's subjects, and all of the subjects in the simulation estimated Bob's responses to the same set of questions employed in the original study.

Table 1 shows the mean ratings for the key question given by the subjects in all three conditions of both the original Festinger and Carlsmith experiment and the present simulation. The key question required subjects to rate Bob's attitude toward the tasks on a scale from −5 to +5, where −5 means that the tasks were extremely dull and boring, +5 means they were extremely interesting and enjoyable, and 0 means they were neutral, neither interesting nor uninteresting.

The results show that in both studies the $1 and control conditions are on different sides of the neutral point and are significantly different from one another at the .02 level of significance. (In the original $t = 2.48$ and in the simulation $t = 2.60$; two-tailed tests are used throughout this discussion.) In both studies, the $1 condition produced significantly more favorable ratings toward the tasks than did the $20 condition ($t = 2.22$, $p < .03$ and $t = 3.52$, $p < .001$ in the original and present studies, respectively). In neither study is the $20 condition significantly different from the control condition; and, finally, in neither study were there any significant differences between conditions on the other questions asked of the subjects about the experiment. Thus, the inverse relation between amount of compensation and the final attitude rating is clearly replicated; and, even though our conceptual model does not require the interpersonal

TABLE 1
ATTITUDE RATINGS AND INTERPERSONAL ESTIMATES OF
ATTITUDE RATINGS TOWARD THE TASKS FOR EACH CONDITION

	Experimental condition		
Study	Control	One dollar compensation	Twenty dollar compensation
Festinger-Carlsmith ($N=20$ in each condition)	−0.45	+1.35	−0.05
Interpersonal simulation ($N=25$ in each condition)	−1.56	+0.52	−1.96

judgments to actually duplicate those of the original subjects, it is seen that the two sets of ratings are quite comparable on the 10-point scales.

An extended version of the simulation just presented (Bem, 1967) provides additional support for our interpretation, and even more direct support comes from a study by Jones (1966), who obtained subjects' attitudes and observers' judgments in the same experiment and found results comparable to our own. Interpersonal simulations of other forced-compliance experiments indicate that beliefs about external events as well as judgments about internal states like hunger are functionally similar to attitudes in that they, too, can be self-judgments based on the individual's observations of his own overt behavior and the stimulus conditions under which it occurs (Bem, 1965).

ATTITUDES AS A FUNCTION OF FREE CHOICE

The dissonance theorists have uncovered a second phenomenon which is amenable to the self-perception interpretation: the re-evaluation of alternatives following choice. In studies of this phenomenon, a subject is permitted to make a selection from a set of objects or courses of action. The dependent variable is his subsequent attitude toward the chosen and rejected alternatives. It is typically found that the subject enhances his rating of the chosen alternative following his choice and lowers his rating of the rejected alternatives. An experiment by Brehm and Cohen is illustrative (1959).

In their experiment, school children were permitted to select a toy as a gift for themselves and were then asked to rate their liking for several toys, including the alternatives they had chosen and rejected in making their selection. These ratings were then compared to initial ratings obtained a week before the experiment. The displacement effect appeared as predicted: Chosen toys were displaced in the more favorable direction; rejected toys were generally displaced in the unfavorable direction.

To interpret this phenomenon as a self-perception effect, consider two hypothetical observers, each charged with trying to estimate a child's ratings of the various toys. Let us assume that the first observer has not seen the child whose attitudes he is attempting to judge engage in any behavior with respect to the toys; the second observer, however, has just seen his child select one of the toys as a gift for himself. Note that the comparison between the first and second observers parallels, respectively, the pre-choice and post-choice ratings of the toys made by the child himself in the original experiment. It seems likely that the second observer would estimate the child's attitude toward the chosen toy to be more favorable and his attitude toward the rejected toys to be less favorable than would the first observer simply because the second observer has some behavioral evidence upon which to base differential estimates of the child's attitudes toward the alternatives. If one now regards the children themselves as observers of their own choice behavior and their attitudes as inferences from that behavior, one arrives at a prediction of the displacement effect reported by Brehm and Cohen: Chosen toys will be displaced upward in the post-choice ratings and rejected toys will be displaced downward.

We tested this conceptual analysis in an interpersonal simulation in which 24 college students served as control subjects by estimating how an 11-year-old boy might rate several different toys. The toys were selected from the list reported by Brehm and Cohen (1959) and were rated on the same rating scales. An additional 96 college students served as experimental subjects by again rating the attitudes of an 11-year-old boy, but they were told that the child had selected one of the toys as a gift for himself. The subjects were told which toy had been selected and from which alternatives he had been permitted to choose.

The results clearly supported our analysis. The chosen toy, which had a mean control-group rating of 3.5 on the five point "liking" scale, rose over half a scale point to 4.0 in the experimental-group estimates of the child's attitudes. That is, the observers who knew that the child had selected the toy as a gift for himself rated it as significantly better liked than did the control subjects. Similarly, the rejected alternatives were displaced significantly in the downward direction toward the "dislike" end of the scale. The total displacement effect was significant well beyond the .001 level ($t = 9.11$). Elsewhere (Bem, 1967) we have presented an internal analysis of the data from the Brehm and Cohen experiment and our simulation which further supports the self-perception model of this phenomenon.

As noted earlier, the technique of interpersonal simulation provides, at best, a sufficiency test or plausibility argument for our theory. In addition, the complex stimulus manipulations employed in cognitive dissonance experiments are often subject to several interpretations, a point frequently noted by critics of the research (e.g., Chapanis & Chapanis, 1964). For example, monetary payoffs have both informational value as well as reinforcement value in a forced-compliance experiment, a fact that has produced a tangle of conflicting findings. (See McGuire, 1966, for a review.)

For these reasons, we sought more direct support for the self-perception model by "raising stimuli from birth" in the laboratory that would have no functional properties other than those we have imputed to the stimulus manipulations in the dissonance studies. In addition, it seemed desirable to utilize a design in which each subject was his own control and provided a complete replication of the experiment. For example, in one of the studies reported in Bem (1965), subjects were first trained to tell the truth in the presence of one colored light and to tell lies in the presence of another. Later in the experimental session, subjects were required to state attitudes with which they disagreed; one of the two colored lights was illuminated as each attitude statement was made. If attitudes are based, in part, on the individual's observation of his own behavior and the stimulus context in which it occurs, then subjects should subsequently endorse the attitude statements that they had uttered in the presence of the "truth light" significantly more than attitude statements they had made in the presence of the "lie light." The lights, in short, should influence their own self-credibility. The results support this hypothesis, and furthermore, no subject could report any awareness of the control exerted by his statements or the lights over his subsequent attitudes. The same technique was employed in another study to demonstrate that an individual can be induced to believe in "false confessions" he has made, but only if they are uttered in the presence of the "truth light" (Bem, 1966). Finally, Bandler, Madaras & Bem (in press) have demonstrated that subjects will rate electric shocks as more uncomfortable if they have observed themselves escaping from the shocks rather than enduring them, the same inference that an outside observer of their behavior would draw.

In sum, the studies described here lead us to conclude that attitudes function as the dependent variable in the attitude-behavior link through the mechanism of description. That is, the functional relation between the antecedent behavior and the consequent attitude is — to the extent that internal stimuli are not controlling — the relation between an event and an individual's description of that event. Attitudes are self-descriptions. I like brown bread because I see myself eat it.

BEHAVIOR AS A FUNCTION OF ATTITUDES

The problematic nature of the relationships between attitudes and behavior appears to be appreciated only when a set of data fails to confirm the common preconception that attitudes should behave like independent variables and cause behavior. Data which show the reverse causal sequence, like that discussed above, receive widespread attention and comment, whereas data consistent with the behavior-following-attitude sequence are apt to be dismissed as obvious. Indeed, theoretical discussions usually concern themselves with why the expected causal chain sometimes fails to occur, and they usually conclude that the behavior is determined by many situational factors and, hence, the control exerted by the attitude is swamped. We accept this general conclusion, but should like to re-open the inquiry into the possible mechanisms by which such control might be present at all. How might self-descriptions function as directives to behavior?

One suggested mechanism stems from research on the directive functions of speech, a topic which has received its most recent examination from Soviet investigators. For example, Luria (1961) has suggested that children learn to guide their own behavior by "internalizing" the directive speech of their parents. After complying with the parental command, "Put on your coat," the child is sometimes heard to repeat a similar instruction to himself on later occasions when no parent is present. Similar observations are described by Skinner (1957). Observation also suggests that parents often incorporate attitudinal descriptions within their commands in a thinly veiled attempt at justification. For example, "You don't like dogs; just leave him alone!" Even as adults we are told by our hostess, "You like brown bread. Take two slices."

We should now like to speculate that attitudes, as self-descriptions, can become "internalized" variants of the attitudinal descriptions used by parents to instruct or control the behavior of their children;

and, it is in this sense that we can expect to find a causal link between attitudes, as the independent variables, and behavior. Such a proposition is rather difficult to test, however, because the link, whatever mechanism produces it, is known to be weak, and one can expect large individual differences in the effectiveness of such self-instruction. Indeed, it seems reasonable to suppose that self-instruction should be no more effective than the interpersonal instruction from which it is derived. But, if this speculation has any merit, then there should be a positive correlation between a child's behavioral response to interpersonal instruction disguised as an attitude statement and his response to a self-instruction of the same form. The experiment described below was conducted as a first approximation to a test of this hypothesis. The dependent variable selected was the daily consumption of brown bread by a population of institutionalized boys.

Two experimental treatments were designed. In the self-instruction treatment, the techniques of programmed instruction and audio-visual stimulus presentation were employed to induce each subject to respond repeatedly with the phrase, "I like the brown bread." In the interpersonal instruction treatment, a narrator simply presented the statement "You like brown bread" repeatedly while the subject was exposed to the same visual materials employed in the self-instruction treatment. In neither treatment was there any explicit persuasion of any other kind or any communication concerning the merits of brown bread.

The predicted functional equivalence of self-instruction and interpersonal instruction is sought in a day-by-day comparison of matched pairs of subjects. The experimental design is thus comparable to single organism research in that the dependent variable is sampled repeatedly over time, and each matched pair is its own control. A control group, as such, was not employed.

METHOD

Forty-eight mentally retarded boys, the entire population of a private institution, were formed into matched pairs on the basis of chronological age, IQ, and mental age (i.e., the product of CA and IQ). Members of each pair were randomly assigned to one of the two experimental treatments.

Each subject served in an experimental room, while seated at a desk which held an audio-visual device (Graflex). This device contains a glass-screen viewer and tape recorder; color slides are projected on the screen in synchrony with the sound track. Remote controls enabled the experimenter, located in an adjacent room, to stop and start the machine at any time and to repeat the sound sequence associated with the slide on the screen. At the end of the session, the subject was paid 25 cents.

Self-Instruction Treatment

As soon as the subject was seated and the experimenter had left the room, the sound track began:

> Hi! I am going to show you some pictures about food and ask you some questions about them. Everytime you answer a question the right way, you will win a gold star. If you answer all the questions the right way, we will give you one penny for every star you have won. So, if you answer all the questions the right way, then we will give you 25 cents when you are through. If you don't answer a question, the machine will just wait until you do answer it. If you don't answer the right way, the machine *may* ask you the same question again so you can try to give the right answer. Are you ready? Here is the first picture.

The program of slides was divided into three parts. The first sequence was designed to evoke the response "yes" to the question, "Do you like brown bread?" It began with a picture of ice cream and the narration, "Here is some ice cream. Do you like ice cream?" When the correct response was made, a gold star (reinforcing slide) appeared and the narrator said, "Good for you. You have just won the first gold star." Successive slides repeated the same question with white cake, brown cookies, brown cake, and finally, brown bread. Reinforcement was always contingent upon the overt response, "yes," or an equivalent response. The second sequence was designed to evoke the response, "I like the brown bread," to the question, "Which do you like: White bread or brown bread?" This sequence began with, "Here is a picture of some castor oil medicine and some brown bread. Which do you like: Castor oil medicine or brown bread?" Successive slides presented brown bread versus the alternatives of cauliflower, asparagus, hard dry crackers, buttermilk rolls, burnt toast, and white bread which was mutilated. Two final slides in this sequence were photographed in the school dining room and showed the bread tray with brown and white bread on it as seen by the subjects at mealtime. Reinforcement was contingent upon a stated preference for the brown bread. The third sequence was designed to increase the amount of brown bread selected. It began: "Here is a plate with a little bit of ice cream and a plate with a lot of ice cream. Which do you like: A little bit or a lot?" This format was repeated with brown cookies, brown cake, and brown bread; the last picture had again been taken in the dining room. Reinforcement was contingent on a stated preference for "a lot." The program ended with the statement: "Because you got all the answers right, you have won 25 gold stars and have earned 25 cents." The entire program consisted of 36 slides and took 6 minutes to complete when there was no stopping or repeating of items.

Interpersonal Instruction Treatment

In this treatment, reinforcement slides were not shown, but all other slides were identical to those used in the response treatment. The narration began:

> "Hi! I am going to show you some pictures now about food. All you have to do is sit quietly and listen while I show them to you. If you pay attention to all the pictures and listen quietly, we will pay you 25 cents after you are all through. Are you ready? Here is the first picture. [Picture of ice cream was projected.] You like ice cream. Here is a picture of some ice cream."

The same format was used throughout. For example, in the second sequence, the narrator would say, "You like brown bread. Here is a picture of some burnt toast and some brown bread," and in the third sequence, the narrator would say, "You like a lot of brown bread. Here is a tray with two servings of brown bread, a little brown bread and a lot of brown bread." The sequence of 19 slides ended with: "Since you have paid attention and listened quietly, you have earned 25 cents." This program took 3 minutes to complete, and the subject heard the statement "You like brown bread" 11 times. The tone of voice was casual, matter-of-fact. There was no information communicated regarding the merits of brown bread in either treatment.

The Dependent Variable

Subjects ate their meals together in groups of four or five at small tables. All food was served at the tables with the exception of bread and milk, which the subjects picked up from the food counter as they filed into the dining room. The bread tray always contained two open loaves of bread, one white and one brown (whole wheat); subjects were free to return to the counter at any time for additional helpings. A member of the school staff recorded the number of slices of each kind of bread taken by each subject at the noon and evening meals of each day. A count of bread wrappers and leftover slices at the end of each meal yielded a total bread consumption which verified the totals on the recording sheets. A further check after each meal indicated that, in virtually every case, all slices that were taken were eaten. In the one or two cases when this was not true, the uneaten slices were subtracted from that subject's total. The subjects were not permitted to obtain bread for others nor to trade food around the table.

Data collection began on a Monday and continued over the next weekend, when the experimental programs were administered, and through the following Thursday, after which subjects returned to their homes for the weekend. The school dietitian matched the Monday through Thursday menus exactly, meal for meal, for the two comparison weeks of observation (e.g., the menu for the Monday dinner meal of the pre-treatment week was identical to the menu for the Monday dinner meal one week later.) The daily routine of the subjects was essentially the same from Monday through Thursday of both weeks. Finally, matched pairs were rarely seated together at the same tables, although this could not be completely controlled at every meal.

RESULTS

During the pre-treatment week, an average of 2.09 slices of brown bread was consumed per day by each of the 48 subjects. The four consecutive daily means were 2.38, 1.92, 2.21, and 1.85, and examination of individual records also indicates that brown bread consumption maintained a fairly stable baseline. Changes in brown bread consumption for each subject are computed by subtracting his consumption for each pre-treatment day from the matched post-treatment day, yielding individual change scores uncontaminated by differences in daily menus.

It will be recalled that subjects were grouped into matched pairs on the basis of chronological age, IQ, and mental age. Table 2 displays the resulting correlations between matched pairs and confirms that the subsequent random assignment of paired partners to the two treatments produced groups which were comparable on these control variables; none of the differences approaches significance. Table 2 also shows that the product-moment correlations between each of the control variables and the total post-treatment change in brown bread consumption for the two matched groups are comparable. Differences between the corresponding correlations are not significant nor are any of the correlations significantly different from zero. Finally, there is no significant correlation between the brown bread consumptions of the matched pairs during the pre-treatment week ($r = .22$).

Our speculation concerning the functional equivalence of the two forms of "attitudinal" instruction was examined by computing product-moment correlations between the matched pairs of subjects on their post-treatment increase in brown bread consumption. The

TABLE 2

CONTROL VARIABLES AND THEIR PRODUCT-MOMENT CORRELATIONS WITH POST-
TREATMENT CHANGE IN BROWN BREAD CONSUMPTION FOR THE MATCHED GROUPS

Control variable	Interpersonal instruction group ($N=24$)	Self-instruction group ($N=24$)	Product-moment correlation between matched pairs
Chronological Age			+.76
Mean (Years)	12.06	12.59	
S.D.	2.42	2.17	
Versus consumption change	−.28	−.24	
IQ			+.90
Mean	63.3	61.3	
S.D.	13.7	13.1	
Versus consumption change	+.01	+.18	
Mental Age			+.92
Mean (Years)	7.6	7.7	
S.D.	2.2	2.2	
Versus consumption change	−.22	−.17	

correlation between consumption changes for the four post-treatment days combined is +.55 ($p < .01$). It will be recalled that prior to the experimental treatments, there was no significant correlation between the brown bread consumptions of matched pairs ($r = +.22$). Moreover, post-treatment changes in brown bread consumption are not correlated with initial brown bread consumptions ($r = .00$).

The strongest evidence for the comparability of the two treatments appears on the Monday following the experimental manipulations, the first day for which matching pre-treatment data are available. On this day, the correlation between matched pairs on changes in brown bread consumption from the previous Monday is +.71 ($p < .001$). It will be recalled that subjects were exposed to the experimental treatment for only 6 minutes in the self-instruction condition and for only 3 minutes in the interpersonal instruction condition. The +.71 correlation was obtained 2 days, or 6 meals, following these experimental manipulations. Thereafter, the correlation between matched pairs declines monotonically to +.36 ($p < .10$) and below on subsequent days.

Internal analyses of the data indicate that the two treatments are also comparable in terms of the absolute size of their effects. One such analysis in displayed in Table 3. In this table, subjects in the interpersonal instruction treatment are divided into two subgroups, those who increased their brown bread consumption over the matching pre-treatment day and those who did not. The statistical analysis is then performed upon the subgroups of their matched partners who were exposed to the self-instruction treatment.

It is seen in Table 3 that the two subgroups of subjects in the self-instruction treatment do show significant and opposing changes in brown bread consumption parallel to those of the defining interpersonal instruction subgroups. The separation between the two subgroups is significant ($t = 3.52$; $p < .01$). The mean consumption changes of the self-instruction subgroups do not differ significantly from the corresponding means of the interpersonal instruction subgroups. (Because of the way the subgroups are defined, one-sample tests are employed to test subgroup differences from hypothetical means equal to the means of the interpersonal instruction subgroups.) These similarities between the two groups also diminish on subsequent days.

Discussion

The results of this study are consistent with the hypothesis that attitude statements can serve as self-instructions in the way that interpersonal instructions do. The experiment does not, of course, provide a very strong test of the opening speculations. Most serious, perhaps, is that the design is similar to that of the interpersonal simulations of the dissonance studies in that it involves testing for the equivalence of two experimental outcomes. Methodologically, this is like trying to prove the null hypothesis. The brown bread

TABLE 3
FIRST-DAY CHANGES IN BROWN BREAD CONSUMPTION FOR SUBJECTS IN THE SELF-INSTRUCTION TREATMENT WHOSE MATCHED PARTNERS IN THE INTERPERSONAL INSTRUCTION TREATMENT INCREASED OR DID NOT INCREASE THEIR FIRST-DAY CONSUMPTION

	Interpersonal instruction treatment	
Self-instruction treatment	Increased ($N=10$) (Mean change $=+2.60$)	Did not increase ($N=14$) (Mean change $=-1.14$)
Increase over matched pre-treatment day (Mean slices per S)	$+2.00$	-1.86
Significance of difference from zero	$t=3.00, p<.02$	$t=-2.35, p<.05$
Significance of difference from mean of interpersonal instruction subgroup (1 sample tests)	$t=0.90$, n.s.	$t=0.90$, n.s.

study, then, must be regarded only as a plausibility demonstration of our self-instruction hypothesis.

With this reservation in mind, we tentatively conclude that the observed weak causal link between antecedent attitudes and consequent behavior is produced by the acquired self-directive function of attitudinal self-description.

The evidence, we believe, is clear in supporting our theory of self-description as a mechanism for producing the behavior-to-attitudes causal sequence. We are less confident of our understanding of the attitude-to-behavior sequence. In short, we can be certain that we like brown bread because we eat it. It may also be that we eat brown bread because we like it.

References

Bandler, R. J., Madaras, G. R., and Bem, D. J. Self-observation as a source of pain perception. *Journal of Personality and Social Psychology,* in press.

Bem, D. J. An experimental analysis of self-persuasion. *Journal of Experimental Social Psychology,* 1965, **1,** 199-218.

Bem, D. J. Inducing belief in false confessions. *Journal of Personality and Social Psychology,* 1966, **3,** 707-710.

Bem, D. J. Self-perception: An alternative interpretation of cognitive dissonance phenomena. *Psychological Review,* 1967, **74,** 183-200.

Brehm, J. W., & Cohen, A. R. Re-evaluation of choice alternatives as a function of their number and qualitative similarity. *Journal of Abnormal and Social Psychology,* 1959, **58,** 373-378.

Campbell, D. T. The indirect assessment of social attitudes. *Psychological Bulletin,* 1950, **47,** 15-38.

Chapanis, N. P., & Chapanis, A. Cognitive dissonance: Five years later. *Psychological Bulletin,* 1964, **61,** 1-22.

Festinger, L. *A theory of cognitive dissonance.* Stanford, Calif.: Stanford University Press, 1957.

Festinger, L. & Carlsmith, J. M. Cognitive consequences of forced compliance. *Journal of Abnormal and Social Psychology,* 1959, **58,** 203-210.

Fishbein, M. A behavior theory approach to the relations between beliefs about an object and the attitude toward the object. In M. Fishbein (Ed.) *Readings in attitude theory and measurement.* New York: Wiley, 1967, Pp. 389-400.

Heider, F. *The psychology of interpersonal relations.* New York: Wiley, 1958.

Jones, E. E., & Davis, K. E. From acts to dispositions. In L. Berkowitz (Ed.), *Advances in experimental social psychology. Vol. 2.* New York: Academic Press, 1965. Pp. 219-266.

Jones, E. E., & Harris, V. A. The attribution of attitudes. *Journal of Experimental Social Psychology,* 1967, **3,** 1-24.

Jones, R. G. Forced compliance dissonance predictions: obvious, non-obvious, or nonsense? Paper read at American Psychological Association, New York, September 1966.

Luria, A. R. The genesis of voluntary movements. In N. O'Connor (Ed.) *Recent Soviet psychology.* New York: Liveright, 1961. Pp. 165-185.

McGuire, W. J. Attitudes and opinions. *Annual Review of Psychology,* 1966, **17,** 475-514.

Osgood, C. E., Suci, G. J., & Tannenbaum, P. H. *The measurement of meaning.* Urbana, Ill.: University of Illinois Press, 1957.

Schachter, S., & Singer, J. Cognitive, social, and physiological determinants of emotional state. *Psychological Review,* 1962, **69,** 379-399.

Skinner, B. F. *Science and human behavior.* New York: Macmillan, 1953.

Skinner, B. F. *Verbal behavior.* New York: Appleton, 1957.

Staats, A. W., & Staats, C. K. Attitudes established by classical conditioning, *Journal of Abnormal and Social Psychology,* 1958, **57,** 37-40.

Valins, S. Cognitive effects of false heart-rate feedback. *Journal of Personality and Social Psychology,* 1966, **4,** 400-408.

PART III: COGNITIVE INTEGRATION THEORY CONTRIBUTIONS TO ATTITUDE THEORY

9

Psychological Perspective and Attitude Change[1]

THOMAS M. OSTROM
DEPARTMENT OF PSYCHOLOGY
OHIO STATE UNIVERSITY
COLUMBUS, OHIO

HARRY S. UPSHAW
DEPARTMENT OF PSYCHOLOGY
UNIVERSITY OF ILLINOIS
CHICAGO, ILLINOIS

What does it mean when an individual identifies his own attitude with a descriptive label such as "very pro-Negro"? For some, it may mean that they actively participate in civil rights activities; for others, it may mean that they believe in black supremacy; and for others, it may mean that they react with price and admiration upon reading a history of the Negro race. The language which people use to describe their attitudes (using terms such as pro and con, favorable and unfavorable, like and dislike, modified by words such as slightly, moderately, and extremely) summarizes a matrix of feelings, beliefs, and policy orientations which the individual holds regarding the attitude object. Such descriptive labels are used most frequently when people are in the early stages of friendship or are not interested in discussing the issue in depth. Only with more extensive discussion is the description of an attitude elaborated to include the specific ideas and reactions which form its substance. Indeed, some people on some topics would find it difficult to elaborate their attitudes beyond such simple descriptions.

In examining the influence of attitudes on behavior, the label which an individual selects to identify his attitude appears to have consequences independent of those stemming from the specific beliefs

[1]The preparation of this chapter was supported by a grant to T. M. Ostrom from the Mershon Committee on Education in National Security and by a grant to H. S. Upshaw from the National Science Foundation.

217

and feelings he may hold toward the attitude object. The selection of reading materials, the choice of television programs, and the initial phases of friendship may all be influenced by such summary attitudinal labels. Frequently, the individual has no information about objects in his world beyond such descriptive classifications. Indeed, there are some gatherings, such as the Republican and Democratic national conventions, in which the primary binding element appears to be a common label rather than similarity of political beliefs. In voting behavior, Campbell, Converse, Miller, and Stokes (1960) have found that candidate preference is predominantly determined by such classifications as Republican-Democrat and Conservative-Liberal, rather than by the congruence between one's personal beliefs and the candidates' advocated policies. Interpersonal attraction is strongly influenced by the similarity of attitude labels with which people describe themselves (Byrne & Nelson, 1965; Newcomb, 1961).

The role of language in attitude expression also plays a part in resolving attitudinal discrepancies which arise when friends discuss a mutually relevant attitude object or when an individual receives a persuasive communication. As an example, the exchange of opinions between two friends sometimes takes the following form: Bill, upon expressing his attitude that Ethel is a very attractive woman, learns that his friend Frank disagrees with him. Bill then comments that he didn't mean that Ethel was the most attractive woman in the world, but that he thought she was pretty nice. Bill's reply is in kind, "Well, I've known some pretty ugly ones in my day, and compared to them, she's not so bad." With one or two further adjustments in terminology, the dispute ends with Bill and Frank agreeing that Ethel is a "moderately attractive" woman.

In this illustration, the two participants have manipulated the language they used in describing their attitudes as a way of establishing congruence between their positions. The main point to be gleaned is that the discrepancy resolution did not entail discussion of or modification of beliefs about any of Ethel's specific characteristics. Despite their final agreement on how to label Ethel's overall attractiveness, Bill and Frank may still have disagreed on such specific attributes as her figure, the amount of makeup she wears, and the beauty of her wig.

Just as a person may change his attitude label without changing any specific beliefs, there are conditions in which a label change may produce a change in beliefs and policy orientations. A person may discover, for example, that some of his prior beliefs are incompatible with a newly acquired label, and that maintenance of the label requires modification of those beliefs.

Phrased in stimulus judgment terms, the attitude labeling process is one in which the individual is judging his own attitude as a unitary stimulus. However, the object of judgment is a compound stimulus made up of a complex of beliefs and values, feelings and policy orientations. The correspondence between the properties of the stimulus (attitude content) and the judgment made of that stimulus is the focus of the present chapter. Although it is normally thought that a change in content of an attitude will directly lead to a change in its judgment, the correspondence appears to be far more complex than this. Through processes to be described, attitudes can be revised in terms of their composition and yet produce no shift in label; judgment changes can be observed when content is unaltered; and a shift in judgment sometimes leads to, rather than being produced by, content changes.

The correspondence between the stimulus properties of attitudes and the classification assigned it are analyzed below in terms of judgmental principles drawn from research on reference scale behavior. A model of psychological perspective (Ostrom, 1966; Upshaw, 1962, 1965, 1968; Volkmann, 1951), developed in the context of social judgment, is employed as the conceptual basis for studying this relationship. This is one of the few judgmental formulations which accounts for both the origin and unit parameters of reference scale formation and change (Ostrom, 1966; Upshaw, 1968).

A PERSPECTIVE MODEL FOR ATTITUDES

The term perspective has taken on a variety of meanings in the past, depending on whether it has been used by historians, artists, sociologists, political scientists, or psychologists. The present discussion adopts Volkmann's discussion (1951) of perspective as its point of departure. Volkmann maintained that one important objective of education is to teach people to employ a common perspective when discussing issues or describing their world. The primary device, Volkmann argued, for accomplishing this is to establish common end anchors for defining a judgmental scale. That is, when learning how to use a set of labels, such as those ranging from "very pro-Negro" to "very anti-Negro," people define or anchor the extreme categories with specific beliefs, feelings, and policies regarding the Negro. So, for example, some people may define "very pro-Negro" as absolute equality between the races, whereas others define it as black supremacy; and at the opposite end, some may identify the "extremely anti-Negro" category with such beliefs as the Negro doesn't know his place, where others might anchor it with the more extreme position that all Negroes should be shipped back to Africa. Thus, for Volkmann, an individual's perspective is characterized by the extremity of the stimuli which anchor his two end categories.

Whereas Volkmann, from the point of view of education, invoked this concept of perspective in the analysis of all absolute judgments, the present discussion is restricted to judgments of one's own attitude. Certain special features must be noted when the stimulus object being judged is a personal attitude. First, the attitude must be considered a compound rather than a simple stimulus. It is made up of many elements, each of which implies a positive or negative evaluation of the attitude object. Second, the elements which make up that compound stimulus are not yet well understood. It is suggested that beliefs, feelings, and policy orientations all contribute. Finally the composition and structure of an attitude is not a static quality as, for example, is a physical stimulus in a standard psychophysical setting. Attitude content has a fluid quality in which the prominence of different elements and their interrelationships are capable of adjusting to the individual's needs as well as to external demands. This group of attitude-relevant elements, whatever may be their specific composition and structure, will collectively be referred to as the *content* of one's attitude in the present chapter.

The judgmental language with which an individual describes his attitude and that of others will be termed the *attitude rating scale.* Such a scale has the following properties: (a) it refers to a single dimension the nature of which is conveyed by terms such as pro-anti and favorable-unfavorable, which define the evaluative poles, and (b) it implies a set of graded quantitative values with respect to that dimension. The gradations between the poles of the dimension are often designated by such modifiers as very, maximally, slightly, and moderately.

Perspective is defined as the range of content alternatives an individual takes into account when rating his own attitude. Thus, for any attitude issue, an individual's perspective would be defined by what he considers to be a very positive and a very negative attitude. The content which represents the two extremes of a person's perspective are assumed to anchor the end points of the corresponding rating scale. A scale position or category is considered anchored if the individual has prejudged its content; a content cognition is considered anchored if its rating scale placement has been predetermined. Content positions which anchor the ends of an individual's rating scale are termed perspective end anchors. Perspective is viewed as an individual difference variable which, in absence of external factors, remains stable over time. However, perspective can be influenced by relevant experiences and thus is considered to be situationally modifiable.

The fundamental proposition of the present model is that perspective mediates the relationship between attitude content and rating. It is postulated that frame of reference effects, whether they derive from context, residual, or focal stimuli (Helson, 1964), operate by affecting the extremity of perspective end anchors. Thus, perspective end anchors are seen as controlling the major properties of the judgmental reference scale which the individual adopts in the rating of his attitude. The origin, or midpoint, of the rating scale is assumed to be a function of the average content values of the end anchors, and the unit of the rating scale (the range of content encompassed by the typical rating category) is a function of the difference between the two perspective end anchors. Thus, the individual's self rating is determined by his attitudinal content evaluated in the context of his own perspective. If he assesses his personal content to fall three-quarters of the distance between his two perspective end anchors, he will assign a rating to his attitude which falls three-quarters of the way between the two end rating categories.

In the typical psychophysical judgment situation, the central dependent variables reflect reference scale shifts as manifested by judgments of stimuli. The quantity inherent in the stimulus objects is an unchangeable attribute of each stimulus. However, when the stimulus being judged is one's own attitude, the critical properties of that stimulus (the content of attitude) are changeable. When the content of one's own attitude is the object of judgment, the individual has under his own control the stimulus properties of that object. By rejecting old beliefs and adopting new behaviors, the object of judgment takes on new stimulus characteristics. Rating an attitude before and after content change is analogous to judging two different compound stimuli.

The perspective model, in establishing the correspondence between content and rating, relates them in a dynamic fashion. A shift induced in content, rating, or perspective will result in a change in one or both of the remaining quantities. To illustrate some implications of the perspective formulation, consider an individual who shifts his attitude content as a result of learning new information. One of two consequences is predicted to follow: either he will change his rating in the same direction that content changed, or he will revise his perspective end anchors so that the new content matches the old rating. In the context of a specific attitude issue, assume the individual had shifted the content of his attitude toward the Negro from a position of "separate but equal" to "complete equality between the races" and had previously rated his attitude as moderately pro. Equilibrium would be reestablished either through rerating himself as very pro or through retaining his prior rating and changing his pro-Negro end anchor from equality to black supremacy.

This formulation has several direct implications for understanding attitude change phenomena. Content and rating emerge as conceptually and operationally distinct forms of attitudinal response, each having different but overlapping determinants. Further, both content and rating appear to have separate consequences for attitude-derived behavior. Of equal importance is the introduction of perspective as a variable in the domain of attitude research; perspective is assumed to operate as an independent variable as well as a dependent variable. As an independent variable, perspective can become a determinant of content and rating changes; as a dependent variable, perspective can be modified as a way to reconcile attitude discrepancies. The anti-communist discovers his views are less extreme than he thought (rating change) upon reading the perspective-widening literature from the John Birch Society and the Minutemen, but retains his beliefs; the political moderate advocates more restraint in the speed of school integration (content change) as the national temperament becomes more conservative, while retaining his moderate rating. The earlier cited example of Bill and Frank discussing Ethel's attractiveness illustrated how people might reconcile rating discrepancies by adjusting their perspectives while leaving their specific content beliefs unchanged.

At least four assumptions are made by the perspective model. The first is that people can reliably order attitude content on the evaluative dimension which underlies the rating scale. This includes their own personal content, content attributed to others, content adopted as perspective end anchors, and any other content positions relevant to the attitude issue. The evaluative dimension is assumed to have the properties of an interval scale, so that the concept of distance between attitude content position and end anchors is meaningful. Data relevant to this assumption were first reported in 1932 by Hinckley, in which the judgments made of attitude statements by different groups were compared. Although there has been considerable research of late (e.g., Ostrom, 1966) over the question of group differences in ability to evaluate attitude content, no research in social judgment has examined whether the individual, over repeated trials, typically maintains a reliable ordering.

The second assumption relates to the potency of end anchors in determining how rating categories are applied to attitude content. Although early research in social judgment and psychophysics (e.g., McGarvey, 1943; Volkmann, 1951) established the effectiveness of end anchors in defining a rating scale, their relative influence in comparison to other potential anchors is yet to be determined. Data relevant to this question are presented and discussed below.

The third assumption required by the present formulation is that individuals, in evaluating their own attitude content as a compound stimulus, base this judgment on the average evaluation derived from all the components of content. This assumption was made by Thurstone (1928) in his techniques for measuring attitude and it has been supported by Anderson (1968) in his recent work on impression formation.

Lastly, it is assumed that the individual need not be fully aware of his attitude content in order for that content to influence his self-rating. Although the degree of awareness may affect the weight given any particular element, phenomenal representation is not considered a necessary feature of content.

TESTS OF THE PERSPECTIVE MODEL

A variety of derivations have been made from the perspective model of attitude judgment. In the six sections below, specific hypotheses are formulated and tested empirically. The first four sections are devoted to testing the predicted associations between perspective, rating, and content; to demonstrating that perspective can be experimentally manipulated; and to examining the effect of perspective on content and rating change. The fifth section takes a variable of traditional importance in the area of attitude change, communication discrepancy, and analyzes it from the point of view of the perspective model. The final section examines the role of anchors other than perspective end anchors as they influence the relationship between content and rating.

THE CONTRIBUTION OF PERSPECTIVE TO ATTITUDE RATINGS

The importance of attitude content as a determinant of rating has been well-established; people who consistently emit pro responses describe themselves as possessing a pro attitude. This functional relationship between content and rating is symbolically expressed in Eq. 1, where C represents the position of attitude content on the underlying evaluative continuum and R denotes the rating of one's

$$R = f(C).$$ (1)

attitude on a parallel evaluative scale. It is the contention of the present formulation that Eq. 1 is an oversimplification that omits the contribution of perspective in determining attitude ratings. The relationship between empirical estimates of rating and content would be expected to improve considerably with the addition of information about the rater's perspective on the issue.

The manner in which perspective operates to influence the rating reference scale is portrayed in Eq. 2. Rating is viewed as a function of the content position location, expressed as a proportion of the distance between the upper (U) and lower (L) perspective end anchors. When content position is equal to the upper perspective end anchor, the rating would be placed in the most extreme position at the upper

$$R = f\left(\frac{C - L}{U - L}\right).$$ (2)

end of the rating scale; when content falls half way between the two end anchors, the middle rating position would be endorsed. Thus, the perspective model predicts a strong positive relationship between the ratio on the right side of Eq. 2 (as calculated from observed estimates of C, U, and L) and the rating which the subject assigns to his attitude.

Two studies (Ostrom, 1964, 1968b) were conducted to test the hypothesis that Eq. 2 is superior to Eq. 1 in predicting self-ratings. The studies were structurally identical, differing only in the topic used. In both cases, material was presented on a novel topic from which the subject could formulate a content belief, rate his overall attitude, and develop perspective end anchors. In the first study a case history was presented which described the background of a man convicted of making bomb threats to a hospital. The content measure was the length of prison sentence (number of years) the subject believed was appropriate for this criminal; the rating was a judgment of personal leniency-sternness; and the perspective end anchors were indexed by the number of years which the subject believed represented a maximally lenient and a maximally harsh prison sentence. The second study provided a description of a summer job at a resort hotel and asked the subject to indicate how much he felt he personally would earn at such a job (content), how high or low he would rate his earnings (rating), and how many dollars corresponded to very high earnings and to very low earnings (end anchors). Sixty-six and 61 subjects participated in the two studies, respectively.

The predictive power of Eq. 1 and 2 was compared in each study. The ratio in Eq. 2 was computed directly from the numerical content and perspective information each subject provided. The results showed, for the bomb threat study, that the direct correlation between content and self-rating was .51, whereas the prediction of rating on the basis of Eq. 2 produced a correlation of .90. In the second study, the prediction of rating from content produced a correlation of .34 and the addition of perspective end anchors in the form of Eq. 2 resulted in a correlation of .72. Figure 1 shows the percent of self-rating variance accounted for by Eq. 1 versus Eq. 2.

These data indicate that the contribution of perspective in accounting for the way people describe their attitudes is substantial—the explained variance is increased more than threefold (see Fig. 1).

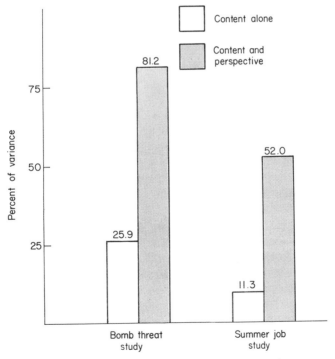

FIG. 1. Percent of variance in self-ratings due to content alone compared with content combined with perspective.

THE ASSOCIATION BETWEEN CONTENT, RATING, AND PERSPECTIVE

The perspective formulation emphasizes that rating, content, and perspective exist in a dynamic relationship such that, when one of the entities is altered, a new equilibrium will be established involving a change in at least one of the others. This formulation, then, has implications not only for the rating of attitudes, but also for the manner in which perspective end anchors and content position changes occur. From Eq. 2 it can be seen that content changes should directly produce rating changes when the perspective end anchors remain constant. Also, as the upper perspective end anchor becomes greater, holding content and lower perspective end anchor constant, self-rating will decrease in magnitude. If Eq. 2 is rewritten so that the remaining quantities (C, U, L) become, in turn, the dependent variables, then similar predictions can be made regarding how each of these other three quantities can be modified.

Equation 3, as an example, is the product of an algebraic transformation on Eq. 2, assuming the functional relationship in Eq. 2 is of a linear form. It places content position as the dependent variable. Inspection of Eq. 3 results in the prediction that a content change

$$C = f[L + R(U - L)]. \tag{3}$$

would be produced either by increasing the upper perspective end anchor while holding rating and lower perspective end anchor constant, or by increasing self-rating when perspective is held constant.

In a similar fashion, two additional equations can be written in which the perspective end anchors are the dependent variables. From these four equations, predictions can be made regarding the correlation between each pair of the four variables, when holding the other two variables constant. In doing this, six bivariate relationships emerge in which each variable is correlated against the other, partialing out the influence of the remaining two. A more complete exposition of these partial derivatives is provided by Ostrom (1964, 1968b). The predicted direction of the bivariate relationships, either positive or negative, can be summarized by noting that all partial correlations involving content position are predicted to be positive in sign and the other three should be negative.

A set of predictions was made from the four prediction equations in addition to those involving the sign of the partial correlations. Given data for content, rating, and end anchors, an expected value was computed for each on the basis of the four equations. Eq. 3, for example, provided a theoretical estimate based upon the observed rating and end anchor information. For each of the four equations, then, the expected value for its dependent variable was computed and compared against the empirically obtained value. In all cases, the expected values and the empirical values were required by theory to be significantly correlated in a positive direction.

The two sets of predictions outlined above were tested with the data gathered in the studies described in the preceding section: the bomb threat study and the summer job study. The observed content, rating, and perspective end anchors of those studies were used to test both the partial correlation predictions and the predicted correspondence between observed and expected values of each variable.

The signs of all partial correlations, six from each study, were found to be in the predicted direction with ten of the twelve coefficients reaching satisfactory levels of significance ($p < .05$). The correlations between the upper and lower perspective end anchors of each study, while in the predicted direction, were not statistically significant. Eight of the twelve partial correlations were above .50 (in absolute value); the lowest observed was .12 between the two end anchors in the summer job study, and the highest was .84 between content and lower end anchor in the bomb threat study.

The second set of hypotheses was tested by examining the correspondence between the expected and predicted values of content, rating, upper perspective end anchor, and lower perspective end anchor. For both studies, all correlations proved to be positive in sign and, with the exception of the lower end anchor from the summer job study, all were statistically reliable ($p < .01$); seven of the eight correlations were higher than .60, the highest being .94 and the lowest .18. The relationships observed for ratings and for content were generally higher than those found for the two end anchors.

These data clearly supported the derivations which stemmed from the postulate that content, rating, and perspective are interrelated not only in a dynamic fashion, but in the specific fashion described by Eqs. 2 and 3. Adequate prediction of each of the four variables was made on the basis of the remaining three. Furthermore, the signs of the partial correlations were predictable on a priori grounds, the relationship being strongest for the variables of content and rating.

THE EFFECT OF PERSPECTIVE ON SELF-RATING

The preceding sections reviewed empirical support for the perspective model's predictions regarding the association between rating, content, and perspective. However, the model assumes that the relationships are more than associative; they are causal, requiring experimental tests for confirmation. To test the influence of perspective on self-ratings as hypothesized in Eq. 2, it was necessary to employ a setting in which content and one perspective end anchor could be held constant. Two studies were conducted which differed in the attitude issue, the manner in which perspective was manipulated, and the technique used to implement the required controls.

In the first study (Upshaw, Ostrom, & Ward, 1968), attitude toward the Negro was chosen as the topic and an equal-appearing intervals measure served as the index of attitude content. The equal-appearing intervals scale assesses the evaluative location of a person's attitudinal beliefs in terms of a standard frame of reference and, therefore, provides a measure of content on a scale of measurement which is invariant over respondents. The topic of attitude toward the Negro was specifically chosen because of the comparatively high level of commitment the subjects (students at the University of North Carolina) had toward their content positions; an appropriately chosen perspective manipulation would be expected to have little effect on such well-established content.

Perspective was manipulated through information regarding students' peer group attitudes. Subjects were brought into the laboratory and informed that in a survey of the present student population the most pro-Negro attitude encountered was "When the chains of prejudice are finally cast off, the Negro will emerge as the finest embodiment of American virtues," and the most anti-Negro attitude encountered was "The Negro will always remain as he is—a little higher than the brutes." A second group of subjects was told that the most pro-Negro attitude was "I believe that the Negro is entitled to the same social privileges as the white man," and were given the same anti-Negro attitude as the first group. The only difference between the two conditions, then, was the extremity of content attributed to the most pro-Negro students on campus. In the first group that content expressed a belief bordering on black supremacy and in the second group it expressed the less extreme position of equality among races. It was predicted that because of a widened perspective, self-ratings would shift more in the anti-Negro direction when the peer group statement expressed black supremacy than when it represented equality.

Using a pre-post design, it was found that the experimental manipulation produced no differential effect on content scores. The self-rating, however, was significantly influenced ($p < .05$; $df = 1/24$); the wide perspective group, that which received the more pro-Negro peer group information, was found to change their rating in the anti-Negro direction (moving, incidentally, in a direction opposite to that expected on the basis of the conventional predictions regarding peer group influence). The narrow perspective group, that which received the less pro-Negro peer group content which espoused equality between the races, rated themselves more favorably than the wide perspective group. This finding, then, verified the hypothesized negative relationship between upper perspective end anchor and rating as described in Eq. 2.

The second study (Ostrom, 1968a) conducted to test Eq. 2 employed the bomb threat case history described several sections above. After reading the case history of a man found guilty of phoning a bomb threat to a large metropolitan hospital, subjects were asked to state their content position in terms of the number of years they, in the role of judge, would sentence the offender to prison. A commitment induction was introduced at this point in the form of asking each subject to write a half-page statement justifying the length of prison sentence he chose. Next, a perspective manipulation was introduced by supplying the subject with the purported range of prison sentences legally available to the judge who actually tried the case. The narrow perspective condition represented the range as extending from 1 to 5 years and the wide perspective condition indicated the range was from 1 to 30 years. The subjects were further told that they were to base all subsequent answers on their own personal beliefs on the matter and to disregard the legal range. Manipulation of the legal range of punishment served as a prestige influence attempt in modifying the subject's upper perspective end anchor, while simultaneously holding the lower perspective end anchor constant at 1 year. Subjects were then asked to indicate their self-rating on a scale of leniency-sternness regarding the degree of punishment they, in the role of judges, believed was just for the convicted man. Finally, a measure of perspective was included as a manipulation check; subjects were asked to indicate how many year's imprisonment they personally considered to be "maximally lenient" for this type of criminal offense and how many years corresponded to "maximally stern."

The perspective manipulation proved highly successful; although almost no difference existed between the groups in identifying their "maximally lenient" end anchor (at about half a year), the upper perspective end anchor averaged 23 years for the wide group and 7 years for the narrow group. These data, then, established the theoretically essential point that perspective is subject to modification by such situational factors as prestige influence.

It was found that subjects in the wide perspective condition rated themselves as much less stern than did the subjects in the narrow range condition ($p < .01$; $df = 1/96$); the difference was most pronounced for subjects whose original content position was a long prison sentence. This latter result was expected in that the stern end of the reference scale was most significantly affected by the perspective manipulation. For subjects who initially advocated a sentence of 5 years, those in the narrow perspective condition rated themselves on the average as "extremely stern" and those in the wide range condition described their attitude as "slightly lenient." The causal relationship described in Eq. 2 between perspective and rating was supported by these data.

THE EFFECT OF PERSPECTIVE ON CONTENT CHANGE

The perspective formulation suggests that a manipulation of perspective can influence an individual's attitude content (see Eq. 3). A man committed to a self-descriptive label, it was predicted, would adopt content consistent with his present perspective. Under conditions in which self-rating and one perspective end anchor are invariant, the higher the other perspective end anchor becomes, the higher content the individual should be willing to endorse.

The case history format described in the preceding study was adopted to test the present hypothesis (Ostrom, 1968a). When subjects finished reading the case history about a man convicted of making bomb threats, they were asked to rate how stern or lenient they, as judges, would be in sentencing this man to prison. This was immediately followed by a request to write a paragraph describing why they recommended their particular degree of sternness. Following this induction of commitment to their initial self-rating, subjects were exposed to a perspective manipulation; half of the subjects learned the legal range of sentences was from 1 to 30 years, while the other half were told it was from 1 to 5 years. After the requisite disclaimer cautioning them to base their judgments on their own personal beliefs, subjects were asked to state the actual number of years and months they as judges would sentence the offender to prison. To check the perspective manipulation, subjects were asked at the end to indicate the number of years and months they believed corresponded to the "maximally lenient" rating category and to the "maximally stern" rating category.

As in the preceding study, the perspective manipulation was highly successful; there was little difference between the groups at the lenient end and very large differences at the stern end. A highly significant effect was found between the two perspective conditions in terms of the attitude content adopted by the subjects ($p < .01$; $df = 1/76$). Subjects in the wide perspective condition advocated more years imprisonment than did those in the narrow perspective condition, the difference being largest for subjects who initially rated themselves toward the stern end of the scale. Figure 2 presents the number of years imprisonment as a function of perspective condition and original self-rating. For example, subjects who rated themselves as "very stern" advocated an average of 7 years imprisonment if they were in the wide perspective condition, but only 3 years imprisonment if they were in the narrow perspective condition. These results demonstrate the influence of perspective as a determinant of the content of one's attitude.

An Analysis of Communication Discrepancy

The perspective formulation has implications for several of the basic problem areas in attitude research. One such area is the effects

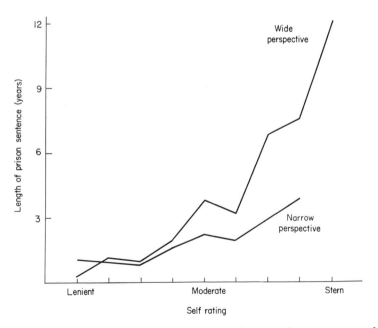

FIG. 2.   Length of advocated prison sentence as a function of perspective condition and original self-rating.

of communication discrepancy on attitude change. An analysis of the discrepancy problem in terms of the perspective model produces two major considerations: (a) two types of communication discrepancy can be seen to exist, discrepancies associated with content and with ratings, and (b) communication discrepancy can affect perspective which, in turn, can serve as a mediating factor in determining the type and extent of attitude change. Rating and content changes may in large part be produced from reference scale changes resulting from communications.

Very little theoretical work has been conducted in the past to determine what qualitative differences exist between various kinds of communications. The present formulation suggests that communications can be prepared with their emphasis on a change in content, on a change in rating, or on a change in both combined. The magnitude of discrepancy in a content-oriented communication would be determined by the difference in the evaluative implication of the beliefs and policies presently held by the recipient and those advocated in the communication. Discrepancy on the basis of ratings would be determined by the scale distance or number of categories between the rating advocated and the rating presently endorsed by the recipient of the communication. Regarding the effects of such communications, it would be expected that when content change alone was advocated, the effect would be primarily on attitude content; a communication which advocated rating change alone should have its influence primarily on rating. A communication which advocated rating and content change simultaneously implicitly advocates that the particular rating be anchored by that particular content. Thus, a communication which advocates a "very stern" sentence of 30 years is implicitly anchoring the very stern rating category with a content of 30 years. Such a communication should affect both content and rating to varying degrees, depending on what effect the communication has on perspective.

Communications can influence perspective either by introducing new content material which is outside the individual's original perspective, or by establishing a correspondence (anchor) between content and rating which is incompatible with the subject's present reference scale. To illustrate the latter, consider an individual whose perspective runs from 1 to 10 years for a certain type of crime and who encounters a credible communicator advocating a "moderate" punishment of exactly 10 years. This implicitly communicates a new perspective to the subject along with the direct influence exerted on his rating and content. As a result, he may abandon his prior upper-perspective end anchor of 10 years and replace it with a content position of, say, 15 or 20 years. The question posed by the present model is that of the degree to which the effects of communication discrepancy on content and rating change can be accounted for in terms of perspective shifts.

In an unpublished study by Upshaw, subjects read materials describing the case of a man convicted of manslaughter arising from an automobile accident. The case history included a section which described the decision rendered by the actual judge trying the case; this constituted a persuasive communication from a high prestige source. Subjects were then asked to express their own views about the appropriate disposition of the case. The relevant portion of the experimental design was a 2×11 factorial in which rating discrepancy and content discrepancy were the two factors. The rating factor had two levels; the judge described himself as either stern or lenient. The content factor had eleven levels; the judge advocated a specific length of prison sentence ranging from 1 to 51 years by intervals of 5 years. Following the case history, subjects were required to report how stern or lenient they would be in sentencing the offender to prison and how many years their sentence would be. To provide an index of the subjects' entire reference scale relating content and rating, a final section required the subjects to rate each of a set of prison sentences in terms of its sternness or leniency.

An analysis of the content measure showed that, while length of prison sentence was significantly affected by the sentence-length manipulation ($p < .01$; $df = 10/396$), it was unaffected by the rating manipulation. In the analysis of leniency-sternness ratings it was found that only the rating manipulation was influential ($p < .01$; $df = 1/396$); manipulation of the judge's sentence length did not affect this measure. These data, then, indicate that of the two kinds of discrepancy, each has its primary influence on the response task which matches the nature of the discrepancy variation. When content was varied, holding rating constant, only content was affected; when rating was varied, holding content constant, only rating was affected. It was found for both content and rating that attitude change was a direct function of the direction and magnitude of discrepancy. These findings suggest that in the design of persuasive communications the propagandist must take into account the type of attitudinal response he wishes to alter, be it content or rating.

According to the perspective formulation, if a manipulation influences content and not rating, or vice versa, a concomitant shift should occur in the reference scale relating content to rating. In the present study data were collected which permitted the computation of the two main parameters of each subject's reference scale, the origin and unit. If subjects altered their perspectives to accommodate the discrepant communications, then post hoc elimination of reference scale differences between experimental conditions should reduce or remove the direct effects of communication discrepancy on attitude. Two multiple covariance analyses were performed in which reference scale origin and unit were the covariates; content was the dependent variable in the first and rating was the dependent variable in the second. It was found that when reference scale differences were controlled through covariance, all the earlier observed significant effects were eliminated. Thus in the present study, communication discrepancy, whether it be in terms of content or rating, produced no effects beyond those which could be accounted for by communication-induced changes in the reference scale.

MULTIPLE ANCHORS AND ATTITUDINAL EXPRESSION

The perspective model of attitude judgment is founded upon the assumption that perspective end anchors mediate the relation between content and rating judgments. The influence of perspective end anchors has been demonstrated in past judgmental research through experimental introduction and manipulation of end anchors (e.g., McGarvey, 1943; Volkmann, 1951). While this research has established that perspective end anchors can be potent determinants of reference scale formation and change, it is a more complex task to demonstrate that end anchors are, in fact, the major determining anchors in the self-rating situation.

The problem of assessing the presence of de facto anchors was confronted in a recently completed study by Ostrom. He reasoned that determination of existing anchors, rather than potential anchors, required the assessment of properties other than influence on judgment. Ease of production was selected as a property of anchors that could be subjected to independent assessment. Based on the earlier definition of an anchored scale position as one which contained prejudged stimuli, it was expected that content illustrations of a particular category should come to mind more readily if that category had been previously anchored with content.

Although the present formulation focuses on end anchors, the works of Helson (1964) and Sherif (C. W. Sherif, Sherif, & Nebergall, 1965; M. Sherif & Hovland, 1961) suggest other possible anchors in attitude ratings. Helson's theory of adaptation level assumes that rating-scale behavior can be explained on the basis of how the middle of the reference scale, or its adaptation level, is defined. Thus, it might be expected that the midscale or neutral attitude-rating category would be anchored to the content dimension. Sherif's research has emphasized the importance of one's personal attitude or content beliefs as an "internal" anchor. In the vocabulary of the present formulation, Sherif's research suggests that one's own attitude content has been prejudged in terms of the rating scale.

In Ostrom's unpublished study, subjects were asked to read a list of 9 descriptive rating labels ranging from "very pro-fraternity" to "very anti-fraternity" and, for a second attitude issue, "very pro-church" to "very anti-church." They were next requested to write one specific content belief for each of the rating categories. Immediately following the completion of each statement, the subject was asked to indicate on a rating scale how easy or difficult it was for him to construct the content statement for that category. The dependent measure, then, was this easiness rating assigned to each category; anchored categories should receive significantly higher easiness ratings.

The effect of end anchors and midscale anchors can be seen in Fig. 3. An analysis of variance showed for each issue that the effect due to rating categories was highly significant ($p < .01$; $df = 8/640$); the ratings assigned to the end and middle categories were significantly easier than the rating assigned the remaining categories.

The influence due to judges' own attitude was next examined. Upon completion of the statement-writing task, judges were asked to indicate which category best described their own attitude. This information was used to classify subjects into three attitude groups: pro, neutral, or anti. It was found (see Fig. 4) that the own attitude classification significantly interacted with the rating category factor ($p < .01$; $df = 16/640$). The form of the interaction indicated that pro subjects found it easier to write pro statements than anti statements, whereas anti subjects found it easier to write anti statements compared to pro statements. A slight effect was found for the neutral subjects which indicated that they found it easier to write neutral statements than either pro or anti. Although Fig. 4 is an average over the two issues, the same pattern was found for each issue separately.

To the extent that the easiness rating accurately reflects the extent of anchoring of a rating category, these data indicate that the rating scale is anchored not only at the ends, but also at midscale and at the location of one's own attitude. These findings were corroborated in a second study which used as its dependent measure the choice of

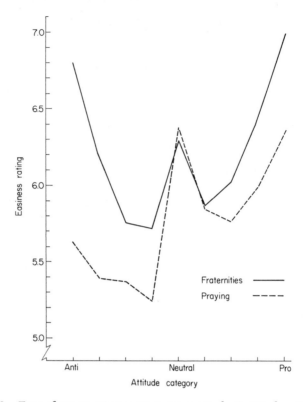

FIG. 3.   Ease of constructing content statements for 9 attitude categories.

whether to write or not to write on any given category. The data, although not yet fully analyzed, substantiate the pattern of results indicated in Figs. 3 and 4.

This finding of multiple anchors has several possible interpretations in terms of the perspective model. One potential interpretation is that the content which comprises these additional anchors is totally dependent upon perspective; the midscale (adaptation level) anchor could be formed through selection of content midway between the two perspective end anchors, and the rating category into which one's own attitude content is anchored may similarly be governed by prior established perspective end anchors as described in Eq. 2. A second possible interpretation is that midscale and own attitude anchors have independent determinants. In this case their location could not be determined from knowledge of perspective end anchors alone. A third interpretation is that perspective end anchors are the primary determinants of the reference scale, but that midscale and own-attitude anchors act as additional determinants under special circumstances. Boundary conditions imposed on the perspective model by such considerations have yet to be specified.

DISCUSSION

The present chapter confronts the problem of how people go about applying a summary label to their attitudes and the reciprocal effects that rating has on the content of attitude. Although the underlying attitude influences both the content a person agrees with and the general manner in which he rates his attitude, frame of reference effects contribute in a significant fashion to the correspondence between content and rating. The position taken in the present model of attitudinal perspective is that these effects of frame of reference can

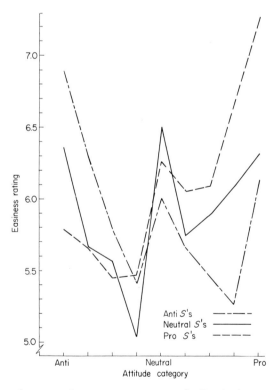

FIG. 4.   Ease of constructing content statements for 9 attitude categories as a function of subjects' attitudes.

be adequately summarized through knowledge of only two parameters, the individual's upper and lower perspective end anchors.
The perspective parameters have been shown to be dynamically
related to an individual's rating and content position. Thus, while
previous research on judgmental phenomena in attitudes (e.g., C. W.
Sherif *et al.*, 1965) has treated the reference scale as a dependent
variable, the present orientation emphasizes its importance as an
independent variable.

CONTENT AS A STIMULUS

A problem not directly dealt with in the present analyses is that of
determining exactly what properties of the stimulus are being evaluated when the subject makes his self-rating; that is, what are the elements or components which make up the stimulus object being
judged. The present formulation adopted the assumption that an attitude is a compound stimulus which can be discriminated from other
subjective quantities. The composition of that compound stimulus
was collectively referred to as attitude content; it was assumed that
the evaluative character of content could be located on the psychological dimension defined by the rating task.

Investigators in attitude research have emphasized different aspects
of content in their theoretical analyses. As a molar approach, content
has been divided into cognitive, affective, and conative components
(Harding, Kutner, Proshansky, & Chein, 1954; Rosenberg & Hovland,
1960). Content may be defined as an implicit mediating response
which determines evaluative meaning in semantic space (Osgood,
Suci, & Tannenbaum, 1957). Content may consist of the salient beliefs which the individual holds regarding the attitude object (Fishbein, 1967). Schachter (1964), studying such emotional states as
euphoria and anger, found that physiological arousal combines with
situational cues to influence self-ratings. Bem, in this volume, dis-
cusses the contribution of both private, internal stimuli and public,
overt behavior to the self-description of attitudes.

If attitude content is a compound stimulus, it becomes important
to ask how the elements of content combine when the individual
makes a single rating of his overall attitude. Recent research of Norman Anderson (1968) on impression formation is relevant to this question. Anderson's research is concerned with the manner in which the
composition of content, in the form of beliefs about a hypothetical
individual's personality characteristics, influences the rating of
liking. He finds that ratings are determined by the average evaluative

weight provided by each cognition, a finding consistent with the present formulation. It should be noted that in all of Anderson's research perspective is experimentally held constant. A common frame of reference is induced in all subjects through the device of providing them experience with a standard set of personality descriptions immediately prior to the experimental variations. While this form of control was necessary for Anderson's purposes, the data of the present chapter indicate that the factor of perspective adds substantial understanding to attitude ratings as they more naturally occur.

COMMITMENT

In the application of a model which is characterized by mutual interdependence among its several components, the influence of supplementary variables must be considered in order to predict what effects the change of one component will have on the others. Many of the present predictions were derived from the assumption that one variable affects another only when the remaining two are "held constant." The problem of holding two variables constant was accomplished for experimental purposes either through the persuasive assertion that "the lenient perspective end anchor *is* one year," through asking subjects to commit themselves by writing a justification of their initial positions, or through selecting an issue on which a person's content stand was well-ingrained. A whole array of external factors may ultimately be relevant in determining which components of this system are most susceptible to change when equilibrium has been disrupted. Factors such as commitment, ego involvement, importance, certainty, salience, and social support may all enter into making content, rating, and perspective relatively impervious to influence.

Although commitment was induced in several of the studies through asking subjects to justify the position they adopted, neither commitment nor any other factors producing resistance to change has yet been experimentally varied in a test of the perspective model. It is expected that the model's predictions would be supported most strongly when the two controlled variables were "held constant" through induction of high commitment and least strongly under conditions of low commitment. It appears likely at the present time that a concept of relative commitment, regardless of the source of that commitment, will be required to account for all of the relationships in this system. That is, when a person is neither commited to his content nor to his rating, both might change when perspective is modified. In fact, data collected by Upshaw (1964) indicate that a widened perspective can simultaneously produce positive change in content and negative change in self-rating. It would further be expected that if the same perspective manipulation was introduced when the subject had high commitment to both content and rating, little or no modification of either will occur. In fact, under these conditions it would be expected that the perspective manipulation itself would be rejected and little or no perspective change would result. This analysis, then, suggests that a technique for inducing resistance to change in any of the four elements of the present model would be to induce prior commitment to the other three variables. In such a way, resistance to persuasion directed toward specific beliefs could be introduced without overt mention of those beliefs. Indeed, this seems to be the device used by political propagandists who defend the "moderate" character of their platforms by repeatedly pointing to extremists of the right and left.

ALTERNATIVE JUDGMENTAL MODES

The rating of attitude content can take many forms. Scales of pro-con, agree-disagree, positive-negative, and for-against all offer alternative judgment languages in which content can be represented. One could even go outside these verbal rating modes and have individuals match their evaluative content with the brightness of a light by controlling a variable rheostat, or with the volume of water dipped into a beaker.

The perspective model can be adapted to any judgmental mode. Correspondence between content and the judgmental mode would be determined by identifying the two points on the response dimension which the individual equates with his perspective end anchors. In a similar manner, the correspondence between any pair of judgmental modes can be established by determining how one scale is anchored in terms of the other. Thus, not only does the perspective model establish the correspondence between content and rating, but it also permits prediction of responses on one rating mode from responses on another.

The influence of attitude on general judgmental processes is an area which has received wide research attention (cf. Bieri, 1967). However, the application of judgmental principles to the perception of one's own attitude has received much more limited attention. The perspective formulation, based on principles of judgment, finds that not only does attitude content affect the judgment of an attitude, but that the judgment, once made, can influence the attitude content. It was further suggested that content and rating, as alternative forms of attitude expression, have separate consequences for subsequent behavior.

References

Anderson, N. H. A simple model for information integration. In R. P. Abelson *et al.* (Eds.), *Theories of cognitive consistency: A sourcebook.* Chicago: Rand McNally, 1968 (in press).

Bieri, J. Attitudes and arousal: Affect and cognition in personality functioning. In C. W. Sherif and M. Sherif (Eds.), *Attitude, ego-involvement and change.* New York: Wiley, 1967. Pp. 178-200.

Byrne, D., & Nelson, D. Attraction as a linear function of proportion of positive reinforcements. *Journal of Personality and Social Psychology,* 1965, 1, 659-663.

Campbell, A., Converse, P., Miller, W., & Stokes, D. *The American voter.* New York: Wiley, 1960.

Fishbein, M. A behavior theory approach to the relations between beliefs about an object and the attitude toward the object. In M. Fishbein (Ed.), *Readings in attitude theory and measurement.* New York: Wiley, 1967. Pp. 389-400.

Harding, J., Kutner, B., Proshansky, H., & Chein, I. Prejudice and ethnic relations. In G. Lindzey (Ed.), *Handbook of social psychology.* Vol. II. Reading, Mass.: Addison-Wesley, 1954. Pp. 1021-1061.

Helson, H. *Adaptation-level theory.* New York: Harper, 1964.

Hinckley, E. D. The influence of individual opinion on construction of an attitude scale. *Journal of Social Psychology,* 1932, 3, 283-296.

McGarvey, H. R. Anchoring effects in the absolute judgment of verbal materials. *Archives of Psychology,* 1943, No. 281.

Newcomb, T. M. *The acquaintance process.* New York: Holt, 1961.

Osgood, C. E., Suci, G., & Tannenbaum, P. H. *The measurement of meaning.* Urbana, Ill.: University of Illinois Press, 1958.

Ostrom, T. M. The relationship between attitude content, self rating, and perspective. Doctoral dissertation, University of North Carolina, 1964.

Ostrom, T. M. Perspective as an intervening construct in the judgment of attitude statements. *Journal of Personality and Social Psychology,* 1966, 3, 135-144.

Ostrom, T. M. Perspective as a determinant of attitude change. *Journal of Personality and Social Psychology,* 1968, in press. (a)

Ostrom, T. M. A mathematical model of the self-rating scale. Unpublished manuscript, Ohio State University, 1968. (b)

Rosenberg, M. J. & Hovland, C. I. Cognitive, affective and behavioral components of attitudes. In C. I. Hovland & M. J. Rosenberg (Eds.), *Attitude organization and change.* New Haven: Yale University Press, 1960. Pp. 1-14.

Schachter, S. The interaction of cognitive and physiological determinants of emotional state. In L. Berkowitz (Ed.), *Advances in experimental social psychology.* Vol. 1. New York: Academic Press, 1964. Pp. 49-80.

Sherif, C. W., Sherif, M., & Nebergall, R. E. *Attitude and attitude change.* Philadelphia: Saunders, 1965.

Sherif, M., & Hovland, C. I. *Social judgment.* New Haven: Yale University Press, 1961.

Thurstone, L. L. Attitudes can be measured. *American Journal of Sociology,* 1928, **33,** 529-554.

Upshaw, H. S. Own attitude as an anchor in equal-appearing intervals. *Journal of Abnormal and Social Psychology,* 1962, **64,** 85-96.

Upshaw, H. S. Opinion change versus reference scale change in the study of attitudes. American Psychological Association Convention, Los Angeles, 1964.

Upshaw, H. S. The effect of variable perspectives on judgments of opinion statements for Thurstone scales: Equal-appearing intervals. *Journal of Personality and Social Psychology,* 1965, **2,** 60-69.

Upshaw, H. S. The personal reference scale. In L. Berkowitz (Ed.), *Advances in experimental social psychology.* Vol. 4. New York: Academic Press, 1968, in press.

Upshaw, H. S., Ostrom, T. M., & Ward, C. D. Content versus self rating in attitude research. Unpublished manuscript, University of Illinois at Chicago Circle, 1968.

Volkmann, J. Scales of judgment and their implications for social psychology. In J. Roher and M. Sherif (Eds.), *Social psychology at the crossroads.* New York: Harper, 1951. Pp. 273-294.

10

Implications of
Commodity Theory for Value Change[1]

TIMOTHY C. BROCK
DEPARTMENT OF PSYCHOLOGY
THE OHIO STATE UNIVERSITY
COLUMBUS, OHIO

In the wide gamut of . . . problems of every society, there is then, a common dominant element throughout—one pervasive, inescapable, inevitable fact: *scarcity*. That is the starting point of our analysis, and behavioral consequences stemming directly or indirectly from it is our subject matter.

—ALCHIAN & ALLEN[2]

Recurrent and pervasive problems of organizational and political life stem from the selective distribution of messages. Analysis of some of these problems led to the formulation of a rudimentary commodity theory that relates selective social communication to value formation and attitude change. In part, the theory promotes a psychological conceptualization of traditionally economic variables such as supply, demand, and utility.

In the following sections some instigating problems of selective communication will be illustrated; commodity theory will be stated;

[1]Sponsored by Advanced Research Projects Agency, monitored as AF-AFOSR-1159-66. I am greatly indebted to A. G. Greenwald and T. M. Ostrom for their suggestions and criticisms. The present development of commodity theory has benefited from the contributions of H. L. Fromkin. The assistance of Dallas M. Cullen and R. M. Yoder is acknowledged with gratitude.

[2]Alchian, A. A. & Allen, W. R. *University Economics*, p. 2. Belmont, Calif.: Wadsworth, 1967.

243

pertinent empirical studies will be examined; and, finally, some inadequacies will be noted with suggestions for revision.

It is manifestly impossible to be communicating everything one knows to all potential recipients all of the time; similarly, of course, it is impossible to be seeking information on all topics from all sources at all times. That there are constraints enforcing selectivity is too obvious to require any documentation here. But what are the psychological consequences and antecedents of selectivity? The theory to be described attempts to provide some answers in a form that may have explanatory value over and beyond those concerns which instigated its formulation. Selective communication refers here not only to the formal conveying of messages but, more generally, to *social relations of whatever kind* in which some information or some experience is or may be selectively distributed or enjoyed. Furthermore, the theory is concerned not only with the selective giving of information but also with the causes and effects of perceived selectivity and with the evaluation of withheld information.

ILLUSTRATIVE PROBLEM AREAS

Selectivity in the reception and transmission of information is an ubiquity of social life that continues to elude satisfactory theoretical understanding. Selective *receptivity* to information has attracted considerable experimentation and there have been attempts at generalization (Brock, 1965, pp. 17–18) but all the data can not yet be ordered to any single model (Brock & Balloun, 1967; Freedman, 1965; Freedman & Sears, 1965; Lanzetta & Driscoll, 1966; Lanzetta & Kanareff, 1962; Mills, 1965). The other side of the coin, the determinants and consequences of selective *transmission,* is even less clear. Aside from intriguing descriptive accounts (Goffman, 1959; Shils, 1956), the literature contains no encompassing explanation of the causes and effects of communication selectivity and of the antecedents of pressure for disclosure of withheld information.

Selective communication shades into secrecy as forces compelling withholding and opposing disclosure increase in magnitude. In *The Torment of Secrecy,* Shils (1956) has cogently rewritten some of the recent political history of the United States by exhibiting the agony, concern, and destruction attending a national preoccupation with secrecy and loyalty. *The Torment of Secrecy* insightfully delineates the psychological consequences of secrecy and the subtle relationships between secrecy, pluralist traditions, privacy, and extremism. For example, pressure for disclosure increases during crisis: "The unrealistic obsession with secrecy—and all its attendant passions for publicity and uniformity—receives a powerful stimulant in a situation in which there is a heightened rational necessity for an efficient and functioning system of information security [Shils, 1956, p. 35]." Danger begets fear of internal conspiracy and consequent pressure for complete publicity. Shils refers here, not to simple curiosity or inquisitiveness, but active attempts to elicit information from or about others when strong forces opposing the communication of that information are perceived to exist. Vigilantist tactics of the John Birch Society illustrate how a group perceiving high, constant threat may actively seek information which normally is held private. Incomplete communication, withholding information, and pressure for concealed information are psychological processes that seem inextricably involved with the set of concerns rubricized as national security (Shils, 1956).

A second set of concerns leading to the present commodity theory stemmed from consideration of the inadequacies of extant economic theories of consumption. The situational determinants of preference and "taste" have yet to be discovered and stated explicitly; one consequence of this gap is that these obvious *variables* in economic life are often treated as *constants*. In *The Sociology of Economic Life*, Smelser (1963, especially pp. 93–94) commented on this point in an overview of the historical development of consumption theories. From discussions such as Smelser's it became clear that there was a need for psychological theoretical treatment of situational factors such as "scarcity" which may influence tastes and preferences. Incomplete distribution of materials, withholding of products, and effort to obtain withheld products are behavioral processes that affect economic outcomes and that may be understandable in the same theoretical terms which can be applied to withheld information, pressure to obtain concealed information, and so forth.

A final species of problem, which influenced the formulation of the theory, concerns the effects of organization on social interaction. Smelser (1963, p. 85) described organizational communication in terms that make clear the important role of selectivity and the need for a theoretical framework within which to understand the consequences.

> A fundamental condition for effective operation in a bureaucracy is a free flow of information and orders. If information is misunderstood, lacking altogether, distorted in passage, or too slow in arriving, confusion, uncontrolled suspicions, and normative conflict arise. Many studies of industrial bureaucracy have uncovered typical points of bottleneck and distortion in the passage

of information. Up and down the line the problems are distortion and omission at each level; subordinates "cover up" information they do not wish to have known by their superiors, and foremen "soften" orders out of sympathy with workmen. Particularly disturbing to most bureaucracies is the practice of "jumping the line"—i.e., sending information and grievances from low levels in the hierarchy of authority directly to high levels, thus subverting the ability of the middle levels to control or censor this information.

COMMODITY THEORY

"Commodity" is defined to mean anything which has usefulness to the possessor and which can be conveyed from person to person. Usefulness implies that the commodity is seen by the possessor as having potential relevance to his needs and interests; he is an interested possessor. There are two principal premises: first, that any commodity will be valued to the extent that it is unavailable; second, that threat increases commodity-seeking behavior and the tendency to withhold commodities from others. Unavailability refers to scarcity and to the degree of effort seemingly needed to obtain the commodity. Threat has been tentatively defined as situational variation which leads the individual to anticipate decrement in physical or social well-being. Since the threat premise has received little development thus far it will not be further discussed in this chapter.

The partial development of commodity theory to be presented here is limited to symbolic or informational stimuli and to messages or experiences, which hold interest for an individual in his role as recipient or communicator or both. The value of such stimuli is defined as their effectiveness or potency for affecting attitudes and behavior. The more a recipient values a prospective experience the more he will seek it out and prefer to have it rather than some other experience. The more a recipient values a message the more likely it is that the message will be effective in changing his attitudes and behavior. Here, "value" and "effectiveness" are synonyms. Stated more generally, the value of a commodity is its weight, or the extent to which it accounts for response variance when compared to other stimuli.

In order to specify how a commodity acquires an increment in value, it has been convenient to invent a term, *commodification*, to refer generically to situational variations which are likely to augment the perceived unavailability of an object. These variations are ones which induce perception of scarcity, delay, transmission restriction, and so forth; they are fully delineated below in the statement of the propositions of the theory. The complete definition of commodification is constituted by the propositions presented later which specify what situational variations will enhance the perceived unavailability of an object. At this point it is sufficient to emphasize that commodification is a property of the stimuli and not of the recipient. Hence, commodification is not synonymous with acquire value.

Before the value of an item would be expected to increase with increase in its commodification, the person needs to be at least a potential possessor of the item, the item has to have potential usefulness for him, and the item has to be conveyable from person to person. The theory is limited to commodities as defined above, that is, to objects (messages, experiences, things, etc.) characterized by usefulness and conveyableness. Where usefulness and/or conveyableness of an object is absent, low, or ambiguous, then it will be unclear that that object is a commodity in the present sense and, consequently, it will also be unclear whether the theory is applicable. Stated in other words, it will be unclear whether the subject was an interested possessor of an object unless that object was demonstrably relevant to his needs or interests and clearly conveyable. Thus, for example, where a message has been presented in a commodified fashion (see below) but the recipient was not interested in the message topic, the situational commodification would not be expected to augment that message's effectiveness. Even if an instance could be found in which an object, that held no prior interest for an individual, increased in value as a consequence of commodification, this result would not be evidence for or against commodity theory because there was, by definition, no commodity and no interested possessor to begin with.

The availability assumption did not appear implausible but there was no pretense that it is congenial with either the data or theories of economic history. It may be that there are conditions in which useful items are not valued more to the extent that they are unavailable. It was assumed that such occurrences, which clearly contradict the first premise of commodity theory, are infrequent enough to be considered exceptions, at least in so far as the theory can be applied to interpersonal behavior. Nevertheless, the premises of the theory were not accepted as "givens" but were considered subject to test along with the empirical propositions.

Propositions Developed from the Unavailability Premise

A population of propositions was surveyed which intuitively seemed to reflect the force against communication, aura of limited disclosure, scarcity, and improbability-of-receipt connotations of "unavailability." The eight propositions presented here met at least two of the following criteria: they seemed likely to illumine selective communication; they reflected differences that "make a difference" according to convincing phenomenal accounts (e.g., Shils, 1956); and they could be tested against available data. Confining exactitude in definition and ultimate rigor in derivation were not sought at this beginning stage. Each proposition begins with "a message will increase in effectiveness." This clause is considered interchangeable with "an experience will increase in value." It has not yet seemed necessary to adopt Rosen's (1966) distinction between a "material commodity" (it is relinquished in a transaction) from "informational commodity" (not relinquished in a transaction). Rosen's distinction, while interesting and generally cogent, is left untreated by the theory: the bulk of the pertinent studies deal with informational commodities.

SCARCITY

Hypothesis a: a message will increase in effectiveness as the perceived number of co-recipients, relative to the total number of potential co-recipients, declines.

Scarcity is likely to be impressed upon the recipient as the number of actual recipients, from the total number of those who are potentially interested in receiving the message, declines. Effectiveness would then be expected to approach a maximum when the recipient believes that he alone, from a pool of interested recipients, has been informed: the larger the pool, the larger the effect.

The same type of reasoning would apply to an experience or to possession of an object. If an individual is afforded an experience that is withheld from some other interested co-enjoyers of that experience, the valuation of the experience will increase as the number of co-recipients declines relative to the pool of potentially interested co-recipients. "Many are called but few are chosen." expresses commodification. In a similar vein, information scarcity would be salient if the recipient perceives that few other communicators exist who could have disclosed the same information. Hence, one is led to the following hypothesis.

Hypothesis b: a message will increase in effectiveness to the extent the recipient perceives that few other communicators exist who might have delivered the same message.

Of course, maximum effectiveness would result from a paucity of both recipients and communicators, that is, from maximum perceived secrecy (Shils, 1956). At a more material level, a person may perceive that not all housewives in his community can prepare Duckling Montmorency. Consequently, his enjoyment of this dish, when it is served to him at a dinner party, may be increased by his perception that, indeed, in very few other homes is he likely to encounter that particular specialty. "The World's Only . . .!", the common tourism appeal, expresses this aspect of commodification in another way.

EFFORT

Hypothesis c: a message will increase in effectiveness the greater the degree of coercion upon the communicator needed to bring about disclosure.

Information that is actually widely held may be functionally in short supply. The greater the force that must be exerted on the communicator (threat, bribe, cajoling, punishment) to obtain disclosure, the greater will be the effectiveness of the disclosed information.

Hypothesis d: a message will increase in effectiveness the greater the perceived effort involved for the communicator, either to conceal the information or to transmit it.

A communicator, wishing to conceal information, may take precautions to prevent disclosure. A message somehow received from a communicator, who has taken effortful precautions, should be more potent than a message from a communicator whose protective steps have been less elaborate and/or easy to implement. In general, where a message is transmitted at "cost" to the communicator, it will be especially effective provided cost does not imply greater distribution and, hence, availability.

Similarly, the effort *put out by a recipient* to obtain information will increase the value of the information under certain conditions (Cohen, 1959). Hence hypothesis *e* follows.

Hypothesis e: a message will increase in effectiveness the greater the magnitude of the recipient's effort to obtain the information or to understand (decode) it.

Since the effort put forth to obtain or decode a message may be due to the value of the message, experimental verification of hypothesis *e* requires independent manipulation of effort. Hypothesis *e* assumes that ease of obtaining information is psychologically in inverse relationship to felt unavailability.

Thus, effort to withhold or to transmit and effort to obtain or to understand were viewed as fundamentally important determinants of commodity value.

RESTRICTION

The recipient may be made aware of reasons limiting disclosure. For example, the message or experience may be labeled "confidential," "secret," "restricted," and so forth. Or it could be hinted that the message contained information that was damaging to some person or group. Other things equal, items accompanied by such labels should be more effective than items not so accompanied because these labels heighten perceived unavailability. This leads to hypothesis *f*.

Hypothesis f: a message will increase in effectiveness in proportion to the amount of accompanying reasons opposing disclosure.

Hypothesis g: a message will increase in effectiveness the greater the restrictions set by the communicator on further transmission.

Restriction on subsequent communication requires the recipient to implement the partial unavailability of the information by cooperating in selective transmission. Consequently, a message which can be transmitted freely to anyone would be least effective, other things being equal. If a person must not tell anyone else about a particular experience that experience will have greater weight for him than an experience which is unaccompanied by a secrecy request.

DELAY

Delay is a further means of conveying unavailableness. The use of delay to provoke the appreciation of the recipient is a well-known strategem used, for example, by the courted and by the bureaucrat. Quick access to a nubile woman or an official signifies their diminished status in many cultures.

Hypothesis h: a message will increase in effectiveness the greater the delay by the communicator.

In sum, the propositions developed from the unavailability premise concerned scarcity (who has it to give and who will get it), effort to withhold and to obtain, and situational constraints (reasons opposing or limiting communication, delay, and restriction on transmittal).

COMMODITY THEORY, "COST" MODELS, "EXCHANGE" THEORIES, AND INFORMATION CONTENT

Note that the definition of value used here is different from that used in decision-making and economic models. For example, Lanzetta and Kanareff (1962, p. 460) stated that information has value to the extent that it increases the probability of choosing the alternative which yields the most favorable outcome. In commodity theory the value of information is proportionate to its effect on the recipient whether the outcome for the recipient is favorable or unfavorable. The two kinds of information value can overlap but they need not.

Another distinction between commodity theory and utility theories concerns the role of information cost. Lanzetta and Kanareff (1962) as well as Marschak (1954), Stigler (1961), and many others, define the value of an inquiry partly in terms of the time, money, and/or effort needed to acquire the information. In commodity theory a "cost" concept clearly applies to some propositions (e.g., c and e) but not readily to others (e.g., a and g). Even where applicable (e), however, note that according to the utility theorists (Lanzetta & Kanareff, 1962; Marschak, 1954) recipient's cost should reduce the net value of the acquired information. In contrast, commodity theory predicts that information effectiveness and impact will increase with increase in the recipient's cost. Furthermore, decision process theories usually highlight the cost to the recipient, whereas commodity theory, in several of its propositions, assigns importance to the recipient's perception of the communicator's cost. Consequently, the concept of information cost, as delineated by other theories, did not seem advantageous for the present commodity theory. It appeared doubtful that competing predictions could be generated.

Costs and gains are the warp and woof of the "exchange" theories (Adams, 1965; Blau, 1964; Homans, 1961; Thibaut & Kelley, 1959). These conceptual frameworks have not yet been articulated sufficiently to enable discovery of many meaningful points of contact with commodity theory.

In its present development, the theory is not directly concerned with message content (or type of experience) as a variable of primary interest, because boundaries had to be set somewhere and systematic theoretical treatment of content, although ultimately important to a definitive analysis of selective communication, would have delayed and complicated experimentation beyond tolerable limits.

Two sections follow. The first contains published evidence germane to the theory; most of this evidence has been collected by other investigators whose efforts, of course, were not directed at testing commodity theory. The second section summarizes unpublished tests of the theory carried out by the writer and his associates.

PUBLISHED EVIDENCE

SCARCITY

The major finding of a well-known experiment by Kelman (1953) appeared understandable in terms of hypothesis a, concerning paucity of co-recipients. In Kelman's experiment, school children in their classes were offered rewards for writing a discrepant essay and the dependent variable was attitude change in the direction of favoring the essay position that was requested by the experimenter. The reward offered was a movie pass. In the Few Recipients condition, the experimenter said "I know you would all like to see the movie. I wish I could give passes to all of you, but unfortunately I only have five for your whole class. So only five of the people who write essays in favor of jungle stories [the discrepant position] will be able to see the movie [p. 193]." In the Many Recipients condition, the experimenter said, "I have enough passes for everyone in the class, and I am sure that everyone can get one. If everyone here just tries his best to write good essays in which he favors jungle stories, then the whole class will get passes. . . . The movie will be shown right here in school, during school hours, and your whole class can go together [p. 194]." Note the ready availability of the movie in the Many Recipients condition—it would be shown right in the school and the class could stay together—whereas no mention of easy access to the movie was made in the Few Recipients condition.

Clearly, commodification of the prize and the associated essay-writing behavior was greater under Few Recipients than under Many Recipients. The results were confirming: more favorable attitude change was shown under Few than Many Recipients. This finding was obtained for both those who did and those who did not comply by writing the discrepant essay. Offering a scarce incentive for advocating a position increased the value of that position more than did offering an incentive that would be available to everyone. The Kelman data offered strong support for commodity hypothesis *a*.

Brehm, Stires, Sensenig, and Shaban (1966) recently hypothesized that

"the elimination of a choice alternative will tend to increase the attractiveness of that alternative to the person who is about to make the choice. Two experiments, in which college students rated the attractiveness of four recordings of music in order to be able to choose one for themselves, found that *the third most attractive record increased in attractiveness when it became unavailable as one of the choice alternatives.* In order to rule out alternative explanations of this finding, the second experiment included a condition in which some subjects were given no prior freedom to choose which record they would receive. The results of this second experiment indicated that the tendency to see the eliminated record as more attractive occurred only when subjects had prior freedom to choose which record they would take [p. 301, our italics]."

The results of their second experiment led Brehm *et al.* to emphasize that the "prior freedom to choose the eliminated alternative accounts for the increased attractiveness [Brehm *et al.*, 1966, p. 312]." The Brehm *et al.* choice manipulation probably affected the prospective possessors' interest and involvement. In the Choice condition subjects were told "you may choose one of the four albums from which you hear selections today"; under No Choice, "we will have a limited number of records so we're going to give them out randomly. You would receive one of the four albums from which you hear selections today." It seemed reasonable to the present writer that the random allocation made the No Choice subjects less interested and concerned about possessing the commodity than the Choice subjects. Consequently, the Choice data were considered clearly pertinent to commodity theory. In this experiment, the subject did not, of course, actually receive the "eliminated" record but he listened to it and evaluated it. Thus, a message was registered and attitude toward the message was affected by the attendant constraints in the theoretically expected fashion. Brehm (1966) has reported other experiments producing comparable outcomes.

"Brehm, McQuown, and Shaban (Chapter II, Brehm, 1966) obtained a small and unreliable tendency for increased desire to see a movie eliminated from among three movies as choice alternatives. . . . That a more personal elimination has similar effects was shown by Hammock and Brehm (1966). Their experiment found that when there are only two choice alternatives and the less attractive of them is arbitrarily eliminated by an 'assistant,' rank preference of the eliminated item tended to increase while rank preference of the remaining gift item tended to decrease. Similar effects were obtained when the preferred alternative was eliminated [Brehm, 1966, p. 120]."

Hence, these selected experiments from the Brehm laboratory supported the general unavailability premise and the scarcity notions of propositions *a* and *b*.

EFFORT

Brock and Becker (1965) performed an experiment pertinent to propositions *d*, communicator effort to conceal, and *f*, accompaniment of the message by reasons opposing disclosure.

> College women heard an experimenter take a rigged phone call in which he advocated an event which was either neutral, unacceptable, or acceptable to the listeners. For one-half the listeners, the experimenter took the call in their presence and, for the others, he ran around to his office saying 'I can't talk about that here.' The dependent variable consisted of opinions on compulsory ROTC, increasing, and decreasing tuition. Overheard communications were especially effective for involved listeners when the advocated position was acceptable. However, overhearing was not more effective for the unacceptable propaganda [p. 654].

Thus, in direct support of proposition *d*, a communicator, who made an effort to conceal his message, was more effective than a communicator who made no attempt at concealment. This finding was restricted to acceptable information; when the message was undesirable, that is, the recipients were not "interested possessors" of the advocated conclusion,[3] there was no effect of attempted concealment.

Obviously, permanently withheld information is a commodity that is more unavailable than temporarily withheld information. Consequently the general prediction was that a communicator, who is perceived to be permanently withholding information, will be more influential than a communicator perceived to be only temporarily withholding information. The dependent variable in a pertinent study by Becker and Brock (1966) was male college students' estimates of

> "their scores on an alleged femininity test. A high score was considered unfavorable. In a 2×2 design, scorer orientation, friendly vs. hostile, and withholding of femininity score, permanent vs. temporary, were the independent variables. The principal finding concerned the effect of *permanently* withholding information, as compared to temporarily withholding information, from prospective recipients on the perceived favorableness of the information.

[3]However, persons can, of course, be interested possessors of undesirable information if the information is useful and relevant. Hence, the present interpretation may appear questionable. The point is discussed below.

Prospective recipients considered information more favorable when it was withheld by a communicator with a friendly orientation and less favorable when it was withheld by a communicator with an unfriendly orientation [Becker & Brock, 1966, pp. 147 and 153].

These differences, which were replicated, were *not* obtained under temporary withholding or in appropriate control groups. In sum, permanent withholding enhanced the effectiveness of the communicator. If what was withheld was expected to be unfavorable, because of what the subject had learned about the communicator's orientation, then it was considered more unfavorable when the withholding was perceived as permanent; if what was withheld was expected to be favorable, because of the communicator's orientation, then it was considered more favorable when the withholding was perceived as permanent rather than temporary. Note that in the Becker-Brock experiment, commodification affected extremeness of favorableness or unfavorableness, rather than "value" as previously defined.

In addition to affording confirmation to the general unavailability premise, the findings lent support to propositions *d*, communicator concealment, and *h*, communicator delay.

Anecdotal evidence for hypothesis *d*, concerning communicator effort, was found in Merton's classic analysis of Kate Smith's bond-selling radio marathon (1946). Smith's grueling eighteen-hour marathon effort apparently validated her sincerity for the audience. Her "sacrifice" made her message especially effective.

Besides an obvious sacrifice, cost to the communicator may be perceived by the recipient when the communicator espouses a position that is contrary to his own or that is contrary to the position of his audience. Presumably it requires less effort to advocate what one believes rather than the opposite and less effort, one may guess, to present a communication that is desirable to an audience rather than one that is manifestly undesirable to the audience.

An experiment by Walster, Aronson, and Abrahams (1966) supported their hypothesis that "any communicator, regardless of his prestige, will be more effective and will be seen as more credible when he is arguing for a position *opposed* to his own best interest, than when arguing for changes obviously in his own best interest [p. 325]." In their study Walster *et al.* gave high school subjects a communication advocating increasing or decreasing the power of the courts; the communication was attributed to either a criminal (who would stand to gain from decreasing, and to lose, from increasing courts' power) or to a prosecutor (who would gain from increasing, and lose, from decreasing courts' power). The results showed that the communicator who argued against his own interest was more effective and was considered more credible and more likely to make the respondents feel they were influenced. Clearly it is costlier to a communicator to disparage his own interests than to advocate his own interests. The concept of cost to the communicator was made especially clear by Walster *et al.* as they reconsidered a portion of the data from the classic experiment of Hovland and Weiss (1951).

> One of the communications utilized by Hovland and Weiss discussed the possibility that there would be a decrease in the number of movie theaters, as a result of inroads made by television. In one condition, the investigators attributed the communication to *Fortune* magazine (previously rated as high in credibility); in the other, they attributed it to a female gossip columnist (previously rated low in credibility). On this issue, with these communicators, there was no significant difference in opinion change; actually, there was a small difference favoring the low credibility source.
>
> To speculate on the reasons for the insignificant data is a precarious occupation. Nonetheless, it can sometimes be rewarding. One possibility is that the credibility of the communicator may not be simply a function of his abstract characteristics but, rather, may be dependent upon an interaction between his characteristics and the nature of the communication. In the above example, the gossip columnist, although generally untrustworthy, may have been far more effective than *Fortune* magazine when she was arguing that the movie industry was rapidly declining. In this situation, she was arguing against her own best interests. This could have raised her effectiveness in this specific instance tremendously, in spite of the fact that she was rated as untrustworthy in the abstract. In effect, since the members of the audience were aware that if her thesis was correct (and if her communication was effective) it would be to her own disadvantage, they were likely to take her very seriously and to change their opinions accordingly [Walster *et al.*, 1966, p. 306].

Cost to the communicator would also be perceived when the communicator delivers a message that is manifestly undesirable to his audience; such a communicator should be more effective. This hypothesis was tested recently by Mills and Jellison (1967).

> College students read a speech favoring tripling truck license fees. Some were told it was delivered to railway men (desirable condition), others, that it was delivered to truck drivers (undesirable condition). Agreement with the communicator was lower in the desirable condition than the undesirable condition [Mills & Jellison, 1967, p. 98].

Very recently Jellison (1967) reported an experiment in which perceived communicator effort very likely affected acceptance of the communicator's message.

An experiment was designed to test the hypothesis that a communicator is more influential when he changes his position than when he maintains the same position if he has had the opportunity to reconsider his position, but is less effective when he changes his position if he has not had the opportunity to reconsider it. The second position was supposedly taken 20 minutes after the first position or immediately after the first position. The results supported the hypothesis [Jellison, 1967, p. 530].

Clearly, reconsideration for twenty minutes required more effort from the communicator than did immediate adoption of the second position with no reconsideration. The results appeared to support not only commodity hypothesis *d,* dealing with communicator effort, but also hypothesis *h,* concerning the enhanced effectiveness of delay by the communicator. In follow-up research based on Jellison's experiment, communicator effort and communicator delay should be unconfounded.

The results of the Mills and Jellison (1967), Jellison (1967), and Walster *et al.* (1966) experiments appeared in accord with the commodity theory proposition relating message effectiveness to communicator effort. This conclusion would be more certain if (a) these experiments had included measures of the subjects' perceptions of how difficult it was for the communicators to take the position they did, how much effort was entailed, what negative consequences they might incur, and so forth, and (b), if it had been demonstrated that communicators taking contrary or undesirable or reconsidered stands were perceived as incurring more psychological cost. Although the experiments were not conducted to test commodity theory or, for that matter, *any* theoretical view, commodity theory appeared to provide a useful set of principles in terms of which to think about these data.

Wicklund, Cooper, and Linder (1967) reported an experiment directly pertinent to commodity proposition *e,* concerning recipient effort.

Subjects in two conditions were led to expect to hear a tape recorded communication in which the speaker was to argue for a viewpoint contrary to the subject's opinion. Effort was varied between these two conditions through use of different intervals of delay. In one condition, the subjects expected a delay of 15 minutes before exposure to the communication, in the other condition, a delay of one minute was expected [p. 419].

In the 15-minute condition the delay would carry the subject ten minutes beyond the 30 minutes for which he was to receive experimental credit as an introductory psychology student. Opinion change was measured immediately after the effort inductions. If commodity theory is correct, subjects anticipating a long precommunication delay might enhance their valuation of the forthcoming communication and, consequently, change their opinions in the direction to be advocated. This is precisely what happened. Opinion change in the direction of the stand to be taken by the communication was reliably greater in the 15-minute than in the one-minute delay and control (no communication) conditions.

Wicklund *et al.* (1967) reported another experiment concerned with proposition *e*, the recipient's effort in exposing himself to information. Each male undergraduate subject was told that the purpose of the experiment was to "test the relationship between a person's heart rate and his ability to recall certain aspects of a communication. We have here a tape recording of a speech given by Senator Eugene McCarthy of Minnesota in which he advocated the elimination of draft deferments for college students. We are going to have you listen to the speech and then answer some questions concerning what you have heard [p. 423]." The subject was informed that since the experiment was investigating the effects of increased heart rate on recall ability, it would be necessary to undergo a physical exercise in order to increase heart rate, viz., to run in place for seven minutes in order to increase cardiac activity. In a Low Effort condition the subject was told that the experiment was concerned with the effects of decreased heart rate and was led to expect to rest in his chair for seven minutes, "to depress heart rate." No running or listening took place, of course; the opinion change measures were obtained immediately. In support of the commodity prediction, mean change in the direction of the anticipated communication was greater in the High Effort than in the Low Effort and Control Conditions.

Ostrom (1966) has also reported an experiment concerned with proposition *e*, the recipient's effort to obtain information.

> Each subject sequentially encountered three different persuasive communications under three different levels of physical effort. These were combined in a 3 × 3 latin square design. An after-only self rating of own attitude served as the dependent variable. Physical effort was manipulated by requiring subjects to continuously rotate a crank handle while reading a persuasive communication. A greater number of revolutions per minute was required in the higher effort conditions. The manipulated level of r.p.m.'s had to be maintained to keep the communication in view. The two questions used as a check on the effort manipulation showed significant differences with both p levels less than .001. The mean effort ratings were in direct accordance with the manipulated levels of effort. Mean self ratings of agreement increased directly as a function of effort for two of the issues used. The over-all effort main effect fell just short of the .05 level of significance [Ostrom, 1966, pp. 3 and 6].

Ostrom discussed his results in conjunction with comparable findings by Cohen (1959) and Zimbardo (1965). He concluded, in support of proposition *e*, that greater recipient effort does lead to greater acceptance of the communication and that this finding represented a "continuity with the general effort-value literature [p. 6]."

A further test of hypothesis *e*, concerning recipient effort, was seen in a recent article by Sears (1967). In both Sears' conditions which are pertinent to commodity theory, the subjects expected to discuss the economy with an expert on economic matters who held a position that was discrepant from the subjects' own by virtue of its extreme pessimism. In the High Critical Partner condition the prospective discussion partner was described as highly critical, easily annoyed with uninformed persons, easily disgusted with naive questions, withering in his replies, etc. In the Low Critical Partner condition, the description of the discussion partner was considerably softened so that he would be seen as warm, helpful, and understanding without, at the same time, sacrificing any intellectual standards. Subjects in both conditions read an essay ostensibly written by the prospective discussion partner and then indicated their own attitudes about the economy, the principal dependent variable. Several Checks on the Partner manipulation indicated clearly that encountering the High Critical Partner was expected to be more effortful than the Low Critical Partner: for example, the former was seen as less easy to get along with than the latter. The main finding was in accord with commodity theory: greater opinion change in the direction advocated was obtained under High Critical Partner, the condition likely to evoke more recipient effort.

Recipient effort may also be created by a barrier, something which impedes or resists the individual's obtainment of a goal object. However, the notion that a barrier enhances desire for a goal object has encountered mixed empirical support as Brehm notes (1966, p. 76) in his review of the literature. Brehm (pp. 76–77) describes in detail an unpublished study by Wright (1934) which did seem to show that when a person is the interested potential possessor of an object, the value of the object increases as it becomes physically remote and, hence, more effortfully attainable.

At the time of Wright's study, female students served as waitresses for other students in the women's dining hall of Duke University. Dishes of food were picked up by the waitress from a serving table three feet deep, placed on serving trays, and then carried into the dining room. The following study was concerned with how the waitresses selected items for themselves. Unknown to these waitresses, Wright arranged to have desserts placed on the pick-up surface in two rows, one close to the front (within easy reach), the other 18 inches further back (more difficult to reach). Then, when these girls picked up desserts for themselves, a tally was kept of the frequency with which they chose from the front, easy, or back, more difficult, row. These arrangements and observations were made on several different occasions. On each occasion only one kind of dessert was served and the portions were approximately equal.

It was found that on over 14 occasions on which observations were made 60 % of the choices were from the more distant row. It is also of interest that when the more attractive desserts were involved, 62 % of the selections were from the back row, while only 58 % were taken when the less attractive desserts were served.

Wright's data provided only a suggestive trend in the direction of the hypothesis that a distal goal object will be more attractive than a proximal goal object *if* the subject is very interested in possessing that particular goal object. An experiment by Brehm and Hammock (Brehm, 1966, pp. 78 – 80) included conditions in which differences were more clearly produced in how interested the subjects were in obtaining the focal object.

Elementary school subjects were individually taken to a small room in the center of which was a table approximately 2 feet wide and 6 feet long. The subject was asked to stand about six inches from one end of the table, facing it.

The procedure then consisted of asking the subject some introductory questions about his interests in order to relax him, telling him that he would receive a piece of candy, and then asking him to point to which of two pieces he thought was best, one of these pieces being near to him, the other, far. In the No Choice condition before pointing to which was best, he was given his piece of candy for doing so, while in the Choice condition he was told he could have either of the two pieces on the table for pointing to which was best. The candies were after-dinner mints which differed only in color: the two placed on the table were yellow and pink, and in the No Choice condition, the one given prior to the judgment was green. The positions of the yellow and pink mints were rotated within conditions.

From a commodity point of view, the significant difference between the conditions was in whether or not the subjects were interested possessors of one of the mints on the table. In the No Choice condition the subject already has his piece of candy; therefore, preference, as a function of distance, would only be expected in the Choice condition. According to Brehm (1966, p. 80) "the results were that 25 out of 53 subjects in the No Choice condition or 47 % said the far candy was the better. In the Choice condition, 33 out of 51, 65 % of the subjects, said the far one was the better." This difference was significant at the 12 % level. Apparently, then, in spite of earlier mixed outcomes pertaining to the barrier-enhancement hypothesis, it is possible to set up conditions in which the effect can be demonstrated.

DELAY AND RESTRICTIONS

In a study exhibiting clearcut differences between experimental conditions, Mischel and Masters (1966) concluded: "the present results indicate that in our culture unattainable positive outcomes may be more valued than those which are attainable and that the unavailability of a positive outcome enhances its perceived desirability [p. 395]." The conclusion was based on a field experiment in which

children viewed a film which was interrupted near the climax on the pretext of a damaged fuse. The probability that the film could be resumed was either 1, .5, or 0. Measures of the film's value were administered before and after the interruption. Thereafter, the fuse was 'fixed' and all subjects saw the remainder of the film, with final value ratings obtained at the end. The hypothesis that the nonavailability of a reward increases its value was supported. Subjects who were given a 0 probability for seeing the remainder of the film increased their evaluation of it more than those in the other groups, and this increase was maintained even after the entire film was shown [Mischel & Masters, 1966, p. 390].

The Mischel-Masters experiment provided strong support for the general unavailability premise as well as specific support for proposition g concerning delay. In the zero probability condition, the film was undoubtedly perceived as *greatly* delayed; the experimenter's confederate, ostensibly the "district electrician," said "It takes a special fuse for this circuit, and there are none around here . . . I can't possibly fix it . . . [p. 392]."

From the commodity viewpoint two elements of the Mischel-Masters experiment were especially noteworthy. The desirable quality of the message was particularly apposite; the children were interested possessors of something relevant and useful to them. The film was described as an "exciting space movie" and the film showing and interruption occurred in a context in which the children were expected repeatedly to mark their opinions and evaluations on rating sheets. Second, the message, the film, was received by all subjects: everyone actually got the commodity.

Turner and Wright (1965) reported two pertinent experiments; the first replicated Aronson and Carlsmith (1963) while the second included treatments that could be considered pertinent to commodity theory. The subjects were young children, about 6 to 8 years old. After the children had ranked five of six toys, the experimental conditions of interest here, "never" and "later," were introduced.

"In both the 'never' and 'later' conditions the experimenter left the room for 7 minutes carrying with her the third ranked toy. In the 'never' condition the experimenter told the child that he could play with any of the toys except the critical toy, which he could not ever play with. In the 'later' condition the experimenter said, 'You can't play with this toy now, but when I come back and we finish the game, I promise that you'll get a chance to play with it.' When the experimenter returned to the room the child was told that he would get a chance to play with the toys again a little later, but first they would play the 'choosing game' again. In the never condition, the instructions varied: the child was told that after he had reranked the toys he could have another chance to play with the toys except, or course, the forbidden toy [Turner & Wright, 1965, pp. 129–131].

The results in the "later" condition were in accord with commodity theory, particularly proposition g, concerning delay: more children increased their ranking of the critical toy than did not change or decreased their ranking. The results in the "never" condition were apparently opposed to what would be expected from the unavailability premise: 13 out of 16 subjects decreased their ranking of the critical toy. The writer considered the Turner-Wright experiment apposite to his theory because the commodity, play with the toys, was "conveyable" and the children were undoubtedly interested possessors of that experience. The "never" condition, which yielded results inconsistent with the permanent withholding effects obtained by Mischel and Masters (1966) and Becker and Brock (1966), may be discountable. In this condition, the second ranking of the toys was accompanied by special instructions which emphasized that play with the critical toy was "forbidden." Since two of the other toys were unquestionably more attractive anyway, it seemed reasonable to infer that the child was, at this point, so dissuaded from the critical toy that he could no longer be considered an "interested possessor." If this explanation is acceptable, then pertinent portions of the Turner-Wright study have lent further support to the theory.

The essential findings of the Aronson-Carlsmith (1963) and Turner-Wright (1965) experiments were recently replicated by Pepitone, McCauley, and Hammond (1967) with procedural modifications that permitted deciding among various alternative interpretations of the Aronson-Carlsmith effect. In the Pepitone *et al.* experiment severe threat was based on the promise of a flashlight. Mild threat was based on the promise of two marbles. Either gift would be received only if the subject refrained from playing with any toy left on the table while the experimenter was out of the room. Pepitone *et al.* concluded as follows:

Accordingly, one might propose that there is something like an economic process in the child whereby the price of playing with the forbidden toy — and thus the value of it — is seen by the child to be equivalent to the value of the promised toy he will lose for disobeying. Under strong threat based on conditional promise of a flashlight, then, the worth of the forbidden toy is increased by pricing it at the value of the valuable gift promised. Under weak threat, based on conditional promise of marbles, the worth of the forbidden toy should be priced at the value of marbles. If the marbles were generally seen as less valuable than the original value of the forbidden toy, and the flashlight was generally seen as more valuable, the pricing mechanism would suffice to explain both the increase and decrease in value of the forbidden toy.

Such an economic process would predict that threat based on possible loss of a gift even more valuable than a flashlight would lead to a greater increase in evaluation of the forbidden toy than occurs under threat based on loss of a flashlight. This outcome, it should be noted, is not only beyond the range of dissonance explanation but would raise doubt about the validity of the dissonance interpretation applied to decrease in evaluation under mild threat [p. 228].

It is evident that the Pepitone *et al.* discussion is quite similar to commodity hypothesis *f*: an experience increases in value in proportion to the amount of reasons opposing commerce with the focal object. It is of interest that Pepitone *et al.* were led independently to posit the sort of psychoeconomic process that is emphasized by commodity theory.

In sum, more than a dozen investigations have supported one or more of the eight propositions developed from the unavailability premise. No empirical results pertinent to proposition *c*, concerning coercion exerted upon the communicator, have been found. However, descriptive accounts of military and police interrogation provide suggestive anecdotal evidence for the high value accorded information which is divulged only after coercive treatment of a prisoner. No studies pertinent to proposition *g*, concerning restriction on transmission, were located. Both propositions *c* and *g* were subjected to experimental examination in our laboratory as described below.

The publicly available studies considered in this section represented diverse theoretical predilections. The present commodity theory appeared to be a superior conceptual framework because it could account for most of the evidence considered while the particular model for each study was rarely appropriate to other studies in the group. Thus, the present theory exhibited a desirable generality in its ability to encompass hitherto unrelated empirical domains. The next section summarizes the results of several unpublished studies which serve to illustrate the potential of the commodity framework for suggesting new relationships.

SUMMARY OF UNPUBLISHED EVIDENCE

SCARCITY

An experiment by Brock and M. Yoder was designed to test commodity propositions *a* and *b:* a message will increase in effectiveness to the extent the recipient perceives the number of recipients as small; a message will increase in effectiveness to the extent the recipient perceives that few other communicators exist who might have delivered the same message. In a 3×2 before-after design, the dependent variable was the difference between the subject's ranking of one particular poetic couplet before and after exposure to a communication praising the poetic quality of that particular couplet. The first factor was the number of co-recipients. One-third of the subjects was given instructions aimed at inducing belief that they and few others received the communication; one-third was given instructions to believe that they and a moderate number of others received the communication; and one-third was given instructions to believe that they and many others received the communication. The second factor was the number of potential communicators of the disclosed information. Half the subjects received a communication in which it was stated that the communicator had shared the information with no one; half the subjects received an identical communication in which it was stated that the communicator had already shared the information with many others. The communication was a letter written ostensibly by an aesthetics expert; a portion of the communication praised a couplet which was obviously bland, inane, and without poetic quality. The subjects were 82 undergraduates recruited from introductory psychology classes.

The experimental manipulations were effective but an initial analysis of the data did not provide support for hypothesis *a* and a trend, which was in the direction predicted by hypothesis *b*, was only marginally reliable, at about the .12 level. Postexperimental protocols indicated that approximately half of the subjects in each experimental treatment explicitly mentioned unwillingness to change the ranking of the focal couplet. The protocols suggested that a more sensitive test of the hypotheses would exclude those subjects who ranked the critical couplet last and were actively unwilling to change. This reduction of the sample, of course, limited generalization of the findings to subjects whose judgments were susceptible to change. The first hypothesis implied that favorable opinion change (in the advocated direction) would decrease linearly as the perceived number of co-recipients increased. The obtained result was a marginally reliable ($p < .07$) quadratic effect. In accord with the hypothesis, favorable change was greater under Small Number of Co-Recipients than under Medium Number of Co-Recipients: the t test was marginally significant at about the .08 level. However, contrary to the hypothesis, favorable change was greater under Large Number of Co-Recipients than Medium Number of Co-Recipients. These differences did not correspond straightforwardly to the theoretical prediction. In spite of this ambiguity, it was found that manipulating the number of perceived co-recipients had some differential effect upon acceptance of the persuasive message. The nature of the relationship remained as a problem for subsequent research.

The second hypothesis was reliably ($p < .05$) supported: change in the direction advocated under Few Potential Communicators exceeded favorable change under Many Potential Communicators.

In sum, the Brock-Yoder experiment provided equivocal support for hypothesis a that specified an inverse relationship between number of co-recipients and acceptance of the message. Hypothesis b, valuation increases with paucity of potential communicators, was supported: the effect was marginally present in the unselected sample and reliably present in the selected sample.

SCARCITY AND RESTRICTION

Yoder (1967) investigated hypotheses a, concerning the effects on value of availability to potentially interested co-recipients, and h, concerning the effects on value of restrictions set by the communicator upon further transmission. An additional hypothesis was that the value of a prospective experience will be enhanced with increase in the number of potentially interested participants that have expressed a desire for that experience.

One hundred and fifty undergraduate psychology students were randomly assigned to the eight cells of a $2 \times 2 \times 2$ factorial design. Subjects were led to believe that they were to be selected to observe ongoing research projects at Ohio State University. They were further told that the project to which they would be assigned would depend on their score on an educational interest test, their personal ranking of ten possible research sites, the number of observers that could be handled at each site, and the number of subjects who ranked each research observation site as their first choice.

The three independent variables were: number of others who ranked as first choice the research observation to which a subject was assigned; the availability of the research observation to which a subject was assigned; and the restrictions on subsequent transmission of information about the research observation.

The first hypothesis was that the greater the number of others who ranked the assigned research observation as most desirable, the greater would be the subject's evaluation of the observation opportunity. The second hypothesis predicted that the subject's evaluation would increase as the availability of the observation decreased. The third hypothesis predicted that evaluation would increase as restriction on comm unication increased.

The experiment was in booklet form. The subjects first read that the study was an attempt to improve undergraduate teaching methods through undergraduate observation of current faculty research projects. The subjects then read a description of four factors which would supposedly determine to which of ten research projects they would be assigned. (See above.) Subjects then took the "educational interest" test and ranked the research projects in terms of personal preference. While these tests were supposedly being graded and assignments being made, subjects engaged in a filler task. Actually all assignments had been made in advance with all subjects assigned to observe the same research project and also randomly assigned to one of the eight experimental conditions.

The manipulation of the independent variables was contained in the assignment sheet. Subjects read that they had been assigned to the "turbulent flow" project because of (a) their score on the educational interest test, (b) their ranking of the projects, (c) the fact that a large amount (or a small amount) of other prospective observers had ranked the turbulent flow project as their first choice, and (d) the fact that the turbulent flow project has facilities for a large number (or a small number) of observers. Half the subjects read that the turbulent flow project was a restricted one and were required to sign a secrecy oath. The other subjects read that some projects were restricted but that the flow project was not one of these.

The next page of the booklet contained two questions designed to measure the dependent variable. The first determined how willing the subject was to switch to another project; the second, how valuable the subject felt his participation in the project would be.

Checks on the manipulations indicated that they were effectively induced. The first hypothesis was not supported for either measure of the dependent variable. The second hypothesis was reliably supported for the "value" dependent measure and the directions of differences on the "willingness to switch" measure were all in accord with the hypothesis, although the overall statistical test was not significant.

The third hypothesis was reliably supported for both dependent measures. In summary the study supported the predictions that unavailability (hypothesis *a*) and communication restriction (hypothesis *h*) enhance the value of an experience.

SCARCITY AND SOCIAL DEMAND

In the above Yoder experiment (1967), number of interested nonpossessors did not have the expected effect and the support for hypothesis *a* was partly marginal. In order to clarify the relationship between unavailability and interested nonpossessors, both of these factors were varied in an experiment by H. L. Fromkin and Brock. The hypothesis was that message effectiveness will be greatest when the recipient perceives the number of other recipients as small and, at the same time, the number of interested nonpossessors as large.

Since subjects in Yoder's experiment (1967) unexpectedly ranked the focal research observation, "turbulent flow," as the project they were least interested in observing, it was likely that the subjects did not perceive the observation experience as potentially useful.[4] It was therefore unclear if the research observation was properly a "commodity" and, consequently, unclear if commodity theory was applicable. Therefore, to test the theoretical requirement of usefulness, the Fromkin-Brock study employed a message about a salient and relevant issue for some subjects and a message about a less relevant and more peripheral issue for others. It was expected that the pattern of results would approximate a second-order interaction which reflected all three variables; increase in the perception of the number of interested nonpossessors was expected to enhance the effects of unavailability only when the issue was salient and relevant.

The Fromkin and Brock study was a naturalistic field experiment conducted among 97 staff members of a large private summer camp. The three independent variables, two levels of each, were number of other recipients, number of interested other nonpossessors, and attitude issue. The first attitude issue, staff curfew, was considered interesting and important by the staff members; in contrast, the second attitude issue, camper visitors, was low in interest and importance.

The unavailability manipulation was varied just before the presentation of the message when two staff members (actually confederates)

---

[4]Unfortunately, Yoder's (1967) "interest" measures were in the form of ranks which did not permit assessing the absolute level of intensity of interest or perceived usefulness.

were asked to leave (to remain) because only 10 staff members (all 150 staff members) were to hear the message. The number of interested nonpossessors was varied by giving the subjects a false report about the number of staff at other camps who had demonstrated their interest in the message by completing an extensive 5500-word essay task as required "homework" in order to receive the message. Subjects in the curfew issue condition heard a persuasive message advocating a more stringent curfew for all staff members; in the visitors issue condition, the message opposed campers being visited by elderly adults and very young children.

The dependent variable was a change score from respective control means, which reflected the amount of influence exerted by each message. A marginally reliable second-order interaction and appropriate simple effects comparisons corroborated the hypotheses. Recipients, who expressed high prior interest in the issue and who perceived the issue as at least moderately important to them, were reliably more influenced by a message when the number of other recipients was perceived as small and the number of other interested nonpossessors was perceived as large. This finding was not demonstrated for recipients of the second issue, that is where recipients expressed low prior interest in the issue and where recipients perceived the issue as unimportant.

The Fromkin-Brock study provided good support for the unavailability hypothesis *a* and has shown, further, that the perceived usefulness of a message is an important determinant of the applicability of commodity principles.

EFFORT AND RESTRICTION

The only commodity proposition for which no empirical data existed was hypothesis *c:* a message will increase in effectiveness the greater the degree of coercion upon the communicator needed to bring about disclosure. This hypothesis, together with hypothesis *g*, concerning transmission restriction, was studied in the following experiment conducted by H. L. Fromkin.

Ninety-five subjects who volunteered to participate in a psychological study of interviewing techniques, were randomly assigned to individual cubicles equipped with earphones and a dial system. First, subjects completed a questionnaire measuring student attitudes toward cheating. The questionnaire allegedly originated in the "Office of Academic Affairs." Responses to the questionnaire provided a baseline for the dependent variable. Next, subjects were instructed to "evaluate *one* of several actual interviews conducted in real life settings." All subjects heard a tape-recorded interview of a dean questioning a student who had been caught cheating during exams. The first independent variable, amount of coercion, was manipulated as the number of threats needed to induce the student to describe an incident from his past. The second independent variable, number of transmission restrictions, was manipulated as the number of other persons that the student said could be told about the revealed incident. The third independent variable, the nature of the revealed information, was whether the incident showed something honest or dishonest about the student's character.

The dependent variables were the subjects' overall evaluations of the student: (a) how honest was the student being interviewed; and (b) how serious a violation of university rules did this student commit. The manipulations were successful but the results showed, unexpectedly, that the student, in response to the initial threats from the dean, was perceived as arguing "convincingly" that the incident from his past was irrelevant. Postexperimental checks revealed that the subjects thought the dean should not use information about the student's past in judging the current cheating incident. Indeed, the data showed that the subjects tried not to use the information about the past incident in making their own evaluations of the student. However, the information did affect their evaluations in subtle ways. For example, restrictions on further transmission of the information served to remind subjects of the information's "illegitimacy" and attenuated use of the information while coercion increased use of the information.

Analysis of the perceived honesty data showed a significant ($p < .05$) main effect due to the nature of the information revealed by the student. The student was perceived as more honest after disclosing information about his honesty than after disclosing information about his dishonesty. In addition, a marginally reliable Coercion × Transmission Restriction interaction ($p < .10$) revealed that the predicted effect of coercion occurred only under the Low Restriction condition. Here, where the information was considered legitimate, subjects incorporated *more* information (favorable or unfavorable depending upon honesty condition) into their overall impression when the information was disclosed after a great deal of coercion than when the information was disclosed after little coercion.

Analysis of the perceived seriousness-of-offense data showed a similar significant interaction ($p < .05$). Subjects perceived the student's violation as *more* serious (or *less* serious, depending upon honesty condition) when the information was disclosed after a great deal of coercion than when the information was disclosed after little coercion.

Again, this effect of coercion occurred only under the Low Restriction condition when subjects perceived that use of the information was "legitimate."

In sum, the interactions of the Fromkin experiment, although not totally consistent with *a priori* expectations, have shown that coercion and transmission restriction affect the weight given disclosed information in ways that are influenced by whether or not the information is perceived as legitimately usable in the recipients' judgements. Hypothesis *c* received qualified support.

REVIEW AND EVALUATION

A commodity theory relating selective social communication to value formation and change has been presented and partially tested. Little work has been done yet on derivations stemming from the threat premise; the bulk of the available experimental evidence concerns propositions associated with the unavailability premise. The results of more than twenty published and unpublished experiments have tended to support a list of eight hypotheses. Proposition *a*, valuation increases with decrease in the perceived number of recipients, received unambiguous support from Brehm *et al.* (1966), Kelman (1953), and Fromkin and Brock (unpublished), and partial support from Brock and Yoder (unpublished) and Yoder (1967). Proposition *b*, valuation increases as the perceived number of potential communicators declines, received indirect support from Brehm *et al.* (1966) and direct support from Brock and Yoder (unpublished). Proposition *c*, concerning coercion of the communicator, received qualified support from Fromkin (unpublished). Proposition *d*, valuation increases with increased perception of communicator effort, was strongly supported by Brock and Becker (1965), Becker and Brock (1966), Walster, *et al.*, (1966), Mills and Jellison (1967), and Jellison (1967). The idea that recipient effort will increase message effectiveness, proposition *e*, was supported by Ostrom (1966), Wicklund *et al.* (1967), Wright (1934), Sears (1967), and Brehm and Hammock (Brehm, 1966, pp. 78–80). In the Brock-Becker (1965) experiment, force against disclosure accompanied the more effective message, in support of proposition *f*. Proposition *f* was also supported by Pepitone *et al.* (1967). In support of proposition *g*, a reliable enhancing effect of restricted transmission was found by Yoder (1967) and restriction reliably interacted with coercion upon the communicator in a study by Fromkin (unpublished). Proposition *h*, valuation increases as the message is increasingly delayed, has been well-documented (Becker & Brock, 1966; Mischel & Masters, 1966; Pepitone *et al.*, 1967; Turner & Wright, 1965; Wicklund *et al.*, 1967).

The above studies notwithstanding, there are still major conceptual and evidential problems with the present commodity theory. Its characterization as "rudimentary" must be maintained until some of these problems have been solved and until time has permitted more experiments directed primarily at the theory. The bulk of the cited studies were not inspired by commodity notions and this has meant that the present interpretation of these studies has been strained: in some instances, interpretation of the studies was "forced" to fit the commodity mold. Those of our unpublished studies that were directly aimed at the theory have been marred by weak results. As a consequence, it has not seemed worthwhile at this point in time to attempt to relate commodity theory to other more robust theories (frustration, reactance, dissonance) that to some extent share independent and dependent variables with commodity theory. Instead, some of the major conceptual problems will be discussed.

Ambiguity attends the notion "interested possessor." With respect to several studies (Brehm *et al.*, 1966; Brock & Becker, 1965; Turner & Wright, 1965), interested possessor was invoked to differentiate various portions of the results as to their theoretical pertinence. It was proposed that, when prospective recipients are uninterested in particular information, commodity propositions are inapplicable. It was clear that individuals were interested in seeing an exciting film (Mischel & Masters, 1966), learning about their femininity (Becker & Brock, 1966), listening to a "folk" album (Brehm *et al.*, 1966), and playing with an attractive toy (Turner & Wright, 1965). However, why should a student be considered an uninterested possessor of the information that the faculty wants to "triple tuition" (Brock & Becker, 1965). Although unpleasant, such information is relevant and useful to him and, hence, it satisfies the present definition of informational commodity. Rather than limiting the applicability of the theory to positive messages, it seemed preferable to acknowledge that very unpleasant information can elicit defensive reactions which may countervail commodity principles. Another resolution was suggested by the Becker-Brock (1966) data: intensification of commodity aspects of information exchange will increase and make acceptable whatever message import was expected from the communicator's orientation. If that import was favorable to the recipient, commodity inductions will make it more positive; if it was unfavorable, commodity inductions will render the import of the message more negative. This possibility is supported by the previously described studies of Wicklund *et al*

(1967), wherein subjects anticipated listening to speakers who would advocate unacceptable states of affairs (e.g., no draft exemption). Of course, future empirical research will have to decide among these proposed clarifications.

In retrospect, it has seemed unnecessarily restrictive to equate value and effectiveness. Message effectiveness refers primarily to yielding whereas value has implications as well for attention, comprehension, retention, and action. Each of these five processes could be affected by commodification. Another potential broadening of the applicability of commodity theory was suggested by the Kelman experiment (1953) where the commodification concerned not the message itself but the accompanying incentive. Hence, a liberalized formulation would concern the derivative effects of commodification upon processes associated with the focal process.

A more serious problem for the theory concerns the assumed underlying psychological mechanism. Suppose it can be demonstrated with sufficient clarity and reproducibility that persons will react to commodification (unavailability, scarcity, effort, delay, restriction) in the ways predicted by the theory. These demonstrations will not tell us *why* commodified information is preferred or *why* commodified communication is especially effective. At present the theory lacks a dynamic explanatory principle. It has been noted that the recipient must be an interested possessor, actually or potentially, of the information or experience to be commodified, before commodity principles are expected to obtain. However, this qualification, as already noted above, has been applied in an unsatisfactory ad hoc fashion. An additional concept was required. What motivational force would lead individuals to prefer stimuli that are unavailable, restricted, effortfully obtained, effortfully communicated, and so forth?

An interesting speculative possibility is that possession of commodified information or experience or objects contributes to the individual's sense of uniqueness, of separate identity (Erikson, 1954; Frank, 1955; Fromm, 1941, 1955; Horney, 1937). A person who has information that is not widely shared will feel himself to be more different from other persons than the possessor of information that is known by all. In general, the greater the need to have attributes which are different from the attributes possessed by others, that is, the greater the need to be unique, the greater will be the valuation and effectiveness of commodified stimuli. (In line with this suggestion, threat, the other major premise of the theory, may be redefined to mean anticipation of decrement in viable individualized personal control of the physical and social environment.) Need uniqueness seems to be a motivational state that is readily susceptible to both measurement and manipulation. If the uniqueness-identity hunch is correct we will be enabled to design experiments in which commodity principles do *and* do not obtain, and thereby, commodity theory will have gained a dynamic explanatory principle. The words of e. e. cummings (letter, 1955) may be appropriate — "To be nobody-but-yourself in a world which is doing its best night and day, to make you everybody else — means to fight the hardest battle which any human being can fight; and never stop fighting!"

References

Adams, J. S. Inequity in social exchange. In L. Berkowitz (Ed.), *Advances in experimental social psychology.* Vol. 2. New York: Academic Press, 1965. Pp. 267-299.

Aronson, E., and Carlsmith, J. M. Effect of the severity of threat on the devaluation of forbidden behavior. *Journal of Abnormal and Social Psychology,* 1963, **66**, 584-588.

Becker, L. A., and Brock, T. C. Prospective recipients' estimates of withheld evaluation. *Journal of Personality and Social Psychology,* 1966, 4, 147-154.

Blau, P. M. *Exchange and power in social life.* New York: Wiley, 1964.

Brehm, J. W. *Theory of psychological reactance.* New York: Academic Press, 1966.

Brehm, J. W., Stires, L. K., Sensenig, J., and Shaban, J. The attractiveness of an eliminated choice alternative. *Journal of Experimental Social Psychology,* 1966, **2**, 301-313.

Brock, T. C. Commitment to exposure as a determinant of information receptivity. *Journal of Personality and Social Psychology,* 1965, **2**, 10-20.

Brock, T. C., and Balloun, J. L. Behavioral receptivity to dissonant information. *Journal of Personality and Social Psychology,* 1967, **6**, 413-428.

Brock, T. C., and Becker, L. A. Ineffectiveness of "overheard" counterpropaganda. *Journal of Personality and Social Psychology,* 1965, **2**, 654-660.

Cohen, A. R. Communication discrepancy and attitude change: A dissonance theory approach. *Journal of Personality,* 1959, **27**, 386-396.

Erikson, E. H. Growth and crises of the "health personality." In C. Kluckhohn and H. A. Murray (Eds.), *Personality in nature, society, and culture.* New York: Knopf, 1957. Pp. 185-225.

Frank, L. K. *Individual development.* New York: Doubleday, 1955.

Freedman, J. L. Preference for dissonant information. *Journal of Personality and Social Psychology,* 1965, **2**, 287-289.

Freedman, J. L., and Sears, D. O. Selective exposure. In L. Berkowitz (Ed.), *Advances in experimental social psychology.* Vol. 2. New York: Academic Press, 1965. Pp. 58-97.

Fromm, E. *Escape from freedom.* New York: Farrah & Rinehart, 1941.

Fromm, E. *The sane society.* New York: Rinehart, 1955.

Goffman, E. *The presentation of self in everyday life.* New York: Doubleday, 1959.

Hammock, T., and Brehm, J. W. The attractiveness of choice alternatives when freedom to choose is eliminated by a social agent. *Journal of Personality,* 1966, **34**, 546-554.

Homans, G. C. *Social behavior: Its elementary forms.* New York: Harcourt, 1961.

Horney, K. *The neurotic personality of our time.* New York: Norton, 1937.

Hovland, C. I., and Weiss, W. The influence of source credibility on communication effectiveness. *Public Opinion Quarterly*, 1951, **15**, 635-650.

Jellison, J. M. The effect of whether a communicator changes his position and his opportunity for reconsideration upon opinion change. *American Psychologist*, 1967, **22**, 530. (Abstract)

Kelman, H. C. Attitude change as a function of response restriction. *Human Relations*, 1953, **6**, 185-214.

Lanzetta, J. T., and Driscoll, J. M. Preference for information about an uncertain but unavoidable outcome. *Journal of Personality and Social Psychology*, 1966, **3**, 96-102.

Lanzetta, J. T., and Kanareff, V. T. Information cost, amount of payoff, and level of aspiration as determinants of information seeking in decision making. *Behavioral Science*, 1962, **7**, 459-473.

Marschak, J. Toward an economic theory of organization and information. In R. M. Thrall, C. H. Coombs, and R. L. Davis (Eds.), *Decision processes*. New York: Wiley, 1954. Pp. 187-220.

Merton, R. K. *Mass persuasion*. New York: Harper, 1946.

Mills, J. Effect of certainty about a decision upon postdecision exposure to consonant and dissonant information. *Journal of Personality and Social Psychology*, 1965, **2**, 749-752.

Mills, J., and Jellison, J. M. Effect on opinion change of how desirable the communication is to the audience the communicator addressed. *Journal of Personality and Social Psychology*, 1967, **6**, 98-101.

Mischel, W., and Masters, J. C. Effects of probability of reward attainment on responses to frustration. *Journal of Personality and Social Psychology*, 1966, **3**, 390-396.

Ostrom, T. M. Physical effort and attitude change. *American Psychologist*, 1966, **21**, 692. (Abstract); Paper read at Psychological Association Convention, New York, September 1966. (Also mimeo, Ohio State University, 1966)

Pepitone, A., McCauley, C., and Hammand, P. Change in attractiveness of forbidden toys as a function of severity of threat. *Journal of Experimental Social Psychology*, 1967, **3**, 221-229.

Rosen, S. The comparative roles of informational and material commodities in interpersonal transactions. *Journal of Experimental Social Psychology*, 1966, **2**, 211-226.

Sears, D. O. Social anxiety, opinion structure, and opinion change. *Journal of Personality and Social Psychology*, 1967, **7**, 142-151.

Shils, E. A. *The torment of secrecy*. Glencoe, Ill.: Free Press, 1956.

Smelser, N. J. *The sociology of economic life*. Englewood Cliffs, N. J.: Prentice-Hall, 1963.

Stigler, G. J. The economics of information. *The Journal of Political Economy*, 1961, **69**, 213-225.

Thibaut, J. W., and Kelley, H. H. *The social psychology of groups*. New York: Wiley, 1959.

Turner, E. A., and Wright, J. C. Effects of severity of threat and perceived availability on the attractiveness of objects. *Journal of Personality and Social Psychology*, 1965, **2**, 128-132.

Walster, E., Aronson, E., and Abrahams, D. On increasing the persuasiveness of a low prestige communicator. *Journal of Experimental Social Psychology*, 1966, **2**, 325-342.

Wicklund, R. A., Cooper, J., and Linder, D. E. Effects of expected effort on attitude change prior to exposure. *Journal of Experimental Social Psychology*, 1967, **3**, 416-428.

Wright, H. F. The influence of barriers upon the strength of motivation. Unpublished doctoral dissertation, Duke University, 1934.

Yoder, M. R. The effect of unavailability and communication restriction upon the evaluation of a prospective experience. Unpublished master's thesis, Ohio State University, 1967.

Zimbardo, P. G. The effect of effort and improvisation on self-persuasion produced by role-playing. *Journal of Experimental Social Psychology,* 1965, **1**, 103-120.

11

Attitude Change from Threat to Attitudinal Freedom[1]

JACK W. BREHM
DEPARTMENT OF PSYCHOLOGY
DUKE UNIVERSITY
DURHAM, NORTH CAROLINA

When one considers the possible range over which attitudes may vary on issues such as the need for foreign aid, the amount of support appropriate for education, the advisability of hastening racial integration, etc., and the inability of anyone to persuade the general population to one side or the other on such issues, it is plausible to conclude that persuasion is at best generally ineffective. What accounts for this ineffectiveness has been the subject of various discussions (e.g., Hovland, 1959; McGuire, 1964), but the problem cannot yet be set aside as understood. While the present paper can offer no general solution, it will attempt to show that there is at least one previously overlooked factor that can account not only for considerable resistance to change, but even for boomerang effects.

The factor in question, called "psychological reactance" (Brehm, 1966), is a motivational state that operates in opposition to inducing forces such as persuasive communications. In general terms, the theory asserts that when a person's freedom to engage in a particular behavior is eliminated or threatened with elimination, the individual

[1] I would like to acknowledge my indebtedness to two students, Russell Jones and Robert Wicklund, from whose unpublished papers I have borrowed freely in writing the present chapter. I also wish to thank the National Institute of Mental Health for their support of research reported here (MH-11228).

will experience psychological reactance, a motivation directed toward the re-establishment of the lost or threatened freedom. Where attitudes are concerned, it is assumed that the individual normally feels free to adopt a position for himself and that any attempt to force him to adopt a particular position constitutes a threat to that freedom. The more important that freedom to the individual, and the greater the pressure to adopt a particular position, the greater will be the magnitude of reactance. Since reactance leads to attempts to re-establish freedom, the greater the reactance, the greater will be the individual's tendency to move away from the position he is pressured to take. The remainder of this paper delineates some of the freedoms there are in regard to attitudes, the conditions under which these freedoms are important, how threats to these freedoms may occur, and, finally, what the consequences of the resulting reactance may be.

WHAT FREEDOMS ARE THERE WITH REGARD TO ATTITUDES?

Prior to any private or public commitment on an issue, the individual presumably feels free to seek information that would be helpful in deciding what position to take. At this point the individual is objectively free to adopt any position on the issue, but psychologically it would be more appropriate to say that the freedom to adopt any position is of no importance since the meaning of holding any position is unclear. On the other hand, a freedom of relatively great importance when one does not have information that allows one to decide upon a position is that of suspending judgment. When the individual feels he cannot yet decide on a position, then, any attempt to make him do so threatens his freedom to suspend judgment and should result in arousal of reactance and consequent attempts to avoid making a decision and to continue to withhold judgment. Since pressure to take a position may also be seen as an attempt to preclude further seeking of relevant information, the freedom to seek such information may be threatened. A consequence, of course, would be an increased desire to have more relevant information regardless of which side of the issue it supported. In the special case where the pressure to take a position implies that one side of the issue should be supported rather than the other side, the threat to freedom of information seeking will be greater for the "other side" and the increased desirability of information supporting the "other side" will be greater than of information supporting the first side.

Suppose, for example, that a person has just obtained his Ph.D.

in computer programming and simulation in psychology and joins a psychology department in which the staff is split over whether or not to expand the program in clinical. We can easily imagine that this person would feel incompetent to adopt a position on the issue and would value the freedom to seek information on both sides. Any pressure on him to adopt a position, such as in a staff vote on the issue, would be resisted until he could acquaint himself with the pros and cons. The more pressure put on him, the more he would resist acting and the more attractive would become the relevant information. Furthermore, pressure from a person known to favor expanding the clinical program would have the effect not only of increasing resistance against voting for expansion but also of increasing the desirability of information against expansion of the program. In effect, premature pressure to take a stand will tend to result in avoidance of doing so, and pressure to take a particular position will tend to produce increased interest in information supporting the opposing position.

THE EFFECT OF HIGH COMPETENCE

The individual's confidence in his ability to make good judgments on an issue will tend to increase as he acquires more relevant information and as he learns from similar judgments that his decisions are "correct" or satisfying. To see why this is true, let us consider a person confronting a choice between two plain white boxes that at first glance appear to be identical. Given that one box contains a valuable prize and the other contains nothing, it is important to the individual to make the right choice; but as long as he cannot make a meaningful discrimination between them, being able to choose one rather than the other has no importance. Now suppose this person is given a series of such choices and he finds that although the boxes appear similar, he is in fact almost always able to choose the one containing the prize. Given enough successful experience, he will become convinced that he is competent to make a meaningful choice and the freedom to choose will acquire importance for him. Before finding himself to be competent to choose correctly, any suggestion by another person about which box he should choose would be seen as possibly helpful information and, although it would interfere with his freedom to decide for himself, would arouse little if any reactance since being able to choose would have little importance. But after gaining a feeling of competence regarding which box to choose, any suggestion by another, although it might still be seen as possibly helpful, would also arouse relatively great reactance since it would interfere with a relatively important freedom. While the "rational" decision under the latter circumstances would be to pool one's own judgment with that of the other's suggestion, so that if the two agreed the suggestion would be followed, the reactance aroused by the interference with freedom to choose would push the individual to reassert his freedom — in this case most effectively done by rejecting the suggestion.

The case with regard to attitudes is similar except that the attitudinal dimension must be conceived of as discriminable positions on an issue. It is not necessary, in terms of the theory, to assume that the positions lie on a single dimension, but it is convenient to make and try to meet this assumption for purposes of experimentation. Thus, for example, we might assume that on a given issue there are two discriminable positions, pro and con, and that holding one position means something different to the individual from holding the other. To the extent that the individual can make meaningful discriminations between positions, he should feel competent to decide which position he would adopt and/or which position he would reject.

There are, it should be clear, two distinguishable sources of the importance of freedom to adopt one's own position. The first is the feeling of competence the individual has that he can make a meaningful choice on the dimension in question. The second is the actual difference he finds between positions once he has had time to study them. It would be possible, for example, that a person might feel quite capable of making a judgment on a given issue prior to studying it only to find that there were no important differences for him between positions. Before studying the positions, the individual would feel that the importance of the freedom to choose his own position would have been relatively great, whereas after finding there were no significant differences, the individual would feel that the importance of the freedom to choose among them would be relatively low. On the other hand, the individual may have little confidence in his ability to make a meaningful discrimination among positions prior to studying them, but find that after study, he could make quite important distinctions for himself. In this case, the importance of the freedom to select or reject a given position would be a function of the final attractiveness of that position, the importance being greater as his liking or disliking for it increased.

In summary, when a person has not yet had a chance to study all of the relevant information on an issue, the more competent he feels to make a good judgment, the more important is it to him to be free to adopt his own position. Thus, given a feeling of high competence, the greater is the threat to the individual's freedom to decide for himself, the greater will be his reactance and the more he will consequently tend to act counter to the threat. Where felt compentence is low, a threat to the individual's freedom to decide for himself should have relatively little effect on his tendency to act conversely.

Whether competence is initially low or high, study of the alternative positions on an issue will eventually determine the importance of the freedom to select or reject each. Where it can be assumed that there is a single dimension on which the positions are ordered, then the freedom to hold the most attractive position, that is, the one preferred by the individual, will be most important and the importance of the freedom to hold other positions will decrease as they become increasingly discrepant from the preferred position. Conversely, the importance of the freedom to reject the preferred position will be low or nonexistent, and the importance of the freedom to reject other positions will increase as they become more discrepant from the preferred position. Two propositions follow: (1) the magnitude of reactance aroused by pressure to adopt a particular position varies directly with the discrepancy between that position and the one which is preferred; and (2) the magnitude of reactance aroused by pressure against taking a particular position varies inversely with the discrepancy between that position and the one which is preferred.

The re-establishment of freedom when reactance has been aroused by pressure to adopt a particular position occurs by not complying, or, more strongly, by movement away from the advocated position. Similarly, if the pressure is to avoid a particular position, restoration of freedom will take the form of moving toward that position. In either case there should be a corresponding change in the perceived value of the position: the position one is pressured to take should become less attractive, the position one is pressured to reject should become more attractive.

When a person is motivated by reactance to change his position on an issue, he may also seek information supportive of that change, be receptive of such information, and be resistant to information that is disconfirmatory. These tendencies toward selective exposure to information would be strong, however, only where it was difficult to adopt the desired position because of lack of rational support. In the more usual case in which arguments and facts are already known for any given position, one might expect some re-evaluation of the relevant information but little tendency for selective information seeking or exposure. Whatever selective information seeking and re-evaluation of information takes place would, of course, tend to support the newly adopted position and give it greater permanence. In any case, change that occurs as a function of reactance may in the absence of other forces be expected to persist.

PUBLIC AND PRIVATE COMMITMENT

Commitment to a particular position tends to eliminate one's freedom to adopt other positions. While it is almost always conceivable that a person may change his position on an issue, public commitment may, in connection with implied punishments, virtually eliminate this freedom. Whether this commitment is private, deriving from a decision or emotional response, or public, deriving from one or more reward or punishment contingencies, the greater the degree of commitment, the greater is the threat to one's freedom to adopt a different position (or reject the one to which the commitment is made), and with high degrees of commitment, freedom is virtually eliminated. Commitment therefore has the capacity to arouse reactance and the effects of this arousal should be observable.

However, commitment to a specific position implies that there is explicit restraint against changing from that position, and for that reason it is not possible to say that the resultant tendency to change away from the position (in order to restore freedom) is a direct function of the degree of commitment (threat). True, the magnitude of reactance should increase as the degree of threat increases but so does the resistance against change. What may be predicted is that the desirability of the position to which one becomes committed will tend to decrease immediately subsequent to the commitment, and the desirability of alternative positions will tend to increase. Because these effects would tend to increase postcommitment dissonance (Festinger, 1957), they should be rather short-lived. Successful dissonance reduction will eventuate in giving up the freedom to adopt other positions, or at least in minimization of the importance of the freedoms given up. In the final analysis, a person who is thoroughly committed to a position no longer feels free to adopt other positions and should experience little or no reactance from being pressured to do so. For example, a baseball fan who lives in Boston may be so affectively attached to the Boston Red Sox that he could never favor any other baseball team in comparison. Though he might generally favor the underdog in sporting events, he would not be free to favor an underdog against his Red Sox. Thus, if someone put pressure on him to favor the underdog rather than is favorite team, little or no reactance should be aroused in him.

In general, a threat to freedom may be defined as the perception by an individual that there is pressure on him to behave in a specific way, in this case, to adopt or reject a position on an issue. Perceptions of pressure may arise in various ways, some of which will be listed here.

Perhaps the most direct pressure is that exerted by one person's telling another person explicitly that he should adopt or avoid a given attitudinal position. This form may appear a little bizarre at first glance since it does not fall within the traditional kinds of communications studies in attitude change research. However, reflection on "real-life" situations quickly reveals how commonly direct attempts at attitudinal control occur. It is not unusual, for example, that a parent tells his child what positions to adopt or reject on a variety of issues such as smoking cigarettes, drinking alcohol, using drugs, having premarital sexual experience, believing in God, etc. In turn ministers tell parents which positions to adopt and reject on these same kinds of issues, as do social and political leaders in various degrees. Another set of explicit pressures may be found in advertising. Direct attempts to eliminate attitudinal freedom seem common indeed.

IMPLIED PRESSURE

Many communications from one person to another (or to an audience) have the intent of getting the listener to adopt or avoid a particular position but do not use the explicit form of telling him what to do. While this type of attempted pressure is less likely to be perceived as a threat to one's freedom to decide for oneself, it still may be so perceived and thereby be capable of arousing reactance. What controls whether or not a persuasive communication is perceived as a threat is not entirely clear, but it can be said that any perceived intent to influence should be seen as a threat to one's attitudinal freedom. Among those factors which give rise to the perception that there is an intent to influence are: (1) that the communicator has something to gain by having his position adopted; (2) that the communication is more one-sided than is warranted by what the communicatee knows; (3) that there are systematic errors in the communication which favor the position advocated; (4) that the communicator tries too hard (by using emotional appeals, repetition of arguments, etc.) to have his case accepted; (5) and that the communicator draws a conclusion unwarranted by his communication. Hence, the presence of any of these factors in a communication should tend to arouse reactance and a consequent tendency to resist influence or move away from the advocated position.

INFORMATION AND SOURCE EXPERTNESS

It should not be construed that just because a communicator is obviously trying to influence his audience that significant reactance will be aroused and boomerang attitude change will ensue. Consider, for example, the case of the Surgeon General endorsing the statement that cigarette smoking causes lung cancer. In this case the communicator cites facts and arguments which are not easy for his audience to refute, and he is considered by his audience to be highly expert and unbiased in regard to the subject matter. Nevertheless, it is clear that the intent of the communicator is to influence his audience to adopt a particular position on the issue of smoking, and his communication should therefore be perceived as a threat to the freedom of his listeners to make up their own minds on the issue. According to the present analysis, there should indeed be some reactance aroused in members of his audience, and there should be some consequent resistance to acceptance of his position. At the same time, however, the audience has relatively low felt competence on the issue since the most important facts are highly technical, and the facts and arguments themselves tend to lead to the conclusion advocated by the communicator. Thus there are good reasons for complying with the persuasive attempt despite any resistance due to reactance, and one would therefore expect that the dominant tendency produced by the persuasive attempt would be in the direction of compliance. However, if the importance of the attitudinal freedom were high despite the high credibility of the communicator, then the magnitude of reactance would be great and there should be relatively great resistance to positive change, and perhaps there would be negative change.

RELEVANT EVIDENCE

Relevant research has been reviewed and appraised elsewhere (Brehm, 1966) and will only be summarized here. In particular, three lines of research were found to lend general support to a reactance analysis of attitude change. First, there are several experiments (e.g., Allyn & Festinger, 1961; Freedman & Sears, 1965; Kiesler &

Kiesler, 1964) which demonstrate that forewarning the audience of the communicator's intent to influence them tends to result in reduced attitude change. Second, there are experiments (e.g., Festinger & Maccooby, 1964) which show that distracting the audience when there is an obvious intent to influence tends to produce increased attitude change. Third, a pair of experiments by Walster and Festinger (1962) show that overheard communications produce more positive change than normally delivered communications, apparently because the audience is unable to infer that an overheard communication is intended to influence. These three lines of research, then, fit rather neatly into the view that the perception of intent to influence arouses reactance and a resultant tendency to reject the advocated position.

TESTS OF IMPLICATIONS FROM REACTANCE THEORY

Attitude change purely as a function of reactance should be away from the position advocated. However, as has been explained previously, reactance is conceived as a counterforce and therefore cannot occur in the absence of a force to comply positively. The typical attitude change paradigm is therefore inadequate to show the effects of reactance per se since the dependent variable of amount of attitude change is normally the resultant force of the pressure to change positively and whatever reactance effect there may be. Since reactance effects can be expected to surpass pressure to change positively only under special conditions, what one would expect to find normally would be a reduction in positive effects rather than actual negative change. This is indeed the pattern observed in the research cited on intent to influence, although interestingly enough, there are instances of negative change consistent with reactance theory and unexpected by the investigators (e.g., Kiesler & Kiesler, 1964).

Initial tests of the effects of reactance on attitude change were designed to show that an explicit attempt to threaten the freedom of the communicatee to select his own position would reduce the effects of an otherwise persuasive communication, and, hopefully, even produce a boomerang effect. Two experiments, reported in detail in Brehm (1966), will be briefly described.

In the first experiment, designed and conducted by Mary L. Brehm, college students in a large lecture course were first asked to fill out a questionnaire which measured their attitudes on several issues related to education, including the experimental issue "De-emphasis on intercollegiate athletics." A week later the experimenter entered the same class and ostensibly as part of the same general study of student views of educational issues, asked the students to read a communication and fill out another questionnaire. The experimental materials were prepared in booklet form, each booklet containing a written persuasive communication preceded by an explanation that described it as having been made by a college student at a national conference. The communication was two-sided, well-reasoned and nonemotional, but argued strongly in favor of intercollegiate athletics, ending, "I conclude that, if anything, we need an even stronger program of intercollegiate athletics."

Unknown to the subjects, two forms of the communications were distributed among them. Both forms were as described above, but one, the High Threat form, had at the end the following additional statement by the communicator: "You, as college students, must inevitably draw the same conclusion."

The questionnaire that followed the communication contained the item from the prequestionnaire designed to measure one's attitude toward the experimental issue, as well as items designed to measure perceptions of the communicator and communication.

The results of this experiment showed that the Low Threat communication did indeed produce positive change while the High Threat did not. However, the difference between conditions was not statistically reliable unless subjects who had initially neutral attitudes were deleted. Deletion of those with initially neutral attitudes makes good theoretical sense since for them, it is likely that the freedom to adopt or reject any given position would have low importance and they should therefore experience little reactance from being told what they must conclude. Nevertheless, this deletion was carried out post hoc and the resulting effect must therefore be viewed with some caution. For that reason, a replication with some elaboration was carried out.

The elaboration consisted of a variation of the status of the communicator relative to the communicatee cross-cutting the High—Low Threat variation in the communication. A different issue, "greater use of teaching machines in education," was used and the communicators were described either as a "prominent educator here at the University" or as a local "high school student who received a national award for an essay on this issue." Otherwise, the rationale and method were the same as before, utilizing a pre-post design, a well-reasoned communication that wound up strongly in favor of teaching machines, and, in the High Threat condition, an additional sentence saying that the subjects must agree.

The results for the High Status communicator confirmed the findings of the previous experiment—that is, the Low Threat communication produced positive change and the High Threat produced no change. Although an even stronger difference was expected for the Low Status communicator because of the "illegitimacy" of his telling college students what to conclude, in this condition there was no difference at all between High and Low Threat conditions, both yielding positive change. Since the High Threat from the Low Status source was perceived as relatively inappropriate by the subjects, this failure to show a reactance effect apparently illustrates that a direct attempt to threaten one's freedom must be accompanied by implicit or explicit power that makes the threat meaningful.

It is noteworthy that a postexperimental questionnaire revealed no differences between conditions in either experiment on perceived fairness of the presentation, expertness of the communicator, position of the communicator, or bias in his position. Apparently the factors commonly associated with differential attitude change do not account for the obtained differences between high and low threat conditions.

These two experiments, then, lend some support to our analysis of attitudes in terms of their associated freedoms and possible threats thereto. They show that when a person is exposed to a persuasive communication, the inclusion of an explicit attempt to tell him what to believe results in resistance to acceptance of that persuasive message.

PRESSURE TO COMPLY

As has been indicated, the threat to a person's freedom to adopt a particular position on the issue need not be in the explicit form of telling him what he must do; any explicit pressure to change should be capable of threatening the individual's attitudinal freedom. Explicit pressure to change, then, should produce resistance to change in proportion to the pressure and the importance of the freedom to decide one's own position. The following experiment, designed and conducted by Brehm and Krasin (and reported in Brehm, 1966), demonstrates the point.

College students, individually contacted, were asked to fill out a 12-item questionnaire to measure their attitudes on various current event issues. Their answers were given on an 11-point rating scale running from "disagree strongly" to "agree strongly." Each was again contacted the following day and told that the Psychology Department was interested to see if he could predict the position of another person on two of the issues from knowledge of how that person had answered on the other 10 issues. The subject was then given a copy of the questionnaire on which were marks to indicate how a student "from an eastern university" had answered items 1 through 5 and 7 through 11. The subject was to predict that person's responses to the two unchecked items, and then he was to go back and again give his own position on each issue. Subjects who completed this procedure were in the Low Threat condition. The High Threat condition was identical except that at the end of the above procedure the subject was told, "We are sure you will be greatly influenced by the opinions stated, and that your answers this time will tend toward those of this student." On the ten items on which the other person's positions were marked some answers were made to coincide with the position of the subject on his first questionnaire, while the others were made to deviate by 1, 2, or 3 scale points, always in the direction of the opposing side of the issue.

The Low Threat condition constitutes a typical social influence experiment in which knowledge of the position of another, somewhat prestigeful person can be expected to produce change toward the other person's position and in an amount proportional to the discrepancy between positions. In the High Threat condition, however, the pressure to change positively is made explicit and presumably varies directly with the discrepancy size. Thus, in High Threat we may expect increasing resistance to change as discrepancy size increases, with the difference in positive attitude change between discrepancy sizes 1 and 3 being less than the comparable difference in the Low Threat condition.

The results were as expected. In the Low Threat condition there were increasing amounts of positive change as discrepancy size increased, while in the High Threat condition there was very slight positive change with a discrepancy size of 1, no change with a discrepancy size of 2, and slight negative change with a discrepancy size of 3. The difference in mean change between discrepancy sizes 1 and 3 in the High Threat condition (−.20) was different from the comparable difference in the Low Threat condition (+.42) at the 5% level by analysis of variance.

Aside from yielding support for our expectations, this experiment is interesting when compared to the experiments on forewarning of intent to influence. In those studies, the reduced positive change due to forewarning is usually explained theoretically as due to defensive arguments rehearsed by the communicatee when he learns he is to be confronted with counter-attitudinal persuasion. But in the present experiment there is neither counter-attitudinal persuasion nor, actually, time to think about arguments at all. It is unlikely that the present results have anything to do with content aside from knowledge of the position one holds and knowledge of the other person's position. Our argument is that the results of the present experiment are due to arousal of reactance and that the same process can account for similar effects where counter-attitudinal persuasion is involved. Whether or not our argument is correct remains to be seen from future research.

FELT COMPETENCE

The role of felt competence in the arousal of reactance has been described at some length. Felt competence, it will be recalled, can make freedom to choose important to the individual prior to his having specific knowledge about the alternatives available. Theoretically, when a person feels high competence in regard to selecting a position for himself on an issue, the greater is the pressure on him to adopt a specific position, the more reactance he should experience and the greater should be his tendency to move away from that position. When a person feels low competence, pressure to take a specific position should arouse relatively little reactance regardless of the magnitude of the pressure. The following experiment by Robert Wicklund and myself (1968) was designed to test these hypotheses.

Male college students were recruited in groups of four to take part in a test of social judgment. When the subjects arrived for their experimental session they were arranged so that they could not communicate with each other, and the experimenter then explained the importance of social judgment and how the test was arranged. The test was said to be in two parts, the first of which would consist of two brief biographies and several questions pertaining to each. The second part would consist of biographical information, to be read to them by the experimenter, about two applicants, Al and Paul, for the position of dormitory advisor at a university. This information, they were told, would be given them in six separate sets after each of which they would be asked to make evaluations of the two applicants.

While the subjects prepared for the second part of the test, their performance on the first part was ostensibly scored by the experimenter. Prior to starting the second part of the test, subjects were given their own test score from the first part and ostensibly because they would be interested to know how others were doing, they were also given the deciles within which the other three members of their group had scored. The scores were actually fictitious, of course, and were used to manipulate the subjects' feeling of competence to make relevant judgments about biographical materials. To create low competence, subjects were told their own score was the 46th percentile while those of the other three subjects were all between the 90th and 100th percentile. To create high competence, subjects were told their own score was at the 94th percentile and those of the other subjects were all between the 90th and 100th percentile. The reported scores for the other subjects were always the same in order to control the apparent expertness of them regarding the judgmental task.

The second part of the test was then begun and following each set of information about Al and Paul, subjects were required to fill out a questionnaire containing the question: "To what degree do you believe one applicant is better qualified than the other?" Their answers were recorded on a 30-point scale labeled at one end "Al definitely superior to Paul" and at the other end "Paul definitely superior to Al."

After two of the six sets of information had been given and their corresponding questionnaires completed, subjects were told to review the information and then, prior to going on, they would fill out another evaluation questionnaire in case they wanted to change their judgments. They were also told that since people were generally interested to know what others thought at this stage, each was to write an anonymous statement of his position on a piece of paper and that these would then be distributed around the group so that each person would see what one other person in the group thought. In the course of collecting and distributing these statements, the experimenter substituted prearranged notes designed to manipulate the degree of threat to the individual's freedom to decide for himself. The low threat note simply said, "Paul is the best advisor" while the high threat note said, "There is no question about it. Paul is the best advisor." The third evaluation sheets were completed immediately after these notes had been distributed.

Two more sets of information were read, followed by evaluation questionnaires, and then a form was given which was designed to measure subjects' perceptions of the note-sender. At this point the procedure was finished and subjects were disabused.

The design, then, was a variation of high and low threat to attitudinal freedom within levels of high and low felt competence to make relevant judgments.[2] Measures of attitudinal position were taken immediately before and after the threat procedure. In addition, a control condition was run using the high competence manipulation but where the threat notes were not delivered. This condition provides an assessment of attitude change for subjects who felt high competence but were not subjected to any sort of influence information.

Before looking at the results of this study, let us consider briefly what the method has attempted to do. Subjects were first led to believe, from false scores on the first part of the test, that they were low or high in their competence to make accurate judgments of the kind required. They were then given preliminary information on the issue of the second part of the test and, because they were still to receive much more information, they could not yet decide that one position was clearly better than another. It was at this point that they received a note indicating what another, highly competent, member of the group believed and for some subjects this note announced "There is no question about it." While this statement may appear to be and probably is a relatively weak manipulation of threat to attitudinal freedom, it also had to appear plausible and not arouse other motives. Finally, because the attitude measures were given immediately before and after the influence attempt one may attribute the obtained change to threat itself rather than to some combination of intervening events. This becomes rather important when one wishes to see whether or not there is an absolute boomerang effect in the attitude change, as opposed to resistance to positive change.

Table 1 reports mean attitude change for each condition including the control. As was expected, for subjects who felt high competence, high threat produced negative attitude change significantly different

TABLE 1

MEAN ATTITUDE CHANGE IN THE EXPERIMENTAL CONDITIONS AND CONTROL

Experimental groups	Control	High Threat	Low Threat
High Competence	−.21[a]	−2.37	.07
Low Competence	−	.76	2.14

[a] Negative change is away from the position supported by the note.

[2] The design also involved separate replications and the reader is referred to the journal article for details.

from the slight positive change produced by low threat ($F = 6.41$, $p < .025$). For subjects with low felt competence, all attitude change is positive and there is no reliable difference as a function of threat ($F < 1$). The main effects of both competence and threat were reliable ($p < .025$ or better), but the interaction was not.

The control condition permits an assessment of whether or not the negative change observed with high competence and high threat is a true boomerang. This comparison showed that the high competence high threat negative change, -2.37, was reliably greater than that in the control, $-.21$, ($t = 2.00$, $df = 132$, $p < .05$). Thus, the results rather clearly demonstrate a force to change negatively under conditions of high competence and high threat.[3]

It may be helpful to dwell for a moment on what makes the present study interesting. First, the theory, while not unique in predicting a boomerang attitude change, does pretend to specify conditions under which relatively great negative change should occur. Second, the predicted boomerang effect was actually produced and in the condition where it was expected. Third, the threat which produced the boomerang might well be considered subtle and weak and by its success indicates a rather potent motivational process underlying the negative change. Fourth, the conditions under which the boomerang occurred minimized any kind of precommitment to a position since the individual still expected to receive the bulk of the relevant information on the issue. Because the initial position was relatively weak, neither can the boomerang effect easily be interpreted as a dissonance effect (cf. Cohen, 1962). Fifth, the social influence (and threat) supported the side initially held by a majority of subjects. Thus, a contrast phenomenon (Sherif & Hovland, 1961) will not easily account for the results. In summary, this study suggests that reactance theory may be quite helpful in understanding and predicting negative attitude change and its effects.

THE EFFECT OF IMPLIED THREATS TO FREEDOM

An interesting aspect of reactance theory is the assertion that freedoms may be threatened by implication, for if this assertion is

---

[3] It will be recalled that additional information was given to subjects after the effects of the message were measured, and further measures of the dependent attitude were made. Though these further measures might have reflected persistence of the effects produced by reactance, they showed only a small tendency for the effects to persist. This relative lack of persistence may have been due, of course, to the introduction of further information which, as shown by the Control condition, strongly affected the dependent attitude.

correct then one might expect rather dramatic reactance effects from relatively minor threats or eliminations of freedom. One form of this proposition is that a threat to the individual's freedom to make any particular decision may also imply that future similar decisions are subject to the same threat. For example, suppose a college student felt he knew what he wanted out of college and could therefore decide which courses to take, but at the beginning of his first semester his roommate tried to influence his choices. The point, of course, is that there are to be new decisions at the beginning of seven more semesters and these future freedoms will also be subject to the influence attempts of the roommate. Thus, the reactance experienced by our example student should be magnified by the implied threats to his future decisions and should be out of proportion to what should occur from the explicit threat to his immediate freedom.

When a person is asked to write a statement in support of one side or the other of an attitudinal issue, we may assume that if he is free to choose either side, normally he will select the side on which he stands. Suppose, however, that though he believed he could choose either side, someone then told him he had to write in support of one side and not the other. If the person who told him which side on which to write had the power to enforce the direction, then the individual's freedom to choose would have been eliminated. However, his *attitudinal* freedom to adopt his own position would not be eliminated but only threatened by the implication that he should uphold a particular position rather than its opposite. Thus, the individual could attempt to restore his freedom of attitude by moving away from the position he was forced to uphold in his written statement. The tendency to move away from the forced position will, of course, be a direct function of the magnitude of reactance which, in turn, is a direct function of the number of freedoms threatened by implication. Given that a person's choice is forced on a particular issue, his tendency to change his attitude away from the forced position should be greater if it is possible that he will be forced to uphold a particular side on other issues than if there is no such possibility. This analysis of attitude change as a function of implied threats to freedom was tested in the following experiment by John Sensenig and myself (1968).

Our intention was to force a person arbitrarily to support one side of an attitude issue after he had been led to believe he could influence the decision about which side he would support. In one condition (Low Threat) it was impossible that the person could be forced on four future decisions, while in a second condition (High Threat) it was possible for the individual to be subjected to the same arbitrary decision on all four future decisions. To make sure negative attitude change could be attributed to the threat to freedom, a Control duplicated the High Threat condition except for the threat; in this condition subjects were consulted prior to being told which side they were to support.

College females from an introductory psychology class were scheduled two at a time for a research project as part of their course requirement. The two subjects were told that the study concerned people's opinions and they were first asked to fill out a questionnaire to measure their opinions on 15 issues in current events. Their position on each issue was indicated by a check mark on a 31-point scale labeled "strongly agree" at one end and "strongly disagree" at the other.

It was then explained that while the questionnaire indicated their positions on the issues, it did not reveal why they held these positions and that we were concerned with what sort of arguments they might use in support of one side or the other. For this reason, they were to write short essays in support of one side or the other on five of the fifteen issues.

The design required giving the subjects the impression that (1) they had some influence over which side of each issue they would support in the written essay; (2) the other subject would actually have the power of decision either on only the first issue or on all five issues; and (3) the other subject either would or would not take the subject's own preference into account in making the decision about which side he would have to support. These requirements were met by telling subjects we were interested in comparing the arguments they used and that this could be done only if they both wrote on the same side of the issue. Some subjects were told that this comparison would be necessary only on the first issue and that on the remaining four issues each could write on whichever side he preferred. Others were told they would both have to write on the same side of all five issues. In all cases, subjects were given the impression that by chance drawing, the other subject had been given the power to decide which side they would both write on. To make them think they had some power to influence the decision, they were told that the other subjects could solicit their preference before making the decision.

Three conditions were run. In the Control condition subjects were under the impression the other person would decide which side they would both write on for all five issues, and that on the first issue the other person wanted to take the subject's preference into account before deciding. In the Low Implied Threat condition, subjects were under the impression that the other person would decide for them only on the first issue, but on that issue that the other person made the decision without taking account of their own preference. In the High Implied Threat condition, subjects were under the impression that the other person would make the decision on all five issues and, as in the Low Implied Threat condition, that the decision on the first issue was made arbitrarily without reference to the subject's preference. In all three conditions the subjects were actually assigned to support the side they favored.

Finally, the subjects were requested to indicate again their position on the issue just prior to writing their statement. Once they had finished their essay, and prior to going on to the second essay, they were asked to fill out a questionnaire designed to measure their impressions of the other person and their perceptions of the manipulations. This completed the procedure and an explanation and catharsis were carried out.

The results were as expected. The Control condition, which should have produced some tendency to become more positive toward the side of one's initial position since it informed the subject that the other person preferred the same side, produced a mean change of +1.37. The Low Implied Threat condition, which should have produced some reactance and consequent tendency to reject the forced position, yielded a mean change of −.27, which was not reliably different from the Control condition but in the expected direction. In the High Implied Threat condition, in which the magnitude of reactance should have been relatively great, the mean change was −4.17, significantly different from the Low Implied Threat condition at the 1% level ($t = 2.70$) and from the Control condition at better than the .1% level ($t = 3.83$).

To make sure that the implication manipulation did not affect perceptions of the other person and thereby confound the attitude change effects, subjects were asked to evaluate both the likeability and competence of the other. Since the mean response to both questions is nearly identical in all three conditions there is no apparent reason to believe that differential perceptions of the other were created by the manipulation of threat. As far as can be seen, then, this experiment confirms our analysis of attitude change as a function of reactance aroused by differential implied threats to freedom.

References

Allyn, J., and Festinger, L. The effectiveness of unanticipated persuasive communications. *Journal of Abnormal and Social Psychology*, 1961, **62**, 35-40.

Brehm, J. W. *A theory of psychological reactance.* New York: Academic Press, 1966.

Cohen, A. R. A dissonance analysis of the boomerang effect. *Journal of Personality,* 1962, **30**, 75-88.

Festinger, L. *A theory of cognitive dissonance.* Stanford, Calif.: Stanford University Press, 1957.

Festinger, L., and Maccoby, N. On resistance to persuasive communications. *Journal of Abnormal and Social Psychology,* 1964, **68**, 359-366.

Freedman, J. L., and Sears, D. O. Warning, distraction, and resistance to influence. *Journal of Personality and Social Psychology,* 1965, **1**, 262-266.

Hovland, C. I. Reconciling conflicting results derived from experimental and survey studies of attitude change. *American Psychologist,* 1959, **14**, 8-17.

Kiesler, C. A., and Kiesler, S. B. Role of forewarning in persuasive communications. *Journal of Abnormal and Social Psychology,* 1964, **68**, 547-549.

McGuire, W. J. Inducing resistance to persuasion. In L. Berkowitz (Ed.), *Advances in experimental social psychology.* Vol. 1. New York: Academic Press, 1964. Pp. 191-229.

Sensenig, J., and Brehm, J. W. Attitude change from an implied threat to attitudinal freedom. *Journal of Personality and Social Psychology,* 1968, in press.

Sherif, M., and Hovland, C. I. *Social judgment.* New Haven: Yale University Press, 1961.

Walster, E., and Festinger, L. The effectiveness of "overheard" persuasive communications. *Journal of Abnormal and Social Psychology,* 1962, **65**, 211-218.

Wicklund, R. A., and Brehm, J. W. Attitude change as a function of felt competence and threat to attitudinal freedom. *Journal of Experimental Social Psychology,* 1968, **4**, 64-75.

12

Attitude Change through Discrepant Action: A Functional Analysis[1]

REUBEN M. BARON

DEPARTMENT OF PSYCHOLOGY
WAYNE STATE UNIVERSITY
DETROIT, MICHIGAN

At the outset it should be noted that the theoretical pretensions of a functional approach must of necessity be modest. A functional analysis is not likely to yield an elegant hypothetico-deductive system. Indeed, previous attempts to utilize a functional approach to analyze attitudinal phenomena have never yielded more than typologies (e.g., Katz, 1960; Katz & Stotland, 1959; Kelman, 1961; M. B. Smith, Bruner, & White, 1956).

A FUNCTIONAL ANALYSIS OF DISCREPANT ACTION AND ATTITUDE CHANGE

Although a functional approach to attitudes is quite general in its ramifications, this chapter will be devoted to applying this mode of analysis to a particular sub-domain in the area of attitudes — changes

[1]The writing of this chapter was partially supported by Grant GS-1342 from the National Science Foundation. The author wishes to acknowledge his debt to Herbert C. Kelman. Many of the present notions stem from direct collaboration, others from his stimulation. He is, however, absolved from any misconceptions that may be contained in this chapter, the final responsibility for the present formulation being mine. The experimental work reported here was carried out collaboratively with Herbert C. Kelman, John Sheposh, and Eugene Johnson. Portions of this chapter were presented at a symposium on "Alternatives to Consistency Theories" held at the September, 1967 meeting of the American Psychological Association in Washington, D. C.

in attitudes which are occasioned by the performance of actions which are discrepant from one's previously existing attitudes or values. The basic assumption of this functional approach is that knowledge of inconsistency comes to serve, through considerable prior learning, as an internal stimulus for the possible existence of a threat to the individual's ability to achieve certain of his goals, or of an *occasion to enhance* his ability to achieve such goals. Inconsistency serves as a signal to the individual that various coping mechanisms, such as his current evaluations or categorizations of himself, his social environment, or the nonsocial environment may not be maximally useful or correct. Attitude change reactions to inconsistent behavior may be viewed as attempts by the person to reduce or eliminate possible shortcomings in his ability to establish successful means-end relations. That is, inconsistency becomes an occasion for attitude change when the implication of discrepancy is that current attitudes fail to provide the most effective basis for goal attainment.

The major basis for any discomfort or tension which accompanies or results from processing discrepant inputs is likely to reside in the fact that inconsistency requires us to review evaluative judgments that have already been filed away in a cognitive dead letter file. Rather than talking of inconsistency as an autonomous motive, it would seem more useful to see the motivational implications of inconsistency as stemming from its signal properties—the new information that inconsistency provides concerning the adequacy of existing coping mechanisms. Inconsistency or dissonance seems to offer a prime example of what Hunt (1963) has referred to as "Motivation inherent in information processing" or what Hebb (1955) has described as the "secondary drive value of cognitive processes."

In process terms, this kind of functional approach involves specifying the kinds of transformations that discrepant inputs go through as they are related by the individual to existing motivational systems. The first step in the individual's analysis of the discrepant input may be the kind of causal analysis suggested by Bem (1967; see also his chapter in this volume). That is, when a person sees his discrepant behavior as constrained by external factors this judgment essentially renders the inconsistency as irrelevant—as without important implications for existing motivational systems.

On the other hand, if a person interprets his behavior as reflecting a "true" attitude, then he is left with the problem of reconciling this interpretation of his attitude with his knowledge concerning his original evaluation of the attitude object. This kind of conflict may, in turn, be labeled by the person as a threat to his existing goals. For example, he may become concerned about his status within certain reference groups and/or see his attitude-discrepant behavior as a serious threat to his personal integrity or worth. It is a basic assumption of the present approach that how a person will resolve such a conflict will depend, at least in part, on the particular pre-existing motivational system that is engaged (e.g., self-esteem motives are likely to involve different resolutions than affiliative motives). A major difference then, between the present analysis of the attitudinal effects of discrepant behavior and the dissonance theory approach, is our stress on the *source* as well as the amount of discomfort present.

Using this kind of functional approach one may analyze existing studies involving discrepant actions. My examination of this literature suggests that at least three qualitatively different kinds of psychological dilemmas have been lumped together under the single rubric of dissonance motivation.

MORAL DILEMMAS

The first class of adjustive problems involves situations where a person is induced to engage in behavior which is likely to violate societal values concerning what is "moral" conduct in this situation. Although it is difficult to escape cultural relativism in defining the dimensions of moral behavior, in Western society at least, moral conduct may be inferred ". . . by reference to the consequences of an act for others, and, to a less definitive extent by reference to the intention of the act [Aronfreed, 1964, p. 216]." Thus, acts which involve intentionally harming another person, either in a physical or psychological sense, would be classified as immoral by these criteria. It should also be noted that an action is assumed to have moral implications only if the actor is capable of making "articulate distinctions between right and wrong or good and bad [Aronfreed, 1964, p. 215]." For an act of intentional harm to be considered unambiguously immoral it is also probably necessary that it be *unprovoked*. That is, any cues as to the innocence, helplessness, etc., of the "victim" are likely to heighten the moral dilemma created by an act of intentional harm.

The following are examples of "forced compliance" dissonance studies, which by the above criteria, involve the induction of immoral behavior: the shocking of a helpless victim (Brock & Buss, 1962, 1964; Glass, 1964); inducing a person to lie and thereby betray a peer (Carlsmith, Collins, & Helmreich, 1966; Festinger & Carlsmith, 1959); provoking a subject to insult an innocent stranger

(Davis & Jones, 1960); and tempting children to cheat in a situation where improving one's score involves disadvantaging "honest" test takers (Mills, 1958).

Following the general approach of Aronfreed, the author will attempt to specify the kinds of responses that are likely to be instigated by moral transgressions in Western society. Because a good number of these responses are likely to involve internal states, it is difficult to entirely avoid the pitfalls of phenomenology. It is possible, however, to isolate relatively common attributes of moral responses as follows: the violation of a moral value is assumed to arouse a state of anticipatory anxiety concerning punishment which is accompanied by a cognitive component involving the person's characterization of his actions as "bad" or "wrong." This affective-cognitive configuration involving anxiety and self-criticism can be described as a guilt reaction. This is probably not a useful strategy, however, because while self-criticism is a likely reaction to a moral transgression, it does not exhaust the individual's means of coping with "moral anxiety." Indeed, Aronfreed (1961) finds: (1) no one moral response is an invariant reaction to a moral transgression; and (2) different moral responses are associated with different child-training practices. Other common responses to a moral transgression found by Aronfreed are as follows: *confession*—which involves an expression of remorse for one's actions or intentions; *reparation*—which involves the removal or amelioration of injurious consequences; and *modification of future behavior*—involving a commitment to act more acceptably in the future. While this listing is not exhaustive, it is reasonably representative of the kinds of responses that may be evoked by an action which violates a moral value. An adequate conceptual or operational definition of a moral dilemma cannot be tied to the occurrence of any single moral response. From the present point of view, the occurrence of phenomenal guilt represents a sufficient but not a necessary condition for the existence of a moral dilemma.

While the attitudinal implications of the arousal of a moral dilemma are importantly contingent on situational constraints and individual difference factors, a general hypothesis is possible. Thus, it may be expected that if a moral dilemma is created, a person's evaluation of his actions as bad or wrong will preclude task enhancement (that is, increased interest in or enjoyment of the immoral action) as a mode of resolution of the dilemma. Indeed, it is likely that persons experiencing a moral dilemma will emphasize the negative attributes of the task situation, since if they can convince themselves that some suffering was involved, this is likely to reduce their "moral anxiety" (i.e., the more a person suffers, the more he may feel he has expiated his immoral deed).

HEDONIC DILEMMAS

We may now turn to a class of situations for which, on the other hand, task enhancement is the most likely mode of tension reduction. Like the moral dilemma, these situations may be described in value terms but the values at issue are *hedonic* rather than moral in character. In this kind of situation, what is involved is a utilitarian value concerning not "doing something for nothing." Discomfort is produced on the basis of a reward-cost operation — a hedonic calculus is involved. The root of a person's dilemma here is how to justify his foolish behavior or bad bargain. The person is motivated to find "hidden attractions" in order to make what he just did seem more palatable or acceptable, hence Weick's (1966) term "task acceptance dilemma" to describe this kind of situation. In contradistinction to the moral dilemma situation, Ss are thus motivated to emphasize the positive features of the task or act and de-emphasize the negative features. The kinds of operations that may be used to instigate this kind of hedonic dilemma may be illustrated by dissonance studies involving the performance of tasks which are boring, useless, intrinsically unpleasant (e.g., eating grasshoppers), and/or effortful under conditions of insufficient external justification (e.g., reward).

A further comparison between moral and hedonic dilemmas may be helpful. Moral dilemmas are more likely than are hedonic dilemmas to arouse central concerns of the individuals. For example, moral violations are more likely to arouse self-esteem motives. If the above assumption about differential centrality is correct, then it may be expected that behavior discrepancies involving moral dilemmas will be more emotionally upsetting, have their effects dissipate more slowly over time, lead to greater changes in other attitude and value systems, and be more likely to result in behavioral as well as cognitive change. Kelman and Baron (1968b) further suggest that reactions to hedonic dilemmas are more likely to involve memorial readjustments rather than genuine cognitive change. That is, reactions to hedonic dilemmas are seen as involving more transitory adjustments involving a selective recall of positive features rather than a basic re-evaluation of any distal object.

CONSENSUAL VALIDATION DILEMMAS

Another class of situations having a different motivational dynamic from the moral or hedonic dilemma may also be distinguished. Here, the person's behavior is discrepant from an attitude rather than a value. That is, what is involved is an organization of beliefs, affects, and behavior orientations focused on a *specific* object or situation rather than a general trans-situational belief concerning a preferable mode of conduct or end-state (see Rokeach, 1967, for an excellent discussion of the differences between attitudes and values in these terms). Attitude-discrepant behavior produces discomfort not because it is intrinsically immoral or unpleasant but because it raises doubts in the person concerning the validity of his initial attitudes. That is, an act such as improvising counterattitudinal arguments, either orally or in a written communication, is likely to both generate new inconsistent cognitions and *make salient for the person any inconsistencies which already exist within his cognitive system.* In this kind of situation, the locus of discomfort most likely will be a concern over the correctness of one's initial opinions. The person's affective reactions are likely to be characterized by doubt and uncertainty, a situation which is likely to trigger certain cognitive needs to establish what is a correct or valid opinion. Corrective strategies are likely to take the form of social comparison processes rather than attempts at reparation or task enhancement; hence we may describe this situation as involving the dilemma of consensual validation. Studies in which various student populations were induced to write counterattitudinal essays on such themes as (a) Ohio State playing in the Rose Bowl (Rosenberg, 1965); (b) the actions of the New Haven Police against Yale students (Brehm & Cohen, 1962); (c) becoming a Catholic (Brock, 1962); or (d) the virtues of modern music (Collins & Helmreich, 1965), are illustrative of consensual validation dilemmas, as are the recent role-playing studies of Janis and his associates (Elms & Janis, 1965; Janis & Gilmore, 1965).

In addition to criteria involving the nature of the act and the focusing on attitudes rather than values, the notion that a social comparison process is implicated suggests some interesting differences in the kinds of interpersonal cues that subjects in moral and consensual validation dilemmas are likely to focus on — given the fact that in both dilemmas interpersonal cues should be important. For example, it may be expected that greater attitude change will occur in the direction of a model (e.g., an influencing agent) whose content expertise is higher than his "moral purity" when a consensual validation dilemma is prepotent, while the reverse pattern should obtain when a moral dilemma is dominant. This kind of derivation follows from the assumption that moral and consensual validation dilemmas are likely to differentially engage self-esteem and cognitive motives. For example, some of Pepitone's work (1964) involving the induction of immoral behavior suggests that behavior which violates a moral value is more likely to cause a lowered self-evaluation than to instigate informational needs. On the other hand, the arousal of a consensual validation dilemma is more likely to increase a person's need for certainty (Brim, 1955) than it is to lower his self-esteem.

When a situation involves behaviors which both violate a moral value and are discrepant from some specific attitudinal stand, the resolution process is likely to involve a decision rule which gives priority to resolving one's moral dilemma. This kind of derivation rests on the assumption that while important values may determine (i.e., induce) attitudinal positions, the reverse is seldom, if ever, true (cf. Rokeach, 1967). Thus, it may be hypothesized that attitude change is a more likely mode of resolution in a situation where both attitude and value inconsistencies exist, i.e., values are assumed to be more stable than attitudes.

A COMPARISON OF DISSONANCE AND FUNCTIONAL THEORY INTERPRETATIONS

Another way to distinguish among these dilemmas is to stress the different effects that such standard dissonance parameters as reward, effort, and choice are likely to have for persons experiencing different dilemmas. Thus, it can be argued, in contradistinction to dissonance theory assumptions, that in moral dilemmas, the greater the reward, the greater the psychological discomforts. That is, the knowledge of having allowed oneself to be "bought off," of having accepted a bribe, may actually increase one's feelings of guilt. Similarly, the greater the effort (physical or psychological), the less the discomfort. That is, the knowledge of having suffered while carrying out the immoral deed may serve to mitigate one's feelings of guilt. In the case of hedonic dilemmas, on the other hand, it is expected that the effects of reward and effort will fit the traditional dissonance model. That is, less discomfort will be created when there is high reward and low effort.

While variations in effort may have important effects on moral and hedonic dilemmas, they are likely to be less crucial for consensual validation dilemmas. Similarly, while choice and commitment may be of central significance to the arousal of discomfort when there are moral violations, they are somewhat less important for consensual validation dilemmas, and essentially irrelevant for hedonic or task acceptance dilemmas (cf. Freedman, 1963, for a demonstration of the irrelevance of a choice manipulation for a hedonic dilemma situation).

Finally, it should be noted that although dissonance theory (cf. Brehm & Cohen, 1962) suggests that there will be greater attitude change in the induced direction with an unattractive than an attractive inducing agent, our analysis of this problem suggests that this derivation should be limited to situations involving a hedonic dilemma. Consider, for example, a situation where a moral dilemma is induced. It is suggested that particularly where the attractiveness manipulation involves a trustworthiness dimension, more attitude change will be produced by an attractive than an unattractive inducing agent. In this kind of situation, the basis of the inducing agent's power to change S's attitude is likely to be his perceived ability to reduce S's "moral anxiety" or "guilt." If a person is troubled about the morality of his behavior, he is not likely to turn to another person for guidance when the trustworthiness of the other person is suspect. Where the inducing agent is attractive and S is able to infer that the inducing agent's attitudinal position is similar to the one implied by his discrepant behavior, attitude change in the direction of the inducing agent's position may reduce a person's guilt. Let us assume, for example, that the immorality of a person's act resides in his deceiving a fellow student into adopting an attitudinal position that S has always felt was repugnant. In this kind of situation, any information that will allow S to believe that the other attitude is a reasonable one is likely to reduce his feeling that what he did was immoral (i.e., psychologically harmful). It is suggested that in this situation an attractive agent becomes relevant as a source of inputs into S's re-examination of his attitudes toward the issue, a re-examination motivated by this particular kind of moral dilemma. By reinterpreting his attitudinal position so as to move it closer to the agent's, S is enabled to change the meaning of his act so as to make it less "wrong." If, on the other hand, the inducing agent is an unattractive person, moving toward his point of view is not likely to help matters; it may even serve to increase S's moral anxiety. Indeed, the possibility of a contrast effect exists, with the result that S will become even more entrenched in his initial position (cf. Kelman & Eagly, 1965).

The dynamic in a consensual validation dilemma is not too dissimilar except that here the individual will focus on the ability of the inducing agent to satisfy his cognitive needs. Assuming that S has a positive self-image, he is more likely to define an attractive inducing agent as similar to himself across a number of dimensions than an

unattractive agent (cf. Stotland & Hillmer, 1962). In the absence of
any objective source of validation, Ss who have a cognitive need
aroused concerning the validity of their opinion are more likely to
move toward the attitudinal position of similar than dissimilar
persons since the former are likely to provide a more stable basis of
social comparison (cf. Festinger, 1954). The above effects should
emerge most clearly when the attractiveness manipulation bears on
the expertness of the inducing agent.

It follows from our kind of functional analysis that every mode of
handling inconsistency is not likely to be equally relevant for all
problems. For example, Kelman and Baron (1968b) distinguish between attitudes toward the discrepant action itself, which usually
involve attitudes toward the experimental task and attitudes toward
the object of the action, which typically involve some substantive
issue. It is suggested that while change in task attitudes is the most
appropriate type of attitude change when hedonic dilemmas are
instigated, changes directed toward the object of the action or the
substantive issue are more important for consensual validation
and moral dilemmas. Thus, while with a hedonic dilemma we
expect more positive attitude change toward the task with an unattractive than an attractive agent, we expect no effect of variations
in attractiveness for hedonic dilemma Ss when attitudes toward a
content issue are measured, i.e., the ability of an inducing agent to
serve as a *communication source* is an irrelevant dimension to such Ss.

The derivation involving change in task attitudes rests on the usual
dissonance reasoning. That is, a person is assumed to experience
more discomfort as a function of perceptions involving insufficient
justification when an unattractive as opposed to an attractive person
asks him to perform an unpleasant task of little value, thereby increasing his motivation to seek justification for his behavior in
"hidden" positive features of the task.

Thus, even when a functional analysis follows the dissonance
theory derivation, it suggests an important qualification: predictions
of attitude change should not be applied indiscriminately to task and
issue attitudes; the prediction should be tied to the particular problem
the individual is faced with. Different modes of resolution should
not automatically be assumed to be interchangeable.

INCONSISTENCY AS A SOURCE OF POSITIVE MOTIVATION

It should be noted that inconsistencies are not always seen as
threats to existing goals. Inconsistencies may be perceived as pro-

viding a person with an opportunity to enhance his relationships with the environment, either in the sense of improving his level of inter-personal functioning (e.g., opening up new reference groups) or his intrapsychic adjustments, such as providing a more accurate concep-tion of himself or the external environment. Under circumstances where the possibility of goal enhancement exists it is suggested that (a) the person may not label his affective reaction in negative terms or experience discomfort, i.e., he may experience the kind of positive affective reactions that White (1959) has suggested accompany oppor-tunities to successfully manipulate one's environment (see also, Byrne & Clore, 1967, for a discussion of effectance motivation); and (b) persons may engage in behavior which is designed to maintain or even increase the existing level of inconsistency. For example, consider a situation where a person has always wanted to engage in a given behavior but has refrained because of some internal inhibi-tion or fear of external sanction, such as a Catholic student who has always favored birth control but has been afraid to speak out on this issue. This student suddenly finds himself in a study which requires him to debate a pro-birth control position. Once the initial barrier, which in the past has prevented the discrepant behavior from spon-taneously emerging, is overcome, the person realizes that a higher level of cognitive and/or social functioning is possible. He may then seek to amplify the change process by actively proselytizing the virtues of his new position, thereby cutting himself off from any possibility of backsliding into his old position.

THE STRUCTURE OF THE PSYCHOLOGICAL FIELD IN A FUNCTIONAL ANALYSIS OF INCONSISTENCY

Up until this point the major burden of the present functional analysis has been upon showing how qualitative differences in the type of motivational system instigated by discrepant behavior are likely to produce qualitatively different modes of resolution. To provide a fuller picture of how a functional approach may be used to make predictions concerning modes of resolution, it is also necessary to explore the *structure* of the psychological field (cf. Kelman & Baron, 1968b, for a fuller discussion of the role of structural parameters). This analysis will focus on specifying whether the inconsistency will be confronted or avoided and whether the outcome of the resolution process will be inconsistency maintenance or reduction (See Figure 1).

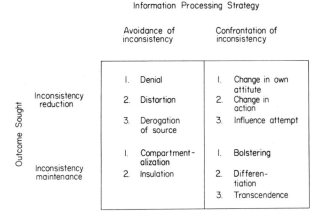

FIG. 1. Modes of resolving inconsistency differentiated by (a) the nature of the information processing strategy used, and (b) the nature of the outcome sought (after Kelman & Baron, 1968b).

Inconsistency-Reduction versus Inconsistency-Maintenance

In Kelman and Baron (1968b), it was suggested that to the extent that the inconsistent elements are linked to the *same* motivational system (i.e., goal, value, need or attitude) rather than two *different* motivational systems, the inconsistency dilemma is likely to be handled by the use of inconsistency reduction mechanisms. By the same token, it is suggested that when inconsistent elements are linked to different needs, goals, values, or attitude objects which are more or less equally important to the individual, maintenance will be sought. By way of further explication, it may be noted that when inconsistencies are predominantly tied to a single goal, the behavior systems are impacted so that goal locomotion is impossible unless the inconsistency is removed or reduced.[2] When the inconsistency involves separate goals, response systems linked to these goals may be instigated independently. This allows the person to make some locomotion toward one goal without necessarily blocking progress toward the other.

[2]Interestingly enough, E. E. Jones and Gerard (1967, p. 181) have independently arrived at a very similar conclusion as to the basis of inconsistency reduction. The core of their analysis is the assumption that cognitive change occurs because ". . . the individual presses toward an unequivocal behavior orientation (UBO)"—i.e., he has a need to act in an unconflicted way.

This distinction between the arousal of single and multiple motivational systems also has implications for the range of effects that should be measured. If there is reason to believe that more than one motivational system is instigated a range of dependent effects which are linked to the particular adjustive problem(s) confronting the individual should be investigated. For example, in the Festinger and Carlsmith study (1959), Ss in the $20 and $1 conditions may have had different dilemmas made prepotent by the reward variation. Ss receiving $1 are more likely to feel hedonically deprived and less likely to see their behavior as immoral than are Ss in the $20 condition. If this line of reasoning is correct, we expect that $1 Ss will focus their resolution on convincing themselves that the task was really useful, while $20 Ss will be more concerned with finding ways to reduce the immorality of their deed (e.g., by changing their values toward the immorality of deceiving someone in the name of science, or seeking ways to apologize and/or make reparation to the deceived peer). Of all these possible modes of resolution only Ss' task attitudes were measured and a general conclusion drawn as to the negative relationship between reward and subsequent attitude change. The author suspects, on the other hand, if changes in Ss' values concerning the morality of deception were measured a more favorable position would have been found for the $20 Ss. The implication of a functional analysis is that there is no general relationship between reward and evaluative change; the form of the relationship will depend on the specific motivational implications of the reward parameter.

Avoidance versus Confrontation

Whether inconsistencies are likely to be avoided or confronted is assumed to be a function of: (a) availability parameters and; (b) whether long or short term commitment to the discrepant behavior is entailed. In some situations it is relatively easy to avoid the implications of the inconsistency because the stimuli are relatively ambiguous or because the source of the inconsistent information has low status. Availability may also be related to differences in personality predispositions. Some persons (e.g., high authoritarians) may have a greater capacity or motivation to deny inconsistencies. Whether the individual views the inconsistency as of relatively short duration or whether he expects to have to contend with it over an extended period of time is likely to be an important determinant of whether avoidance or confrontation mechanisms will be used. When a person's commitment to a discrepant action is relatively long term, central motivational systems involving the individual's self-concept are likely to be engaged. A long-term commitment to a discrepant action increases the likelihood that the individual will have to face repeated reminders of his inconsistent behavior. Under these conditions, an individual is likely to anticipate having to justify his action to both himself and others. When the person is primarily concerned with preparing himself for future actions, confrontation mechanisms (e.g., attitude change) are likely to be more useful than avoidance mechanisms (e.g., denial). On the other hand, short-term inconsistencies are likely to promote an orientation toward reworking the past rather than preparing for the future. For example, when it is not likely that the person will have to live with the implications of the inconsistency, he is likely to try to distort his memory or interpretation of the inconsistent event.

Some Suggestive Experimental Evidence

We may now review some experimental results that bear on the functional model of attitude and value discrepant behavior that has been presented. Because these studies were planned and carried out before the theoretical notions the author has presented were fully worked out, they should be regarded as exploratory, as sources of our hypotheses as well as sources of evidence testing them. The research program to be described represents a joint venture on the part of Professor Herbert C. Kelman, the author, and our students. Because a number of the more refined derivations concerning differences among hedonic, moral, and consensual validation dilemmas had not been worked out at the time of this research, there are important omissions in the kind of data that were collected. Because of this we failed, with the exception of Sheposh's Prisoner's Dilemma study (below), to obtain good independent evidence bearing on the Ss' interpretation of their dilemmas. Therefore, in some cases we have been forced to infer the nature of the intervening process, i.e., the type of dilemma, from the characteristics of the discrepant act and the pattern of dependent variable effects that emerged.

Attractiveness of the Inducing Agent and Attitude Change

To test the dissonance derivation that when an individual is induced to take action discrepant from his attitude, he is more likely to manifest attitude change in the direction of the induced action if the agent is unattractive than if he is attractive, Kelman and the author carried out two experiments. In both experiments, attractiveness of the inducing agent was the independent variable, and attitude change subsequent to a discrepant action was the dependent variable. Also, in both experiments, subjects were given a choice between engaging in the induced action or withdrawing from it (the dropout rate was about 25 % and was not differential between experimental conditions). It should also be noted that in each study, the inducing agent specifically associated himself attitudinally with the action he was inducing so that he served not only as an inducer of action, but also as a *communicator of attitudes*. (This was accomplished by having the experimenter mention his membership in an organization known to be favorable toward the induced action.)

Aside from these similarities, the two studies used rather different situations and ways of operationalizing the common conceptual variables. In one study, subjects were asked, in the dead of winter in Ann Arbor, to distribute pro-peace leaflets with which they did not agree (initial attitude was inferred on the basis of an earlier attitude questionnaire), on busy downtown street corners. (It should be noted that this study was carried out before the war in Viet Nam was a "hot" issue.) After they had committed themselves to this action, but before they performed the deed, the experimenter began to reveal himself as either a very attractive or a very unattractive person. For example, in the Unattractive condition E was very rude and insulting to a stooge who interrupted him while he was explaining the details of how to distribute the leaflets. In the Attractive condition E was very understanding and patient. Subjects then actually distributed the leaflets. After returning from the leaflet distribution, subjects completed an attitude questionnaire (a before-after attitude change design was used) and answered a variety of other questions regarding their reactions to the situation.

In the second experiment, subjects who opposed interracial marriage were asked to write essays favoring it, with the understanding that they would later participate in a discussion with a group of Southern students using the essay as notes. After they had committed themselves to participation, subjects were "allowed to overhear" either a very favorable or very unfavorable description of the experimenter which was carried out by "stooge" subjects when the E left the room on some pretext. After completing the essays, subjects again filled out attitude questionnaires and answered other questions concerned with their perceptions of the experiment and the experimenter. Before presenting the specific results of these studies, the following should be noted: (1) In both studies the manipulations were effective; subjects rated the attractive E significantly more favorably than the unattractive E. (2) Subjects in both studies were able to accurately assess E's attitude position. (3) Subjects in both studies experienced a relatively high degree of perceived choice. In both studies undergraduate volunteers at the University of Michigan were used as subjects. In the leaflet distribution study both males and females were used. In the interracial marriage essay study, the original investigation utilized males as subjects, but subsequent replications involved two female samples, and one additional male sample. (Further details concerning procedures, sample size, etc., of all of the above studies will appear in a forthcoming monograph by Baron, Kelman, Sheposh, and Johnson.)

While the findings based on these two different paradigms were somewhat ambiguous, they showed definite trends in opposite directions. In the essay writing paradigm, it was the attractive inducing agent who appeared to produce the greatest amount of attitude change. This effect was found for the two replications involving female subjects and with the initial male sample. The finding was not replicated with a subsequent male sample, where an insignificant trend in the opposite direction was found. Combining the results of separate t test comparisons for the two independent replications involving females (Stouffer's technique as described in Mosteller and Bush, 1954, was used), we find this effect reliable at less than the 1% level, when the initial p's were at the .01 and .10 levels, respectively. In the leaflet-distribution study, on the other hand, the dissonance hypothesis tended to be confirmed. That is, subjects who complied with the unattractive inducing agent showed greater attitude change than those who complied with the attractive agent. This effect was obtained for both males and females on an item dealing specifically with an action component of a militarism attitude ($F = 4.11$, $p < .05$). On items dealing with more abstract belief components, the dissonance effect reached significance only with the males ($p < .05$, by simple effects test).

In attempting to reconcile these contradictory findings, Kelman and the author speculated about the meaning of the two situations created in the two experiments, on the basis of our observations of the subjects' reactions and of their answers to various postexperimental questions. It seemed that in the leaflet-distribution experiment, the subjects were not very much bothered by the content of the leaflets they were distributing. Even though we had reason to believe that they initially disagreed with the content of the leaflet, they seemed to find it relatively innocuous and sufficiently ambiguous so as to arouse very little discomfort. Moreover, they seemed to accept the experimenter's statement that the content of the leaflet was irrelevant (since this experiment was introduced as an attempt to explore emotional reactions to leaflet distribution), and they paid little attention to the content. The act of distributing leaflets, however, did bother them considerably. Since none of the subjects had engaged in this kind of activity before it is not hard to understand why they would find such behavior embarrassing. In addition, they had to stand on a street corner on what happened to be a cold winter day.

In the essay writing paradigm the opposite conditions appeared to prevail. The subjects were obviously not very much bothered by the act of writing essays as such. There were, however, clear indications that many of them were upset by the content of the act in which they were asked to engage—by the fact that they were writing in favor of interracial marriage, and that these essays would then be used to convince others of that position. Indeed, it may very well be that female subjects found this particularly disturbing, which might account for the fact that the results appeared more consistent for the females than for the males. That is, the females may have entered the experiment with more inconsistencies in their attitudinal systems than the males; such inconsistencies may have been brought to Ss' level of awareness by the requirements of the counterattitudinal essay writing.

In terms of my present thinking, I would say that the leaflet distribution study created both a strong hedonic dilemma and a somewhat weaker consensual validation dilemma, while the essay-writing study had a consensual validation dilemma as the main process mediating attitude change effects, although some subjects may have experienced some of the guilt associated with the violation of a moral value (e.g., a couple of subjects who had recently come from the South started writing, stopped, and refused to continue!).

Now let us turn to the first study in our research program that was designed to test the "hypothesis of differential dilemmas."

A STUDY OF THE EFFECTS OF MORAL AND HEDONIC DILEMMAS ON ISSUE AND TASK ATTITUDES

The study to be described here was an attempt to demonstrate that the effects of variations in the attractiveness of the inducing agent on issue and task attitudes are moderated by the specific type of inconsistency dilemma that is created for the person. Specifically, it was designed to test the following hypothesis: when the inconsistent behavior involves violation of a moral value, there will be more attitude change when an attractive rather than an unattractive inducing agent is present. On the other hand, when the person's primary concern is hedonic, i.e., involves an unpleasant task, there will be greater attitude change when an unattractive rather than an attractive inducing agent is present.

It also follows from a functional analysis that Ss experiencing qualitatively different inconsistency dilemmas may focus their resolutions on qualitatively different aspects of the experimental situation. Thus, it is hypothesized that Ss experiencing a moral dilemma will show greater changes on the specific issue at hand, while hedonic inconsistency Ss will be more concerned with task re-evaluations. Finally, in order to test the limits of the hypothesized effects, a variation in the intensity of the aroused dilemma was employed. It was expected that the differential effects of attractiveness hypothesized above would be most pronounced for the High Arousal conditions.

GENERAL DESIGN

The issue used in this study was whether the state government should have the final voice in determining who should speak on state campuses. This issue was salient at the time because a number of state schools were under pressure by the state legislature to refuse Herbert Apthaker, an avowed-communist, permission to speak on campus. A pilot questionnaire administered four months before the start of the experiment indicated that approximately 80% of the undergraduate Introductory Psychology classes (both male and female) were opposed to state control.

Seventy-two female undergraduate students in Introductory Psychology from Wayne State University served as subjects. The Ss were nonvolunteers who served as part of a course requirement. Two parallel 2×2 factorial designs were employed, one for arousal of a moral dilemma, the other for arousal of a hedonic dilemma. In each design, one factor was the degree of arousal of the dilemma (high versus low) and the second was a variation in the experimenter's attractiveness (attractive versus unattractive).

An after-only procedure was employed, with the two major dependent variables being attitudes toward state control over campus speakers and task attitudes (i.e., how interesting, pleasant, valuable, etc., the task was). In all conditions, the experimenter was portrayed as being favorable toward state control over selection of campus speakers — a position at variance with that of the majority of the subject population (this linkage was established by having the experimenter mention his membership in an organization known to favor state control over campus speakers).

Arousal of a Moral Dilemma

Ss were informed via taped instructions that the study was concerned with investigating the effects of social influence on a person's attitudes. They were told that this was to be accomplished by means of an interview procedure. For each interview session, one S was to be randomly selected as the interviewer (S_1), while the other would serve as the interviewee (S_2). S_1 was then told to interview S_2 from a prepared set of questions. Additionally, she was to positively reinforce statements which were pro-state control over selection of campus speakers, i.e., she was to say "that's good," "that's fine," "that's interesting," or "Mhmm" after each such statement made by S_2 (S_2 was a *male* confederate, preprogrammed to gradually increase the number of pro-state control statements he made as the interview progressed). In order to heighten the S's moral dilemma, she was informed that S_2 was an active member of a campus civil rights organization and that because of her reinforcing behavior, changes in S_2's attitude might result which would generalize to his behavior outside the laboratory. That is, it was assumed that Ss would experience a moral dilemma if they were made to believe they had "brainwashed" a fellow student.

In the High Arousal condition, S_1 was instructed to reinforce every statement S_2 uttered that was favorable to state control. In the Low Arousal condition, 1 out of every 4 of these statements was to be reinforced. In addition, Ss in the Low Arousal condition were instructed to use "Mhmm," a rather vague positive reinforcer, while high arousal Ss used more clearly defined positive reinforcers such as "that's good," "that's fine," or "that's interesting." It was assumed that the immorality of S's behavior would be more salient in the High Arousal condition where she would be constantly and clearly reinforcing a discrepant position. Under such conditions Ss should experience a greater personal responsibility for manipulating the interviewee's attitude. After the nature of S's "immoral" act was detailed, she was given the option of participating in the experiment or withdrawing from it.

Arousal of a Hedonic Dilemma

In the Hedonic condition, S was informed via taped instructions that she was participating in an experiment concerned with an anal-

ysis of the interview process. She would be asked to analyze statements from a taped interview. S was told that she would hear a student
undergoing an interview on the issue of state control over the selection of speakers on college campuses. Specifically, her task was to
tally the number of nouns and verbs in each sentence. S was informed
that this would be an index of the complexity of the interviewee's
statements. Only the interviewee's responses were on tape; the questions were omitted. However, written sets of the questions were made
available to S. The content of the interviewee's responses were identical to those given in the Moral Dilemma condition. At this point in
the experiment, S was given the option of continuing or leaving.

The only difference between high and low arousal groups in the
Hedonic condition was the inclusion of white noise in the High
Arousal condition. It was assumed that the inclusion of white noise
would make the S's job more effortful and difficult—in our terms,
more hedonically unrewarding.

Manipulation of Attractiveness

After S_1 had agreed to continue, the attractiveness of the experimenter was manipulated with the aid of S_2. In both the Moral and
Hedonic Unattractive conditions, the following procedure was followed: E noticed S_2 reading the college newspaper and then proceeded to make some disparaging remarks about the caliber of the
paper. E then departed, leaving the two Ss alone, after telling them
that the experiment would start in a few minutes. At this point, S_2
asked S_1 if she knew E. After S_1 said she did not, S_2 described E as a
very unfair and unreasonable instructor who S_2 felt was unqualified
to teach.

The identical procedure was executed in the attractive conditions,
except that E did not make any comments about the college newspaper. When E left the room, S_2 remained and asked S_1 if she knew E.
After S_1 said she did not, S_2 described E as a fair and interested instructor who enjoyed teaching.

RESULTS

Before detailing the attitude data, the following should be noted.
There were no differences among the experimental conditions in perceptions concerning volition. On a five point scale the average score
was 3.8, with 4 indicating Ss felt free not to participate "to a fair
extent" and 1 indicating Ss did not feel free at all. Postexperimental

questionnaire items also confirmed that Ss were aware of the experimenter's organizational affiliation and attitude on the state control issue.

The evidence concerning the effectiveness of the attractiveness manipulation is, however, more ambiguous. The conditions involving the arousal of a hedonic dilemma provided good evidence based on responses to 7 point semantic differential scales of the effectiveness of the attractiveness manipulation. Within the Hedonic conditions Ss exposed to an "attractive" E found the experimenter more considerate, pleasant, sensitive, good, fair, attractive, and warm than did Ss exposed to an unattractive E (all p's at the .05 level or less by t test). Within our Moral Dilemma conditions, however, the perceptual data failed to show any clear cut difference between the Attractive and Unattractive E conditions; Ss in both conditions evaluated E relatively favorably, although on the average, Ss in the Attractive condition were slightly more favorable toward E than were Ss in the Unattractive condition. Because of the clear cut differences we found for Moral Ss between attractiveness conditions on attitude change (to be presented below), the lack of a significant difference on these postexperimental self-report scales should not be taken as an indication that the attractiveness manipulation was ineffective.

Because a full report of the experimental data is now in preparation, only the findings directly bearing on our hypotheses will be presented.

Attitudinal Effects of the Moral Dilemma[3]

The major findings for the Moral Dilemma conditions were as follows: a significant attractiveness × arousal interaction ($F = 6.11$, $p < .025$) was found on the "state control" issue. As hypothesized, a simple effects analysis revealed that there was a more favorable attitude toward the state control issue for the attractive than the unattractive agent under conditions of High Arousal of the dilemma ($F = 11.19$, $p < .01$). No differences were found for the Low Arousal conditions (See Table 1). Within the Moral Dilemma conditions, the

---

[3]Attitudes toward the state control over campus speakers were assessed by presenting Ss with the sentence "The state government should have the final power to determine which speakers will appear on state campuses." This sentence was followed by a series of statements expressing reactions to it, including evaluative statements (such as, "This appeals to me," or "This is not a good idea"), with subjects asked to express their degree of agreement on a 6-point scale. Attitudes toward the task were assessed by using a series of 7-point Semantic Differential scales such as pleasant-unpleasant and interesting-boring. These separate scale judgments were summed to give us a composite task evaluation score.

TABLE 1
MEAN EVALUATION OF STATE CONTROL ISSUE FOR THE
MORAL DILEMMA CONDITIONS[a]

| | Arousal of dilemma | |
Attractiveness of E	High	Low
Attractive	4.16	2.67
	(1.07)	(1.01)
Unattractive	2.63	2.74
	(1.06)	(0.73)

[a]There are 9 subjects per cell. Standard deviations are reported in parentheses. Higher scores indicate increasing favorableness toward state control over campus speakers.

task attitude results yielded a similar pattern of effects, although the significance levels were lower. Thus, the attractiveness × arousal interaction only reached the .10 level of significance. There was no significant effect of the attractiveness variable on favorability of task attitude in the Low Arousal conditions, while under the High Arousal conditions, Ss confronted by an attractive E evaluated the task more favorably than Ss confronted by an unattractive E ($p < .05$, simple effects test).

Attitudinal Effects of the Hedonic Dilemma

As hypothesized, there were no significant effects on the state control issue for the attractiveness variations under the Hedonic conditions. Also, as predicted, a significant interaction was obtained involving the attractiveness and arousal variables on Ss' task attitude ($F = 9.30$, $p < .01$). A specification of this interaction by simple effects tests revealed one expected and one unexpected finding (See Table 2). As hypothesized, high arousal hedonic dilemma Ss showed a more favorable task attitude when confronted with an unattractive than attractive E ($F = 4.27$, $p < .05$). However, instead of an attenuated effect under low arousal, we found a reversal, i.e., more favorable task evaluation for the attractive than the unattractive agent condition ($F = 5.03$, $p < .05$).

Although this reversal was unexpected, it may be interpreted as consistent with some recent investigations that have found reversal effects under conditions of low dissonance arousal, i.e., a positive relationship between a justification parameter and attitude change. For example, Carlsmith *et al.* (1966) found incentive effects in their

TABLE 2
MEAN EVALUATION OF TASK FOR Ss IN HEDONIC
DILEMMA CONDITIONS[a]

	Arousal of dilemma	
Attractiveness of E	High	Low
Attractive	4.32	4.35
	(0.96)	(0.87)
Unattractive	5.20	3.40
	(0.74)	(1.00)

[a]There are 9 subjects per cell. Standard deviations are reported in parentheses. Higher scores indicate more positive task evaluations.

low dissonance arousal conditions (i.e., the conditions involving anonymous essay writing). Similarly, Linder, Cooper, and E. E. Jones (1967) and R. A. Jones and Brehm (1967) have found a positive relationship between reward and attitude change under low choice conditions.

DISCUSSION

The minimal conclusion that seems compelled by the attitudinal results of this experiment and the findings of the initial "street corner pamphlet" and "essay writing" studies is that *the dissonance derivation concerning a general negative relationship between attractiveness and attitude change in the forced compliance area must be qualified.* Our data suggest that the dissonance effect occurs only when the experimenter poses a hedonic dilemma for the Ss. What we have not demonstrated clearly, I think, is the motivational properties of our nonhedonic conditions. That is, there is probably reason to suspect that even in the "social reinforcement" study we did not separate out moral and consensual validation types of motivation, e.g., self-esteem motives and needs for certainty. Part of the problem stems from the attempt of Kelman and myself (Kelman & Baron, 1968a) to view forced compliance situations in terms of a simple dichotomy of moral versus hedonic dilemmas. It was in this context that the present study was designed. A second problem pertains to the type of "moral" manipulation we used. While the cognition that, "I have freely chosen to manipulate a fellow student's attitude and behavior concerning an issue of importance to him" would seem to be an immoral act by our definition, i.e., an act which involves the intentional inflicting of psychological harm, it is questionable whether the primary reaction of most Ss in this situation involved the arousal of moral anxiety. It is quite possible that this situation aroused more cognitive types of needs, i.e., doubts concerning the correctness of one's initial attitude rather than a concern with the goodness or badness of one's behavior, or that both types of motivations were equally salient.[4]

MORAL AND HEDONIC DILEMMAS IN A PD GAME

A study recently completed by John Sheposh (1967), under the writer's direction, is relevant to the present hypotheses in that (1) it represents the first test of our functional typology of attitude-discrepant behavior in a nonpersuasive context (see Weick, 1966, for a discussion of the importance of distinguishing between persuasive and nonpersuasive tasks in understanding consistency phenomena); and (2) Sheposh used operations which allowed him to achieve an arousal of a moral dilemma which is relatively unconfounded by issues of consensual validation.

METHOD

Since the details of this complex study will appear in a forthcoming monograph (Baron, Kelman, Sheposh, & Johnson), only the main features of procedure and results will be presented. Ninety-six female Ss were run in pairs in partial fulfillment of a three-hour research requirement. The experimental situation involved a mixed motive game of the type known as a Prisoner's Dilemma (PD). Although Ss were led to believe they were playing against each other, feedback was actually controlled by E.

A moral dilemma was created by inducing Ss to betray or double-cross their opponent in the PD game, and thereby illegitimately

---

[4]This is not to say that other motivational concerns might not have been instigated by this situation. For example, Ss might experience discomfort because they felt "ashamed" of themselves for acting in a manner discrepant from their attitudes. A "shame" dilemma of this type would be expected to lead to somewhat different problems from those created by moral and consensual validation dilemmas, e.g., Ss might become concerned with what the interviewee thought of them — their needs for social approval may become prepotent. Since it will probably never be possible to rule out all alternate arousal patterns, all that can be done is to establish empirically what are the most likely motivational concerns to be aroused by a given discrepant behavior. We can then move by successive approximation to more purified situations where we will be able to establish experimental control over possible confounding sources of motivation.

profit at the opponent's expense. Ss were instructed to play cooperatively for the initial trials to create an atmosphere of trust, and then, on a preprogrammed basis, betray the other S by adopting a competitive strategy. In the Hedonic condition Ss were induced to adopt a strategy of cooperation which would result in their obtaining minimal payoffs with the knowledge that the other S was maximizing at their expense. In contrast to the moral instructions which stressed that the Ss' behavior represents a violation of trust, the hedonic instructions emphasized that S's behavior might be described in terms of "letting oneself be played for a sucker."

After their role was explained, both moral and hedonic Ss were given an option of staying or leaving. Within each of the dilemmas, two common conceptual variables were manipulated: effort and duration of the discrepant role commitment. Essentially, the effort manipulation involved asking Ss in the High Effort condition to not only keep a tally of the other's responses (as low effort Ss do), but also to estimate the probability that the other Ss will make a cooperative choice, and the utility of such a choice to them. High effort Ss were also asked to calculate the product of these two values. The duration of commitment variation involved telling Ss they would have to perform their role either only this once (short term) or two other times in the future (long term). Dependent variables included Ss' affective reactions to the dilemma (e.g., phenomenal guilt, self-disapproval, etc.), evaluations of their role and of the experiment and the other player, estimates of the number of positive consequences Ss saw themselves and the other person receiving, changes on a social responsibility scale, and performance in a new one-trial PD game following the experiment proper.

HYPOTHESES AND RESULTS

The major hypotheses can be grouped into two categories: (1) those concerning the type of dilemmas that were produced and (2) those concerning the type of resolution likely to be employed.

Before presenting the major dependent variable data, the following should be noted. There were no differences in perceived choice among the experimental conditions, with all Ss experiencing a relatively high degree of freedom from external pressure. Second, the effort manipulation appears to have been successful. That is, regardless of variations in type of dilemma, or extent of commitment, Ss in the High Effort conditions perceived that their role performance was more effortful than Ss in the Low effort conditions ($F = 7.48$, $p < .01$).

Defining the Dilemma

The present distinction between moral and hedonic dilemmas suggests that there will be qualitatively different affective reactions for Ss experiencing a moral as opposed to a hedonic dilemma. Moral dilemma Ss are hypothesized to experience intropunitive emotions (such as phenomenal guilt and self-disapproval), while hedonic Ss are assumed to be concerned with dimensions involving how unrewarding the experience was.

In order to test these notions a three step procedure was followed: (1) responses to a number of items involving Ss' affective reactions were intercorrelated and factor analyzed; (2) the results of this factor analysis were used to form composite score indices which included scales that loaded heavily on the major factors; and (3) $2 \times 2 \times 2$ analyses of variance involving type of dilemmas, effort, and duration of commitment were done on these indices.

Three major factors emerged: (a) Factor I can be described as an intropunitive factor—heavily loaded by items involving phenomenal guilt, annoyance with self, perceived disapproval of others, and self-disapproval; (b) Factor II is a general arousal factor involving feelings of uneasiness and non-relaxation; and (c) Factor III is loaded strongly by a boredom item and an item involving the feeling that this is a worthless chore. An analysis of variance of a composite score based on the self-punitive scales of Factor I revealed that moral dilemma Ss were significantly more self-critical than hedonic dilemma Ss ($F = 16.71$, $p < .001$). An analysis of the composite score suggested by Factor II revealed that moral Ss reported more general discomfort than hedonic Ss ($F = 9.90$, $p < .01$). No significant differences between moral and hedonic Ss were found on an index based on Factor III (the disinterest factor).

While the above evidence seems to support our notions concerning the antecedents and consequences of a moral dilemma, we are left without a clear picture of the psychological reactions of the hedonic Ss. That is, the affective items designed to tap the utilitarian aspects of Ss' dilemmas (perceived foolishness of one's behavior, and recognition of the worthlessness of one's behavior) did not differentiate between moral and hedonic Ss. However, a look at the results of some open-ended questions which required Ss to list the positive and negative consequences of participating in this study suggests that Ss in the Hedonic condition did feel that the study was less rewarding than Ss in the Moral condition. It was found that hedonic Ss saw the other person as accruing more positive consequences from the experiment than did moral Ss ($F = 6.29$, $p < .025$). An index based on subtracting the total number of positive consequences attributed to the other from the total number of positive consequences attributed to oneself revealed that hedonic Ss had a relatively smaller favorable balance of outcomes than did the moral Ss ($F = 4.55$, $p < .05$). Thus, in terms of absolute and relative estimates, hedonic Ss perceived the other as benefiting more from the experiment than did moral Ss.

The Role of Effort in the Arousal Process

As part of the general conceptualization of a moral dilemma, it was suggested that if a person can convince himself that he expended a good deal of effort while carrying out an immoral deed, this might serve to mitigate his feelings of guilt or moral anxiety. This derivation can be contrasted with the dissonance reasoning which would predict greatest discomfort in the high as opposed to low effort cell. Within the Moral conditions it was found that low effort Ss tended to experience more guilt than high effort Ss ($F = 2.78$, $p < .15$). Low effort Ss were also significantly more annoyed with themselves than were high effort Ss ($F = 6.22$, $p < .025$.).

These data suggest that effort may function to reduce rather than increase one's feelings of discomfort when a moral dilemma is aroused. In line with a dissonance theory approach we found that within the Hedonic conditions high effort Ss felt more uneasy than low effort Ss ($F = 5.55$, $p < .05$).

The Effects of Commitment Duration on the Arousal of Discomfort

Within the Moral Dilemma conditions short-term commitment Ss tended to experience the negative consequences of the dilemma more intensely than long-term Ss, while the reverse appeared to be true in the Hedonic conditions. Short-term commitment Ss in the Moral conditions experienced more embarrassment ($F = 4.41$, $p < .05$) and saw more negative consequences for themselves as a result of their behavior ($F = 4.45$, $p < .05$) than did long-term Ss. On the other hand, within the Hedonic conditions, long-term Ss were less relaxed than were short-term Ss ($F = 6.25$, $p < .025$). These findings suggested that the moral dilemma Ss may have interpreted our long-term instructions as offering them the possibility of interacting with the person they had just betrayed. That is, they may have experienced less discomfort because unlike the short-term Ss, they perceived the possibility of apology and/or reparation. Since hedonic Ss were not likely to be thinking in these terms, anything that increased the duration of this unpleasant situation was likely to create greater discomfort.

THE RESOLUTION PROCESS

Subjects played a one-trial postexperimental PD game which provided an opportunity to cooperate with or retaliate against the fictitious opposing player. It was hypothesized that hedonic Ss would make significantly greater use of the retaliatory strategy than would moral dilemma Ss and that this difference would be strongest in the long-term conditions. As hypothesized, 54% of the long-term hedonic Ss made a noncooperative (retaliatory) choice, while only 17% of the long-term moral Ss did so ($p < .01$, by Critical Ratio test). There were no significant differences between short-term moral and hedonic Ss (18% versus 20%).

These findings support the notion that long-term moral Ss are oriented toward making reparation to the other Ss while long-term hedonic Ss are oriented toward getting even.

From our general functional analysis, it may be recalled that it was suggested that Ss who had engaged in an immoral act would be less likely to enhance the positive features of their behavior than Ss who had experienced a hedonic dilemma. In order to test this hypothesis an "attractiveness of role behavior" index was constructed based on a factor analysis of intercorrelations of Ss' responses to semantic differential scales involving an evaluation of their role in the experiment. Individual scales involving ease, goodness, and pleasantness of role performance loaded heavily on this factor. As hypothesized, it was found that hedonic Ss stressed' more of these positive features than did moral Ss ($F = 5.08, p < .05$).

Evaluation of the Other Player

Earlier it was suggested that the Moral Dilemma Long-Term conditions may have been interpreted by Ss as providing the possibility of future interaction and thereby providing an opportunity for apology and/or reparation. If Ss were thinking in these terms, we would expect a more favorable evaluation of the other player to occur in the Long- rather than Short-Term Commitment Condition. As predicted, within the Moral conditions, we found a lower evaluation of the other in the short- rather than long-term cells ($F = 8.28, p < .01$). This finding is consistent with Pallak's (1966) finding that within his High Shock Conditions there was more derogation of the victim under low rather than high expected confrontation. The notion that when a moral dilemma is involved there will be more derogation of the victim when no further confrontation is anticipated is also supported by the results of Davis and Jones (1960).

It would seem then, that within the Moral Dilemma Short Term conditions, a person's guilt or embarrassment about his behavior may be somewhat rationalized by a relatively negative evaluation of the other person. Such a resolution does not seem to be functional if a person expects to either confront the other person again or to perform this same immoral behavior on subsequent occasions. Within the Hedonic conditions, we found that long- and short-term Ss did not differ in their evaluations of the other person.

It appears clear from Sheposh's results that moral and hedonic dilemmas produce different affective, cognitive, and behavioral reactions both in terms of patterns of arousal and resolution. There was also some evidence that the variables of effort and duration of commitment showed differential patterns of effect depending on the type of dilemma. In summary, the general patterns of effects Sheposh found are more compatible with propositions derivable from a functional model than they are with hypotheses suggested by dissonance theory.

A Concluding Statement

If the present results do nothing else, they make untenable the notion that a single process mediates all the attitudinal effects of discrepant action. Viewed in this way, the phenomenon of attitude change through discrepant action becomes an arena for the operation of many processes, the specifications of which depend on ". . . the nature of the situation in which the discrepant action took place, the nature of the attitudes that were 'violated' by the action, and the motivational implications of that violation [Kelman, 1967, p. 4]." What emerges from such an orientation is an attempt to specify under which conditions inconsistent behavior renders one's present attitudes obsolete as coping mechanisms. Attitude change is now seen more as a preparation for the future than as an attempt to justify the past. The message of such a functional approach is not simple, but neither is the phenomenon.

References

Aronfreed, J. The nature, variety, and social patterning of interalized responses to transgression. *Journal of Abnormal and Social Psychology,* 1961, **63,** 223-240.

Aronfreed, J. The origin of self-criticism. *Psychological Review,* 1964, **71,** 193-219.

Bem, D. J. Self perception: An alternate interpretation of cognitive dissonance phenomena. *Psychological Review,* 1967, **74,** 183-200.

Brehm, J. W., & Cohen, A. R. *Explorations in cognitive dissonance.* New York: Wiley, 1962.

Brim, O. G., Jr. Attitude content-intensity and probability expectations. *American Sociological Review,* 1955, **20**, 68-76.

Brock, T. C. Cognitive restructuring and attitude change. *Journal of Abnormal and Social Psychology,* 1962, **64**, 264-271.

Brock, T. C. & Buss, A. H. Dissonance, aggression and evaluation of pain. *Journal of Abnormal and Social Psychology,* 1962, **65**, 197-202.

Brock, T. C., & Buss, A. H. Effects of justification for aggression and communication with the victim of post aggression dissonance. *Journal of Abnormal and Social Psychology,* 1964, **68**, 403-412.

Byrne, D., & Clore, G. L., Jr. Effective arousal and attraction. *Journal of Personality and Social Psychology Monograph,* 1967, **6**, 1-18 (Whole No. 638).

Carlsmith, J. M., Collins, B. E., & Helmreich, R. L. Studies in forced compliance: I. The effect of pressure for compliance on attitude change produced by face-to-face role playing and anonymous essay writing. *Journal of Personality and Social Psychology,* 1966, **4**, 1-13.

Collins, B. E., & Helmreich, R. Studies in forced compliance: II. Mechanisms of attitude change. Unpublished mimeo, 1965.

Davis, K., & Jones, E. E. Changes in interpersonal perception as means of reducing cognitive dissonance. *Journal of Abnormal and Social Psychology,* 1960, **61**, 402-410.

Elms, A. C., & Janis, I. L. Counter-norm attitudes induced by consonant versus dissonant conditions of role playing. *Journal of Experimental Research in Personality,* 1965, **1**, 50-60.

Festinger, L. A theory of social comparison processes. *Human Relations,* 1954, **7**, 117-140.

Festinger, L., & Carlsmith, J. M. Cognitive consequences of forced compliance. *Journal of Abnormal and Social Psychology,* 1959, **58**, 203-210.

Freedman, J. L. Attitudinal effects of inadequate justification. *Journal of Personality,* 1963, **31**, 371-385.

Glass, D. Changes in liking as a means of reducing cognitive discrepancies between self esteem and aggression. *Journal of Personality,* 1964, **32**, 531-544.

Hebb, D. O. Drives and the C. N. S. (conceptual nervous system), *Psychological Review,* 1955, **62**, 243-254.

Hunt, J. McV. Motivation inherent in information processing and action. In O. J. Harvey (Ed.), *Motivation and social interaction: Cognitive determinants.* New York: Ronald Press, 1963. Pp. 35-94.

Janis, I., & Gilmore, J. The influence of incentive conditions of the success of role playing in modifying attitudes. *Journal of Personality and Social Psychology,* 1965, **1**, 17-27.

Jones, E. E., & Gerard, H. B. *Foundations of social psychology.* New York: Wiley, 1967.

Jones, R. A., & Brehm, J. W. Attitudinal effects of communicator attractiveness when one chooses to listen. *Journal of Personality and Social Psychology,* 1967, **6**, 64-71.

Katz, D. The functional approach to the study of attitudes. *Public Opinion Quarterly,* 1960, **24**, 163-204.

Katz, D., & Stotland, E. A preliminary statement to a theory of attitude structure and change. In S. Koch (Ed.), *Psychology: A study of a science.* Vol. 3. New York: McGraw Hill, 1959. Pp. 423-475.

Kelman, H. C. Discrepant action and attitude change: A functional analysis. Colloquium presented at the University of Oregon, April 1967; and at the University of California, Santa Barbara, May, 1967.

Kelman, H. C., & Baron, R. M. Inconsistency as a psychological signal. In R. P. Abelson *et al.* (Eds.), *Theories of cognitive consistency: A sourcebook.* Chicago: Rand McNally, 1968, in press. (a)

Kelman, H. C., & Baron, R. M. Determinants of resolving inconsistency dilemmas: A functional analysis. In R. P. Abelson *et al.* (Eds.), *Theories of cognitive consistency: A sourcebook.* Chicago: Rand McNally, 1968, in press. (b)

Kelman, H. C., & Eagly, A. H. Attitude toward the communicator, perception of communication content, and attitude change. *Journal of Personality and Social Psychology,* 1965, **1,** 63-78.

Linder, D. E., Cooper, J., & Jones, E. E. Decision freedom as a determinant of the role of incentive magnitude in attitude change. *Journal of Personality and Social Psychology,* 1967, **6,** 245-254.

Mills, J. Changes in moral attitudes following temptation. *Journal of Personality,* 1958, **26,** 517-531.

Mosteller, F., & Bush, R. B. Selected quantitative techniques. In G. Lindzey (Ed.), *Handbook of social psychology.* Vol. 2. Reading, Mass.: Addison-Wesley, 1954. Pp. 289-334.

Pallak, M. S. The effect of aggression on interpersonal attractiveness. Paper presented at the Eastern Psychological Association, New York, April 1966.

Pepitone, A. *Attraction and hostility.* New York: Atherton Press, 1964.

Rokeach, M. A theory of organization and change within value and attitude systems. Presidential address to the Society for the Psychological Study of Social Issues, American Psychological Association, September 1967.

Sheposh, J. Reactions to moral and hedonic dilemmas in a prisoners' dilemma game. Unpublished doctoral dissertation, Wayne State University, 1967.

Smith, M. B., Bruner, J. S., & White, R. W. *Opinion and personality.* New York: Wiley, 1956.

Stotland, E., & Hillmer, I. L. Identification, authoritarian defensiveness and self esteem. *Journal of Abnormal and Social Psychology,* 1962, **64,** 334-342.

Weick, K. E. Task acceptance dilemmas: A site for research on cognition. In S. Feldman (Ed.), *Cognitive consistency: Motivational antecedents and behavioral consequents.* New York: Academic Press, 1966. Pp. 225-255.

White, R. W. Motivation reconsidered: The concept of competence. *Psychological Review,* 1959, **66,** 297-334.

13

A Conflict-Theory Approach to Attitude Change and Decision Making[1]

IRVING L. JANIS
DEPARTMENT OF PSYCHOLOGY
YALE UNIVERSITY
NEW HAVEN, CONNECTICUT

LEON MANN
DEPARTMENT OF SOCIAL RELATIONS
HARVARD UNIVERSITY
CAMBRIDGE, MASSACHUSETTS

Although a rational animal, man as a decision-maker can seldom claim to make purely rational judgments. Oversimplifications, distortions, evasions, and gross omissions of relevant considerations are likely to arise whenever an important life decision is being made. Most people spend much time and energy mulling over the issue when they have to make a personal decision concerning such matters as marriage and divorce, choice of career, seeking a cure for a disease, or making a move that will affect the social and economic welfare of their families. But they frequently fail to think through carefully all the relevant pros and cons of each of the alternatives open to them. Nor is their final ranking of the available alternatives always in accord with their expected utility. The deviations from rational models of maximal utility and minimax solutions become increasingly apparent to those psychologists whose research leads them to look into decisional conflicts that arise outside of the laboratory. Obviously we need studies of how people actually do make up their minds when they have to make personal decisions that have important implications for their future. In such investigations, it soon becomes

[1] This chapter presents in somewhat modified form some of the material from our forthcoming book on *Attitudes and Decision Making*, which we expect to publish in 1969 or 1970. The preparation of this chapter was facilitated by Grant No. MH-08564 to the senior author from the National Institute of Mental Health, U.S. Public Health Service, for research on tolerance for self-imposed deprivations.

apparent that the theoretical models derived from research on students' reactions to laboratory games are inadequate and that we need a framework that will enable us to take account of motivational and emotional factors that interact with cognitive processes in decision making.

The present approach, which we call "conflict theory" (Janis, 1957, 1959, 1968a 1968b; Mann, Janis, & Chaplin, 1967) views the decision-making process as a sequence of stages which start off with attitude changes induced by challenging information that motivates constitutes his current policy. We view successful challenges as having the effect of arousing interest in social communications containing new information and persuasive messages concerning the desirability of alternative courses of action, since the person has become motivated to find an adequate solution to the problem posed by the challenge. This theoretical approach also gives considerable emphasis to the decision-maker's capacity to resist impressive persuasive communications and signs of social disapproval after he has committed himself to a course of action. We assume that such resistance is determined partly by the way the person has resolved the predecisional conflicts generated when he was thinking about the antithetical pro and con considerations before he made his choice.

The conflict-theory viewpoint has grown out of concepts and hypotheses evolved in the course of carrying out psychological research on motivational processes in decision making. This has been particularly so for the determinants of the modes of conflict resolution as observed in studies of personal decisions, such as whether or not to obtain a divorce following a marital crisis, whether or not to accept an attractive job offer that will determine one's career line, whether or not to accept a physician's advice to undergo a surgical operation, and whether or not to go on a diet or try to give up cigarette smoking (Janis, 1957, 1959, 1968a; Janis & Mann, 1965; Mann, 1967b; Mann et al., 1967). We draw heavily upon the closely related area of research on attitude change processes generated by exposure to persuasive communications (Hovland, Janis, & Kelly, 1953; Janis, 1968b; Janis, Hovland, Field, Linton, Graham, Cohen, Rife, Abelson, Lesser, & King, 1959). Of special relevance for our approach is the large number of studies in experimental social psychology bearing on the concept of *social commitment* and its relevance for problems of the stability of attitudes and decisions (Festinger, 1957, 1964; Kiesler, 1968; Lewin, 1951).

The main point of departure for our conflict-theory analysis of attitude change and decision making is an earlier analysis of motivational aspects of decisional conflicts in terms of opposing reactions evoked during exposure to persuasive messages (Janis, 1957, 1959, 1968a). Among the major questions discussed in the earlier papers are the following:

1. What distinctive stages in the decision making process can be discerned that make a difference in the decision maker's responsiveness to persuasive messages intended to influence his attitudes toward alternative policies (courses of action)?

2. What are the main classes of pro and con considerations (incentives) that enter into decisional conflicts?

3. What are the main modes of conflict resolution that are in the repertoire of the average person and that can be selectively influenced by social communications?

In this chapter, we shall summarize briefly the tentative answers to these three questions, as outlined in the earlier papers. We shall also examine some of the ramifications of the conflict-theory approach for several additional problems that we have not hitherto discussed in detail.

STAGES IN THE DECISION MAKING PROCESS

Most discussions of personal decision making distinguish between two major phases in the decision process — the predecision and postdecision phases (see Festinger, 1964). However, a finer classification from the standpoint of a conflict theory analysis of the decision process differentiates among five sequential stages through which a person goes in moving toward a successful decision (see Janis, 1968a):

Stage 1: Appraisal of a Challenge

The decision-making process begins when the individual is exposed to persuasive information that challenges his current course of action or inaction by calling attention to important losses that will ensue if he does not change. This gives rise to a type of attitude change that involves a temporary personal crisis. The inconsistency between the new information and the person's current plans and commitments can generate an acute conflict about continuing his present policy.

Stage 2: Appraisal of Alternatives

The decision maker focuses his attention on each recommended course of action, which he initially evaluates from the standpoint of whether it can meet the challenge; in addition, he scans his memory for alternatives considered to have a good chance of averting or minimizing the losses made salient by the challenge.

Stage 3: Selection of the Best Alternative

The decision maker proceeds to a more thorough evaluation of each of the surviving alternatives in an effort to select the best available policy. The balance-sheet model to be described shortly is most applicable to this stage. By scanning and weighing each alternative in terms of its advantages and disadvantages, the decision maker attempts to select the one that will best meet his personal criteria for maximal gains and minimal losses. A *maximization of net gains* formula would be the likely basis of choice in many utilitarian decisions, but other formulae, such as the *minimization of serious losses*, might also be used frequently in social decisions when the individual is more prepared to reduce his utilitarian gains to avoid offending or embarrassing other persons. Under certain conditions, a "satisficing" formula may be adopted (cf. Cyert, Simon, & Trow, 1956); this seems especially likely when there are many potential alternatives that seem almost equally attractive at the outset. In such instances the person may simply choose the first one drawn to his attention which meets his minimum requirements. The latter strategy involves much more superficial scanning and less cognitive work than the other two. Thus the duration and intensity of mental activity during Stage 3 depends upon the type of evaluative strategy the decision maker is using, which, in turn, depends upon external information and cues that arouse the real possibility of anticipatory regret. In general, this stage is characterized by lack of commitment even after the decision maker feels certain that he has made his definite choice. Thus, he continues to be responsive to new information indicating that he may have miscalculated and will find it relatively easy to change his mind, in contrast to the next stage when he will become much more resistant to information that is inconsistent with his selected course of action.

Stage 4: Commitment to the New Policy

The person announces or reveals his intended course of action to others — usually his friends first, then others, saving potential critics for the last. This is the beginning of the postdecisional phase, when the individual anticipates loss of self-esteem and social disapproval if he fails to carry out the new policy. Although there may be wide individual differences in the degree to which commitment motivates people to assimilate and consolidate the new policy with a minimum of inconsistency, there is a general tendency to avoid negative feed-back, to adduce new reasons that bolster the decision, and to "spread" the attractiveness of the alternatives (see Festinger, 1964; Gerard, Blevans, & Malcolm, 1964; Malewski, 1962). Postdecisional bolster-ing is likely to be most pronounced when the alternatives had been initially close in value during Stage 3, making it difficult to arrive at the decision (see Mann, 1967a).

Stage 5: Adherence to the New Policy Despite Negative Feedback

This stage is parallel to Stage 1, except that when adherence occurs, challenging information is discounted or minimized. The persevering decision maker refutes or ignores arguments that might change his attitudes bearing on the desirability of the new policy; he continues to bolster his decision. For example, Greenbaum, Cohn, & Krauss (1965) found that after receiving negative information about perfor-mance on a chosen task, the committed subjects showed increased positive attitudes toward the task. Other modes of conflict resolution used to preserve the new policy include changing one's social net-work and proselytizing to others about the wisdom of the choice. These modes of resolution are especially likely to occur when there is a long time lag between the overt commitment and putting the decision into action and when the decision maker is exposed to negative social feedback without being able to refute the criticisms by pointing to the advantages of the chosen alternative that have already materialized.

Of course, the five stages which we have outlined cannot be sharply differentiated, especially for relatively minor, nondeliberate deci-sions. Often a decision maker will approach the task quite casually and will tend to coalesce or even omit some of the stages. However, the conceptualization of a five-stage model provides a useful frame-work for analyzing the problems that arise when people make ego-involving decisions to which they feel deeply committed.

SOME IMPLICATIONS OF THE ANALYSIS OF STAGES

The five-stage sequence provides a set of categories for describing qualitative differences in responsiveness to internal and external sources of conflict that may help focus psychological research on relevant microprocesses and facilitate the search for the more subtle interacting variables that give rise to anomalous and seemingly unlawful effects. Elsewhere (Janis, 1968a) the five stages in the decision-making process have been discussed from the standpoint of their implications for attitude change. A gradual change in eight different attitude components is expected as the decision maker goes through the five successive stages. These implications are summarized in Table 1, which shows how the various patterns of attitude change might form a unitary (Guttman-type) of scale. One of the main suggestions that follows from this analysis is that the five stages might be used as a set of categories to differentiate the varying degrees of success of different types of exposures to persuasive messages that are intended to evoke changes in attitudes and action. At one extreme are the inputs that merely succeed in opening up the issue, without carrying anyone beyond the first or second stage. For example, an experiment by Janis and Terwilliger (1962) showed that a strong-threat version of a factual pamphlet on smoking and lung cancer elicited more psychological resistance and somewhat less attitude change than a milder threat version, but the latter version succeeded only in making some of the smokers feel uneasy and doubtful about continuing to smoke cigarettes (Stage 1 or Stage 2). None of the smokers were induced to go so far as to decide that the best policy would be to cut down on cigarette consumption. In contrast, our more recent research shows that when an emotional role-playing procedure is used, many subjects are not only strongly challenged but show the changes that go along with the later stages of the decision-making process (Janis & Mann, 1965; Mann, 1967b; Mann & Janis, 1968). In this procedure, strong fear is aroused during a psychodramatic performance in which the subject plays the role of a patient who is given the bad news (by the experimenter, enacting the role of a physician) that a supposed x-ray examination has revealed cancer of the lung and that immediate surgery is necessary. Follow-up data (Mann & Janis, 1968) indicate that the one-hour psychodramatic procedure succeeds in inducing a sizeable proportion of the subjects to go through all five stages of the decision-making process; 18 months later these subjects were still sustaining the decision to cut down on smoking, which was made at the time of the experimental session, despite the withdrawal symptoms and other negative feedback they subsequently encountered (Stage 5).

The five-stage schema may also prove to be useful for classifying varying degrees of receptivity among members of any audience exposed to the same persuasive message. The way a person responds to new arguments and appeals intended to induce him to adopt a new course of action probably varies considerably, depending upon whether the informational inputs are creating a cognitive conflict

TABLE 1

TYPES OF ATTITUDE CHANGE ACCOMPANYING EACH STAGE IN MAKING A DECISION TO ADHERE TO A RECOMMENDED POLICY Inferred from Studies of Heavy Smokers Who Decided to Stop Smoking after Being Exposed to Publicity about the Surgeon General's Report on Smoking and Lung Cancer[a]

Components of attitude change (new beliefs, value judgments, and dispositions toward recommendation, R)	Initial attitude of complacency	Stage 1 Positive appraisal of challenge	Stage 2 Positive appraisal of recommendation (R)	Stage 3 Selection of R as the best alternative	Stage 4 Commitment to decision to adopt R	Stage 5 Adherence to R despite negative attack
Overt behavior						
1. Acts in accordance with R following major challenges to the new attitude?	No	No	No	No	(?)	Yes
2. Acts in accordance with R under normal circumstances?	No	No	No	No	Yes	Yes
Verbal evaluation of R						
3. Feels willing to act in accordance with R?	No	No	No	No	Yes	Yes
4. Believes R is best available means?	No	No	No	No	Yes	Yes
5. Believes R is a satisfactory means worth considering?	No	No	No	Yes	Yes	Yes
6. Selectively responsive to subsequent communications about R? (Accepts assertions that R is an effective means)	No	No	Yes	Yes	Yes	Yes
Verbal evaluation of threat						
7. Believes the threat is serious?	No	Yes	Yes	Yes	Yes	Yes
8. Selectively responsive to subsequent communications about the threat? (Accepts assertions that the threat is serious)	No	Yes	Yes	Yes	Yes	Yes

[a] From Janis, 1968a.

for the first time (challenge stage) or are introducing additional incentives at a later state, when the individual already feels regretful about his earlier decision and is intensively searching for a satisfactory alternative.

> The stage of the decision making process at which a person is currently located is probably a major determinant of (a) the degree of interest he will have in exposing himself to one or another type of information relevant to the decision and (b) the degree to which he will be positively or negatively influenced by the information if he is exposed to it. The analysis of stages . . . has some obvious implications for receptivity to new information about the positive gains to be expected from adopting the recommended policy. For example, a new bit of antismoking information (such as 'doctors have found that the average person experiences less fatigue if he gives up smoking') will meet with indifference or high resistance before Stage 1 is completed; but if the same new bit of information is presented to the same person when he is at Stage 3 or 4, it will elicit great interest, and will be carefully mulled over and evaluated. If presented at a still later stage (after Stage 4 is completed), it will be highly welcome and promptly assimilated with hardly any critical reflection about it.
>
> An entirely different sequence would be expected from a bit of information that argues in the direction of rejecting the recommendation (e.g., 'doctors have found that most people who give up smoking become chronically overweight'). Before Stage 1, the average smoker would have little interest in such information, but if brought to the focus of his attention in a captive audience, it would be readily assimilated into his cognitive structure. During Stages 2 and 3, the smoker would display much more interest and would evaluate the information in a relatively unbiased way. But then, after Stage 4, the ex-smoker would avoid such information if possible. If he could not escape it, he would be highly skeptical and would try to refute it.
>
> In order to test the generality of the above hypotheses—and of the entire schema of stages . . . —it will be necessary to investigate many different types of decisions, in addition to the smoking decision that has furnished most of the empirical basis so far [Janis, 1968a].

The relationship between stages in the decision process and receptivity to persuasive messages probably can be tested in attitude change experiments in which identical information inputs are presented at various time intervals before and after a choice has been made. (We currently have such a study underway.) Perhaps by taking account of the different stages in decision making during which cognitive conflicts are aroused, it will be possible to resolve some of the contradictions among attitude change experiments on such issues as the primacy versus recency controversy, the effects of fear appeals on acceptance of recommendations and the effects of overt role playing or forced compliance on attitudes and decisions.

We regard the five-stage sequence as part of the framework for a conflict-theory analysis of changes in attitudes and decisions. This sequence points up the continuity of past, current, and future decisions. Every current decisional conflict is viewed as starting out with some relatively powerful form of negative feedback or challenge (Stage 1) that makes the person doubtful about his preexisting policy which, for a short or long period, had survived the onslaughts of earlier challenges (Stage 5). When negative feedback can no longer be contained—as a result of impressive evidence of unforeseen losses, social criticisms, or excessively costly commitments—the person can no longer quickly terminate the postdecisional conflict and revert to a relatively complacent attitude concerning his prior actions and commitments. Stage 5 is then superseded by Stage 1, which may lead to a new decision. Thus, today's regret about yesterday's decision constitutes a postdecisional conflict; it is also a predecisional conflict if it gives rise to a new commitment tomorrow.

SOURCES OF DECISIONAL CONFLICT: THE BALANCE SHEET MODEL

The five-stage sequence provides a context for the balance sheet model, which is intended as a schema for a microanalysis of the positive and negative incentives that enter into predecisional choice (in Stage 3) and of the new incentives added by social commitments (in Stage 4), all of which are assumed to influence the long-run stability of the decision (Stage 5).

The major types of considerations that enter into any decisional conflict can be classified into four main categories with respect to the anticipated favorable or unfavorable consequences of choosing a given alternative (see Janis, 1959):

1. Anticipated utilitarian gains or losses for self
2. Anticipated utilitarian gains or losses for significant others
3. Anticipated approval or disapproval from significant others
4. Anticipated self-approval or disapproval

For most personal decisions in everyday life the main considerations in these four categories are likely to be conscious anticipations mediated by verbal symbols. Occasionally, however, an important consideration may be temporarily preconscious, but readily accessible to consciousness if someone calls it to the decision maker's attention. Hence, by and large, these considerations usually are subject to social influence through informational inputs and persuasive arguments presented either in the mass media or in direct interpersonal discussions. (In exceptional cases, an important consideration is not accessible to awareness due to the operation of repression or other defense mechanisms, in which case the person is unlikely to take full account of it in his attempts to resolve his decisional conflict unless he goes through special therapeutic procedures.)

In most of the important decisions that a person takes throughout his life history, all four types of considerations are relevant to some extent and the outcome is presumably determined by the relative strength of these incentives. Decisional conflicts are conceptualized in terms of a balance sheet containing weighted positive and negative values corresponding to the potential gains (positive incentives) and potential losses (negative incentives) that are anticipated by the decision maker when he evaluates each alternative open to him. At present, the art and science of quantitatively assessing the positive and negative incentive values that enter into decisional conflicts is not very well-developed. Consequently, we cannot expect to use a balance sheet schema to predict which choice a person will end up making (e.g., whether he will accept or reject a new policy recommended in a persuasive message). Nevertheless, the balance sheet schema does appear to be useful for predicting certain other aspects of postdecisional behavior, such as the modes of conflict resolution the person will display and the way he will respond to counterattitudinal communications during the postdecisional period. Examples of these implications of the model will be presented shortly.

In order to clarify the types of pro and con considerations that are likely to enter into a schematic balance sheet at the time when a person is making a personal decision, let us examine Table 2. The entries in this table are based on interview data from a heavy smoker who participated in one of our preliminary experiments on changing smoking attitudes and habits. The balance sheet provides for the eight basic types of anticipations that are assumed to enter into any decision to adopt a new course of action. Each relevant entry in the positive incentive (+) rows involves potential gains that are expected from retaining the original policy or from adopting one of the alternative new policies; each relevant entry in the negative incentive (−) rows involves expectations of potential losses. The entries in the plus rows would give rise to some degree of approach motivation, which can be conceptualized as a vector in the direction of accepting the given policy; whereas the entries in the minus rows would be assumed to give rise to some degree of avoidance motivation, which can be conceptualized as a vector in the direction of rejecting the policy.

The middle-aged man whose decisional conflict is dissected in Table 2 had shown three main reactions to the series of persuasive communications that had recently appeared in the mass media, generated by the United States Surgeon General's Report (1964) on smoking and lung cancer. These three reactions are represented in Table 2 by the use of italic type in the appropriate cells of the balance sheet: (1) He had become highly concerned about the possible damage he might be creating to his future health if he were to continue smoking. (This is classified as increasing the negative incentive value of the original policy by adding to the anticipated utilitarian losses to the self.) (2) As a result of reading an impressive article about a famous person who developed lung cancer, at a time when the subject was already partially influenced by other communications on the same topic, he confided in several friends that he was concerned about the harmful effects of his smoking and was going to do something about it. (This partial commitment to several friends, from whom he would anticipate at least a mild degree of social disapproval if he were to remain a heavy smoker, is represented in Table 2 as another type of negative incentive that makes for rejection of his original policy.) (3) The very same act of committing himself to change his policy—which was spontaneous and genuine, rather than a matter of momentary verbal compliance with social pressures from the friends—engendered a special form of ego-involvement. He would now anticipate a loss of self-esteem from failing to keep his word. (This self-commitment to change his smoking habit which arises from anticipated self-disapproval from failing to live up to his own standards of conduct is represented as a third type of negative incentive that also makes for rejection of his original policy.)

These three considerations generated by the series of persuasive anti-smoking communications constituted a strong challenge to his preexisting complacent attitude ("I like to smoke, I've been doing it for 20 years, and there is no good reason why I shouldn't keep on"). The three components that were influenced by the publicity about the Surgeon General's report, it will be noted, are embedded in a complex matrix of other positive and negative incentives. All the remaining entries in the balance sheet are based on inferences from interviews concerning the various considerations he was taking into account when he was trying to make up his mind about which alternative course of action he was going to adopt. At that time this man was

TABLE 2

HYPOTHETICAL BALANCE SHEET AT THE STAGE WHEN A TENTATIVE DECISION IS BEING MADE

Examples of Conflicting Cognitions Verbalized by an Average Smoker Whose Complacent Attitude Has Been Challenged by Publicity about the Surgeon General's Report on Smoking and Lung Cancer

Alternative courses of action (policies)	Positive or negative incentive values	Type of Cognition				Final judgment
		Anticipated utilitarian consequences		Anticipated approval or disapproval		
		For self	For significant others (Spouse, friends, family, reference group	From self	From significant others	
1. Original policy (Continue smoking about one pack per day)	+	Provides daily pleasure; sometimes relieves emotional tension.	By relieving tension, it helps me get along better with my family and fellow workers	I pride myself on not scaring easily.	My statistician friend, to whom I expressed concern about the surgeon general's report, will be pleased that I do not accept correlation as proving causation.	Unsatisfactory—wants to change if a satisfactory alternative is available to provide a net gain (or less net loss).
	−	Possibility of my developing a lung cancer; it will make ordinary respiratory illness more serious; costs money.	Family would also suffer if I were to become a cancer victim.	If I don't live up to my commitment, I shall feel like an untrustworthy, weak character; if I ever develop a serious respiratory illness, I'll feel guilty about having ignored the medical evidence.	Several friends will lose respect for me, since I committed myself when I told them I was going to change my smoking habits; my family doctor and other antismoking friends will continue to disapprove.	
2. New recommended policy (Stop smoking)	+	Chances of lung cancer will be greatly reduced; respiratory illness will be less troublesome; money could be put to good use.	Family will be more secure if I reduce chances of lung cancer and other respiratory diseases; also my abstinence might exert a good influence on our children to avoid becoming smokers.	I shall feel satisfied with myself for living up to my commitment; also, taking action on the basis of new evidence shows that one is mature, realistic, and intelligent.	My friends will see that I am living up to my commitment; my family doctor and a few antismoking friends will strongly approve.	Mixed attitude—Prefers a less conflictful alternative if available.

					My statistician friend will think I am stupid.	
	−	Unsatisfied craving will be unpleasant; I'll be more irritable and angry; might develop severe anxiety symptoms; might become overweight, which would be as unhealthy as smoking.	I already cause enough trouble to my spouse without becoming even more irritable and tense; this could be the last straw that breaks up our home.	I might lose my temper more often, which would make me feel like a heel.		Most satisfactory — Ready to adopt this policy since no available alternative is more attractive.
3. Alternative compromise policy (Smoke only one-half pack per day)	+	Same as No. 2 to a milder degree, *with risk of cancer greatly reduced.*	Same as No. 2 to a milder degree.	Same as No. 2 to a milder degree.	Same as No. 2 to a milder degree.	
	−	Same as No. 2 to a milder degree, with no anticipated problem of becoming overweight; in addition, *a slight risk of lung cancer.*	Same as No. 2 to a milder degree.	Going only part way may show a lack of self control.	My family doctor and several friends will not approve of this compromise.	Satisfactory — but less attractive than an available alternative.
4. Alternative nonrecommended policy (Switch to filtered cigarettes, one pack per day)	+	Same as No. 2 to a milder degree, except that no money saved and *not sure risk of lung cancer reduced at all.*	Same as No. 2 to a milder degree.	Same as No. 2 to a milder degree.	Same as No. 2 to a milder degree.	
	−	Same as No. 2 to a much milder degree; but in addition, *the same drawbacks as No. 1 to a somewhat milder degree, since filters are not recommended.*	Same as No. 2 to a milder degree.	Same as No. 3 to a stronger degree.	My family doctor and several friends will not approve of this compromise.	

still smoking heavily, but was dissatisfied about it and kept telling himself that one day soon he was going to change.

THE BALANCE SHEET AS A PREDICTOR OF VULNERABILITY TO COUNTERATTITUDINAL COMMUNICATIONS

Although the balance sheet model illustrated in Table 2 is still incomplete in many ways, it can be used to generate at least a few crude predictions, particularly in connection with reactions of regret and readiness to backslide when counterattitudinal communications and other forms of negative feedback are encountered after the person has begun to carry out the new policy. One of the main assumptions of conflict theory is that a decision maker's vulnerability to post-decisional feedback is dependent upon the gaps in his thinking during the predecisional stages. For example, if a decision were based on only one type of consideration — say the utilitarian consequences for the self, as may often happen in career decisions when a man decides to change jobs because of higher pay and better working conditions — the gaps in the third and fourth columns of the balance sheet would lead us to predict that he will be particularly vulnerable to criticisms from his social network of family and friends and also to any postdecisional event that makes him realize that he has violated his own personal standards of moral conduct. Similarly, if only social considerations were intensively scanned before the decision — as often happens when a person is invited to join a social club — he will be highly vulnerable to negative feedback about utilitarian considerations after he has made the decision (e.g., when he is informed that there are hidden costs of membership).

Prior research, particularly on postdecisional regret about having decided to accept a physician's recommendation to undergo surgery, provides some support for the assumption that the stability of a decision during the postdecisional period depends partly on the degree to which the various sources of negative feedback have been worked through in advance. The immunizing effects of taking account of the negative consequences of a decision, which can be stimulated by authoritative information about the painful consequences to be expected during the postoperative period, are suggested by relevant correlational data obtained in studies of surgical patients (Janis, 1958, pp. 274–296.). From a survey of several hundred young men who had recently undergone a surgical operation, a number of relationships were observed showing a link between amount of preoperative information (of the type that could be expected to help a person to anticipate and work through the subsequent negative feedback) and tolerance for the frustrations, pains, discomforts, and other stresses of the postoperative period. The negative feedback following acceptance of a physician's advice to undergo surgery is, of course, extremely powerful and makes many patients change their attitudes toward the physician and regret their decision.

The men who were least informed about the unpleasant consequences in store for them were found to have been relatively free from worry before the operation. But then, when subjected to the impact of the stresses of the postoperative period, they became much more upset, angry, and hostile toward the medical staff than the others. These unprepared patients were also less cooperative when the nurses or interns tried to give them an injection or to carry out some other routine postoperative treatment; this negative attitude and uncooperative behavior was tantamount to reversing their earlier decision to allow the hospital staff to take over their medical care.

Egbert, Battit, Welch, and Bartlett (1964) conducted an experiment in order to follow up on this correlational evidence and its implications concerning the increase in subsequent stress tolerance created by "working through" the major sources of stress in advance. They tested the prediction that a group of surgical patients given appropriate preparatory communications before their operations will show better adjustment to the stresses of the postoperative period than an equivalent group of patients given no special preparatory communications other than the information ordinarily available to any hospitalized patient. This prediction was tested in a carefully controlled field experiment with 97 adult surgical patients at the Massachusetts General Hospital. Neither the surgeons nor the ward nurses were told about this experiment, to make sure that the experimental (informed) and control (uninformed) patients would receive equivalent treatment in all other respects.

On the day of the operation both groups required about the same amount of narcotics, but on each of the next five postoperative days, the experimental group required significantly less than the controls. In fact, the requests for medication to relieve their pains were so infrequent from the well-informed patients that their postoperative narcotic requirements were reduced by about one-half, as compared with the uninformed control group. Moreover, "blind" ratings from an independent observer, which were obtained for slightly more than half of each group, showed that the patients in the experimental group were in better emotional and physical condition than the controls. Further evidence of the more rapid improvement of the well-informed patients is provided by data on duration of hospitalization. Completely unaware of the experimental or control treatments received by the patients, the surgeons decided that the well-informed patients were well enough to be sent home much sooner than the uninformed—an average of 2.7 days earlier. In line with the earlier correlational findings, the investigators also noted that the uninformed controls made many more complaints to the staff.

Thus, the experiment provides systematic evidence in support of the conclusion, derived from the earlier studies, concerning the positive value of advance information about the negative consequences of making a decision to undergo surgery. This is a striking illustration of the general proposition that the more complete the "work of worrying" during the early stages of making a decision, the greater the tendency to adhere to the decision when challenging provocations are encountered after the person has committed himself to it. Additional evidence of the immunizing effects against counterattitudinal attacks is provided by the experimental studies reported by McGuire (1964).

We can conceptualize the working through process as involving intensive unbiased scanning of all the relevant types of considerations that enter into the balance sheet. If it is true that the degree to which unbiased scanning is carried out during the predecisional stages has an important influence on the stability of the decision, we must consider the following key question: What are the *determinants* of intensive scanning during the predecisional period? In order to answer this question, we find it necessary to introduce some additional theoretical postulates concerning conflict dynamics.

BASIC DECISIONAL CONFLICTS

According to conflict theory, a decision is "any verbal or overt action which is socially defined as a commitment to carry out a specified task or to adhere to a particular course of action in the future [Janis, 1959, p. 199]." The concept of decision pertains "to those instances where a person has informed others of his choice and perceives himself as committed to it [p. 202]"; thus it is linked with Lewin's concept of social commitment (1951). Statements of preference and implicit or covert decisions do not fall within the definition, since they have ambiguous implications for commitment. In Festinger's restatement of the dissonance theory of decision making (1964) there is a similar emphasis on the tie between decision and commitment (p. 156). This agreement between the two theories on what constitutes a decision, as will be seen shortly, is important for testing certain of the differential predictions which follow from the two theories.

According to the conflict theory of decision making, the individual is motivated to reduce the tension which arises whenever he has to make an important decision and foresees difficulties ahead if he chooses any of the feasible courses of action. We assume that predecisional choices generally involve two basic types of conflict, each of which is likely to be aroused before a person commits himself to a course of action that is expected to affect his own future welfare (or the welfare of his group or organization): (1) the here-and-now conflict of wanting and not wanting to commit oneself to start carrying out a given course of action; and (2) anticipated conflict in the near future from foreseen or unforeseeable consequences that might engender postdecisional regret from having made a bad decision.

Presumably both types of conflict generate powerful aversive motivational effects, but the modes of escape or resolution of the two types of conflict are quite different. We shall briefly discuss the way we view these two sources of predecisional conflict in order to specify the different types of cues that are likely to give rise to each and the different types of avoidance or coping mechanisms that are likely to be set into motion.

The first source of conflict is assumed to arise whenever a person is being tempted, pressured, or persuaded to engage in a course of action about which he has mixed feelings. This type of conflict, which is likely to be subjectively painful without necessarily being intolerable, can be summarized in the form of a critical verbal formula: "This *plan of action* is *good*, so I *want* to do it; but it is *bad*, so I *don't want* to do it."

Obviously, this type of here-and-now conflict about taking action does not include all instances of cognitive dissonance; rather, it is limited to instances of what could be called "*conative* dissonance" (wanting to do something and wanting to do the opposite).

If we are correct in assuming that every decision maker is motivated to put an end to this conflict as quickly as possible in order to terminate the painful tension it generates, we would expect a variety of evasive mechanisms to be manifested. The main question the distressed decision maker would be asking himself is: "Can I *escape* from this dilemma?" When he expects no penalty for postponing action, the decision maker may feel free to "leave the field" and thus turn his attention to other, less distressing matters. But when he is unable to evade or suppress the dilemma, he will be highly motivated to find at least a temporary solution whereby he can either accept the plan of action as a substantially good one or reject it as a substantially bad one.

Let us now turn to the second source of conflict: whenever a person arrives temporarily at a transformed formula that inclines him to accept or reject a given plan of action while still uncommitted, he is likely to become concerned about preventing or warding off future (postdecisional) conflict, which he knows will be generated if the new plan turns out to be a poor one. The formula which underlies this source of conflict during the third stage of the decision-making sequence would be "I think I know what I want to do, but if I do it I might regret it later."

One of our main assumptions is that whenever a person scans the probable consequences of alternative courses of action, he seeks for a solution that will yield a large discrepancy between the approach and avoidance tendencies that are generating his present dilemma. Thus, he will try to transform all situations where the approach and avoidance vectors are of nearly equal strength into one in which there is a marked discrepancy one way or the other. But most people are prevented from resorting to wishful thinking because of the powerful reality-testing motivations that arise at the point where action is about to be taken. Hesitation, doubt, and scanning for possible negative consequences that might be overlooked—by searching one's memory and by actively seeking out information—are all consequences of stressful training episodes of the following sort that start in early childhood and continue throughout adult life. The decision maker judges that this plan is mainly good; he initiates the action; he then encounters severe social punishment or some other form of negative feedback, such as actual pain or deprivation. Subsequently, he will experience intense conflict when he thinks about this negative feedback from reality as against the overoptimistic beliefs and fantasies that led him to initiate the action. Probably this type of "hard knocks" training, together with other socialization experiences, gives rise to the second type of predecisional conflict, the main feature of which is that the person is motivated to put up with the tension of the first type of conflict while he engages in intensive reflection about the consequences of his intended actions before it is too late. Thus, we assume that although every adult decision maker is motivated to terminate predecisional conflict quickly, he has also learned to be sufficiently vigilant to avoid commiting himself to a course of action until he has carefully considered the possible consequences that could cause him to regret it.

It is important to reiterate that predecisional conflict might be rapidly dissipated if the person were able to ignore the negative consequences that might be in store for him. When a trustworthy authority or representative of a reference group makes a strong persuasive effort to change his attitudes and actions, the person could avoid much distress by making a quick decision to adopt a positive high-discrepancy formula. But when there are cues to future trouble, he anticipates postdecisional regret before he encounters it.

Thus, as soon as the person encounters any pressure to decide for himself, or to make a real choice that involves an element of doubt, he is cued to the possibility of subsequent conflict. Then he begins to scan his memory for possible sources of postdecisional losses and he seeks out information about the consequences. This tendency, which is a product of social training and personality development, can be regarded as another form of the capacity to delay gratification, whereby the person puts up with the current tension of unpleasant conflict in order to arrive at a larger reward (via better decisions) in the future. To be able to tolerate the painful state of predecisional conflict, it is necessary for the person to be able to represent to himself cognitively the notion of regret: "I might regret this if I overlook the bad consequences."

Even when no bad consequences can be pinned down, either through memory scanning or information seeking, the mere fact that it is socially labeled as an "important decision" may be enough to cue the person to the possibility of potential losses when he contemplates a new course of action like changing his career or getting married. We refer to this fear of unknown dangers as the "there-is-the-rub" phenomenon. In order for the crucial cues to evoke the person's anticipation of possible negative feedback ("I just might regret this"), it is necessary for the person to be aware of the fact that he is committing himself, or is about to initiate an action.

Much of the social training everyone receives in commitment reinforces the tendency to stop and think before committing oneself. Time and again, one learns that it is costly to reverse a decision after one is committed to it—that there will be social disapproval as well as imposed penalties. In addition there is likely to be a loss of self-esteem insofar as the decision maker regards himself as having judged foolishly or as having behaved in an untrustworthy manner by failing to keep his word. These considerations can be powerful incentives that enter in whenever a person encounters any cue showing that he is committing himself to an important course of action. He is likely to respond by postponing the decision long enough to think it over, avoiding the temptation to use one of the comfortable low-conflict formulas involving rapid acceptance or rapid rejection of a given choice.

Thus, the second type of conflict and its accompanying images of potentially grave losses motivates the person to put up with the painfulness of the first type. Whenever the second type of conflict is aroused, the person will intensively reflect about the pros and cons of the issue in an objective way (to the best of his ability). He will be motivated to use the full capabilities of his creative powers to work out an adequate solution, and this may lead him to invent a new combination of the conventional alternatives or to work out an addendum to the least objectionable policy in order to prevent undesirable consequences from materializing.

After a person has committed himself to a course of action he generally regards the issue as closed and the second type of conflict subsides. But right up until the last moment (and perhaps for a few moments after the decision is made, as suggested by Walster's [1964] findings), most decision makers may tend to engage in unbiased scanning and avoid bolstering the dominant choice or belittling the unchosen alternatives.

COMMITMENT AND POSTDECISIONAL CONFLICT

Avoidance of the current predecisional conflict and avoidance of anticipated postdecisional conflict are assumed to be tendencies that are always present when a person is making a difficult decision, although each of the tendencies will vary in strength as a function of situational and predispositional variables. At any time during the postdecisional period, either or both types of conflict may be re-aroused by communications that evoke a negative attitude toward the adopted policy. Sometimes even very mild social feedback that does not strongly arouse the first type of conflict will nevertheless succeed in producing attitude changes that give rise to the second type of conflict. This may occur, for example, when a person's recent decision is challenged by a good friend who points out that others will regard his action as violating a group norm. If the friend's prediction is taken as a sign that a great deal of negative social feedback is going to be encountered in the near future, the person will become vigilant, regretful, and inclined to stop bolstering the decision he has recently made. The person will then be motivated to reopen the issue in order to deal with the newly discovered weaknesses of the decision. When this happens, the postdecisional conflict about the old policy becomes equivalent to a predecisional conflict about a new policy, as we suggested earlier.

These postdecisional conflicts are complicated by the added consideration that if one changes his policy he will suffer the cost of breaking his commitments. There is also the related problem of having to admit to oneself and to significant others that one has been misled or has used poor judgment. Thus, even if he feels quite sure that the unexpected negative feedback shows up the old policy as essentially a bad one that should now be rejected, he will be deterred from immediately giving it up and adopting a seemingly better one because of the arousal of anticipatory regret about breaking his commitment. For example, some heavy smokers who have decided to give up smoking are ready to change their minds during the first few days of deprivation, as they experience severe withdrawal symptoms; but they are likely to put up with these painful consequences if they have joined a "no-smoking" group to which they have announced their decision (Janis & Kahn, 1966; Mausner, 1966; J. C. Miller, 1966).

All decisions, as Lewin (1951) has suggested, are "frozen" to some extent by social commitments to one's social network of family, friends, work groups, and acquaintances in the community, even if not sealed by a legal contract. Consequently, whenever an acute postdecisional conflict inclines the person to reverse his decision, he is likely to be restrained by the anticipated social disapproval (and self-disapproval) entailed by failing to live up to expectations. This is, in effect, a special form of the second type of basic conflict: "I now want to change my course of action but if I do I will regret it when others find out that I have gone back on my commitment." It is likely to be a major component of any postdecisional reaction to negative feedback, which induces the person, once again, to engage in relatively unbiased exploration of the pros and cons, just as he did before making the decision. Even when he is so bitterly disappointed that he wants to reverse his decision as soon as possible, he will be inclined to reconsider the issue carefully; he may proceed to engage in intensive, unbiased reflection about the costs of undoing his commitments and adopting an attractive alternative.

The conditions that evoke such a full rearousal of decisional conflict probably occur rarely, except following crises when people make overhasty decisions. The probability of encountering the type of negative feedback that makes for acute regret seems quite low for most life decisions, but it may become fairly high when people are forced to decide on a course of action rapidly without sufficient information about the probable outcome or become so emotionally aroused that they commit themselves impulsively without taking account of the catastrophic consequences that could ensue.

THE CONTINUITY OF PRE- AND POSTDECISIONAL CONFLICTS

Dissonance theorists make a sharp distinction between predecisional and postdecisional conflict. They assume that predecisional conflicts lead to objective appraisals of the pros and cons and that it is only during postdecisional periods that the person engages in cognitive distortions of the kind that enter into dissonance reduction (see Festinger, 1964). Our analysis of the two basic types of decisional conflict leads us to question this view. We expect that either tendency can occur during the predecisional period or during the postdecisional period, depending on whether certain arousal conditions are present or absent. We do agree, however, that generally speaking when a person is visibly in the throes of predecisional conflict he is anticipating some postdecisional regrets (otherwise he wouldn't be so agitated) and hence he is likely to be vigilant and relatively objective in arriving at his final choice. Whereas, during the postdecisional period challenging information or events can make the person momentarily doubt the soundness of his choice, but his dominant tendency usually will be to minimize the conflict or dissonance created by the negative feedback. Here it should be mentioned that we question the universality of another assumption put forth by Festinger and his associates, namely that after committing himself to a new course of action, a decision maker will always reduce dissonance by selectively focusing his attention and thinking on the good features of his choice and/or the bad features of the unchosen alternatives. We agree that there is a strong tendency to bolster the decision after a person has committed himself, but we do not expect that postdecisional bolstering will always be the dominant tendency. Our assumption is that at any time during the postdecisional period, if the person perceives a threat of great impending conflict or regret, he will be provoked into rational reexamination of alternatives.

Our conflict-theory analysis makes the same prediction as Festinger (1964) and his associates for postdecisional challenges that are relatively weak. But, as stated earlier, when the challenges are strong enough to have more than a momentary impact on the person, regret can become such a dominant reaction that the person enters into a new predecisional conflict. Thus, our formulation emphasizes the need to investigate the conditions under which challenges will have strong or weak effects, i.e., will produce a new predecisional conflict as against a sealing over of the potential conflict by sticking to the original decision and bolstering it.

We postulate that the first tendency in response to negative feedback after making a decision is to try to minimize it by adopting some form of cognitive defense (see pp. 354-355 below). For example, if there is some ambiguity about just how bad the negative feedback might be (e.g., a vague warning that one might be socially disapproved by a powerful and important reference group), the person will minimize the probability that it will materialize or play down the bad consequences in one way or another. If this cognitive defense does not work, he may resort to denying that the unfavorable consequence is really bad—for example, by playing down the importance of the group to him, or by playing up the value of having an argument with them so as to establish his independence. In addition, he may use other cognitive defenses, such as expecting his actions to go unnoticed; playing up the good consequences that will counteract the bad; or, if worse comes to worse, denying that what he is doing is something that he wants to do.

Whenever these cognitive defenses are counteracted by impressive information and arguments from respected authorities (or by repeated indications of social disapproval from representatives of a reference group), the decision maker will no longer be able to bolster his decision effectively. He will then find himself in the throes of a postdecisional conflict—wanting and not wanting to carry out the policy to which he had committed himself. The stronger the commitment, the stronger will be the motivation to adhere to the policy and the stronger the negative feedback will have to be to challenge the decision sufficiently to rearouse the conflict.

PRELIMINARY EVIDENCE BEARING ON PREDECISIONAL BOLSTERING

In Festinger's 1964 volume, two experiments (one by Davidson and Kiesler, 1964; the other by Jecker, 1964) are presented as supporting the conclusion that bolstering of the dominant choice does not occur during the predecisional period, but is confined solely to the period after the person has committed himself. In commenting on the results of the two experiments, Festinger states: "One may regard the theoretical question as settled. There is a clear and undeniable difference between the cognitive processes that occur during the period of making a decision and those that occur after the decision has been made. Reevaluation of alternatives in the direction of favoring the chosen or disfavoring the rejected alternative, or both, is a post-decision phenomenon [pp. 30-31]." Later, in drawing the main conclusions of his book, Festinger states: "There is no evidence of any biasing influences before the decision is made [p. 153]."

We do not propose in this paper to undertake a full analysis of the Davidson-Kiesler and Jecker studies in order to evaluate the status of the evidence on the predecisional biasing issue. However, we shall try to indicate why we do not regard these two studies as settling the issue and we shall also discuss some of our own experimental work on this problem (Mann *et al.*, 1967) which points to a different conclusion.

The Davidson and Kiesler experiment required teenage girls to play the role of someone "responsible for hiring a man to become a first vice-president" in a firm they "own and control." Information cards about the fictitious applicants were given to the subjects, one at a time, and they were told that it is "impossible" to reach any decent decision until they had read all 10 cards. But after receiving only 4 cards, they were requested to rerank the candidates. Then they were asked to make their decision. Not surprisingly, there was no evidence of predecisional reevaluation.

Leaving aside the question of whether teenage girls who play the role of a top management executive really undergo a genuine predecisional conflict, there are other ambiguities in the Davidson and Kiesler experiment and this is acknowledged by Festinger. For example, we could interpret the results as supporting the conflict-theory assumption that whenever more information is expected, decision makers will anticipate later conflict from a hasty decision based on incomplete information, and therefore will be inclined to resist any tendency to engage in biased scanning of alternatives or to bolster the most attractive alternative. These conflict-reducing tendencies might become dominant, however, when the decision maker believes that he has all the relevant information for making an adequate decision, even though he knows that he will not have to commit himself until some later time.

Jecker's study, which was designed to avoid the ambiguities created by asking subjects to wait for more information before making their decision, has also been put forth as firmly supporting the dissonance prediction that there is no bolstering of the most attractive alternative before a decision is made. In this experiment high school girls were offered a choice between two phonograph records. Before making their choice some of the girls were given the impression that they had a good chance of receiving both records anyhow (low conflict) and others were led to believe that they had a very poor chance of getting both records (high conflict). After the decision was made, the degree of dissonance was manipulated by telling some of the girls that they actually would receive only one record (high dissonance) and by telling others that they could have both records (no dissonance). When subjects were then asked to rerate the records, only the high dissonance group showed a tendency to reevaluate the alternatives in the direction of bolstering their choice. Since no such tendency was manifested by the postdecisional ratings of the high conflict group, Jecker concluded that there was probably no reevaluation at all before the decision was made. But Jecker's study provides no direct evidence concerning predecisional changes and does not unambiguously support the conclusion that "spreading apart" of the alternatives occurs only postdecisionally. Festinger acknowledges that this study has some weaknesses, but when discussing the ambiguities in the initial experiment by Davidson and Kiesler, he argues that "these ambiguities vanish when one considers both experiments together [p. 30]." It seems to us, however, that no dependable conclusion can be drawn from two such ambiguous experiments, even though there is some nonoverlap in their respective weaknesses. Neither study meets the essential requirements for testing the differential predictions from dissonance theory and conflict theory. (Additional ambiguities are discussed by Zajonc, 1968.)

Since the two experiments by adherents of dissonance theory do not call into question our assumption that, under certain conditions, predecisional bolstering will occur, we consider the issue as unsettled. Moreover, we are able to point to preliminary findings from a study by Mann et al. (1967) which can be interpreted as evidence that undecided decision makers will sometimes attempt a resolution by distorting the attractiveness of the alternatives in order to avoid the unpleasant tension of predecisional conflict.

One of the prime conditions under which we expect this outcome has been mentioned in our discussion of the Davidson and Kiesler experiment. Our hypothesis is that when the decision maker believes that he has obtained all the relevant information for making the decision that will be available to him and yet he is still not altogether confident about the to-be-chosen alternative, he will tend to scan in a biased fashion the desirability of the more preferred alternative and will bolster it, so that it becomes increasingly more attractive than the less preferred alternative. This "spreading of the alternatives" is expected to occur predecisionally, before the person has committed himself, when he knows that he is still free to change his mind if he wishes. On the other hand, when the individual is led to believe that there is the possibility of obtaining new relevant information right up to the time of the decision, he will anticipate the possibility of subsequent regret if he should prematurely bolster one alternative; therefore he will show little or no tendency to spread the alternatives before he is required to commit himself.

In order to test this hypothesis, we designed the following experiment, which was carried out with women students at an Australian university (Mann *et al.*, 1967). The subjects were told that the experiment had to do with the effect of physiological stimulations on ability to carry out intellectual tasks and that therefore they would undergo three different forms of physiological stimulation (movement stimulation, taste stimulation, and auditory stimulation) before being tested on simple arithmetic problems. They were also informed that each of the three stressors had the *possibility* of producing temporary side effects such as nausea, dizziness, headache, and other unpleasant symptoms. Next they were asked to rate the attractiveness of the three types of stimulation, for the purpose of helping us understand their reactions and performance on the intellectual tests. Then, the experimenter took leave to check on the "movement" apparatus which the subjects learned had been giving trouble. When the experimenter reappeared she explained to the subjects that movement stimulation had to be cancelled and that there was now time for only one type of stimulation. The experimenter told them that they would be asked to choose between the two types of stimulation for which the apparatus was still functioning—taste and auditory stimulation. After assuring the subjects that there was no need to make up their minds for the present, the experimenter introduced the "information" manipulation. In one experimental condition, the subjects were led to expect more information; the experimenter said that information about the percentage of people suffering side effects from the different stimulations would be provided later on. In a contrasting condition, the subjects were told that no more information was available. Five minutes later during the waiting period, the experimenter—still acting as though perturbed by the apparatus failure—announced it might be a good idea because of the unexpected change in procedure to obtain another rating of subjective feelings about the physiological tests. After this second predecisional rating, the experimenter told the subjects in both conditions that from looking through the files it was now apparent that the same number of people had suffered side effects from the different stimulations. Each subject was then asked to state her actual choice (for the taste or auditory stimulation) and to estimate her chances of suffering side effects from the chosen and unchosen alternatives.

The results support the predictions from the conflict-theory hypothesis. When the subjects were led to believe that they would receive no additional relevant information, they tended to bolster the to-be-chosen alternative on the rerating, even though it was made clear to them that they were not being asked to make their decision and the rerating was merely a precautionary repetition because of the unforeseen change in procedure. In contrast, the subjects who were led to expect more information relevant to the decision showed significantly less bolstering of the to-be-chosen alternative; in fact, they showed no bolstering tendency at all. The latter finding is consistent with the outcome of the Davidson and Kiesler experiment (1964).

This pattern of results was obtained essentially in two different types of task settings. In one variation the subjects were kept mentally occupied during the predecisional period with an irrelevant cognitive task (Concealed Figures Test) while in the other variation they were asked to try to relax during the same waiting period. Both variations yielded essentially the same outcome.[2] The expectation of further information discouraged predecisional bolstering; the knowledge that there was no more information to be obtained stimulated predecisional bolstering.

It could be argued, of course, that the expectation of no more information makes any predecisional choice equivalent to a final decision. It is conceivable that when a tentative or implicit decision is reported, we are no longer dealing with a purely predecisional process (cf. Aronson, 1968; Festinger, 1964; Weick, 1965). But it should be noted that our subjects were unambiguously informed that they were not committing themselves at that time and hence this argument would require a new definition of the concept of "making a decision," with corresponding redefinitions of the terms predecisional and post-

---

[2]We found no significant difference between the magnitude of bolstering in the mentally occupied condition and in the relaxed condition. This finding appears to be inconsistent with Allen's finding (1965) that less dissonance reduction occurred (during the postdecisional period) when extraneous cognitive activity interfered with the subject's opportunity to think about the alternatives. The discrepancy between our findings and those of Allen might be due to a higher level of concentration required in Allen's irrelevant cognitive activity, or other situational variables, including perhaps the different time periods when the subjects were evaluating the alternatives.

decisional. In any case, our findings do not support the dissonance theory assumption that bolstering of the most attractive alternative occurs only after the decision maker has committed himself to that choice. The findings also call into question the dissonance position that precommitment and postcommitment processes are dynamically different and support our view that the usual differences between the way decision makers behave during the precommitment period and the way they behave during the postcommitment period are attributable to the correlated differences in the conditions that are usually present, which determine the nature of the conflict and the way it is likely to be resolved. One of the heuristic values of the latter assumption is that it leads us to formulate some new theoretical questions that might open up a new species of inquiry concerning aspects of decision making that have hitherto been neglected. Some of the main questions to be answered are these: What are the conditions that determine whether a here-and-now predecisional conflict will be hastily terminated by impulsive, distorted, or biased modes of resolution? What are the conditions that promote the more rational types of resolution, involving unbiased exploration of the available alternatives, objective weighing of the pros and cons, and creative thinking directed toward finding the best possible solution? Under what conditions will negative feedback that momentarily evokes postdecisional regret be rapidly dissipated with no changes in attitude or action? Under what conditions will it induce either: (a) temporary conflict followed by an impulsive reversal of the decision or (b) sustained postdecisional conflict accompanied by unbiased deliberation about the pros and cons of adhering to the decision and of adopting alternative courses of action?

In the remaining sections of this chapter, we shall present a number of hypotheses, based on or suggested by conflict-theory assumptions, that might provide some answers. The hypotheses point up the types of variables that warrant investigation.

ALTERNATIVE MODES OF CONFLICT RESOLUTION

According to our assumption about the two types of basic conflict, the mode of resolution depends on variations in the degree to which each type of conflict is aroused. Whenever the decision maker is preoccupied with the tension of a current conflict—either before the decision is made or after—he will seek to escape from it quickly with a minimum of current distress and effort. Thus he will rely upon evasive or impulsive mechanisms of conflict avoidance. These mechanisms involve superficial scanning of the alternatives, biased appraisals of the pros and cons, and selective bolstering of the most attractive alternative. They may also lead to thought-evasion strategies such as inducing an authority figure to decide for him or relying on coin-tossing or other chance devices for making a choice. All these modes of conflict resolution or evasion make for a quick reduction of the current level of conflict without the tension and work required for careful, intensive reflection. The absence of concern about possible future losses or setbacks will persist until the unvigilant decision maker encounters some powerful form of negative feedback.

When the decision maker anticipates the possibility of future regret about having committed himself to the decision, he becomes preoccupied with ensuring that subsequent conflicts do not develop. Taking account of the high cost of reversal, he will use modes of conflict resolution that involve attempts to prevent potential conflicts in the future and to plan for expected setbacks well in advance. The dominant tendency will be to strive toward rational, unbiased scanning of alternatives and open-minded seeking for relevant information in an effort to arrive at a sound solution that takes into consideration all the likely outcomes. The vigilant decision maker is therefore likely to hit upon a creative solution involving a compromise alternative or a recombination of alternatives. If he cannot discover a seemingly sound solution, he will try out other modes of resolution, which will still be directed toward preventing later conflict, rather than merely escaping current conflict. These, of course, will be painful modes of resolution because the decision maker must retain a high level of awareness and vigilance in order to deal with anticipated negative feedback.

Certain types of information about anticipated losses at a time when a person is undergoing predecisional conflict might function as a goad to anticipatory regret and might lead to inventive solutions to the decisional conflict. In order to arrive at new insights and breakthroughs in attempting to solve the problems of maximizing gains while minimizing losses, it is usually necessary for the decision maker to tolerate the tension of predecisional conflict during a relatively long period of deliberation, which requires resisting the temptation to achieve rapid closure by adopting one or another mode of cognitive defense to reduce the conflict. Effective resolutions are the gains that come from making non-impulsive decisions; they make it worth suffering the pangs of predecisional conflict instead of escaping from it by making a hasty choice.

FACTORS INFLUENCING THE MODE OF RESOLUTION

Whenever a person has to make an important life decision—such as whether or not to get married, to shift to a new career, or to follow a physician's advice about counteracting the threat of disease by cutting down on smoking, drinking, food intake, or some other source of pleasure—certain conditions are likely to produce a relatively low degree of anticipatory regret. In our observations of people facing such decisions, we have noted at least four sets of factors that interfere with effective decision making by inducing the decision maker to approach the task of selecting a course of action in a relatively hasty, superficial manner without engaging in the thoughtful, open-minded, and imaginative mental activity that characterizes the most successful, self-enhancing decisions.

1. *Perceived Remoteness of the Implementation of the Decision*: When a decision maker has the illusion that the time for making the decision or for putting it into action will be a long way off in the future, he is free to imagine or daydream about only the positive consequences of the most attractive choice.

2. *Perceived Absence of Choice*: When a decision maker has the illusion that only one course of action is open to him and believes that no alternatives will become available before he will be required to act, he will spend little time thinking about the issue and may be inclined to try to relax and enjoy it.

3. *Perceived Remoteness of Anticipated Negative Consequences*: When the person is aware of potential losses that could cause future regret from deciding in favor of the most attractive alternative, he will remain relatively uninfluenced by such considerations if he believes that the loss will not materialize within whatever time span he conceives as "the foreseeable future" (e.g., many young persons believe that smoking can cause lung cancer, but ignore this threat because they assume the danger to be at least 20 or more years hence).

4. *Signs of Low Social Importance of the Decision*: When the decision maker has the illusion that no one else will care very much about whether he sticks with his personal decision or that the cost of reversing it will be low, he will be inclined to ignore potential negative consequences since anticipatory regret can be dissipated simply by planning to switch to a new course of action whenever it may become necessary.

By and large, the more important a decision is perceived to be within the decision maker's community or subculture, the less likely that any of the above four conditions will be present. Nevertheless, studies of surgical patients suggest that certain of these conditions may crop up with a surprisingly high frequency, especially when the decision makers are facing serious dilemmas that strongly arouse their emotions. For example, when a physician tells an ill person that he urgently needs a major surgical operation, the patient is likely to have the illusion that he has no choice but to comply immediately. He is likely to think only of the tremendous gains to be expected from warding off the threat of loss of life and escaping from the current disease, pain, and incapacitation. Moreover, the prestige of the authoritative doctor and the impressive institution he represents makes it hard for the patient to consider the possibility that other, equally prestigeful doctors might disagree and perhaps suggest a better alternative. The illusion of having no choice but to comply is further enhanced by time pressures to decide immediately, as when a hospitalized patient is told that tomorrow morning is one of the rare times when the recommended surgeon will be available and when there is an opening in the busy schedule of the operating room. These factors summate to get the person to choose the recommended course of action (surgery) without exploring the unfavorable consequences and without seeking for information about alternative types of treatment that might be preferable.

When none of the above four conditions are met, negative feedback and postdecisional regret will usually be anticipated, which leads a person to mull over the decision, to seek the advice of other experts, and to try to arrive at the best possible solution.

We regard each of the four conditions stated above as extreme values of variables that can range from the extreme that makes for a low degree of anticipatory regret to some optimal value that makes for a high degree of anticipatory regret. Thus, we expect much more information seeking and open-minded deliberation when a life decision is made under conditions where the person is led to believe that (1) the decision will have to be implemented in the fairly near future (but not so immediately that one is under time pressure to decide rapidly); (2) two or more alternative courses of action are available as possible good candidates for his choice (but not so large a number of alternatives that the decision maker feels frustrated by the seemingly hopeless task of evaluating all of them carefully and therefore overreacts by not trying to evaluate any of them carefully); (3) the negative consequences of the most preferred choices might materialize within the near future (although not so imminently as to arouse emotional tension to the point where it interferes with cognitive efficiency or motivates defensive avoidance of the issue); and (4) his commitment to the decision will be regarded by significant others as sufficiently binding so that many persons in his social network will disapprove if he acts as though he were not committed (but without regarding the decision as so binding or so costly to undo that he will be inclined to postpone committing himself as long as possible and to relegate the decision to the remote future).

The parenthetical addenda in the foregoing paragraph call attention to our expectation that many of the critical variables are likely to have a nonmonotonic relation to the degree of open-mindedness and objectivity displayed by the decision maker. It is also conceivable that the degree to which anticipatory regret is momentarily aroused will be found to bear a nonmonotonic relation to cognitive efficiency and inventive problem solving, just as seems to be the case for anticipatory fear. (For a review of the relevant experimental evidence, see Janis, 1967, pp. 187-191.)

In addition to the four variables already discussed, several other conditions can be singled out as potential determinants of an optimally high level of anticipatory regret: (1) when two quite different alternatives are almost equally attractive (so that neither can be bolstered without regret about renouncing the other); (2) when the person is under pressure to decide for himself and believes that he must take full responsibility for the decision; (3) when there is salient, unambiguous information that undermines cognitive defenses that ordinarily enable one to minimize anticipated unpleasant consequences; and (4) when additional information about the consequences of the most attractive alternative is expected well before the time when one will be required to commit oneself to the decision. So far, experimental evidence is available only for the fourth of these conditions (see the discussion on pp. 351-354 above concerning the experiment by Mann *et al.*, 1967). Obviously, it will require an extensive amount of experimental research to investigate the eight variables we have described in relation to the mode of conflict resolution.

Observations from studies of counseling, self-study groups, therapy groups, and psychotherapy suggest that when a person's cognitive defenses are questioned by others, he may become motivated to appraise the alternatives more objectively and arrive at more inventive self-fulfilling decisions concerning his future. Such observations encourage us to hope that a new line of systematic research on the effects of counteracting cognitive defenses will be developed, which might provide some of the missing answers to our questions about the conditions under which a person will adopt a sound decision-making strategy that enables him to face up to the full implications of all the relevant conflict-inducing information available to him. By focusing on the conditions under which various types of cognitive defenses are facilitated or interfered with, in circumstances where people are undergoing attitude changes that lead to new courses of action, we may learn a great deal about how persuasive communications and other informational inputs, as well as personality predispositions, determine which mode of conflict resolution will become dominant.

References

Allen, V. L. Effect of extraneous cognitive activity on dissonance reduction. *Psychological Reports*, 1965, **16**, 1145-1151.

Aronson, E. Comment: Time — past, present, and future. In R. P. Abelson *et al.* (Eds.), *Theories of cognitive consistency: A sourcebook.* Chicago: Rand McNally, 1968, in press.

Cyert, R. B., Simon, H. A., & Trow, D. B. Observation of a business decision. *Journal of Business*, 1956, **29**, 237-248.

Davidson, J. R., & Kiesler, S. B. Cognitive behavior before and after decisions. In L. Festinger (Ed.), *Conflict, decision and dissonance.* Stanford, Calif.: Stanford University Press, 1964. Pp. 10-19.

Egbert, L., Battit, G., Welch, C., & Bartlett, M. Reduction of postoperative pain by encouragement and instruction of patients. *New England Journal of Medicine*, 1964, **270**, 825-827.

Festinger, L. *A theory of cognitive dissonance.* Evanston, Ill.: Row Peterson, 1957.

Festinger, L. (Ed.) *Conflict, decision and dissonance.* Stanford, Calif.: Stanford University Press, 1964.

Gerard, H. B., Blevans, S. A., & Malcolm, T. Self-evaluation and the evaluation of choice alternatives. *Journal of Personality*, 1964, **32**, 395-410.

Greenbaum, C. W., Cohn, A., & Krauss, R. M. Choice, negative information, and attractiveness of tasks. *Journal of Personality*, 1965, **33**, 46-49.

Hovland, C. I., Janis, I. L., & Kelley, H. H. *Communication and persuasion.* New Haven: Yale University Press, 1953.

Janis, I. L. Motivational effects of different sequential arrangements of conflicting arguments: A theoretical analysis. In C. I. Hovland (Ed.), *The order of presentation in persuasion.* New Haven: Yale University Press, 1957. Pp. 170-186.

Janis, I. L. *Psychological stress.* New York: Wiley, 1958.

Janis, I. L. Motivational factors in the resolution of decisional conflicts. In M. R. Jones (Ed.), *Nebraska symposium on motivation.* Vol. 7. Lincoln, Neb.: University of Nebraska Press, 1959. Pp. 198-231.

Janis, I. L. Effects of fear arousal on attitude change: Recent developments in theory and experimental research. In L. Berkowitz (Ed.), *Advances in experimental social psychology*. Vol. 3. New York: Academic Press, 1967. Pp. 166-224.

Janis, I. L. Stages in the decision-making process. In R. P. Abelson *et al.* (Eds.), *Theories of cognitive consistency: A sourcebook*. Chicago: Rand McNally, 1968, in press. (a)

Janis, I. L. Attitude change via role playing. In R. P. Abelson *et al.* (Eds.), *Theories of cognitive consistency: A sourcebook*. Chicago: Rand McNally, 1968, in press. (b)

Janis, I. L., Hovland, C. I., Field, P. B., Linton, H., Graham, E., Cohen, A. R., Rife, D., Abelson, R. P., Lesser, G. S., & King, B. T. *Personality and persuasibility*. New Haven: Yale University Press, 1959.

Janis, I. L., & Kahn, M. Factors influencing tolerance for deprivation. Unpublished progress report, NIMH Grant No. MH 08564, December 1966.

Janis, I. L., & Mann, L. Effectiveness of emotional role-playing in modifying smoking habits and attitudes. *Journal of Experimental Research in Personality*, 1965, 1, 84-90.

Janis, I. L., & Terwilliger, R. An experimental study of psychological resistance to fear-arousing communications. *Journal of Abnormal and Social Psychology*, 1962, 65, 403-410.

Jecker, J. D. The cognitive effects of conflict and dissonance. In L. Festinger (Ed.), *Conflict, decision and dissonance*. Stanford, Calif.: Stanford University Press, 1964. Pp. 21-32.

Kiesler, C. A. Commitment. In R. P. Abelson *et al.* (Eds.), *Theories of cognitive consistency: A sourcebook*. Chicago: Rand McNally, 1968, in press.

Lewin, K. *Field theory in social science*. New York: Harper, 1951.

McGuire, W. J. Inducing resistance to persuasion: Some contemporary approaches. In L. Berkowitz (Ed.), *Advances in experimental social psychology*. Vol. 1. New York: Academic Press, 1964. Pp. 191-229.

Malewski, A. The influence of positive and negative self-evaluation on post-decisional dissonance. *Polish Sociological Bulletin*, 1962, 3-4, 39-49.

Mann, L. The effect of commitment on post-decisional bolstering. Unpublished paper, University of Melbourne, 1967. (a)

Mann, L. The effects of emotional role playing on desire to modify smoking habits. *Journal of Experimental Social Psychology*, 1967, 3, 334-348. (b)

Mann, L., & Janis, I. L. A follow-up study on the long-term effects of emotional role playing, *Journal of Personality and Social Psychology*, 1968, 8, 339-342.

Mann, L., Janis, I. L., & Chaplin, R. The effects of anticipation of forthcoming information on predecisional processes, Mimeographed preprint, 1967.

Mausner, B. Report on a smoking clinic. *American Psychologist*, 1966, 21, 251-255.

Miller, J. C. Effects of leadership style and meeting sequence on emotional responses in smoking groups. Unpublished doctoral dissertation, Yale University, 1966.

United States Surgeon General. *Report on smoking and health*. Washington, D.C.: United States Government Printing Office, 1964.

Walster, E. The temporal sequence of post-decision processes. In L. Festinger (Ed.), *Conflict, decision, and dissonance*. Stanford, Calif.: Stanford University Press, 1964. Pp. 112-127.

Weick, K. E. When prophecy pales: The fate of dissonance theory. *Psychological Reports*, 1965, 16, 1261-1275.

Zajonc, R. Cognitive processes. In G. Lindzey & E. Aronson (Eds.). *Handbook of social psychology*. (2nd ed.) Reading, Mass.: Addison-Wesley, 1968, in press.

PART IV: CONCLUSIONS

other similar definitions may be said to stress the discriminative stimulus function of the attitude object, with minor emphasis on the conditioned stimulus function (since it may be assumed that a portion of the response tendencies in relation to an object may be emotional).

Definitions that refer to readiness to respond but specify an evaluative dimension (Krech et al., 1962; Osgood, et al., 1957; Sarnoff, 1960) appear to lay approximately equal stress on conditioned and discriminative stimulus functions. That is, the tendency to respond favorably, say, may include the tendency to respond with positive emotional reactions (e.g., affection) and instrumental responses (e.g., "striving for" to use Staats' term). It may be noted that definitions in terms of evaluative predispositions serve not only to restrict the range of response tendencies in regard to an object that are considered to comprise the attitude, but also to restrict the range of objects regarded as significant attitude objects. For example, doors would not be significant attitude objects since, although one has a considerable repertory of response tendencies regarding doors, these responses are typically not to be construed in terms of an evaluative dimension.

Attitude definitions that refer to affective reactions to an object (Thurstone, 1931) or to "implicit drive-producing" reactions (Doob, 1947) have apparently focused the conception of attitude on the conditioned stimulus function.

None of the attitude definitions sampled here makes explicit reference to a reinforcing stimulus function. Although those definitions that refer to a conditioned stimulus function may be seen as implying a reinforcing property (due to the acquired reinforcing properties of classically conditioned stimuli), nonetheless such a function is typically not stressed in conceptual definitions of attitude. Staats' own treatment is, of course, an exception to this observation. The question of the relation between reinforcing, discriminative, and conditioned stimulus functions will be considered critically below in connection with a discussion of Staats' chapter.

Perhaps the most widespread, currently, of the various attitude definitions is that which proposes to divide the construct attitude into three components — affects (or emotions), cognitions (or beliefs or opinions), and action tendencies. The definition given by Krech et al. is of this type as are the formulations of Insko and Schopler (1967), Rosenberg and Hovland (1960), Smith et al. (1956), and others. One of the virtues of this type of definition is that it incorporates a conceptual separation of the conditioned stimulus (affect or emotion) and discriminative stimulus (cognition and action tendency) functions of attitude objects. Because this definition facilitates the transition from the conceptual language of attitudes to stimulus-response language, it will be used as the basis for discussing the general field of attitude theory, which employs both of these languages, in the following sections of this chapter.

The point of this brief discussion has been that, despite the many ways in which a conceptual definition of attitude can be and has been stated in words, there are a limited number of themes that are expressed in these definitions. These themes can be summarized, respectively, as the conditioned, discriminative, and reinforcing stimulus functions attributed to attitude objects. The various definitions of attitude can be characterized in terms of which of these three functions is (are) attributed to attitude objects and in terms of what restrictions there are, if any, on the types of responses or stimuli that are considered to be attitudinal.

A FRAMEWORK FOR THE THEORETICAL STUDY OF ATTITUDES

In the first chapter of this volume, Ostrom discussed the diversity of theoretical approaches to the study of attitudes. The intervening chapters have presented a wide sampling of this theoretical diversity. For the most part, the approaches put forth by individual theorists should be construed as elements of a larger body of attitude theory. The remainder of this chapter will consist of an attempt to describe the structure of this larger body of theory. The aims of this description will be (a) to view the position of attitude as a theoretical construct in psychological theory, (b) to allow some conclusions about competition versus complementarity among attitude theories, and (c) to provide a common framework for considering the distinct contributions of individual theorists.

The proposed conception of attitude theory, presented schematically in Fig. 1, is organized around the definition of attitude as a trichotomy consisting of cognitions, emotions, and action tendencies. "Habit" has been substituted for the less specific "action tendency" for purposes of integrating attitude theory with other areas of psychological theory.

In Fig. 1, four areas of psychological theory are designated as especially applicable to the study of attitudes:

1. *Learning theory* offers an account of the processes involved in storing the residues of direct and symbolic experience with an attitude object as habits, cognitions, and emotions. It should be emphasized that Fig. 1 is not intended to represent the content of any specific learning theories. The learning process has been subdivided

under the labels "instrumental learning," "cognitive learning," and "classical conditioning" solely as a means of indicating that one may conceive habit-, cognition-, and emotion-acquisition as theoretically separable processes. Similarly, the labeling of specific categories of antecedent experiences is only intended to be suggestive; it is not meant to imply, for example, that cognitions are acquired only from exposure to symbolic communications or that symbolic communications cannot be involved in emotion-acquisition.

2. *Behavior theory* accounts for performance as a function of learned habits, cognitions, and emotions, in combination with current stimulus conditions. Although no specific interpretation of behavior theory is intended in Fig. 1, a minimal assumption is that all three attitude components enter into the determination of performance. Most versions of behavior theory accord a stop-go function to emotions — either inhibiting or energizing responding. The details of performance (skilled motor reactions) are typically assumed to be organized in the form of habits — specific organizations of efferent activity coordinated with afferent input. The role of cognition is less well agreed upon. For some theorists, cognitive *expectations* consisting of stimulus-response-reinforcer relationships (cf. MacCorquodale & Meehl, 1954; Tolman, 1959) are involved in the organization of performance. For others (e.g., Bandura, 1965; Miller, Galanter, & Pribram, 1960; Nuttin & Greenwald, 1968) the *sequencing* of performance of habit units is organized at the cognitive level.

3. *Theory of cognitive information processing* explains the transformations in information input that occur prior to information storage as the cognition component of attitude.

4. *Theory of component interaction* explains the transformations that occur in attitude components (particularly cognitions) subsequent to storage.[1]

In practice, these four areas of theory can be reduced to two — *learning-behavior theory* and *cognitive integration theory* — in recog-

---

[1]It may be noted that perceptual theory has not explicitly been included in Fig. 1. It is to be understood, however, that the broad heading "cognitive processes" includes perceptual processes. Additionally, no reference has been made here to attitude measurement theory. Psychological measurement theory is, of course, independent of content area and rightly has no place in the present framework. Nonetheless, attitude measurement theorists have frequently made assumptions about attitude processes (see Part II of Fishbein, 1967). Since these assumptions typically concern the manner in which an attitude becomes manifest in behavior (i.e., for purposes of measurement) such theoretical statements can be considered as belonging in the behavior theory area of the present framework.

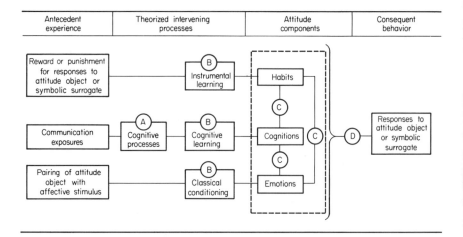

| Antecedent experience | Theorized intervening processes | Attitude components | Consequent behavior |

FIG. 1.   Schematic framework for analysis of attitude theory. The four areas of attitude theory discussed in the text are identified by letters as follows: A, theory of cognitive information processing; B, learning theory; C, theory of attitude component interaction; D, behavior theory. Attitude is identified as a complex consisting of the three intervening constructs enclosed in the dashed rectangle. These component constructs are assumed to be acquired through learning processes from a variety of categories of antecedent experience and, in combination, to determine subsequent performance relating to the attitude object.

nition of substantial overlap in terminology and theoretical principles between learning theory and behavior theory, on the one hand, and between theoretical analyses of prestorage and poststorage processes affecting cognitions, on the other. In learning-behavior theory, the basic discourse is in terms of stimulus and response, and the basic theoretical problem is specification of the mechanisms linking response to stimulus. In cognitive integration theory (as used here), discourse is in terms of cognitive structures and cognitive elements, while the basic theoretical problem is to establish the mechanisms linking elements within structures. In that the various mechanisms currently treated under the "cognitive integration" heading may reasonably be assumed to be learned, it may ultimately be possible to reduce or translate cognitive integration theory to the language of learning-behavior theory. At present, this possibility must be regarded as remote.[2]

_____

[2]To be more specific, before learning-behavior theory can be applied successfully to phenomena of cognitive integration, it will be necessary (a) to determine what are the units from which complex cognitive responses are constructed, (b) to identify the primary discriminative stimuli for cognitive responses, and (c) to adapt learning-behavior principles that typically account for repetitive aspects of performance to explain the flexibility of cognitive integration mechanisms.

IMPLICATIONS FOR ATTITUDE DEFINITION

The portion of Fig. 1 that one chooses to label "attitude" varies with one's definition of attitude. To identify attitude with the total set of object-relevant habits, cognitions, and emotions corresponds to a broad definition of attitude such as Allport's. The popular narrower definitions interpret attitude as designating all or some portion of the evaluative aspect of the set of object-related components. Some theorists (see especially Doob, 1947; Rosenberg & Hovland, 1960, p. 3) prefer to conceive attitude as a hypothetical construct of a unitary nature that mediates three categories of response to the attitude object— affective, cognitive, and "overt action." Figure 1 does not present this view of attitude since it is one that seems more difficult to integrate with learning-behavior theory than is the conception of attitude as identified with the total set (or with some attribute of the set) of object-related habits, cognitions, and emotions, with these components conceived as intervening hypothetical constructs rather than as overt response categories. While it may be acknowledged that one can design response measures to tap the components with satisfactory separation, it does not seem appropriate to view naturally occurring attitude-guided behavior as being so conveniently compartmentalized. Everyday behavior is more properly regarded as a synthesis of cognitive, habitual, and emotional elements; when these components are successfully studied in isolation, it is because the experimenter has satisfactorily designed a situation in which one of the components is the primary determinant of behavior variance while the other two are controlled. The chief advantage to the Doob and Rosenberg-Hovland conceptions is that they contain a built-in explanation for affective-cognitive-behavioral consistency. At the same time, observations of inconsistency (e.g., Festinger, 1964; Greenwald, 1965b) are embarassing to this view. Further, the unitary conception of attitude is not at all necessary to account for observed consistency; the set of habits, cognitions, and emotions identified as attitude in Fig. 1 would be expected to display substantial internal consistency strictly on the grounds that (a) the components all derive from the experience of a single individual, (b) a single learning situation may simultaneously satisfy the conditions necessary for habit-, cognition-, and emotion-acquisition, and (c) a certain portion of the residual inconsistency may be removed by the operation of intercomponent organizing processes.

COMPETITION VERSUS COMPLEMENTARITY AMONG THEORIES

The framework presented in Fig. 1 enables some conclusions about the extent to which various theories may be seen as competing with each other as opposed to complementing one another in the analysis of attitude phenomena. For example, as currently formulated, learning-behavior theories are largely *not* competing with cognitive integration theories. (An exception to this observation—learning versus cognitive integration interpretations of cognitive consistency phenomena—will be discussed on p. 385.) The various cognitive integration theories deal with domains of attitude processes to which, for the most part, learning-behavior theory has not yet been applied with success (see footnote 2). This, it is important to note, is not to say that learning-behavior theories and cognitive integration theories do not deal with the same independent and dependent variables. For example, the attitudinal effects of variables such as incentive and effort can be analyzed in either theoretical context. While different theories make different predictions about the attitudinal effects of these variables (cf. Aronson, 1961; Festinger & Carlsmith, 1959; Janis & Gilmore, 1965; Lott, 1963, these predictions need not be regarded as competing ones; for example, it is possible that predictions from both Hullian theory and dissonance theory about attitudinal effects of effort may simultaneously be valid (see Fromkin, in press). If it happens that data from a given experiment turn out to support only the prediction from dissonance theory, this likely should be interpreted as indicating that the experimental manipulations had tapped more deeply into the domain of dissonance theory than into that of Hullian theory—not that Hull's "competing" theory was invalid.

Competition between theories will be obtained, in general, within each of the two broad areas of attitude theory. Thus, as is well-known, there are competing theoretical interpretations of learning processes. Also, there is room for complementarity within each area of theory as is argued, for example, by those "two-factor" theorists who advocate one set of principles for instrumental learning and another for classical conditioning. Within the cognitive integration area, it is sometimes difficult to determine the degree of competition or complementarity among theories. For example, for the varieties of cognitive consistency theory (most notably, those of Heider, Osgood, and Festinger), it is not clear to what extent the alternative forms are competitive, isomorphic, or possibly complementary by virtue of nonoverlapping domains (cf. Abelson, 1968). Similarly, the extent of competition between cognitive consistency formulations, on the one hand, and those cognitive integration formulations not based on the consistency principle (for example, those presented in Chapters 9 through 13 of this volume), on the other, is not readily apparent. A reason for this difficulty is that the domains of the various cognitive integration formulations have rarely been specified in satisfactory detail. This circumstance is understandable in an area of theory that is in a very active stage of development and is, in effect, in the process of finding its own boundaries. The fact that some boundary-drawing attempts are being made is encouraging (see, for example, the attempts by Aronson and Rosenberg to establish domains for the dissonance and "incentive" formulations, reported in their chapters in Feldman, 1966).

CONTRIBUTIONS TO ATTITUDE THEORY

The organization of chapters in this volume has been guided by some of the considerations that entered into the construction of Fig. 1. It has been convenient to present contributions with a learning-behavior theory orientation first, followed by cognitive integration theory approaches. In reviewing the content of these chapters and attempting to summarize each in terms of its contribution to the larger body of attitude theory, this same ordering will be preserved.[3]

LEARNING-BEHAVIOR THEORY CONTRIBUTIONS: S-R FORMULATIONS

Staats

In Staats' integrated application of learning principles to human motivational phenomena, classical conditioning is considered to be the fundamental process of attitude acquisition. Thus, attitude is defined essentially as an affective or emotional response to a stimulus (attitude object). However, the instrumental learning (habit formation) process plays an essential role in attitude phenomena in that classical conditioning experiences are assumed to occur primarily in the context of instrumental reward or punishment situations; further, a stimulus with acquired attitudinal (emotional) value is assumed to have acquired the power to serve as a positive or negative reinforcer for further instrumental learning. In addition to functioning as an emotional stimulus and a reinforcing stimulus, an attitude object acquires discriminative stimulus function; that is, since certain responses made "to" the attitude object are rewarded, the attitude object comes to serve as a signal that such responses are appropriate. Each of

---

[3]Most of the contributing authors have been kind enough to comment on an earlier draft of these summaries, for which the writer is grateful. Since there have been some revisions and additions subsequent to that earlier draft, it should not be assumed that the contributors necessarily endorse the remarks made about their work.

the three stimulus functions of the attitude object can serve as the basis of a technique for assessing the attitude; however, Staats suggests that it is typically most efficient to observe the verbal behavior that is controlled by the attitude object in its discriminative stimulus capacity. It seems appropriate to treat such verbal behavior as the equivalent of what is identified as the cognitive component of an attitude in Fig. 1. Thus, while Staats prefers to identify the term attitude specifically with the emotional component of Fig. 1, it is apparent that his formulation leads to the prediction of an interrelated attitudinal system of emotions, habits, and cognitions (verbal behavior).

The wealth of illustration provided by Staats, particularly from clinical and educational settings, indicates the ease with which his integrated set of learning principles can be transferred from laboratory to complex natural situations. One area of difficulty in accepting this integrated set of principles, however, concerns the presumed relation between the acquired reinforcing and discriminative functions of attitudinal stimuli.

Consider, for example, the attitude of the white racist toward Negroes. The attitude is clearly a negative one of "striving against" in Staats' terms; the attitude object as discriminative stimulus controls verbal and other behaviors of negative evaluation. However, the attitude may be based on positive reinforcement for anti-Negro behavior; that is, hostile actions may be reinforced by social approval, by pleasurable feelings from unpunished aggression, etc. Thus, as a conditioned stimulus, the Negro as attitude object should be conditioned to positive emotional reactions and should serve as a positive reinforcing stimulus; for this reason, the racist may be expected to take actions that would bring him into the presence of Negroes, thereby allowing him to gain the rewards of exercising his prejudice. In this illustration, clearly, it would not be equivalent to measure the racist's attitude toward Negroes in terms of any of the three stimulus functions; only the discriminative stimulus function would indicate what is commonly agreed on as the negative aspect of the prejudicial attitude.

Additionally, it could be noted that positive attitudes can be learned by combinations of reward for "striving for" and punishment for "striving against." With equal reward and punishment experience, only the discriminative stimulus function of the attitude object would reflect the positive attitude, while the conditioned and reinforcing stimulus functions would, on balance, be neutral or ambivalent.

Although these illustrations appear difficult for Staats' analysis, in fact they can be accommodated within his set of integrated S-R principles simply by an additional extension of the principles to include *response-correlated* stimuli. That is, for positive attitudes, the stimuli (proprioceptive, visual, verbal, etc.) contingent on "striving for" responses would acquire positive conditioned emotional value and positive reinforcing function; those produced by "striving against" responses would acquire negative conditioned and reinforcing value. For negative attitudes, these functions of response-correlated stimuli would be opposite in direction (cf. Mowrer, 1960).

In the further extension of Staats' principles suggested here, an object would be recognizable as the object of a positive or negative attitude primarily in terms of its discriminative stimulus function. The conditioned and reinforcing stimulus functions of the attitude object would depend on the particular combination of learning experiences involving reward and punishment that have contributed to the formation of the attitude and would not necessarily be reliable indicators of the positive or negative aspect of the attitude. These conditioned and reinforcing functions would be borne primarily by response-correlated stimuli that have been more consistently associated with a specific type of reinforcement (reward or punishment) than has the attitude object itself. This conclusion, it may be noted, is consistent with those definitions of attitude that emphasize the discriminative stimulus function of attitude objects with specific reference to evaluative responses.

Lott and Lott

The orientation of Lott and Lott is similar to that of Staats in making reference to the multiple effects of the classical conditioning situation which they take to be the basic mechanism of acquisition of attitudes. (Although their research has concerned only persons as attitude objects, it is apparent that their analysis is potentially more general.) In place of Staats' "discriminative stimulus function" of attitude objects, the Lotts refer to a "motivating" function. The concepts of discriminative stimulus and incentive motivation have much formal similarity in learning-behavior theory, and the difference between Staats' and the Lotts' formulations concerning this point may be interpreted at least in part as a difference between the Skinnerian and Hull-Spence terminologies, respectively, for dealing with a given set of experimental data (cf. Kimble, 1961, pp. 170ff).

In discussing the classical conditioning process by which emotional properties are transferred between stimuli, the Lotts tie their analysis to the anticipatory goal response $(r_g\text{-}s_g)$ mechanism of Hull-Spence theory. Their interpretation of the goal response (R_G) is broad, including "evaluative verbal, autonomic, and central reactions which are only partially overt but which we assume human beings reliably make to rewarding objects or situations (p. 69)." The Lotts further acknowledge that the goal-response mechanism functions strictly as a hypothetical construct in their analysis.

In sum, the Lotts' formulation, like Staats', represents a synthesis of S-R principles drawn from the empirical and theoretical work of Hull, Spence, Skinner, and others. The Lotts have employed the Hull-Spence theoretical language in making their synthesis, while Staats has incorporated some Skinnerian terms. By appropriate translation between the two systems, it may be expected that different theoretical predictions would not be generated. Significant differences between the work of Staats and the Lotts are to be found principally in the types of research problems suggested by their respective formulations.

Rosnow

Rosnow's experiments illustrate the operation of a conditioning process in situations employing sequenced opposing communications with reward or punishment administered at a selected point during the sequence. His interpretation, stated in terms of a "spread of effect," assumes that covert responses of agreeing with a persuasive argument are reinforced by temporal proximity of the argument to a reward and are weakened by proximity of the argument to a punishment. More specifically, Rosnow assumes (p. 94ff) that the stimulus of a persuasive argument elicits an agreeing response and that reward and punishment elicit characteristic goal responses that can positively or negatively reinforce this agreeing response. Rosnow's theoretical paradigm thus corresponds to a rather special "passive instrumental conditioning" experimental situation that has been studied by Konorski (1950), one that is different in several respects from Thorndike's (1933) serial trial and error paradigm for which the spread of effect interpretation has been offered. Thus, there are grounds for doubt as to whether or not Thorndike's spread of effect should be expected (in terms of its original formulation) to generalize to Rosnow's paradigm. Regardless, Rosnow's crucial assumption that persuasive arguments elicit covert agreeing responses can be compared with available data.

In several experiments reported by Greenwald (this volume), the probability of an agreeing response to a persuasive argument was found to be correlated reliably with initial attitude on the issue to which the argument was relevant; there was a strong tendency for subjects to respond by *disagreeing* with arguments opposing their initial attitudes. Thus Rosnow's assumption is apparently invalid when the experimental issue is one for which the subjects have opposing pre-experimental attitudes. On the other hand, Weiss (this volume) reported several experiments in which persuasive arguments apparently functioned as positive reinforcers, suggesting that they may have elicited agreeing responses. Since Weiss' experiments employed issues for which pre-experimental attitudes were weak or absent, it appears that Rosnow's assumption may be valid under conditions of a neutral or nonexistent prior attitude.

Rosnow's spread of effect hypothesis may be useful in interpreting the rather puzzling set of findings obtained in studies employing noncontingent rewards presented near in time to receipt of a persuasive communication (see, for example, Dabbs & Janis, 1965). If Rosnow is correct, such experiments might be interpreted in terms of covert responses to the experimental situation that are selectively strengthened as a function of their proximity to the noncontingent reward. On the other hand, as Rosnow acknowledges, it is possible that a simpler classical conditioning explanation may offer the most satisfactory account of his and other data. In this alternative explanation, the persuasive argument is viewed as a stimulus that acquires the power to elicit a positive (or negative) affective response as a function of its temporal proximity to a noncontingent reward (or punishment).

Weiss

Weiss' chapter presents a theoretical account of attitude formation in which the formal relations among the constructs of Hull-Spence behavior theory are mapped onto the attitude domain. This formulation is easy enough to set into the Fig. 1 framework if Weiss is interpreted as making an equation between *habit* and *opinion response,* and if his experiments are interpreted as demonstrating that opinion responses, like other habits, are acquired as a positive function of numbers of reinforced trials, immediacy of reinforcement, etc. However, Weiss notes that his theorization concerning attitudes may bear only formal similarity to the Hull-Spence theory. Rather than assuming that opinion responses are habits as defined by Hull, Weiss assumes that they function theoretically in the manner that habits function in Hull-Spence theory. If Weiss had chosen to identify his attitude constructs with those of Hull-Spence theory, he would be open to possible criticism due to the content of some of his identifications. For example, equating the presentation of a supporting response with the reinforcement operation might be difficult to justify. However, to point out that presentation of supporting arguments functions as an independent variable in persuasion experiments in the same fashion that reinforcement functions in conditioning experiments is a remarkable observation and one that should not be criticized on the grounds that it stretches the imagination to assume that these two variables are equivalents—Weiss makes no such assumption.

The data reported by Weiss should not be evaluated only in terms of the impressive success of their fit with the predictions derived from the Hull-Spence theory analogy. In the abstractness of Weiss' model, one tends to lose sight of the fact that his experiments provide empirical data with potential significance beyond their service in tests of his theoretical model. It is particularly interesting to note that Weiss' experiments typically involve learning of verbal opinion responses following which the subject is tested for performance of nonverbal responses (most often lever movements) to verbal stimuli derived from the learned opinions. Such data are clearly relevant to the recently developing interest in the relation between cognitive attitude change and change in nonverbal attitude-relevant performance (cf. Festinger, 1964; Greenwald, 1965a, 1965b; Insko & Schopler, 1967). A note of caution is warranted in attempting to generalize Weiss' findings since, as Weiss has been careful to note, one of the boundary conditions of his analysis has been the assumption of neutral or nonexistent prior attitudes. Because Weiss has been careful to select opinion issues that fall within this boundary condition, it may well be that the communications used in his experiments have more of the character of informational communications (such as classroom lectures) than do most persuasive messages.

LEARNING-BEHAVIOR THEORY CONTRIBUTIONS: ECLECTIC FORMULATIONS

Greenwald

Greenwald's chapter concludes by suggesting that attitude modification by persuasive communication may be conceived in terms of the combined operation of two processes: (a) cognitive response to persuasion and (b) cognitive learning. This position was arrived at through an empirical investigation of the adequacy of models of persuasion that assume the cognitive component of attitude to be modified by learning of the content of persuasive communications. Greenwald's experimental findings indicated that the cognitive learning explanation could be successful only if it took into account the communication-recipient's rehearsal of his own cognitive reactions to

committed to a self-rating (e.g., middle-of-the-road) than to his content position, end-anchor change is expected to result predominantly in content position change.

The Ostrom-Upshaw analysis deals with cognitive effects of communications designed to change the audience's end anchors in regard to a particular judgment dimension. While such communications are not common in laboratory attitude change experiments, they occur frequently in nonlaboratory situations. An example is the manipulation of the end points of the judgment dimension pertaining to the pricing of a product in order to influence the buyer's perception of the price he wants to pay. To illustrate, knowing yourself to be very thrifty (self-rating), are you more willing to spend $400 on a color television set if you perceive the price range of color TV sets to be $400-$600 as opposed to $300-$600? It seems possible that communications directed at perspective alteration may derive strong advantages from the fact that the communicator does not appear to be attempting to persuade his audience. An important question regarding perspective-manipulating communications that remains to be answered concerns the stability or persistence of their effects relative to those produced by communications that advocate specific content positions.

Brock

Brock has marshaled a varied collection of evidence to support an empirical relation between perceived unavailability of information and information value. As Brock notes in the conclusion of his chapter, it is possible that a motivational principle may explain this empirical relationship, but it is perhaps premature to identify this motive as, for example, a *need for uniqueness* that can be satisfied by the possession of not generally available information.

Until Brock's "commodity" analysis has been translated more fully from its economic inspiration into psychological theoretical terms, it will be difficult to appraise his "unavailability principle" in terms of some basic theoretical criteria, such as its boundary conditions. For example, life would be difficult if the most attractive objects in one's environment were the most unavailable ones. That is, there must be some psychological force (dissonance reduction?) that complements the unavailability principle under some circumstances, so that available commodities are perceived to be attractive and unavailable ones are rejected ("sour grapes"). Further, if there is a uniqueness need at the basis of the unavailability principle, is this a need dimension along which individuals differ so that commodity manipulations might be expected reliably to be more effective for some individuals than for others?

Irrespective of the answers to these questions, it is obvious that Brock's analysis is directed at one of the basic psychological problems connected with the study of attitudes — specifically, the determinants of acceptance or rejection of potentially persuasive information. In connection with the empirical evidence bearing on Brock's unavailability principle, it may be noted that some of the supporting laboratory findings have produced relatively weak statistical confirmation of predicted effects. Such findings should likely not be held against the practical value of the theory, since it may be decidedly more difficult to manipulate perceived unavailability of information in a laboratory setting than it is in natural situations in which selective communication is the rule rather than the exception.

COGNITIVE INTEGRATION THEORY CONTRIBUTIONS: MOTIVATIONAL FORMULATIONS

Brehm

Brehm's reactance formulation asserts that actual or implied threats to a valued attitudinal freedom (that is, the freedom to arrive at one's own opinion) will create a tendency to reject the position toward which one is being coerced and to accept an opposing position. Reactance, or motivation to re-establish lost or threatened freedoms, is thus assumed to be a directing force for cognitive processes in coercive persuasion situations. Brehm's analysis is somewhat unusual among theories of attitude processes in that the phenomenon it is fundamentally concerned with is lack of change or negative change, rather than positive change, in response to persuasive communications. The reactance formulation is thus a potential competitor with Hovland's (1959) analysis of the ineffectiveness of mass media persuasion attempts and McGuire's (1964) "inoculation" analysis of resistance to persuasion.

A number of questions may be raised concerning the boundary conditions of the reactance formulation. Specifically: (a) As a motivational state, may reactance be expected to vary reliably across individuals, as do other motivational states such as achievement or affiliation? (cf. Brehm, 1966, p. 127) (b) Since the goal condition of reactance motivation is the restoration or exercise of decision freedom, might the intensity of the motive be assumed to decrease following successful exercise of decision freedom? (c) Reactance is hypothesized to apply only to valued decision freedoms. Is there perhaps a complementary motive state, such as dependence, that is satisfied by abdicating one's decision freedom to others? If so, under what conditions would decision freedom be valued and under what conditions would one wish to delegate or abdicate one's decision freedom? (cf. Brehm, 1966, p. 126) (d) What are the persistence characteristics of reactance effects? If one has shifted opinion in response to a threat to decision freedom, will the shift persist in the face of elimination of the threat? In sum, reactance theory raises a number of interesting questions for further research; such research is, in fact, necessary in order to determine the boundary conditions within which reactance manipulations may be expected to affect cognitive processes.

Some interesting translations can be made between Brock's analysis of commodity value and Brehm's reactance formulation. Both analyses start with a boundary condition concerning importance; for Brock, the individual must be interested in possessing a given commodity; while, for Brehm, a given decision freedom must be a valued one. In both analyses, the introduction of a psychological barrier (unavailability for Brock, eliminated or threatened freedom for Brehm) increases the value of whatever is perceived to be on the other side of the barrier. Both authors cite the same types of data in support of their formulations. The chief difference between the two formulations resides in the different psychological interpretations of the effects of the barrier. For Brehm, the existence of the barrier provokes a *negative* motivational state, reactance; reappraisal of the forbidden object or action is conceived as being in the interest of escaping or avoiding a negative condition. On the other hand, Brock's analysis, while not committed to a specific psychological process, implies an approach rather than an avoidance or escape dynamic underlying reevaluation; the object behind the barrier, that is, becomes more *desirable* by perception of its unavailability.

Baron
Janis and Mann

The chapters by Janis and Mann and by Baron both deal with cognitive attitude change as a potential means of reducing or eliminating the discomfort of intrapsychic conflict. The different theoretical approaches offered in their chapters reflect, in part, the different conflict situations to which each is primarily addressed.

The Janis-Mann analysis is set in the context of a five-stage analysis of decision or attitude change: (1) recognition of a challenge to initial attitude, (2) appraisal of alternative responses to the challenge, (3) selection of the best alternative, (4) commitment to the new attitude, and (5) adherence to the new attitude in the face of challenges. It is to be expected that these five stages will characterize the decision or attitude change sequence when the issue is one of major importance, such as giving up smoking, changing careers, or undergoing surgery.

On the other hand, Baron's analysis focuses on a type of conflict that arises (in terms of the Janis-Mann analysis) when the individual has thoughtlessly or inadvertently arrived at stage 4 without having experienced the prior three stages; that is, the individual discovers that he has acted in a fashion inconsistent with a pre-existing attitude. (Such a situation arises with great frequency in social psychology experimentation, as well as in a number of real-life situations in which there is pressure to act hurriedly or when the issue is not initially perceived to be of much importance.)

In both analyses, an essential theoretical device is a classification of the basic pro and con considerations of the conflict situation into a set of categories. For Janis and Mann, considerations are classified as (a) utilitarian outcomes to self, (b) utilitarian outcomes to significant others, (c) self-esteem, and (d) approval by significant others. For Baron, conflicts are classified into (a) hedonic dilemmas, (b) moral dilemmas, and (c) consensual validation dilemmas. Baron's categories can be mapped *approximately* onto those of Janis and Mann by identifying hedonic dilemmas with ones involving utilitarian gains to self and/or significant others, moral dilemmas with those involving self-esteem considerations, and consensual validation dilemmas with those concerning considerations of approval by others.

For Baron, the major theoretical work is done by classifying a case of conflict as primarily involving one or the other of the three dilemma categories and generating differential predictions for cognitive attitude change on this basis. For Janis and Mann, on the other hand, all four of their categories of pro and con considerations are assumed to enter into any major attitude change (with the stability of the new attitude being predicted to increase as a function of the decision maker's thoroughness in dealing with all four), while the major predictions concerning differential effects are generated by means of the five-stage analysis.

It would take too much space here to review the kinds of prediction each analysis can make. In general, however, both analyses predict that conflict is to be resolved by attitude and/or behavior change, and both analyses make predictions concerning the individual's receptivity to specific types of information during the change process as a function of the specific circumstances of the conflict situation. For example, Baron predicts greater receptivity to conflict-resolving information provided by an attractive communicator when the dilemma is in the moral category than when it is hedonic; Janis and Mann predict greater receptivity to negative information bearing on a new policy during the stage of challenge to the old policy than during the stage of commitment to the new one. A fundamental point of both analyses is that there is a broad variety of conditions under which the maintenance of cognitive consistency is *not* a central concern. In the Janis-Mann analysis, such unbiased scanning of information occurs primarily when a person is more concerned with possible future conflict due to unforeseen consequences of a new attitude than with the immediate need to make an attitude-relevant decision. In Baron's analysis, inconsistency is similarly sought and confronted when it is interpreted by the person as providing an opportunity to enhance the adequacy of his intrapsychic or interpersonal functioning.

SUMMARY

Psychology's diverse heritage of conceptual attitude definitions can be reduced to theoretically manageable proportions by reconceptualizing them in terms of one or more of the three stimulus functions of attitude objects that have been identified by Staats. In particular, attitude definitions most commonly make reference to the attitude object's conditioned stimulus function (the object elicits an emotional response) and its discriminative stimulus function (the object serves as a signal for performance of a variety of instrumental responses, particularly ones indicating positive or negative evaluation of the object). The popular three-component definitions of attitude offer the advantage of a built-in distinction between the conditioned stimulus function (emotional component of attitude) and the discriminative stimulus function (cognition component and action-tendency or habit component). The distinction between the cognition and habit components of attitude may be conceived as the distinction, respectively, between verbal and nonverbal instrumental response tendencies regarding the attitude object.

This chapter has divided the body of attitude theory into the two major areas of *learning-behavior theory* and *cognitive integration theory*. Learning-behavior theory has been credited with analysis of the acquisition of attitude components and their role in determining performance, and cognitive integration theory with the information-transforming processes that operate particularly on the cognitive component of attitude. While it thus appears that one may sharply define the boundaries of the two major areas of attitude theory, in fact a number of attempts have been made to apply learning-behavior theory to the domain of cognitive processes. In S-R formulations, such as those of Staats, Lott and Lott, Rosnow, and Weiss, the cognition component of attitude has been formulated in terms of implicit or overt verbal responses conditioned to the attitude object as discriminative stimulus. Although such S-R discussions of cognitive processes are theoretically interesting, they currently appear not to rival analyses formulated outside the S-R framework as devices for understanding and predicting cognitive attitude phenomena. It will require much further theoretical development before the cognition component of attitude can be analyzed as fully in S-R terms as have been the emotion and habit components.

The potential of learning-behavior theory for analysis of attitudinal cognition is perhaps more apparent in the successes of learning-behavior theory formulations that have avoided the restraints of S-R language. For example, Bem's view of attitudes as learned self-descriptions and self-instructions indicates a potentially fruitful direction for further development of learning-behavior theory in its analysis of cognition. In a different direction, Greenwald has found it convenient to analyze the effects of persuasive communications in terms of cognitive responses to persuasion characterized chiefly in terms of an acceptance-rejection dimension; going further in this same direction, McGuire has elaborated a conception of cognitive information processing in persuasion that includes sequential processes of attention, comprehension, and yielding as persuasion mediators.

At best, learning-behavior theory attitude formulations have made probing forays into the domain of cognitive attitude processes. The details of cognitive response to persuasion and cognitive structure of attitudes are presently more successfully analyzed in terms of cognitive integration theories, including the various forms of the cognitive consistency principle and formulations such as those presented in the chapters in this volume by Ostrom and Upshaw, Brock, Brehm, Baron, and Janis and Mann, which assume principles other than consistency maintenance for the direction of cognitive processes.

Cognitive integration theory is currently the most active area of attitude theorization; it is thus appropriate to review briefly the problem of theoretical competition-complementarity specifically for cognitive integration formulations. Two general observations may be offered.

First, there is competition between theoretical statements made with reference to motivational principles directing cognitive processes and those nonmotivationally stated. It is possible to view the appeal or nonappeal to motivational principles as simply a matter of choice of language; for example, one may *describe* consistency of cognitive attitude structure in terms of a need for consistency which is assumed to derive from extensive past training in which cognitive judgments meeting a consistency criterion have been selectively reinforced by the socializing community. In this sense, alternative treatments such as Bem's vis à vis those of dissonance theorists may be regarded as substantively identical. However, motivational constructs can be used as *explanatory* devices in addition to functioning descriptively; in fact, the appeal to motivational principles that serve only a descriptive function is to be deplored. In this sense, Bem and the dissonance theorists are indeed saying something different from one another. Specifically, Bem (see also Hovland & Rosenberg, 1960, pp. 221 −227) explains consistency phenomena in terms of generalized learning to respond to specific types of stimuli (dissonant configurations) with specific types of responses (meeting a consistency criterion); the motivational basis for such learning presumably resides in the needs satisfied by rewards originally used to reinforce such responding. On the other hand, dissonance theorists postulate a motivating property of inconsistency per se and a rewarding property of inconsistency reduction. Since these two competing formulations make many of the same predictions, it is difficult to devise experiments to compare their validity; ideally, one would wish to raise subjects with varied histories of reward for consistent and inconsistent cognitive judgments before putting them into dissonance experiments. Bem's strategy of interpersonal simulation of dissonance experiments is an imaginative procedural alternative that calls into question the necessity for attributing an intrinsic motivating property to inconsistency.

A second observation on competition among cognitive integration analyses concerns the relative accuracy of alternative formulations that apply to the same data domains. Here again, the cognitive consistency formulations, particularly dissonance theory, receive competition from several of the contributions in this volume. For example, Brock would interpret attitudinal effects of effort to receive a communication in terms of his unavailability principle rather than in terms of dissonance; Baron's formulation leads to the observation that inconsistency may be sought when it is interpreted as a signal that a superior level of functioning is possible; Janis and Mann have suggested, in contrast to dissonance theory, that postdecisional cognitive processes will not be biased toward consistency when the decision maker is motivated more to avoid future conflict than to resolve immediate conflict.

CONCLUSION

In the present conception, attitude is a complex psychological construct, built up from the theoretically subordinate constructs, habit, cognition, and emotion. It follows that attitude theory should be regarded as a complex psychological theory, constructed from more basic psychological theories of learning, behavior, and cognitive integration. This conception of attitude theory might serve as a model for theoretical analyses of other complex psychological constructs. That is, it may be useful to view constructs such as *motive* or *trait* similarly as compound organizations of habits, cognitions, and emotions. In constructing such other complex theories, one inevitably must deal with the definitional problem of distinguishing among the domains of the various constructs.

Earlier in this chapter, the task of describing the body of attitude theory was likened to assembling a jigsaw puzzle whose pieces are the contributions of individual theorists. By now, it is clear that the puzzle is no ordinary one; the pieces have pieces; further, the pieces have not been designed to fit neatly together at the edges — in fact most of the pieces don't have sharply defined edges. For these reasons (if the analogy is not yet out of hand), the present attempt has not gone much beyond putting the picture of the puzzle (Fig. 1) on the box that contains the pieces; this at least defines the kind of work needed in order to assemble the puzzle.

References

Abelson, R. P. Psychological implication. In R. P. Abelson, *et al.* (Eds.), *Theories of cognitive consistency: A sourcebook.* Chicago: Rand McNally, 1968, in press.
Allport, G. W. Attitudes. In C. A. Murchison (Ed.), *A handbook of social psychology.* Worcester, Mass.: Clark University Press, 1935. Pp. 798-844.
Aronson, E. The effects of effort on the attractiveness of rewarded and unrewarded stimuli. *Journal of Abnormal and Social Psychology,* 1961, 63, 375-380.
Bandura, A. Vicarious processes. In L. Berkowitz (Ed.), *Advances in experimental social psychology.* Vol. 2. New York: Academic Press, 1965. Pp. 1-55.
Brehm, J. W. *A theory of psychological reactance.* New York: Academic Press, 1966.
Campbell, D. T. Social attitudes and other acquired behavioral dispositions. In S. Koch (Ed.), *Psychology: A study of a science.* Vol. 6. New York: McGraw-Hill, 1963. Pp. 94-176.
Dabbs, J. M., & Janis, I. L. Why does eating while reading facilitate opinion change? An experimental inquiry. *Journal of Experimental Social Psychology,* 1965, 1, 133-144.
Doob, L. W. The behavior of attitudes. *Psychological Review,* 1947, 54, 135-156.
Feldman, S. (Ed.) *Cognitive consistency: Motivational antecedents and behavioral consequences.* New York: Academic Press, 1966.

Festinger, L. (Ed.) *Conflict, decision, and dissonance.* Stanford, Calif.: Stanford University Press, 1964.

Festinger, L., & Carlsmith, J. M. Cognitive consequences of forced compliance. *Journal of Abnormal and Social Psychology,* 1959, **58**, 203-210.

Fishbein, M. (Ed.) *Readings in attitude theory and measurement.* New York: Wiley, 1967.

Fromkin, H. L. Reinforcement and effort expenditure: Predictions of 'reinforcement theory' versus predictions of dissonance theory. *Journal of Personality and Social Psychology,* in press.

Greenwald, A. G. Behavior change following a persuasive communication. *Journal of Personality,* 1965, **33**, 370-391. (a)

Greenwald, A. G. Effects of prior commitment on behavior change after a persuasive communication. *Public Opinion Quarterly,* 1965, **29**, 595-601. (b)

Hovland, C. I. Reconciling conflicting results derived from experimental and survey studies of attitude change. *American Psychologist,* 1959, **14**, 8-17.

Hovland, C. I., & Rosenberg, M. J. Summary and further theoretical issues. In C. I. Hovland and M. J. Rosenberg (Eds.), *Attitude organization and change.* New Haven: Yale University Press, 1960. Pp. 198-232.

Insko, C. A. *Theories of attitude change.* New York: Appleton, 1967.

Insko, C. A., & Schopler, J. Triadic consistency: A statement of affective-cognitive-conative consistency. *Psychological Review,* 1967, **74**, 361-376.

Janis, I. L., & Gilmore, J. B. The influence of incentive conditions on the success of role playing in modifying attitudes. *Journal of Personality and Social Psychology,* 1965, **1**, 17-27.

Kimble, G. A. *Hilgard and Marquis' conditioning and learning.* (2nd Ed.) New York: Appleton, 1961.

Konorski, J. Mechanisms of learning. In *Physiological mechanisms in animal behavior.* (Society for Experimental Biology, Symposium No. 4) New York: Academic Press, 1950. Pp. 409-431.

Krech, D., Crutchfield, R. S., Ballachey, E. L. *Individual in society.* New York: McGraw-Hill, 1962.

Lott, B. E. Secondary reinforcement and effort: Comment on Aronson's "The effect of effort on the attractiveness of rewarded and unrewarded stimuli." *Journal of Abnormal and Social Psychology,* 1963, **67**, 520-522.

MacCorquodale, K., & Meehl, P. E. Edward C. Tolman. In W. K. Estes *et al., Modern learning theory.* New York: Appleton, 1954. Pp. 177-266.

McGuire, W. J. Inducing resistance to persuasion: Some contemporary approaches. In L. Berkowitz (Ed.), *Advances in experimental social psychology.* Vol. 1. New York: Academic Press, 1964, Pp. 191-229.

McGuire, W. J. Nature of attitudes and attitude change. In G. Lindzey & E. Aronson (Eds.), *Handbook of social psychology.* (2nd ed.) Reading, Mass.: Addison-Wesley, 1968, in press.

Miller, G. A., Galanter, E., & Pribram, K. H. *Plans and the structure of behavior.* New York: Holt, 1960.

Mowrer, O. H. *Learning theory and behavior.* New York: Wiley, 1960.

Nuttin, J., & Greenwald, A. G. *Reward and punishment in human learning.* New York: Academic Press, 1968.

Osgood, C. E., Suci, G. J., & Tannenbaum, P. H. *The measurement of meaning.* Urbana, Ill.: University of Illinois Press, 1957.

Osgood, C. E., & Tannenbaum, P. H. The principle of congruity in the prediction of attitude change. *Psychological Review,* 1955, **62,** 42-55.

Rosenberg, M. J. & Hovland, C. I. Cognitive, affective, and behavioral components of attitudes. In C. I. Hovland and M. J. Rosenberg (Eds.), *Attitude organization and change.* New Haven: Yale University Press, 1960. Pp. 1-14.

Sarnoff, I. Psychoanalytic theory and social attitudes. *Public Opinion Quarterly,* 1960, **24,** 251-279.

Smith, M. B., Bruner, J. S., & White, R. W. *Opinions and personality.* New York: Wiley, 1956.

Thorndike, E. L. An experimental study of rewards. *Teachers College Contributions to Education,* 1933, No. 580.

Thurstone, L. L. The measurement of social attitudes. *Journal of Abnormal and Social Psychology,* 1931, **26,** 249-269.

Tolman, E. C. Principles of purposive behavior. In S. Koch (Ed.), *Psychology: A study of a science.* Vol. 2. New York: McGraw-Hill, 1959. Pp. 92-157.

ADDENDUM TO CHAPTER 2 (P. 56)

As the author has indicated (Staats, 1964, 1968; Staats and Staats, 1963), many important aspects of social interaction may be considered in terms of the manner in which one individual serves as a stimulus (actually, a complex of stimuli) for another. The individual's physical appearance—including dress, his actions of various kinds (including language), his associates and other surroundings and accoutrements, his titles, name, and so on—will constitute stimuli that affect other individuals in explicit ways that can be stated in terms of learning principles. One of the general classes of effects of the stimuli that constitute a person involves the elicitation of emotional (attitudinal) responses in the other individual, and the emotional response will then determine the types of overt instrumental behaviors of the individual toward that person.

This statement may be elaborated to suggest that the principles of the A-R-D system will apply to significant aspects of social interaction. That is, the type of social interaction briefly described above may be understood in greater detail and depth through use of the concepts of the A-R-D system. Stimuli which are aspects of the person may be conditioned stimuli (^CS) for an attitudinal response. Because of their attitudinal value, and hence reinforcement value, these stimuli will affect the ability of the person to instrumentally condition the behavior of some other individual. Moreover, the person, because of his reinforcing value, will as a discriminative stimulus control the already learned class of striving behaviors of the individual (providing the person is positively reinforcing). If the person has negative reinforcing value for the individual he will control the "striving away from" class of behaviors.

Author Index

Weiss, R. F., 3, *32*, 100, *107*, 109, 110, 114, 116, 119, 121, 123, 125, 126, 129, 131, 134, 135, 136, 137, *144*, *145*
Weiss, W., 116, 139, *142*, 256, *274*
Welch, C., 341, *359*
Westley, W. A., *274*
Wheeler, L., 110, *145*
White, R. W., 4, 14, 18, *32*, 148, *170*, 297, *326*, 361, 362, 363, *387*
Whiting, J. W. M., 110, *145*
Wicklund, R. A., 257, 258, 270, 271, 272, *275*, 289, *296*
Winer, B. J., *275*
Winokur, S., 37, *66*
Wolpe, J., 110, *145*
Woodworth, R. S., 166, *170*
Wrench, D. F., 92, *107*

Wright, H. F., 259, 270, *275*
Wright, J. C., 261, 262, 271, *274*

Y

Yamaguchi, H. G., 125, *145*
Yoder, M. R., 265, 267, 270, *275*
Young, R. K., 84, 87, 100, *106*

Z

Zajonc, R. B., 4, 12, *32*, 86, 88, 117, 128, *145*, *326*, 351, *360*
Zeaman, D., 125, *145*
Zimbardo, P. G., 259, *275*, *326*
Zimmerman, D. W., 40, *66*
Znaniecki, F., 1, *32*

Subject Index